Praise for *Classroom Discussions* in Math . . .

I thought that the second edition of *Classroom Discussions in Math* was the single best book available for learning about and implementing academically productive talk in the classroom. Now, it's even better: the third edition includes classroom videos from grades K–6! This new edition describes the practices and gives *examples* of them in action in urban classrooms—a window into using talk tools to promote learning.

    If you need to select one resource to help you address the Common Core call for discussion, this is the one to get. If you are working with a study group of teachers interested in transforming their practice, you can combine the third edition with the *Facilitator's Guide*.

—Sarah Michaels, Professor and Chair, Education Department, and Senior Research Scholar at the Jacob Hiatt Center for Urban Education, Clark University, Worcester, Massachusetts

This book has had a direct, positive, and important influence on my math teaching. The ideas are clear and persuasive, and I gained new and important tools for engaging students and improving classroom math discussions. It's a terrific resource!

—Marilyn Burns, founder, Math Solutions

Boston Teacher Residency instructors and coaches have used the resources in the *Classroom Discussions in Math* program to design assignments for residents and for teacher study groups, and as content for the professional learning of the community of BTR coaches. As a result of focusing on student learning and understanding as it is constructed in classrooms through talk, we are getting better at assessing effective teaching. The inclusion of authentic classroom videos in the new edition will help us in this work of making professional learning powerful and precise.

—Lynne Godfrey, Co-Director of Clinical Teacher Education, Boston Teacher Residency

Using this resource in book study groups and then coaching teachers to use the strategies presented has really changed teacher practice.

—Janie Merendino, math coach, Fairmont, West Virginia

(*Continued*)

This new edition of *Classroom Discussions in Math* is my "go-to" resource for helping educators implement strategies that engage *all* students in conversations that can deepen their understanding of mathematics. Video clips clearly demonstrate what productive talk looks like during math instruction, and the suggestions for reflecting on the lessons are extremely helpful. *Classroom Discussions in Math* has transformed my own teaching, profoundly changing how I support English language learners.

—Rusty Bresser, Lecturer and Supervisor of Teacher Education, University of California, San Diego

This book gives teachers concrete tools—*talk moves*—that provide security and a framework to open up discussion in the math classroom. The talk moves will enhance daily conversations, professional development, and most of all the conversations heard in classrooms.

—Lori Murach, math program supervisor, Department for School Improvement, North East ISD, San Antonio, Texas

Classroom Discussions in Math is an essential resource in my elementary mathematics methods course. The talk moves described in this resource provide an inviting and accessible tool for prospective elementary teachers to plan and implement productive mathematics discussions in their clinical experiences. Recognizing the importance of such discussions for their own teaching also encourages them to participate in similar ways as students in their college classrooms, leading them to explore more deeply what it means to teach effectively.

—Edna O. Schack, professor, P-5 Mathematics Education, Morehead State University, Morehead, Kentucky

Classroom Discussions in Math

A **Teacher's Guide** for using talk moves to support the Common Core and more

THIRD EDITION

GRADES K–6

Math Solutions
Sausalito, California, USA

Suzanne H. Chapin | Catherine O'Connor | Nancy Canavan Anderson

Math Solutions
One Harbor Drive, Suite 101
Sausalito, California, USA 94965
www.mathsolutions.com

ISBN-13: 978-1-935099-56-7
ISBN-10: 1-935099-56-6

Editor: Jamie Ann Cross
Production: Denise A. Botelho
Cover design: Jan Streitburger
Interior design: Lisa Delgado, Delgado and Company
Composition: MPS Limited
Cover and Interior images: Cambridge Public Schools, Cambridge, Massachusetts
Videographer: Friday's Films, www.fridaysfilms.com

5   6   7   8   9   10   31   22   21   20   19   18   17   16   15

A Message from Math Solutions

We at Math Solutions believe that teaching math well calls for increasing our understanding of the math we teach, seeking deeper insights into how students learn mathematics, and refining our lessons to best promote students' learning.

Math Solutions shares classroom-tested lessons and teaching expertise from our faculty of professional development consultants as well as from other respected math educators. Our publications are part of the nationwide effort we've made since 1984 that now includes

- more than five hundred face-to-face professional development programs each year for teachers and administrators in districts across the country;
- professional development books that span all math topics taught in kindergarten through high school;
- videos for teachers and for parents that show math lessons taught in actual classrooms;
- on-site visits to schools to help refine teaching strategies and assess student learning; and
- free online support, including grade-level lessons, book reviews, inservice information, and district feedback, all in our Math Solutions Online Newsletter.

For information about all of the products and services we have available, please visit our website at *www.mathsolutions.com.* You can also contact us to discuss math professional development needs by calling (800) 868-9092 or by sending an email to *info@mathsolutions.com.*

We're always eager for your feedback and interested in learning about your particular needs. We look forward to hearing from you.

Math Solutions.
FOUNDED BY MARILYN BURNS

SCHOLASTIC

To the students and teachers of Project Challenge

Brief Contents

(Continued)

Contents

(Continued)

(Continued)

Acknowledgments

In 1998, the authors began to work together on Project Challenge, a program to enhance learning opportunities for urban students with potential talent in mathematics. Suzanne Chapin brought her experience in professional development and mathematics education, Cathy O'Connor brought her background in linguistics and the study of classroom discourse, and Nancy Anderson brought her training in math education and her willingness to try new approaches to mathematical communication in the classroom. This resource grew out of our collaboration. Its contents are based on our years of work in our respective fields, on what we learned during Project Challenge, and on subsequent research and professional development we have done together.

We would like to express our appreciation to the students of Project Challenge and to their families. They inspired us to write down our ideas so others might use them. We are also grateful to all the Project Challenge teachers who so willingly tried new methods and materials, even in the face of pressures from high-stakes testing. They were willing to think deeply about what it means to be talented in mathematics, and to spend many hours in demanding professional development activities. Our profound thanks go to Beth Brogna, Ali Brown, Patty Burge, Lauren Carilli, Roseanne Cataldo, Maureen DeFreitas, Janice Fields, Kathy Foulser, Laura Glavin, Monty Grob, Gina Lally, Mesook Lee, Claire Moran, Magaly Rodriguez, Alice Rourke, Rene Sacco, Sally Siriani, Alissa Stangle, Andrea Taddeo, Henry Utter, Tanya Walsh, and Carol Wolf, as well as other teachers, support staff, project staff, and district administrators who offered time and support of many kinds. Furthermore, we appreciate the advice we received from teachers, professors, professional development experts, and students on what to include in the second edition of *Classroom Discussions*. A special thanks to Jennifer McPherson, Lainie Schuster, Marji Freeman, Linda Honeyman, Chris Brunette, Rusty Bresser, Elizabeth Sweeney and to the many educators who have been using this resource to support talk in the classroom.

Many of the ideas and practices described in this resource came from the work of individuals that Cathy O'Connor has had the opportunity to collaborate with over the past decade. She is very grateful for help and discussion over the years from Lynne Godfrey, Magdalene Lampert, Sarah Michaels, Robert Moses, Pam Paternoster, Lauren Resnick, Vicki Bill, Matthew Robert, Marty Rutherford, and many others.

We are greatly indebted to our funders. Project Challenge itself was funded by the Jacob K. Javits Gifted and Talented Students Education Program (Grant No. R206A980001). The National Science Foundation supported our study of this approach from 2003–2006 (REC-0231893). The opinions expressed in this book do not necessarily reflect the position, policy, or endorsement of the U.S. Department of Education or of the National Science Foundation. And although we are grateful to all of the individuals and institutions cited, none of these individuals or institutions should be assumed to endorse the contents of this volume.

We wish to thank Marilyn Burns, Carolyn Felux, and Jamie Cross from Math Solutions. Marilyn Burns has had a tremendously positive impact on the form and contents of previous editions of this work. Carolyn Felux and Jamie Cross provided us with invaluable guidance, insight, and laughter during the production of this resource as well as the companion facilitator's guide. Thank you to Denise Botelho for crafting a written teacher's guide that is both appealing and informative. Thank you to Perry Pickert and Friday's Films for producing video clips that are pleasing to the eye as well as the ear and full of priceless examples of student discourse.

Our thanks are extended to the administration, faculty, and staff of our three participating school districts: Cambridge Public Schools, Cambridge, Massachusetts; Hartford Public Schools, Hartford, Connecticut; and West Hartford Public Schools, West Hartford, Connecticut. We thank all the teachers who appear on the DVDs: Stephanie Burgess, Rocco Danella, Pat Delaney, Ali Foley, Katelyn Fournier, Lisa Hayward, Ruth Luipold, Kim Luizzi, Amy Moylan, Megan Powers, Kelly Rowan, and Julie Schineller. We are forever indebted to each of you for inviting us into your classroom and providing us with rich, engaging, and thought-provoking examples of productive mathematical discussions. We thank the parents and guardians of the students appearing in these videos. And we especially want to express our gratitude to the students: Everyone who watches these DVDs will learn from your hard work, persistence, good humor, and courage in expressing your thoughts and ideas.

We would also like to express our appreciation to all the students in classrooms across the United States who are trying to make sense of mathematics by talking about key ideas. We are deeply encouraged and inspired by your hard work and consistent efforts to talk productively and animatedly about mathematics! And last, we wish to thank our families whose love and support made this project possible.

Why Use Talk in Mathematics Classrooms?

Five Reasons Talk Is Critical to Teaching and Learning

For the past two decades, the National Council of Teachers of Mathematics (NCTM) has encouraged teachers to use classroom discourse in math classes, to support both students' ability to *reason mathematically* and their ability to *communicate that reasoning*. When teachers commit themselves to *teaching for understanding*, classroom discourse and discussion are key elements in the overall picture.

Why do educators and researchers think that classroom talk has the power to improve both students' learning and ability to reason and teachers' ability to teach? Let's look at what we consider to be five major reasons that talk is critical to teaching and learning.

Five Major Reasons That Talk Is Critical to Teaching and Learning

1. Talk can reveal understanding and misunderstanding.
2. Talk supports robust learning by boosting memory.
3. Talk supports deeper reasoning.
4. Talk supports language development.
5. Talk supports development of social skills.

Reason 1: Talk can reveal understanding and misunderstanding

If students talk about the content they're studying, we can see more clearly what they don't understand . . . and what they *do* understand. This helps teachers adjust their teaching. Some call this *formative assessment*. Getting students to talk about mathematical content is one of the best ways to engage in formative assessment. An additional benefit is that students may *themselves* realize what they don't understand and what they do understand. This allows them to adjust their own reasoning, and over time it may improve their metacognitive abilities.

Reason 2: Talk supports robust learning by boosting memory

Talk is a rich source of information and plays a part in many kinds of memory. When we hear about and *talk* about concepts, procedures, and applications, our memories have more to work with. In classroom discussions, as multiple students discuss the same content, everyone benefits by hearing that content verbalized in different ways, particularly students who may need more time to process mathematical ideas. The social aspects of talk also help students remember content and argumentation: If the teacher makes a claim, some students remember it; some don't. If a student makes a claim and another student contests it or agrees with it, the whole learning event becomes more memorable because of its social significance.

Reason 3: Talk supports deeper reasoning

Learning to reason well takes time. Both children and adults need practice to work out the logic of their ideas and to put together a persuasive argument. And practice with reasoning requires that we have other people to reason with—people who can respond to our own reasoning and share their reasoning with us. In the classroom, teachers can give students that practice by using talk in strategic ways.

Reason 4: Talk supports language development

When talk is used intensively in classes, students may get a richer sense of what words and phrases mean and of when to use them. Their control of complex grammar also improves, in speaking and in reading. For students who are English learners, this is particularly crucial.

Reason 5: Talk supports development of social skills

When teachers use classroom talk a great deal, it gives students a chance to learn about respect and kindness. They learn that it takes time to understand somebody else's reasoning, and that they have to be patient as others struggle to clarify. They also learn that they have to work to make their *own* reasoning clear. Over time, this improves students' social skills and ability to be patient and cooperative with others—and with themselves.

Teacher Reflection: The Benefits of Productive Talk

Mrs. Rowan

I've seen connections between what we talk about during class discussions and students' work on written assessments. I have seen students use strategies on tests that they were not using prior to doing a turn and talk or math discussion. And I've also seen students doing a lot better on assessments. From talking to each other, they know different ways of solving problems, not just the one way that I showed them.

The Typical Classroom

Researchers have found that few American classrooms display consistent or even occasional use of student talk. Instead, most classroom talk consists of the teacher lecturing, asking students to recite, or posing simple questions with known answers. Of course, lecturing, recitation, and quizzing are useful instructional tools. They form the bedrock of most teachers' instructional practice and we would not want them to disappear. However, they have limitations, as do all forms of talk! Our purpose here is to focus on the benefits of discussion.

I Don't Have Time—and What If No One Talks?

Most teachers would agree that the five reasons discussed on the previous pages make sense. So why do so few teachers use talk extensively in their classes? We have learned in our work that many teachers find that creating a discourse-intensive classroom is difficult, because they encounter many obstacles. Here are a few of the most frequent responses—have you heard yourself or your colleagues say something similar?

Common Obstacles to Using Talk Extensively in Classrooms

- We don't have time! It takes time to conduct discussions, and I have a curriculum pacing manual I have to keep up with.

- What if I ask a question and I can't understand what the student is saying? I'll feel like an idiot and the student will be embarrassed. I don't want either of us to feel put on the spot.

- What is there to talk about in math? You have the correct answer. What's to discuss? It's not like a poem or a short story.

- What if no one talks?

- Some of my students are too shy to talk in front of everyone. Some have language-based learning disorders. And some of my students are English language learners. I *can't* ask them to talk.

- I have these two bright students who could talk and discuss for hours. What if they just hog the floor, as usual? I don't want to shut them down, but I want the others to talk too.

These obstacles are real problems, but there are solutions for them. All of the components of *Classroom Discussions in Math* are developed to help you work through these obstacles and bring all of your students into the conversation.

How to Use This Resource

The Components of *Classroom Discussions in Math*

There are two main components of *Classroom Discussions in Math:* a teacher's guide and a facilitator's guide. Ideally, the components are used together to maximize your understanding and facilitation of best talk practices in mathematics learning.

Teacher's Guide

You have in your hands the teacher's guide component of this program, now in a multimedia third edition. This resource is designed for individual use
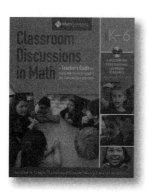
and features forty-six video clips (total viewing time of approximately two hours and twenty-six minutes). Some of the video clips are new to *Classroom Discussions in Math*; others are all-time favorites selected from the video clips included with the facilitator's guide described below. The teacher's guide continues to hold true to the principles and practices shared in the best-selling previous editions (for more on what's new in this third edition see the next page in this section). The teacher's guide can be used separately or with the facilitator's guide.

For a list of which video clip selections in the teacher's guide overlap with the facilitator's guide, refer to the video "Video Clips by Grade" table on page xliv.

Facilitator's Guide

In addition to the teacher's guide, *Classroom Discussions in Math* offers a facilitator's guide for use in settings with multiple participants. The 240-page facilitator's guide includes seventy-five video clips (total viewing time of approximately five hours), twenty professional development sessions, and a CD with session handouts and lessons plans in printable PDF format.
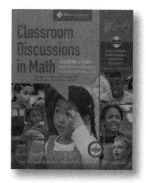
In every chapter of the facilitator's guide, we include references to this teacher's guide to encourage a seamless use of all components. It is our vision that every participant in the facilitator's guide's professional development sessions would also have his or her own copy of this teacher's guide.

What's New to the Third Edition?

Try This Out

In addition to vignettes drawn from real classroom experiences, most chapters now contain one or more sections entitled Try This Out, with specific mathematics problems, questions, and plans that you can use in your classrooms.

Math Talk Tips

In the margins throughout this resource you will now find Math Talk Tips that highlight suggestions and strategies for using specific talk moves, tools, and formats to develop students' mathematical learning.

Video Clips

Perhaps the most important new feature is the presence of video clips that illustrate the principles and practices we discuss in each chapter. Each video clip is accompanied by questions for discussion and further exploration of your own practice. To see which video clips in the teacher's guide overlap with the video clips in the facilitator's guide, refer to the Video Clips by Grade Table starting on page xliv.

Teaching with the Common Core

The mathematical topics highlighted in the lesson suggestions, vignettes, and video clips are aligned with the Common Core State Standards for Mathematics.

Guidelines for Watching Videos of Teaching

The teachers who agreed to be recorded in these videos have complex and challenging classrooms, just like you. When we watch videos of others it is easy to see things that we might do differently. It is then all to easy to move to a critical stance, focusing on what the teacher "should" have done differently. But we have found that such a stance is not helpful for learning.

These videos are not scripted or rehearsed. They are real classroom sessions. Remember that teaching is a complicated activity, in which the teacher is required to do many things at once. As you watch these videos, alone or with others, we recommend following the rules below:

1. Assume that there are many things you don't know about the students, the classroom, and the shared history of the teacher and students in the video.

2. Assume good intent and expertise on the part of the teacher. If you cannot understand his or her actions, try to hypothesize what might have motivated him or her.

3. Keep focused on your observations about what students are getting out of the talk and interaction.

4. Keep focused on how the classroom discourse is serving the mathematical goals of the lesson.

Teaching with the Common Core State Standards

Math Talk and the Common Core State Standards

For more than two decades, the National Council of Teachers of Mathematics has been urging teachers to emphasize communication—talk and writing—as part of mathematics teaching and learning. Their arguments make sense: The mathematical thinking of many students is aided by hearing what their peers are thinking. Putting thoughts into words pushes students to clarify their thinking. Teachers can spot student misunderstandings much more easily when they are revealed by a discussion instead of remaining unspoken.

Recently, the ante has been upped by the introduction of the Common Core State Standards. Now there are even more reasons to use classroom talk and discussion to support math learning. Let's look at these reasons through both the standards for mathematical practice and the standards for mathematical content.

The Standards for Mathematical Practice

Consider just a few of the Mathematical Practices from the CCSS.

Mathematical Practice Standard 3: Construct viable arguments and critique the reasoning of others.

Any teacher knows that this is not a simple goal. How can we help students learn to make claims, support them with evidence, and engage in discussion of counterarguments with others? We believe that the use of *discussion* in a variety of formats is really the ideal (and perhaps only) way to bring this about.

Mathematical Practice Standard 6: Attend to precision.

As the CCSS writers argue, "Mathematically proficient students try to communicate precisely with others." In our experience, the desire and ability to communicate clearly and precisely grows best *in the context of talking with others.* As students engage in productive talk, they learn that it takes effort to get their ideas across. They learn to pay attention to what they don't understand,

and ask questions of others to repair their own understanding. In this environment, they naturally learn to attend to precision.

The Standards for Mathematical Content

It is not just the Mathematical *Practices* that call for discussion. The Content Standards call for it too. As the CCSS writers state:

> Expectations that begin with the word "understand" are often especially good opportunities to connect the practices to the content. Students who lack understanding of a topic may rely on procedures too heavily . . . they may be less likely to consider analogous problems, represent problems coherently, justify conclusions, . . . explain the mathematics accurately to other students, step back for an overview. (2010, 8)

In our experiences in many classrooms where academically productive discussion is common, deeper understanding emerges from the many opportunities students have throughout the year to hear about and talk about the mathematical concepts, procedures, tools, and representations in their lessons.

Lesson Correlations in this Resource

Throughout this resource, we rely on classroom examples to portray the practices and principles of whole-class mathematics discussions. All the mathematics problems that are described in our classroom vignettes and the lessons featured in the video clips are connected to the Common Core State Standards. The connections are listed with grade (K, 1, 2, 3, 4, 5, 6) first, followed by the abbreviated domain, followed by a description of the relevant strand and/or cluster.

Teaching with the Common Core State Standards: Lesson Correlations

Chapter	Discussion Examples: Vignettes and Video Clips	Counting and Cardinality (CC)	Operations and Algebraic Thinking (OA)	Number and Operations in Base Ten (NBT)	Number and Operations – Fractions (NF)	Ratios and Proportional Relationships (RP)	Expressions and Equations (EE)	Measurement and Data (MD)	The Number System (NS)	Geometry (G)
1	Academically Productive Talk in Mrs. Schuster's Third-Grade Class		3.OA Understand properties of multiplication and the relationship between multiplication and division. 3.OA Apply properties of operations as strategies to multiply and divide.							
1	Ms. D's Third-Grade Class		3.OA Represent and solve problems involving multiplication and division.							

Chapter	Discussion Examples: Vignettes and Video Clips	Counting and Cardinality (CC)	Operations and Algebraic Thinking (OA)	Number and Operations in Base Ten (NBT)	Number and Operations – Fractions (NF)	Ratios and Proportional Relationships (RP)	Expressions and Equations (EE)	Measurement and Data (MD)	The Number System (NS)	Geometry (G)
1	Mrs. Sigler's First-Grade Class									1.G Reason with shapes and their attributes. 1.G Distinguish between defining attributes (e.g., triangles are closed and three-sided) versus non-defining attributes (e.g., color, orientation, overall size); build and draw shapes to possess defining attributes.
1	Mrs. Stangle's Fifth-Grade Class				5.NF Apply and extend previous understandings of multiplication and division to multiply and divide fractions. 5.NF Interpret division of a whole number by a unit fraction, and compute such quotients.					

(Continued)

Teaching with the Common Core State Standards: Lesson Correlations *(Continued)*

Chapter	Discussion Examples: Vignettes and Video Clips	Counting and Cardinality (CC)	Operations and Algebraic Thinking (OA)	Number and Operations in Base Ten (NBT)	Number and Operations – Fractions (NF)	Ratios and Proportional Relationships (RP)	Expressions and Equations (EE)	Measurement and Data (MD)	The Number System (NS)	Geometry (G)
3	Working with Place Value, Grade 2			2.NBT Understand place value. 2.NBT Use place value understanding and properties of operations to add and subtract.						
3	Counting and Place Value, Grade 1			1.NBT Extend the counting sequence. 1.NBT Understand place value.						
3	Area of a Parallelogram, $A = bh$, *Grade 6*									6.G. Find the area of right triangles, other triangles, special quadrilaterals, and polygons by composing into rectangles or decomposing into triangles and other shapes.

Chapter	Discussion Examples: Vignettes and Video Clips	Counting and Cardinality (CC)	Operations and Algebraic Thinking (OA)	Number and Operations in Base Ten (NBT)	Number and Operations – Fractions (NF)	Ratios and Proportional Relationships (RP)	Expressions and Equations (EE)	Measurement and Data (MD)	The Number System (NS)	Geometry (G)
3	Perimeters of Rectangles with a Fixed Area, Grade 4							3.MD Recognize perimeter as an attribute of plane figures and distinguish between linear and area measures. 3.MD Solve real world and mathematical problems involving perimeters of polygons, including finding the perimeter given the side lengths, finding an unknown side length, and exhibiting rectangles with the same perimeter and different areas or with the same area and different perimeters.		

(Continued)

Teaching with the Common Core State Standards: Lesson Correlations *(Continued)*

Chapter	Discussion Examples: Vignettes and Video Clips	Counting and Cardinality (CC)	Operations and Algebraic Thinking (OA)	Number and Operations in Base Ten (NBT)	Number and Operations – Fractions (NF)	Ratios and Proportional Relationships (RP)	Expressions and Equations (EE)	Measurement and Data (MD)	The Number System (NS)	Geometry (G)
								4.MD Apply the area and perimeter formulas for rectangles in real world and mathematical problems.		
3	Operations with Decimals, Grade 5			5.NBT Perform operations with multi-digit whole numbers and with decimals to hundredths.						
4	Teaching Addition Strategies, Grade 1		1.OA Understand and apply properties of operations and the relationship between addition and subtraction. 1.OA Add and subtract within 20.							

Chapter	Discussion Examples: Vignettes and Video Clips	Counting and Cardinality (CC)	Operations and Algebraic Thinking (OA)	Number and Operations in Base Ten (NBT)	Number and Operations – Fractions (NF)	Ratios and Proportional Relationships (RP)	Expressions and Equations (EE)	Measurement and Data (MD)	The Number System (NS)	Geometry (G)
4	Teaching Subtraction Strategies, Grade 2			2.NBT Use place value understanding and properties of operations to add and subtract. 2.NBT Explain why addition and subtraction strategies work, using place value and the properties of operations.						
4	Teaching Division Strategies, Grade 5			5.NBT Find whole-number quotients of whole numbers . . . using strategies based on place value, the properties of operations, and/or the relationship between multiplication and division.						

(Continued)

Teaching with the Common Core State Standards: Lesson Correlations *(Continued)*

Chapter	Discussion Examples: Vignettes and Video Clips	Counting and Cardinality (CC)	Operations and Algebraic Thinking (OA)	Number and Operations in Base Ten (NBT)	Number and Operations – Fractions (NF)	Ratios and Proportional Relationships (RP)	Expressions and Equations (EE)	Measurement and Data (MD)	The Number System (NS)	Geometry (G)
4	Connecting Multiplication Strategies and Concepts, Grade 4			4.NBT Use place value understanding and properties of operations to perform multi-digit arithmetic.						
4	Developing Fraction Sense, Grade 4				4.NF Build fractions from unit fractions by applying and extending previous understandings of operations on whole numbers.					
4	Placing Fractions on a Number Line, Grade 6								6.NS Understand a rational number as a point on the number. Find and position	

Chapter	Discussion Examples: Vignettes and Video Clips	Counting and Cardinality (CC)	Operations and Algebraic Thinking (OA)	Number and Operations in Base Ten (NBT)	Number and Operations – Fractions (NF)	Ratios and Proportional Relationships (RP)	Expressions and Equations (EE)	Measurement and Data (MD)	The Number System (NS)	Geometry (G)
									integers and other rational numbers on a number line diagram. 6.NS Apply and extend previous understandings of numbers to the system of rational numbers.	
5	The Pencil Problem, Grade 4		4.OA Use the four operations with whole numbers to solve problems.							
5	The Birthday Party Problem, Grade 3		3.OA Solve problems involving the four operations, and identify and explain patterns in arithmetic.							

(Continued)

Teaching with the Common Core State Standards: Lesson Correlations *(Continued)*

Chapter	Discussion Examples: Vignettes and Video Clips	Counting and Cardinality (CC)	Operations and Algebraic Thinking (OA)	Number and Operations in Base Ten (NBT)	Number and Operations – Fractions (NF)	Ratios and Proportional Relationships (RP)	Expressions and Equations (EE)	Measurement and Data (MD)	The Number System (NS)	Geometry (G)
5	The Coin Problem, Grade 3		3.OA Represent and solve problems involving multiplication and division.							
5	The Field Trip Problem, Grade 1		1.OA Represent and solve problems using addition and subtraction. 1.OA Add and subtract within 20.							
5	The Newspaper Club Problem, Grade 6					6.RP Understand ratio concepts and use ratio reasoning to solve problems.				
6	The Baseball Logic Problem, Grade 4*									

*Indicates a discussion vignette that is intended to demonstrate how productive math talk can be used to support the Standards for Mathematical Practice such as reasoning abstractly and quantitatively, attending to precision, and using appropriate tools strategically.

Chapter	Discussion Examples: Vignettes and Video Clips	Counting and Cardinality (CC)	Operations and Algebraic Thinking (OA)	Number and Operations in Base Ten (NBT)	Number and Operations – Fractions (NF)	Ratios and Proportional Relation-ships (RP)	Expres-sions and Equations (EE)	Measure-ment and Data (MD)	The Number System (NS)	Geometry (G)
6	Four Strikes and You're Out, Grade 3			3.NBT Fluently add and sub-tract within 1000 using strategies and algorithms based on place value, proper-ties of opera-tions, and/or the relation-ship between addition and subtraction.						
6	What's the Same?, Kindergarten							K.MD Classify objects and count the number of objects in each category.		
6	Volume of Rectangular Prisms, Grade 5							5.MD Understand concepts of volume and relate volume to multiplica-tion and to addition.		

(Continued)

Teaching with the Common Core State Standards: Lesson Correlations *(Continued)*

Chapter	Discussion Examples: Vignettes and Video Clips	Counting and Cardinality (CC)	Operations and Algebraic Thinking (OA)	Number and Operations in Base Ten (NBT)	Number and Operations – Fractions (NF)	Ratios and Proportional Relationships (RP)	Expressions and Equations (EE)	Measurement and Data (MD)	The Number System (NS)	Geometry (G)
6	Weighing Fruit, Grade 6						6.EE Apply and extend previous understandings of arithmetic to algebraic expressions.			
7	Making Sense of Scale, Grade 6					6.RP Understand the concept of a ratio and use ratio language to describe a ratio relationship between two quantities.				
7	Making Sense of One-Half, Grade 2							2.MD Work with time and money.		
7	Making Sense of Quarter							2.MD Work with time and money.		
7	Using More and Less to Describe the Data in a Graph, Kindergarten	K.CC Compare numbers.						K.MD Classify objects and count the number of objects in each category.		

Chapter	Discussion Examples: Vignettes and Video Clips	Counting and Cardinality (CC)	Operations and Algebraic Thinking (OA)	Number and Operations in Base Ten (NBT)	Number and Operations – Fractions (NF)	Ratios and Proportional Relationships (RP)	Expressions and Equations (EE)	Measurement and Data (MD)	The Number System (NS)	Geometry (G)
7	Connecting Factors and Multiples, Grade 4		4.OA Gain familiarity with factors and multiples.							
7	Sorting: Attributes of Shapes, Grade 3									3.G Reason with shapes and their attributes.
7	Guess My Object: Attributes of Shapes, Kindergarten									K.G Analyze and compare shapes.
7	Differentiating between Squares and Cubes, Grade 5							5.MD Understand the concept of volume.		
7	Talking About Ratios, Grade 6					6.RP Understand the concept of a ratio and use ratio language to describe a ratio relationship between two quantities.				

(Continued)

Teaching with the Common Core State Standards: Lesson Correlations *(Continued)*

Chapter	Discussion Examples: Vignettes and Video Clips	Counting and Cardinality (CC)	Operations and Algebraic Thinking (OA)	Number and Operations in Base Ten (NBT)	Number and Operations – Fractions (NF)	Ratios and Proportional Relationships (RP)	Expressions and Equations (EE)	Measurement and Data (MD)	The Number System (NS)	Geometry (G)
7	Recording Addition Number Sentences, Kindergarten		K.OA Decompose numbers less than or equal to 10 into pairs in more than one way, e.g., by using objects or drawings, and record each decomposition by a drawing or equation (e.g., 5 = 2 + 3 and 5 = 4 + 1).							
7	Making Sense of Subtraction Symbols, Grade 1		1.OA Represent and solve problems involving addition and subtraction.							
7	Interpreting Numerical Expressions, Grade 5		5.OA Write and interpret numerical expressions.							
8	Analyzing Data from a Bar Graph, Grade 3							3.MD and 4.MD Represent and interpret data.		

Video Clips by Chapter, Including References to Facilitator's Guide

*Indicates that clip in Teacher's Guide features a portion of the clip that is featured in the Facilitator's Guide.
**Indicates that clip in Teacher's Guide features portions of two clips in the Facilitator's Guide.

Chapter	Video Clip	Length	Title	Grade/Teacher	Description	What This Clip Is Labeled in *Classroom Discussions in Math Facilitator's Guide*
1	1A	1:19	Wait Time: Hands down; let him think.	Grade 3/Mrs. Foley	In this clip, Mrs. Foley reinforces respectful behaviours in the midst of a problem-solving lesson.	2.1f
1	1B	1:38	Turn-and-Talk: How many cans of grape juice?	Grade 3/Mrs. Foley	In this clip, Mrs. Foley's students are solving a complicated problem with two kinds of packs of juice cans.	1.2a2*
1	1C	:44	Turn-and-Talk: How do we know those are greater than a whole?	Grade 6/Mrs. Rowan	In this clip, the student Jaehun has just given his thinking about where 7/6 and 13/9 are on a number line. The teacher, Mrs. Rowan, realizes that this was a point of confusion during a previous lesson.	1.2a4
1	1D	:33	Turn-and-Talk: Can everyone turn . . . and repeat that idea?	Grade 6/Ms. Fournier	In this clip, Ms. Fournier asks everyone to practice saying an important idea about ratios.	n/a
1	1E	:42	Revoicing: So you're saying I can't buy one can . . . ?	Grade 3/Mrs. Foley	In this clip, the teacher, Mrs. Foley, asks a student what at least twenty-six cans means.	1.2b2
1	1F	:50	Revoicing: So you multiplied the length . . .?	Grade 5/Mrs. Foley	In this clip, Mrs. Foley's class is working on ways to find the volume of a rectangular prism.	1.2b4
1	1G	1:02	Say More: Can you tell me what you did?	Kindergarten/ Mrs. Luizzi	Mrs. Luizzi's students have just done a turn-and-talk. She asks one student to report what they have talked about.	1.2c1

(Continued)

Chapter	Video Clip	Length	Title	Grade/Teacher	Description	What This Clip Is Labeled in *Classroom Discussions in Math Facilitator's Guide*
1	1H	:39	Say More: Tell me a little bit more.	Grade 3/Mr. Danella	In this clip, Mr. Danella asks a student to give an argument as to why his (Mr. D's) claim is wrong. (This clip also provides a revoicing example.)	1.2c2*
1	1I	1:57	Who Can Repeat? He's not all done yet.	Kindergarten/ Mrs. Hayward	In this clip, Mrs. Hayward's students are working on circling groups of hearts on a card with seven hearts. One student circles only three of the hearts.	1.3a1
1	1J	:48	Who Can Repeat? She was counting by fives.	Grade 1/Mrs. Delaney	In this clip, Mrs. Delaney's class is using a hundreds chart to explore counting patterns.	1.3a2
1	1K	1:46	Who Can Repeat? Finding the volume of a rectangular prism	Grade 5/Mrs. Foley	In this clip, a student gives his way of finding the volume of a rectangular prism. The teacher, Mrs. Foley, asks others to repeat.	1.3a5
1	1L	1:33	Who Can Repeat? How did you know that seven-eighths was greater than three-fourths?	Grade 6/Mrs. Rowan	In this clip, a student explains her reasoning in deciding where to place fractions on a number line. The teacher, Mrs. Rowan, asks others to repeat.	1.3a6
1	1M	1:06	Who Can Repeat? Which table is "the root beer drinkers?"	Grade 6/Ms. Fournier	In this clip, Ms. Fournier asks another student to repeat a classmate's solution strategy to a ratio problem.	n/a
1	1N	:35	Press for Reasoning: Are you sure? How do you know?	Grade 2/Ms. Powers	In this clip, Ms. Powers asks a student to explain her thinking about a strategy for subtracting numbers.	n/a
1	1O	1:14	Press for Reasoning: Can you prove it?	Grade 4/Mrs. Burgess	In this clip, Mrs. Burgess's students are solving a mystery number puzzle. She presses for reasoning several times.	1.4a2

(Continued)

Chapter	Video Clip	Length	Title	Grade/Teacher	Description	What This Clip Is Labeled in *Classroom Discussions in Math Facilitator's Guide*
1	1P	2:42	Press for Reasoning: Why does that work?	Grade 5/Mrs. Foley	In this clip, the teacher, Mrs. Foley, is pressing for reasoning in students' explanations of how they found the volume of a rectangular prism. You will see "Who can repeat?" mixed in with press for reasoning.	1.4a4
1	1Q	:43	Do You Agree or Disagree . . . and Why? Why do you agree with him?	Mrs. Delaney	In this clip, Mrs. Delaney's students are explaining how they counted two nickels and five pennies. Mrs. Delaney asks one student whether he agrees or disagrees with what the previous student said.	1.5b1
1	1R	2:30	Do You Agree or Disagree . . . and Why? Do almost all of the people do their homework before dinner?	Grade 3/ Mrs. Schineller	In this clip, the teacher, Mrs. Schineller, asks her students to turn and talk about whether they agree with the claim that almost all of the thirty-eight people polled do their homework before dinner.	1.5b2
1	1S	1:04	Do You Agree or Disagree . . . and Why? Not to be rude but	Grade 3/Mr. Danella	In this clip, the teacher, Mr. Danella, asks students whether they agree or disagree with Jeda's claim about what numbers would solve their puzzle, and one student disagrees.	1.5b3
1	1T	1:03	Who Can Add On? Would you like to add on to the beginning of her thinking?	Grade 1/Mrs. Delaney	In this clip, Mrs. Delaney's students are discussing ways to add nickels and pennies. One student explains her approach but reaches an impasse. Mrs. Delaney asks for input from others.	1.5a1
1	1U	1:04	Who Can Add On? Who can add on to that?	Grade 2/Ms. Powers	In this clip, Ms. Powers asks a student to add on to a classmate's explanation about linear measurement.	n/a

(*Continued*)

Chapter	Video Clip	Length	Title	Grade/Teacher	Description	What This Clip Is Labeled in *Classroom Discussions in Math Facilitator's Guide*
1	1V	:43	Who Can Add On? What is a rectangular prism?	Grade 5/Mrs. Foley	In this clip, the teacher, Mrs. Foley, is asking her students to weigh in with their understandings of what a rectangular prism is.	1.5a3
2	2A	1:49	Setting Up Classroom Talk Norms: Discussing *Fair Turns* and Repeating	Grade 1/ Mrs. Hayward	In this clip, Mrs. Hayward is working with her kindergarten students to review what constitutes a fair turn—this is her term for a collection of positive behaviors that help students orient to each other's contributions.	2.1a
2	2B	1:21	Setting Up Classroom Talk Norms: How do we agree and disagree?	Grade 4/Ms.Luipold	In this clip, Ms. Luipold discusses with her students how to use the agree/disagree move.	2.1j
3	3A	3:32	Number Patterns on the Hundreds Chart	Grade 1/Mrs. Delaney	In this clip, a number of students count to one hundred using different patterns.	3.1a
3	3B	7:40	Examining Area and Perimeter	Grade 4/Mrs. Luipold	In this clip, students discuss in small groups and as a class some of their thoughts about why the perimeters of rectangles with the same area are different.	3.2b*
4	4A	3:19	Adding Three Numbers	Grade 1/Ms. Moylan	In this clip, Ms. Moylan has students solve addition of three numbers and explain it to their partner. The partner then repeats back what the first student said. Here the problem is 3 + 4 + 2.	1.1b, 8.1b*
4	4B	4:37	Subtracting on the Number Line	Grade 2/Ms. Powers	In this clip, students talk about a number sense strategy for whole-number subtraction.	n/a

(*Continued*)

Chapter	Video Clip	Length	Title	Grade/Teacher	Description	What This Clip Is Labeled in *Classroom Discussions in Math Facilitator's Guide*
4	4C	4:44	Comparing Subtraction Strategies	Grade 2/Ms. Powers	In this clip, students compare two different representations of the same computational strategy.	n/a
4	4D	6:59	Fraction Number Line	Grade 6/Mrs. Rowan	In this clip, students talk about their strategies for locating fractions on the number line.	4.2 and 5.2**
5	5A	6:21	Solving a Multistep Word Problem, Part 1	Grade 3/Mrs. Foley	In this clip, the teacher makes sure students understand all of the statements and facts from the problem.	5.1a*
5	5B	9:35	Solving a Multistep Word Problem, Part 2	Grade 3/Mrs. Foley	In this clip, students share their solution methods to a multistep problem.	5.1b
5	5C	3:39	The Newspaper Club Problem	Grade 6/Ms. Fournier	In this clip, students talk about an important generalization about equivalent ratios.	n/a
6	6A	7:45	Finding Missing Digits	Grade 3/Mr. Danella	In this clip, students talk about what would and would not make a good next guess for the practice game Four Strikes and You're Out.	6.1*
6	6B	7:33	Developing Methods for Volume of Rectangular Prisms	Grade 5/Mrs. Foley	In this clip, students develop and connect two general methods for determining the volume of a rectangular prism.	6.2
7	7A	5:54	Making Sense of One-Half	Grade 2/Ms. Powers	In this clip, students talk about why one-half of an hour and one-half of a dollar are not the same.	n/a
7	7B	4:43	Using the Words *More* and *Less*	Kindergarten/ Mrs. Luizzi	In this clip, students compare the heights of towers made from interlocking cubes.	7.1a

(*Continued*)

Chapter	Video Clip	Length	Title	Grade/Teacher	Description	What This Clip Is Labeled in *Classroom Discussions in Math Facilitator's Guide*
7	7C	5:23	Connecting Factors and Multiples	Grade 4/ Mrs. Burgess	In this clip, fourth graders use classroom discourse to make sense of the connections between factors and multiples; they discuss whether or not the number twenty-eight can be both a factor of twenty-eight and a multiple of twenty-eight.	7.2c*
7	7D	2:07	Defining the Word *Volume*	Grade 5/Mrs. Foley	In this clip, fifth graders work together to define volume. Their teacher, Mrs. Foley, assists them in defining volume as the amount of space an object takes up; it is measured in cubic units.	7.2d
7	7E	6:07	Talking About Ratios	Grade 6/Ms. Fournier	In this clip, students practice talking about ratios using precise mathematical language.	n/a
7	7F	2:56	How Many Groups? How Many Hearts?	Kindergarten/ Mrs. Hayward	In this clip, kindergartners find groups of different sizes.	7.1b*
8	8A	4:57	Turn-and-Talk Modeling	Kindergarten/ Mrs. Luizzi	In this clip, Mrs. Luizzi is working on making turn-and-talk a productive practice for her kindergarten class. She decides to model a turn-and-talk with one of the students and discusses it with the rest of the class.	2.1b
8	8B	1:06	If I Call on You . . .	Grade 6/Ms. Fournier	In this clip, Ms. Fournier gives her students guidance on what to do if she calls on them to speak but they are not ready to respond.	n/a

(*Continued*)

Chapter	Video Clip	Length	Title	Grade/Teacher	Description	What This Clip Is Labeled in *Classroom Discussions in Math Facilitator's Guide*
8	8C	4:57	Analyzing Data from a Bar Graph, Part A	Grade 3/ Mrs. Schineller	In this clip, the teacher, Mrs. Schineller, explains the task to students, works with student pairs to write their conclusions, and prepares them to speak during the whole-class discussion.	8.2a
8	8D	3:53	Analyzing Data from a Bar Graph, Part B	Grade 3/ Mrs. Schineller	In this clip, students discuss conclusions that use the phrase three times as many.	8.2c
8	8E	5:11	Analyzing Data from a Bar Graph, Part C	Grade 3/ Mrs. Schineller	In this clip, students discuss their conclusions that use the phrase more than half.	8.2d*

Video Clips by Grade, Including Demographics

The mathematics lessons on the DVDs were filmed in kindergarten through grade 6 classrooms in Cambridge, Massachusetts, Hartford, Connecticut, and West Hartford, Connecticut. All lessons were filmed in October, the second month of the students' school year. The teachers who participated in this project had a variety of backgrounds but all shared a strong commitment to using math talk to help their students learn. Additional support staff, including math coaches and assistant teachers, also participated in some of the lessons. The lessons focus on mathematical content from the following areas: number sense and operations, algebraic thinking, geometry, measurement, and data analysis. The video clips show excerpts from the lessons. The information in the chart below reflects the demographics of the classrooms during the school year in which the lessons were filmed.

Grade	Teacher	School and Demographics	Video Clips	Lesson Plan (See Appendix B.)
Kindergarten	**Mrs. Luizzi** Mrs. Luizzi teaches junior kindergarten/kindergarten at the Martin Luther King, Jr. School in Cambridge, Massachusetts. In her ten years of teaching, Mrs. Luizzi has taught Sheltered English Immersion (SEI), English as a Second Language (ESL), and Spanish Dual Language Immersion instruction. Mrs. Luizzi believes that math talk empowers her students to learn. She encourages all of her students to share their ideas about math standing with feet square on the ground and voices that are loud and proud.	**Martin Luther King, Jr. School** There are eighteen students in Mrs. Luizzi's junior kindergarten/kindergarten class, seven boys and eleven girls. (In a junior kindergarten, students enter at age 4.) Assistant teacher Mrs. Denise Toomey also takes part in the lesson. The student body at this school in Cambridge, Massachusetts, is composed of 18 percent Caucasian, 46 percent African American, 11 percent Hispanic, and 22 percent Asian. Sixty-one percent of students qualify for free or reduced lunch. Thirty-one percent of students do not have English as their first language.	1G 7B 8A	Using *More* and *Less* to Describe the Data in a Graph
Kindergarten	**Mrs. Hayward** Mrs. Hayward teaches kindergarten at the Kennedy-Longfellow School in Cambridge, Massachusetts. A teacher for more than ten years, she has also taught first, second, and third grades. Mrs. Hayward believes that discussions in math class should capitalize on young children's natural inclinations to talk. She emphasizes that, with effective modeling from the teacher, students' own words become a powerful learning tool.	**Kennedy-Longfellow School** There are twenty students in Mrs. Hayward's class, nine boys and eleven girls. Math coach Ms. Fiona Healy and assistant teacher Ms. Maryann Sprague also take part in the lesson. The student body at this school in Cambridge, Massachusetts, is composed of 33 percent Caucasian, 35 percent African American, 18 percent Hispanic, and 11 percent Asian. Fifty-eight percent of students qualify for free or reduced lunch. Twenty-six percent of students do not have English as their first language.	1I 2A 7F	Decomposing the Number Seven

(Continued)

Grade	Teacher	School and Demographics	Video Clips	Lesson Plan (See Appendix B.)
Grade 1	**Mrs. Delaney** Mrs. Delaney teaches first grade at the Batchelder School in Hartford, Connecticut. She has been teaching for more than thirty years and has worked as a classroom teacher, Title I teacher, and gifted and talented teacher. Mrs. Delaney is passionate about giving all students the time they need to make productive contributions to math discussions. She regularly reminds her students that giving a classmate time to formulate an answer is just as important as raising their hands to give one of their own.	**Batchelder School** There are nineteen students in Mrs. Delaney's first-grade class, ten boys and nine girls. The student body at this school in Hartford, Connecticut, is composed of 4 percent Caucasian, 21 percent African American, 72 percent Hispanic, and 2 percent Asian. More than 95 percent of students qualify for free or reduced lunch. Fifty-two percent of students do not have English as their first language.	1J 1Q 1T 3A	Number Patterns on the Hundreds Chart
Grade 1	**Ms. Moylan** Ms. Moylan teaches first grade at the Amigos School in Cambridge, Massachusetts. A certified Responsive Classroom trainer, Ms. Moylan has ten years of experience as a classroom teacher. She believes that first-grade students can participate productively in mathematical discussions; she recommends providing lots of opportunities for students to practice listening and responding to each other's ideas as an effective tool for deepening their own understanding of mathematical concepts.	**Amigos School** The Amigos School is founded on a dual-language immersion model. Students receive 50 percent English and 50 percent Spanish instruction and are expected to become literate in both Spanish and English. Ms. Moylan teaches the English component of two classes of first-grade students. There are fourteen students in this first-grade class, eight boys and six girls. Assistant teacher Ms. Elba Santiago also takes part in the lesson. The student body at this school in Cambridge, Massachusetts, is composed of 34 percent Caucasian, 7 percent African American, 48 percent Hispanic, and 3 percent Asian. Thirty percent of students qualify for free or reduced lunch. Thirty-seven percent of students do not have English as their first language.	4A	Adding Three Numbers

Grade	Teacher	School and Demographics	Video Clips	Lesson Plan (See Appendix B.)
Grade 2	**Ms. Powers** Ms. Powers teaches second grade at the Maria Baldwin School in Cambridge, Massachusetts. She uses math talk to assess how her students are thinking and learning about math concepts. Ms. Powers believes that the talk moves used in *Classroom Discussions* encourage students to be more active participants in math learning. She has found that conversations among students can be a powerful learning tool for all learners.	**Maria L. Baldwin School** There are twenty-two students in Ms. Powers' class, twelve boys and ten girls. Intern Ms. Brittany O'Neill also takes part in the lesson. The student body at this school in Cambridge, Massachusetts, is composed of 50 percent Caucasian, 25 percent African American, 8 percent Hispanic, and 10 percent Asian. 36 percent of students quality for free or reduced lunch. 18 percent of students do not have English as their first language.	1N 1U 4B 4C 7A	Teaching Subtraction Strategies and Making Sense of One-Half
Grade 3	**Mr. Danella** Mr. Danella teaches third grade at the Kennedy-Longfellow School in Cambridge, Massachusetts. In addition to third grade, he has also taught second, fourth, and sixth grades. Mr. Danella relies on math talk to provide him with ongoing formative assessments of student understanding. He uses what he gleans from partner talk and whole-class discussions to tailor instruction to students' needs.	**Kennedy-Longfellow School** There are eighteen students in Mr. Danella's third-grade class, eleven boys and seven girls. The student body at this school in Cambridge, Massachusetts, is composed of 33 percent Caucasian, 35 percent African American, 18 percent Hispanic, and 11 percent Asian. Fifty-eight percent of students qualify for free or reduced lunch. Twenty-six percent of students do not have English as their first language.	1H 1S 6A	Four Strikes and You're Out

(Continued)

Grade	Teacher	School and Demographics	Video Clips	Lesson Plan (See Appendix B.)
Grade 3	**Mrs. Foley** Mrs. Foley is the mathematics specialist at the Florence E. Smith School of Science, Math and Technology in West Hartford, Connecticut. She has twelve years of teaching experience, including nine years as a classroom teacher for fourth and fifth grades. Mrs. Foley emphasizes the important role that the teacher plays in a math discussion. As she facilitates a discussion, she actively monitors the student talk so that it remains focused on the targeted concepts and skills of the lesson.	**Florence E. Smith School of Science, Math and Technology** There are nineteen students in Mrs. Foley's third-grade class, twelve boys and seven girls. The student body at this school in West Hartford, Connecticut, is composed of 29 percent Caucasian, 18 percent African American, 34 percent Hispanic, and 19 percent Asian. Forty-three percent of students qualify for free or reduced lunch. Twenty-five percent of students do not have English as their first language.	1A 1B 1E 5A 5B	The Birthday Party Problem
Grade 3	**Mrs. Schineller** Mrs. Schineller teaches third grade at the Amigos School in Cambridge, Massachusetts. She has taught for four years and credits talk moves such as "Who can repeat?" for helping all of her students develop understanding of key mathematical ideas. Mrs. Schineller enjoys seeing previously quiet students become active participants in a discussion as the result of these moves.	**Amigos School** The Amigos School is founded on a dual-language immersion model. Students receive 50 percent English and 50 percent Spanish instruction and are expected to become literate in both Spanish and English. Mrs. Schineller teaches the English component of two classes of third-grade students. There are nineteen students in this class, eleven boys and eight girls. The student body at this school in Cambridge, Massachusetts, is composed of 34 percent Caucasian, 7 percent African American, 48 percent Hispanic, and 3 percent Asian. Thirty percent of students qualify for free or reduced lunch. Thirty-seven percent of students do not have English as their first language.	1R 8C 8D 8E	Analyzing Data from a Bar Graph (See Chapter 8)

Grade	Teacher	School and Demographics	Video Clips	Lesson Plan (See Appendix B.)
Grade 4	**Ms. Luipold** Ms. Luipold teaches fourth grade at the Florence E. Smith School of Science, Math and Technology in West Hartford, Connecticut. She has been an elementary educator for more than twenty-five years. Ms. Luipold works diligently to use talk moves in all of her math lessons. She recommends that teachers new to classroom talk start slow, focus on one talk move at a time, and be persistent.	**Florence E. Smith School of Science, Math and Technology** There are twenty-one students in Ms. Luipold's fourth-grade class, eleven girls and ten boys. The student body at this school in West Hartford, Connecticut, is composed of 29 percent Caucasian, 18 percent African American, 34 percent Hispanic, and 19 percent Asian. Forty-three percent of students qualify for free or reduced lunch. Twenty-five percent of students do not have English as their first language.	2B 3B	Perimeters of Rectangles with a Fixed Area
Grade 4	**Mrs. Burgess** Mrs. Burgess teaches fourth grade at the John M. Tobin School in Cambridge, Massachusetts. She is a National Board Certified teacher with thirty-five years of teaching experience. Mrs. Burgess believes that discussions in math class deepen student understanding, and that as students talk about their ideas, they are exposed to strategies that they might not have thought of on their own. With experience, students can then use those strategies in their own work.	**John M. Tobin School** There are nineteen students in Mrs. Burgess's fourth-grade class, nine boys and ten girls. The student body at this school in Cambridge, Massachusetts, is composed of 27 percent Caucasian, 36 percent African American, 13 percent Hispanic, and 17 percent Asian. Fifty-four percent of students qualify for free or reduced lunch. Forty-nine percent of students do not have English as their first language.	1O 7C	Reasoning About Factors and Multiples

(Continued)

Grade	Teacher	School and Demographics	Video Clips	Lesson Plan (See Appendix B.)
Grade 5	Mrs. Foley [See more about Mrs. Foley in the Grade 3 section of this table.]	**Florence E. Smith School of Science, Math and Technology** There are eighteen students in Mrs. Foley's fifth-grade class, ten boys and eight girls. The student body at this school in West Hartford, Connecticut, is composed of 29 percent Caucasian, 18 percent African American, 34 percent Hispanic, and 19 percent Asian. Forty-three percent of students qualify for free or reduced lunch. Twenty-five percent of students do not have English as their first language.	1F 1K 1P 1V 6B 7D	Volume of Rectangular Prisms
Grade 6	Ms. Fournier Ms. Fournier teaches sixth-grade math at the Rindge Avenue Upper Campus in Cambridge, Massachusetts. In her experience, Ms. Fournier has found that hearing the same key idea, restated by several students, gives students an opportunity to think deeply about a particular concept. Ms. Fournier loves when she hears a student say, "Oh I get it," as a result of participating in a class discussion.	**Rindge Avenue Upper School** Ms. Fournier teaches four sections of grade 6 mathematics at the Rindge Avenue Upper School. Students from three of her four classes participated in the filming. The student body at this school in Cambridge, Massachusetts is composed of 44 percent Caucasian, 32 percent African American, 10 percent Hispanic, and 11 percent Asian. Forty-four percent of students qualify for free or reduced lunch. Twenty percent of students do not have English as their first language.	1D 1M 5C 7E 8B	

Grade	Teacher	School and Demographics	Video Clips	Lesson Plan (See Appendix B.)
Grade 6	**Mrs. Rowan** Mrs. Rowan teaches sixth- and eighth-grade mathematics at the Kennedy-Longfellow School in Cambridge, Massachusetts. She has taught elementary and middle grades for fifteen years. Mrs. Rowan stresses the importance of creating a safe environment for productive math discussions and talks regularly with her students about the norms of respectful class discussions. As the school year progresses, she delights when students who were once hesitant to speak in class develop the confidence to explain their ideas, share their confusion, and ask for help.	**Kennedy-Longfellow School** There are nineteen students in Mrs. Rowan's sixth-grade class, five boys and fifteen girls. The student body at this school in Cambridge, Massachusetts, is composed of 33 percent Caucasian, 35 percent African American, 18 percent Hispanic, and 11 percent Asian. Fifty-eight percent of students qualify for free or reduced lunch. Twenty-six percent of students do not have English as their first language. Mrs. Anderson, a coauthor of the book *Classroom Discussions* (Chapin, O'Connor, and Anderson 2009), was a guest in Mrs. Rowan's class on the day of filming.	1C 1L 4D	Placing Fractions on a Number Line

Getting Started
Mathematics Learning with Classroom Discussions

Section Overview

In Chapter 1, "Academically Productive Talk: An Overview," we introduce the four steps of productive mathematics discussions, describing the talk tools and the talk moves you'll need to accomplish those discussions. Using several classroom examples, we also review what students need to know about each talk move and provide suggestions and tips for connecting with students. At the end of Chapter 1, we provide a list of videos exemplifying each talk move at different grade levels for your convenience.

In Chapter 2, "How Do We Begin? Classroom Norms for Productive Talk," we introduce the two major goals of setting up classroom talk norms—respectful discourse and equitable participation—along with reasons that these goals are crucial for success. We also address students' rights and obligations—the ground rules for respectful and courteous talk that must be established and then followed in order for discourse to be effective.

Academically Productive Talk: An Overview

What does productive math talk sound and look like?

(Continued)

About This Chapter

As teachers, we elicit responses from our students in various ways—with questions, commands, hints, jokes, and so on. When students become familiar with our inventory of phrases and expressions, they usually know what we expect of them. Although we rarely stop to think about our most common conversational prompts, they are among our most important instructional tools. From our work in Project Challenge (see Appendix A: The Research: Project Challenge, page 319), we have found it useful to think carefully about these tools: It matters what you say and how you say it.

> **Although we rarely stop to think about our most common conversational prompts, they are among our most important instructional tools.**

[See Appendix A.]

In this chapter we start by giving you a first encounter with a number of examples of talk in action in mathematics lessons. We then provide an introduction to the steps that support productive discussion, followed by the tools—specifically *talk moves*—that make it possible to achieve those steps. We then focus on the actual practice of using these moves. Throughout the chapter, we include examples, strategies, and tips and suggestions for you to use as you get started. Narrative examples, or "cases," illustrate how the basic talk moves look in several different classrooms. Video examples illustrate the moves in action (see the "Summary Tables of Productive Talk Moves" at the end of this chapter). In Chapter 2, "How Do We Begin? Classroom Norms for Productive Talk," we provide detailed plans for how to introduce your students to the practices you'll learn about in this chapter.

[See Chapter 1, Summary Tables]

[See Chapter 2.]

A First Encounter with Examples of Productive Math Discourse

To understand what academically productive math talk sounds and looks like, it's helpful to read and view some especially compelling examples from various grade levels, such as those that follow, that illustrate the benefit of math talk in action in classrooms.

Academically Productive Talk in Mrs. Schuster's Third-Grade Class

The students in Mrs. Schuster's third-grade classroom are discussing a question she has set out for them to consider:

Does the order of the numbers in a multiplication sentence affect the answer? Explain why or why not.

In order to explore this question, students are generating examples of multiplication sentences and testing what happens when they change the order of the factors. Students know many of the basic multiplication facts but have not yet learned an algorithm for multidigit multiplication.

Teaching with the Common Core

3.0A Understand properties of multiplication and the relationship between multiplication and division.

3.0A Apply properties of operations as strategies to multiply and divide. *Examples: If 6 × 4 = 24 is known, then 4 × 6 = 24 is also known. (Commutative property of multiplication.)....*

One student has made a conjecture that the order of the factors does not make a difference—"the answer is the same no matter which number goes first." Students are agreeing with this conjecture by bringing up other examples that work, such as 3 × 4 = 12 and 4 × 3 = 12. Mrs. Schuster then asks if this conjecture works with larger numbers and suggests they use calculators to check. Students are able to generate many examples to verify the conjecture, but explaining *why* the products are the same is not as straightforward as carrying out the multiplication procedure.

As the students work together in pairs, Mrs. Schuster circulates around the room listening. She notices that Eddie has made an interesting comment, so she addresses the class and asks him to repeat it for the whole class.

1. **Mrs. S:** Eddie, I heard you make an interesting claim during your partner work with Sila. It was something about the multiplication sentences: The sentence two times five equals ten, and five times two equals ten. Can you repeat it for the class?

2. **Eddie:** Well, I don't think it matters what order the numbers are in. You still get the same answer. But the multiplication sentences are different because they mean different things.

3. **Mrs. S:** OK, Rebecca, do you agree or disagree with what Eddie is saying?

4. **Rebecca:** Well, I agree that it doesn't matter which number is first, because two times five equals ten and that's the same answer as five times two. But I don't get what Eddie means about the multiplication meaning different things.

5. **Mrs. S:** Eddie, would you say more about what you mean?

6. **Eddie:** Well, I just think that the two times five can mean two groups of five things like two bags of five apples. And five times two means five bags of two apples. And those aren't the same thing.

7. **Tiffany:** [Hand up, waving] But you still have the same number of apples! So they do mean the same!

8. **Mrs. S:** OK, so we have two different ideas here to talk about. Eddie says that order *does* matter, because five times two and two times five can each be used to describe a different situation, like two bags of five apples or five bags of two apples. So the two number sentences mean different things. And Tiffany, are you saying that those two number sentences *can't* be used to describe two different situations?

9. **Tiffany:** No, I mean that even though the two situations are different, the answer is the same.

10. **Mrs. S:** OK, so you're saying that order doesn't matter because the answer is the same? You have the same number of apples?

11. **Tiffany:** Right.

12. **Mrs. S:** OK. We need to think about this. In Eddie's claim, order makes a difference in the situation you're describing. In Tiffany's claim, order doesn't make a difference in the answer we get. So do you think order makes a difference in multiplying two numbers together? Talk to your partner about that question.

Mrs. Schuster is using classroom talk to deepen students' understanding of the commutative property of multiplication. She knows that this mathematical idea may be clear enough for the operation of addition, but that it gets complicated when we introduce multiplication. She knows that in the case of addition, students can easily see that the number sentence 2 + 3 and the number sentence 3 + 2 can be used to describe the same situation. It doesn't really matter whether we mention the three pears or the two apples first. In the case of multiplication, however, if we focus on the particulars of the problem situation, the order of elements in the number sentences suddenly matters. As Eddie points out, two bags of five apples and five bags of two apples are very different.

> Mrs. Schuster is using classroom talk to deepen students' understanding of the commutative property of multiplication. She knows that this mathematical idea may be clear enough for the operation of addition, but that it gets complicated when we introduce multiplication.

Mrs. Schuster knows that this is one of many points in the early grades where students' mathematical reasoning and their appreciation of real-world problem situations can come into apparent conflict. Yet in the long run, students' abilities to use mathematical expressions to model real-world situations will be central to their progress in mathematics and science. She knows that it is therefore worth time and effort to clarify things here in her third grade, and she has chosen to use classroom talk as a tool to support that aim.

Video Clips: Seeing Academically Productive Talk in Various Grades

Watch the following video clips, categorized by grade on the DVD. What do you see happening in each? Does anything surprise you, interest you, or make an impression on you?

Video Clip 7B: Using the Words *More* and *Less* (Mrs. Luizzi, Kindergarten)

Video Clip 6A: Finding Missing Digits (Mr. Danella, Grade 3)

Video Clip 4D: Fraction Number Line (Mrs. Rowan, Grade 6)

BEFORE YOU WATCH THE VIDEOS

To make the most productive use of the video clips, you and any colleagues you are working with should take time to read through the "Guidelines for Watching Videos of Teaching" (see page xxi). For demographics, see page xliv.

Your Turn: Why Use Talk in Mathematics Classrooms?

Read "Why Use Talk in Mathematics Classrooms?" (see the Frontmatter, page xv). Think about your own students and their learning strengths and difficulties. Which of the five reasons for using classroom talk and discussion seem most relevant to your current teaching? Is there an example from your experience that might support one of the five claims?

Quantity of Talk Versus Quality of Talk

Remember, if we simply ask students to talk, without thinking carefully about our purposes, we may end up with irrelevant, hard-to-manage talk that serves no clear academic purpose. Sometimes this aimless talk may be pleasant; sometimes it may be unpleasant. But in either case it probably will not significantly advance student thinking and learning. Instead, for talk to be productive, we believe that it must be carefully integrated with the content of the mathematics lesson. Our goal is not to increase the *amount* of talk in our classrooms, but to increase the *amount of high-quality* talk in our classrooms—the mathematically productive talk.

> Our goal is not to increase the *amount* of talk in our classrooms, but to increase the *amount of high-quality* talk in our classrooms—the mathematically productive talk.

How can we tell when the talk in our classrooms has been productive, and not a waste of time? It seems clear that we can't simply rely on our feelings. Think back to the last time you had a conversation that you enjoyed. It may or may not have been intellectually significant. Obviously, the best conversations—in or out of school—are the ones that are fun and exciting, and also intellectually or personally important. But we cannot use fun and excitement as our only criteria for whether classroom talk has been productive. We have to find ways to recognize and appreciate which forms of talk are most mathematically productive for our students, and for a particular lesson or topic. In this resource, we provide multiple ways for you to develop a sense for when talk is mathematically productive for your students.

Four Steps Toward Productive Talk

As a professional educator, you want to encourage and sustain academically productive talk in your classes. In order to create an atmosphere in which productive discussion can take place, first think about *goals*. Specific moves and tools to support productive talk don't really make sense until you understand what they are supposed to do—how they are supposed to support your goals.

In our observations of teachers who are successful in using classroom talk to support learning, we have seen again and again that they are able to accomplish four specific steps—goals—that are essential to creating the conditions needed to support real discussion.

Four Steps Toward Productive Talk

Step 1: Helping Individual Students Clarify and Share Their Own Thoughts

Step 2: Helping Students Orient to the Thinking of Others

Step 3: Helping Students Deepen Their Own Reasoning

Step 4: Helping Students Engage with the Reasoning of Others

Step 1: Helping Individual Students Clarify and Share Their Own Thoughts

If students are going to participate in the discussion, they have to be able to share their thinking and reasoning out loud in a way that is at least partially understandable to others. If only one or two students can do this, you won't have a discussion, you'll have a monologue or, at best, a dialogue between the teacher and a student.

Step 2: Helping Students Orient to the Thinking of Others

> If a student is simply waiting to speak, and is not *listening* to others and *trying to understand them*, he or she will not be able to contribute to a real discussion.

Many teachers have told us, "My students have no trouble talking about their ideas—they just won't listen to others!" If a student is simply waiting to speak, and is not *listening* to others or *trying to understand them*, he or she will not be able to contribute to a real discussion. A discussion involves sharing ideas and reasoning, so it is important to steer students away from a series of individual, unrelated thoughts. If they can't listen to one another, and hear one another, they won't really be able to engage in productive talk.

Step 3: Helping Students Deepen Their Own Reasoning

Even if students express their thoughts and listen to others' ideas, the discussion can still fail to be academically productive if it does not include solid and sustained reasoning. Some classroom discussions are superficial—most students are not skilled at pushing to understand and to deepen their own reasoning. Therefore, the teacher's role includes continuous and skillful use of the tools that *keep the focus on reasoning*.

Step 4: Helping Students Engage with the Reasoning of Others

The final step involves students actually absorbing the ideas and reasoning of other students and responding to them. This is when real discussion can take off—discussion that will support robust learning.

Productive Talk Moves and Tools

How do the teachers we observe succeeding in discussion accomplish the four steps outlined above? These goals don't just happen by themselves. Moment to moment, these teachers use particular *talk moves* and other tools to help their students in these four activities. In this section we have organized the talk moves within the four steps toward productive talk and provided explanations of how the talk moves will help you achieve your goals.

Talk *Moves* or *Tools*?

The term *talk moves* refers to strategic ways of asking questions and inviting participation in classroom conversations. Each talk move comes from our observation of skilled teachers and their ways of supporting productive talk. In addition, we introduce more general tools that can help you increase the productivity of the talk in your class, such as wait time and stop and jot. Sometimes we will use the umbrella term *talk tools* and sometimes we will refer specifically to the talk moves that are the focus of this resource. You can use whatever term seems most helpful to you and your colleagues!

For each step, we describe a situation that will occur if you decide to use talk intensively in your class—a situation that will *challenge* you as you try to use talk and discussion. We then explain one or more talk moves or other tools that will help you meet the challenge. We illustrate these with a classroom example and explain the teacher actions that support those goals.

Talk Moves That Help Individual Students Clarify and Share Their Own Thoughts

Talk Moves That Help Individual Students Clarify and Share Their Own Thoughts

Wait Time
Turn and Talk
Stop and Jot
Will You Share That
    With the Class?
Say More . . .
So Are You Saying . . . ?
    (Revoicing)

How do we get students to externalize their thinking so that others can respond to it? Part of this work involves setting up classroom norms to ensure that students will feel safe in expressing their thoughts in public. (This is described at length in Chapter 2.) Additionally, it is important to help students get better at saying what they are thinking in ways that can be understood. Very often, students say things that are hard to understand. So what do we do when students are unclear, telegraphic, or vague? Because of time pressures and embarrassment, there is a strong motivation to simply move on. If you simply move on, however, without getting a real understanding of what the student is trying to say, there are downsides:

> So what do we do when students are unclear, telegraphic, or vague? Because of time pressures and embarrassment, there is a strong motivation to simply move on.

- You will not understand students' thinking, and neither will their classmates.

- Students will not get better at explaining their thoughts.

- Students are likely to believe that you don't really *want* to know that they think.

This in turn lowers students' motivation to participate; the whole enterprise of classroom discussion can quickly grind to a halt. Getting students to share their thoughts takes time and attention—but time and attention that are very well worth it!

Ms. D's Third-Grade Class

Imagine that you have asked your students a question, based on something they have read or done recently. We'll use an example from a third-grade class-room here, but you can imagine your own. Ms. D has spent the previous day working with physical materials to get across the idea that even numbers can be shared equally into two groups with no remainder. She starts out the next day with this question:

1. **Ms. D:** So, boys and girls, what do you think? Is twenty-four an even number or an odd number?

She looks out to see twenty-four blank faces and one raised hand. The student with her hand raised is the student who *always* has the answer. Ms. D feels that sinking feeling many of us are familiar with. Are they just not interested? Do they not remember? What now? Should she just repeat the lesson?

> **CCSS**
> **Teaching with the Common Core**
> 3.0A Represent and solve problems involving multiplication and division.

At this point, we would strongly encourage Ms. D to use a talk move: It is highly likely that her students are not respond-ing because *they need time to think—time to put their thoughts into words.* Many students feel intimidated about venturing into the arena of group talk. You can help them become willing to do this, however, with one of four simple but powerful talk tools.

> **MATH TALK TIP**
> **Problem!**
> Only one student volunteers to talk—the student who *always* has the answer.

> **MATH TALK TIP**
> **Solution!**
> Try these: *wait time, turn and talk, or stop and jot.* After turn and talk or stop and jot, use *Will you share that with the class?*

A Closer Look

Talk Tool: Wait Time

This well-known talk tool involves . . . not talking! Wait time, as first described by Mary Budd Rowe (1974), involves waiting at least four to five seconds after asking a question. By counting to five, Ms. D may start to see a few more hands creep up. But in some cases this may not be enough to really open up the conversation. As an alternative, try turn and talk.

Talk Move: Turn and Talk

Turn and talk or partner talk (also sometimes called "think-pair-share") is best used when you have asked a question and no one responds. Some teachers like to give students thirty seconds to a minute to think to themselves (no hands!) and then give students a short time, perhaps a minute or so, to put their thoughts into words with their nearest neighbor.

While this is happening, the teacher circulates and listens to discover what students are thinking. He or she can then go back into the large-group discussion with a better sense of how to proceed, while students have had a chance to clarify their thinking in a low-stress format. When the teacher then asks students to report what they said in their partner talk, many more will feel confident in doing so.

You can see how this supports Step 1: Helping Individual Students to Clarify and Share Their Own Thoughts. Students who are keeping up with the lesson but are hesitant about voicing their thoughts will have a chance to practice their contribution with just one conversational partner. Students who have not understood completely can bring up their questions with their partner, and perhaps formulate a way to ask their questions to the whole class. For many students, particularly those who are English learners, a one- or two-minute turn and talk is invaluable. They can emerge from the partner talk ready to participate in the whole-group discussion.

> For many students, particularly those who are English learners, a one- or two-minute turn and talk is invaluable. They can emerge from the partner talk ready to participate in the whole-group discussion.

Talk Tool: Stop and Jot

Some teachers, particularly in higher grades, like to use writing as a tool for students to gather their thoughts. You can give students a minute to think and to jot down their ideas about a solution method, an estimate of the answer to a problem, or their questions about a problem. When you then return to discuss the problem in more detail, students who are hesitant to speak off the cuff can read from their notes.

Talk Move: Will You Share That with the Class?

If you ask students to turn and talk, or stop and jot, use the opportunity to circulate and see what students are saying or writing. This will give you a sense of where students are in their understanding. You will also be able to call on students whose ideas might form the basis for productive discussion. It is helpful to ask students whether they are willing to share their thinking. When you pose the question to the whole class again, you can call on those students.

Teacher Reflection: Wait Time

Mrs. Anderson

During a year when I co-taught mathematics with another classroom teacher, my co-teacher and I set a goal of improving our wait time. To reach this goal, we first took turns collecting data about each other's wait times. When it was my turn to instruct the class, my co-teacher counted the number of seconds that passed after I asked a question and then called on a student to respond. When my colleague handed me my data, I was shocked to see that my wait times were only one second or less! I set a goal of increasing my wait time to ten seconds. To help me reach this goal, I asked my co-teacher to begin counting after I asked a question and signal me when ten seconds had passed. As I stood in front of the class waiting for my colleague's signal, the ten seconds often felt like hours. But in less than one week, I saw my wait times dramatically improve. Now, more than ten years after that experience, I still count in my head ("one Mississippi, two Mississippi, three Mississippi") after calling on a student. It's still a struggle to be patient enough to make it all the way to ten. But seeing more and more students raise their hands as the seconds tick by motivates me to keep trying and keep waiting.

When her initial question is met with a sea of blank faces, Ms. D chooses turn and talk to try to help her students clarify their thinking. She says, "Why don't you talk about this with the person next to you? Is twenty-four odd or even?" Immediately the room erupts with talk and many students appear eager to share their thinking. After a minute or so, Ms. D reconvenes the class. She does not have the chance to circulate around the class, so she does not know for sure what ideas students remember from the day before or what they think about even numbers.

Ms. D calls on Paulo to share, thinking he will know that 24 is an even number.

2. **Ms. D**: So Paulo, what did you and your partner think? Is twenty-four an even number or an odd number?

3. **Paulo**: Umm . . . we were, um . . . it's odd.

Paulo's answer is wrong. And furthermore, Ms. D doesn't know what Paulo is thinking, so she can't really tell where to go with it. Ms. D could now choose to move on, looking for someone with the right answer. She might choose to tell Paulo that his answer is incorrect and remind him of the previous day's discussion. However, she chooses instead to use another talk move, *Say more. . . .*

MATH TALK TIP

Problem!

The student's answer is wrong, and the teacher isn't clear on what the student is thinking.

MATH TALK TIP

Solution!

Try the talk move *Say more . . .*

A Closer Look

Talk Move: Say More . . .

Frequently, when students say something, it's hard to understand what they are thinking because they seem to be aiming to say the absolute minimum! In order to get them to share their thinking, it is often helpful to use some variant of the *Say more . . .* move:

Who can say more?
Tell us more about what you're thinking.
Would you give an example?

This simple "family" of talk moves is often enough to get the student to expand and provide material for the teacher to work with as he or she attempts to get other students engaged. This move sends the message that the teacher *wants to understand* the student's thinking. It sends a signal that the teacher wants more than just a correct answer. It also potentially gives the student time to regroup and clarify.

Ms. D proceeds to use this variation of the *Say more . . .* move with Paulo.

4. **Ms. D:** Paulo, *can you say more about your thinking?*

5. **Paulo:** Well, if we could use three, then it could go into that, but three is odd. So, then, if it was . . . but . . . three is even. I mean odd. So if it's odd, then it's not even.

Ms. D is confused by this somewhat garbled utterance. However, she knows that students are frequently very unclear, or even impossible to understand. And she wants to understand Paulo's reasoning, in spite of his lack of clarity. So she tries again with another talk move known as revoicing.

> **MATH TALK TIP**
>
> **Problem!**
> What the student is trying to say just gets more confusing as he or she attempts to say more.

> **MATH TALK TIP**
>
> **Solution!**
> Try the revoicing talk move, *So are you saying . . . ?*

A Closer Look

Talk Move: So Are You Saying . . . ? (Revoicing)

When students talk about new content, it's often difficult to understand what they say. But given your goals to improve the mathematical thinking and reasoning of all students, you cannot give up on an especially unclear student. Deep thinking and powerful reasoning do not always correlate with clear verbal expression.

Yet many teachers feel anxiety about continuing to query a student like Paulo: *His thinking seems unclear. If I continue to press him, will I be putting him on the spot and embarrassing him? Maybe I should just move on!* This is a common and understandable reaction to students' lack of clarity. Yet we have to admit that students are often unclear, and that is unlikely to change. Therefore, if you want to use talk in your classroom, you need to find a way to deal with this common situation.

In the revoicing talk move, the teacher essentially tries to repeat some or all of what the student has said, and then *asks the student to verify* whether or not the teacher's revoicing is correct. This talk move is not just a simple repetition of what the student has said. It is a question that is intended to *ask* the student what they mean, in order to leave room for the student to *clarify* the original intention. There are different ways to do this, including the following examples:

So it sounds like you're saying _____. Is that what you're saying?

Let me see if I'm understanding you. Are you thinking that _____?

Teacher Reflection: Revoicing

Mrs. Foley
Sometimes a student will say something and you think you heard what he said but you're not 100 percent sure. So, with revoicing, you can go back and check in with that student to be certain you're clear on exactly what his thinking is. Because whether the ideas are right or wrong, it's important to know exactly what that student is thinking so you can develop his reasoning further.

After hearing Paulo's contribution in (5), all Ms. D could grasp was that Paulo *might* be saying that twenty-four is odd because he divided it by three and got no remainder. She recalls that this is a common misconception among students: If division by two with no remainder yields an even number, then division by three with no remainder must yield an odd number! By phrasing this guess as a question, she is asking Paulo if her understanding is correct. And, by using the talk move wait time before he answers, she gives him a chance to clarify.

6. **Ms. D**: OK, let me see if I understand. So you're saying that twenty-four is . . . an odd number . . . because you divided it by three? Is that right?

Seven or eight seconds go by. Ms. D waits. Finally Paulo answers.

7. **Paulo:** Yeah. Because three goes into it, because twenty-four divided by three is eight.

As it turns out, Paulo verifies that he did intend to claim that twenty-four is an odd number, and he gives his reason. By creating a space in the conversation for Paulo to respond, Ms. D has learned that he probably does hold this basic misconception about even and odd numbers. She has gained a foothold in the discussion that she did not have after simply hearing his contributions in turns (3) and (5). Now Ms. D may include other students in this small and impromptu discussion.

Talk Moves That Help Students Orient to the Thinking of Others

Anyone who has tried to use academically productive classroom talk will know that often, students don't pick up on what has *just* been said! Perhaps they haven't heard it. Perhaps they were thinking about something else. Perhaps their English language competence is not yet strong enough to guarantee understanding on the first hearing. Perhaps the comment was so rich with math content that they need to hear it again to fully get it. Yet if you want to engage students in a learning conversation, they have to orient to others' thinking, and hear it, and understand it. This can be a tall order.

> ### Talk Moves That Help Students Orient to the Thinking of Others
>
> Note that these talk moves do not need to be repeated word for word. In the family of talk moves we refer to as *Who can repeat?*, there are many ways to get the same meaning across. For example:
>
> *Who Can Repeat?*
> Who can say that again?
> Who can put that into their own words?
> Who can restate what [student's name] said?
> Can anyone repeat what they heard [student's name] say?
> Who can say that again for us?
> After a turn and talk: Tell us what your partner said.

> ### MATH TALK TIP
> #### Talk Moves Have More Than One Function
> Many teachers have pointed out that most talk moves have more than one function. For example, the *turn and talk* move can also help students orient to the thinking of others, as we discuss in the Facilitators' Guide.

When a student says something potentially important, you may want to incorporate that into the ongoing discussion. However if the contribution was insightful but dense or other students did not hear it, or were not paying attention, they will not be able to take the next step and think about it. And if teachers are always the only ones who repeat students' ideas, students will not learn that they too are responsible for attending to each other's contributions. There are several ways to express this talk move.

Ms. D's Third-Grade Class

Let's return to Ms. D's third-grade class. Following Paulo's turn in (7), repeated below, the teacher asks, "Who can say that again?"

7. **Paulo:** Yeah. Because three goes into it, because twenty-four divided by three is eight.

8. **Ms. D:** *Can anyone repeat what Paulo just said in his or her own words?* Miranda?

9. **Miranda:** Um, I think I can. I think he said that twenty-four is odd, because it can be divided by three.

> **MATH TALK TIP**
> **Problem!**
> The teacher isn't sure that other students have heard and understood a student's idea.

10. **Ms. D:** Is that right, Paulo? Is that what you said?

11. **Paulo:** Yes.

> **MATH TALK TIP**
> **Solution!**
> Try talk moves in the *Who can repeat?* family.

Now Ms. D can go forward with this idea of Paulo's, assuming that other students have heard and understood. If the idea or contribution is particularly complex, it can be helpful to ask more than one student to put it in their own words. Here, students are getting a moment to understand Paulo's idea, determining the even or odd status of a number by *dividing it by three.* It is this idea that they will have to address going forward, deciding whether they agree or disagree. Notice that Ms. D is not using this talk move as a classroom management device. She is not trying to "catch" students who are not listening. Instead, she is trying to make sure everyone hears the idea and understands it.

Notice that Ms. D is not using this talk move as a classroom management device. She is not trying to "catch" students who are not listening. Instead, she is trying to make sure everyone hears the idea and understands it.

Talk Moves That Help Students Deepen Their Own Reasoning

Talk Moves That Help Students Deepen Their Own Reasoning

There are many ways to ask the question, "Why do you think that?" depending on the age of the student and the topic under discussion. Here are some examples. Can you think of other ways to help students deepen their reasoning?

Press for Reasoning: Why Do You Think That?

What is your evidence?

How did you get that answer?

What convinced you that was the right answer?

Why did you think that strategy would work?

Where in the text is there support for that claim?

Can you prove that to us?

What makes you think that?

I'm not sure I understand. Can you explain it to me step-by-step?

To deepen the focus on reasoning, all students must get used to explaining *why* they say what they say. This is a crucial part of the CCSS Practice Standard 3: *Construct viable arguments*. In many classrooms, students simply provide answers without digging deeper into how they got there. To help students explain their thinking and get better at providing evidence for their claims, you can use a large family of talk moves called *Why do you think that?* Sometimes this family of talk moves is called *press for reasoning*.

CCSS

Teaching with the Common Core

Practice Standard 3: Construct viable arguments.

MATH TALK TIP

Talk Moves Have More Than One Function

As you become more familiar with these talk moves and tools, you will start to use them in different ways to support productive discussions in your own classroom. In the Facilitators' Guide we also suggest using *turn and talk* and *Who can repeat?* to help students deepen their reasoning. What we provide here is just the start.

Ms. D's Third-Grade Class

Let's return to our example. At this point, Ms. D guesses that others will hold the same misconception, and to address it, everyone must be clear about what he is saying. Therefore, she decides to ask Paulo to dig deeper into his reasoning. She knows that

> **MATH TALK TIP**
>
> **Problem!**
> The teacher feels a student needs to take his or her reasoning deeper. How can this happen?

> **MATH TALK TIP**
>
> **Solution!**
> Try one of the talk moves in the *Press for reasoning*; *Why do you think that?* family.

as others listen to him, they will have a better chance to understand what he is saying. If they hold the same misconception, they will get clearer about it, and she can more effectively work to change that misconception.

12. **Ms. D:** So Paulo, can you tell us why that makes twenty-four an odd number? *Can you explain your reasoning?*

13. **Paulo:** Well, you divide by three. And eight is the answer. And there's no remainder. So like . . . even—even is when you divide by two and there's no remainder. So since three is odd, this one is odd.

As you work on deepening and clarifying one student's reasoning, other students need to be following along. Even if the speaker is mathematically correct and concise, that does not mean that everyone will follow it! Many students will tune out as they hear a classmate produce a long and complex piece of reasoning. This is an ideal time to go back to the talk moves and ask, "Who can say that again?" or "Who can put that into their own words?" This helps everyone deepen their own understanding, and thus, the entire class moves forward toward a more academically productive discussion.

> **MATH TALK TIP**
>
> **Problem!**
> Other students may be tuning out as one student focuses deeper on his or her reasoning. How can the teacher help *everyone* deepen their own understanding?

Even in cases where the student is not correct, all students can benefit from understanding the reasoning behind it, particularly when a common misconception is at stake, and you plan to address that misconception shortly. Here, the ideas of the divisor and of *no remainder* are key to clarifying the misconception. Therefore, Ms. D decides to make sure that everyone is following.

> ## MATH TALK TIP
>
> ### Solution!
> Try one of the talk moves and ask students, "Who can say that again?" or "Who can put that into their own words?"

14. **Ms. D:** Wow, Paulo, you said a lot. *Can anyone put that into his or her own words?* Eva?

15. **Eva:** Well, I would say that if a number is even then you can divide it into two groups and there's no remainder. And Paulo said that if you divide it by three, well, three is an odd number. So if you don't get a remainder when you divide it by three, maybe it's . . . odd?

From Eva's reaction, Ms. D guesses that maybe Eva's knowledge of *even* and *odd* is still tenuous and that she would benefit from thinking about this some more, despite the previous day's lesson!

Teacher Reflections: Who Can Repeat?

Ms. Fournier
I ask, "Can someone else repeat that?" or "Who can put that in your own words?" after a student makes a comment that focuses on the main points of the lesson. When a student makes a comment and I hear myself say, "That's a really key idea," that's when I know it's a good time to use this move.

Mrs. Burgess
Sometimes when I ask a student to repeat what a classmate just said, they ask me if they can put it in their own words instead. This is a judgment call I have to make. Sometimes I say, "Sure, put it in your own words." But if someone prior to that student has said something that I think is really important—if that student has really hit the nail on the head—I might say, "You know, really try to repeat what your classmate said."

Talk Moves That Help Students Engage with the Reasoning of Others

Talk Moves That Help Students Engage with the Reasoning of Others

Note that these talk moves do not have to be repeated word for word. There are many ways to get the same meaning across.

What Do You Think About That?
Do You Agree or Disagree . . . and Why?
Who Can Add On?

After everyone hears and understands the claim, and the reasoning behind it, they are ready to take the step of really engaging with that claim. This is where productive discussion can really take off.

The final step toward engaging in academically productive discussion involves students actually working with the thinking and reasoning of others. If a classroom is to function as a community of learners who can learn from one another, they must be able to engage with one another's ideas beyond simply listening and repeating. The talk moves in this session encourage students to discuss mathematical topics in ways that will allow robust learning.

Ms. D's Third-Grade Class

Ms. D decides that students are now ready to engage with what she knows is a misconception that Paulo and others probably hold. So she asks students to take a position on the idea.

MATH TALK TIP

Problem!
The teacher needs to engage students beyond simply listening and repeating.

MATH TALK TIP

Solution!
Try the talk move *Do you agree or disagree . . . and why?*

16. **Ms. D:** So, let me ask you: *Who agrees with what Paulo said, and who disagrees?*

Thirty seconds go by as Ms. D waits for hands to go up. Ms. D has tried hard to let these students know that in their classroom, it is not always going to be the same two or three students who answer all the questions. She has been working on letting them know that she will wait until a number of students think through her question. Finally, Eduardo raises his hand. He is an English learner, and rarely talks. Slowly, he reveals his understanding and deepens the reasoning the class can share.

17. **Eduardo:** Yes, I am not agreeing with Paulo's idea, because if something is even it can be broke into two equal groups. We divide twenty-four in three groups, and we can also divide in four groups. And they don't get no remainder. And we can divide by six, also. So I think we should stay with two groups only for finding even numbers.

A Closer Look

Talk Move: Do You Agree or Disagree . . . and Why?

With this talk move, you are opening up the floor for others to weigh in on the specific question or claim that is being discussed. There are many ways to encourage students to engage with what another student has said:

What do other people think about what he/she just said?

Who agrees or disagrees, and why?

Does anyone have a different way of looking at that?

Does that make sense to you? Why?

Does anyone want to contribute more evidence for that claim?

This family of talk moves really brings students into direct contact with the reasoning of their peers.

Disagreeing with One's Friends

Teachers for grade 4 and above may find that students feel there are social consequences to disagreeing with one's friends. These may impinge on the progress you as the teacher wish to make with academically productive discussions. How can you deal with this issue? Here are some suggestions:

- One teacher we met told us that she and her students worked out another way to say it: Her students say, "I respectfully challenge what Jason said," instead of using the word *disagree.*

- Another strategy includes grouping students together in twos or threes; in at least some cases the group opinion does not carry the interpersonal threat of the single student's disagreement.
- Insist on talking about disagreeing with the person's *idea*, or what he or she *said*, not with the student personally.
- Walk the Line: Set up a line of chairs across the front of the room. Ask the students to place themselves at one end if they agree with the claim at issue, at the other end if they disagree, and in the middle if they don't know how they feel. Then when further arguments and evidence are offered, students can change positions, but they have to explain what made them change their mind. (This activity works best for major questions that are central to the lesson, not a minor claim or issue.)

Teacher Reflection: Giving Evidence, from Math to Reading

Mr. Danella

We talk a lot in math about giving evidence—explaining why you agree or disagree or proving why you've gotten a certain answer. The effects of these conversations show up during reading time when I hear my students pull out important information from a text to support a point that they're making.

So with Eduardo's carefully considered answer, Ms. D has a lot to work with in setting up a discussion. By asking students to take a position, Ms. D has set up a way for all students to engage with this central issue. She has now entertained two claims: 24 is odd, and 24 is even. Each student has provided a rationale of sorts for their position. She is now in a position to throw open the discussion to other students.

How do we invite students in when we sense that the conversation is clear enough, and there is enough common ground, to move forward? To do this, Ms. D decides to use a talk move that is very open, much less specific than

Do you agree or disagree . . . and why? This talk move does not require students to address an immediately preceding claim or statement, but it doesn't preclude that either—it's open.

MATH TALK TIP

Problem!

How do we invite students in when we sense that the conversation is clear enough, and there is enough common ground, to move forward?

MATH TALK TIP

Solution!

Try the talk move *Who can add on?*

18. **Ms. D:** *So who wants to add on to that?* Can someone add more to this discussion?

19. **Jamie:** I agree. Because I thought that we said yesterday that even numbers could be put into two equal groups; they can be divided by two. And I know Paulo said that. But, like, I think you can divide twenty-four by two. And it's twelve with no remainder. So isn't that . . . like . . . even? Like Eduardo said.

A Closer Look

Talk Move: Who Can Add On?

When a student's statement or claim is clear enough for others to easily understand and work with, you have an opportunity to really help students participate in a productive discussion by opening it up a bit. Asking, "Who can add on?" or "Who wants to respond to that?" invites anyone to join in and respond. This move is also appropriate after a student makes a contribution that provides only one step toward a longer and more complex explanation. You can ask other students to add on to the statement as a way to encourage the whole class to work together to produce one coherent and complete explanation. In this way, you are encouraging the focus on reasoning, contributing one's own ideas, and working with the ideas of others, all at the same time! Variations for this talk move include:

Who can add on to what [student's name] just said?

Does someone want to take that idea another step?

Someone else?

Teacher Reflections: Who Can Add On?

Ms. Luipold

Sometimes I get so involved in the mathematics of a lesson that I forget to ask students to repeat or agree or add on. But I find that the more that I use these moves, the more my students remind me to use them. In the middle of a lesson, someone might raise his hand and say, "Oh! I have something to add on here." The better they get at responding to the talk moves, the more they remind me that I need to use them.

Mrs. Delaney

Sometimes my first graders can start an explanation but cannot finish it. But if one student starts, and another one is able to add on, then the first student can pick up new ideas. Because if someone says, "I'd like to add on to what Andrew said," all of a sudden Andrew's ears have perked up because he's hearing his name. And now he's listening to another student say what he thought he was trying to say. So that discussion has actually helped that student go back and think more deeply about his own reasoning.

Summary of Productive Talk Moves

See the "Summary Tables of Productive Talk Moves," (pages 49–63).

In the constructed example from Ms. D's third-grade class that we've used throughout this chapter, Ms. D uses almost all of the talk moves and tools listed in the summary tables on pages 49–63. Although this entire exchange would take only a few minutes, it illustrates how teachers can accomplish the four steps that underlie productive discussion.

In the summary tables we present the talk moves and other tools in terms of what they do for you. If these are tools, we should be able to describe what they do—a bucket is a good tool when you are faced with a flooded basement, but it won't help you pound a nail. For that you will need a hammer. Similarly, if you are trying to get shy students to say something about their thinking, you may need a different tool than you need to get rambunctious students to listen to one another. We also review what your students need to know about each talk move or tool, and we provide strategies for you.

We think it's important to *try only one new thing at a time*. That means that when you introduce new talk moves or discussion practices, you should use them in the context of math that your students *already know*, or at least have a fairly good handle on. That way, students won't be left figuring out these new patterns of interaction while trying to keep track of the new mathematical goals of the lesson. You can avoid this pitfall by talking to your students about each new talk move before you ask students to react to them in appropriate and productive ways.

> **When you introduce new talk moves or discussion practices, you should use them in the context of math that your students *already know*.**

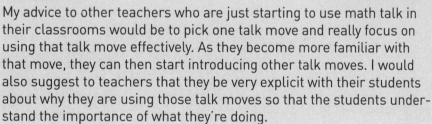

Teacher Reflection: Getting Started with Talk Moves

Mrs. Schineller

My advice to other teachers who are just starting to use math talk in their classrooms would be to pick one talk move and really focus on using that talk move effectively. As they become more familiar with that move, they can then start introducing other talk moves. I would also suggest to teachers that they be very explicit with their students about why they are using those talk moves so that the students understand the importance of what they're doing.

From an early age, students develop generalizations about acceptable ways of participating in social settings. If students enter your class only having experienced traditional mathematics instruction, they may be stymied by questions such as, "Why do you think that?" or "Who can say that again?" And as we all know, students differ! So some will take to these new ways of talking right away, while others will find it more difficult. As we point out in Chapter 2, it's important that you find ways to bring everyone along, or your goals for equitable discussion will not be realized.

See Chapter 2.

Finally, it's important to point out that after you become familiar with these talk moves, you might start to use them in ways that go beyond the basic introduction that we provide here. These moves can all be adapted to

> You may notice that in related publications, such as our *Classroom Discussions in Math: A Facilitator's Guide to Support Professional Learning of Discourse and the Common Core*, we sometimes use slightly different terms or titles for these talk moves. As we work with more teachers, we refine and add to these moves. As you use them in your own classroom, you will probably do the same thing!

your circumstances and your way of talking and teaching. You may notice that in related publications, such as our *Classroom Discussions in Math: A Facilitator's Guide to Support Professional Learning of Discourse and the Common Core*, we sometimes use slightly different terms or titles for these talk moves. As we work with more teachers, we refine and add to these moves. As you use them in your own classroom, you will probably do the same thing!

Additional Case Studies

We offer two additional vignette examples of talk moves being used in first- and fifth-grade classrooms. See the case studies at the end of this chapter.

Teacher Reflection:
Facilitating the Discussion

Ms. Powers

When I facilitate a classroom discussion, I have to think about what I'm going to say while also listening to my students. I have to make sense of what they are saying and decide what I want them to share with the class. It's a lot of hard work, but it's my job to steer the conversation toward where I know we need to go and to use students' ideas to help get us there.

Video Clips: Watching and Analyzing Talk Moves

Now that we have introduced the basic talk moves, let's sharpen our ability to recognize and appreciate the uses of the talk moves. Revisit the video clips you watched earlier in this chapter. What talk moves do you see, and what do you think the teacher is trying to accomplish by using these talk moves in this combination?

Video Clip 7B: Using the Words *More* and *Less* (Mrs. Luizzi, Kindergarten)

Video Clip 6A: Finding Missing Digits (Mr. Danella, Grade 3)

Video Clip 4D: Fraction Number Line (Mrs. Rowan, Grade 6)

BEFORE YOU WATCH THE VIDEOS

To make the most productive use of the video clips, you and any colleagues you are working with should take time to read through the "Guidelines for Watching Videos of Teaching" (see page xxi). For demographics, see page xliv.

What Next?

You have now been introduced to the basics of using classroom talk to support productive discussion. What are the next steps?

See Chapter 2.

- If you are going to try any of the moves introduced above in your own classroom, we strongly suggest that you first read Chapter 2. This will provide you with guidance on the classroom norms needed to introduce your students to these practices in the most positive and productive way possible. We have encountered many enthusiastic teachers who jump in and try to use these talk moves without preparing their students and installing norms for respectful and equitable talk. When things don't go well, they are disappointed and discouraged. We have found that starting with the norms is really important, so we encourage you to work through that material first.

See Section II.

- If you are planning to use discussion in your math class, you will want to think through *what* to discuss and *how* to discuss it. The chapters in Section II are all designed to help you do that. Each chapter focuses on an important aspect of mathematical learning: concepts, computation, procedures, mathematical terminology, and reasoning. In each chapter, you will be given suggestions for how to use discussion to help students with that aspect of math learning. Each contains video cases, *Try this lesson* segments, and tips for using talk. Enjoy!

Discussion and Reflection

1. One of the key skills you will develop in using this resource is the ability to work with students whose contributions are initially unclear, helping them move toward clarity. This kind of work is not easy at first. To prepare for this, try to recall a time when you could not explain your thinking to others because the ideas you were dealing with were new and complex. What would have helped you at that time?

2. This resource will also help you develop the ability to tell when talk in your classroom is academically productive. Can you recall a time when you held a discussion in your class that was not academically productive? What happened? What was it like? Can you recall a time when you held a discussion that was academically productive? What were the qualities of that discussion? Do you remember anything you did to make it productive, or did it just seem to happen spontaneously?

3. Think back in your own education. Can you recall a teacher who made you feel that he or she really wanted to understand what you had to say? Try to picture a conversation with that teacher. What was it like?

4. One of the main goals of using classroom talk moves like those described here is to manage the unavoidable complexity and lack of clarity that occurs when students are learning something new and complicated. Consider each of the talk moves. Could each be useful when you are faced with a student contribution that is completely unclear? Or are some better than others? Construct a situation in your classroom in which you are faced with an uninterpretable response and describe what you would do.

5. In the cases in this chapter and throughout the resource, you will see instances of students making assertions or observations that are mathematically incorrect. In many cases, because the emphasis is on sustaining student discussion and developing deeper understanding, the teacher chooses not to correct or call attention to these mistakes. What are some of the consequences of such choices? Have you had this experience? How did you deal with it? How might you deal with it in the future?

For professional development sessions and additional video clips that go with this chapter, see:

*Classroom Discussions in Math: A **Facilitator's Guide** to Support Professional Learning of Discourse and the Common Core* (Anderson, Chapin, and O'Connor 2011)

ISBN: 978-1-935099-12-3

What Does Productive Talk Look Like?

Mrs. Sigler's First-Grade Class: Experiences with Triangles

In Chapter 1 we used an example from Ms. D's third-grade classroom to introduce you to various talk moves. Following is an additional narrative example, or case, that shows you how talk moves look in action in the classroom. This example is a composite, constructed from a class we have observed. The case begins with a brief description of the mathematical ideas or problems that are central to the lesson, along with a description of what the class has done so far. We then present the interaction in the form of a script, tracking the teacher's and students' contributions to the conversation.

[See Chapter 1.]

"This is a triangle because it just looks right."

Mrs. Sigler's first-grade students are learning about geometric figures. The students have been given a set of polygons to sort into two groups: triangles and other shapes.

Within the set there are many different sizes and kinds of triangles, including scalene, equilateral, isosceles, and right triangles. The triangles are cut out of colored paper and are either red, green, or blue. Other shapes are also in the set—squares, rectangles, hexagons, and parallelograms.

Students are working in groups of four. Mrs. Sigler notices that one group of students has separated the equilateral triangles from all of the other triangles and grouped them alone. They have placed most of the other triangles in the "other" category.

1. **Mrs. S:** I see you've separated the shapes. What is this group of shapes called? [Points to the set of equilateral triangles.]
2. **All:** Triangles!

Teaching with the Common Core

1.6 Reason with shapes and their attributes.

1.6 Distinguish between defining attributes (e.g., triangles are closed and three-sided) versus non-defining attributes (e.g., color, orientation, overall size); build and draw shapes to possess defining attributes.

3. **Mrs. S:** I'd like each of you to explain your thinking to me. I'd like each of you to explain to me why all of the shapes in this group are triangles [points to the equilateral triangles] and all of *these* are *not* triangles [points to some triangles in the "other" group].

4. **Ollie:** This [points to one equilateral triangle] just looks like a triangle.

5. **Mrs. S:** Can you say more? What do you mean?

6. **Ollie:** It's short and fat and just looks right.

7. **Yoon So:** Yeah. This one [points to a scalene triangle] is too skinny and pointy. It isn't a triangle.

8. **Mrs. S:** What do you think, Paul? Do you agree or disagree?

9. **Paul:** Well, you know these are maybe triangles [indicates the group of equilateral triangles] because you know they just look like triangles.

10. **Mrs. S:** Hmm. I'm not sure I'm understanding. Can you tell me more about what you mean? You say they just look like triangles. What does a triangle look like?

11. **Paul:** Umm . . . [Paul looks around the room and then points to a poster of geometric shapes. The shapes on the poster are all regular polygons and the triangle on it is equilateral.] Like that one. See, triangles just look like this [cups hands into the shape of an equilateral triangle]. They're flat on the bottom.

12. **Mrs. S:** Ollie, can you say again what Paul just said?

13. **Ollie:** These are a triangle [cups his hand].

14. **Mrs. S:** What else did he say?

15. **Ollie:** They have to sit on their bottoms—there aren't pointy parts on the bottom.

16. **Mrs. S:** OK. Look at this. [She takes one of the large equilateral triangles from the triangle pile and turns it so a vertex is pointing downward.] Is this a triangle?

17. **Paul:** [Turns the triangle so it is sitting on a side.] Now it is.

18. **Mrs. S:** Sim, you have been very quiet. What do you think? Is this a triangle? [Turns the equilateral triangle around so the point is again facing down.]

19. **Sim:** I don't think so.

20. **Mrs. S:** So you think this is *not* a triangle? Is that right?

21. **Sim:** It's not a triangle.

22. **Mrs. S:** Can you say more? Why do you think it's not a triangle?

23. **Sim:** I don't know. [Long pause.] Maybe it is. Because I can turn it and it looks like a triangle.

Mrs. Sigler has been asking each student in turn to justify their categorization of the equilateral triangles as the only "real" triangles. Mrs. Sigler has seen that the children in this small group have a very restricted idea of what a triangle is. She knows that *this is quite typical for young children*: Their definitions for geometric shapes are based on their visual memory of their previous experiences with that shape. Equilateral triangles are typically used to illustrate the concept of "triangle." One teacher we know calls this the *Sesame Street* level of understanding geometric shapes.

Some readers might find this small-group interchange to be somewhat slow and laborious. Is the teacher really moving the children toward changing their understanding? Yes, but first she must assess what they believe—find out how they think about the question! And to do this, she is getting them to *externalize* their ideas by asking them each to speak in turn—a good example of Step 1: Helping Students Clarify and Share Their Own Thoughts (see page 12).

> Is the teacher really moving the children toward changing their understanding? Yes, but first she must assess what they believe—find out how they think about the question! And to do this, she is getting them to *externalize* their ideas by asking them each to speak in turn.

Notice that with each new contribution, the students' low level of understanding gets a little bit more obvious. Even though the teacher pushes them to justify their categorization of the triangles, they only offer reasons like it "looks right." It doesn't seem that the talk is moving the group very far into new understandings, but at this point, Mrs. Sigler does have a pretty clear picture of the level of this group's understanding. She sees that this classification task has not been an effective instructional activity at this point. She decides to bring out another set of materials the next day.

The next day, Mrs. Sigler brings out a large box of strips made of cardboard of different lengths, with holes at the ends. They can be fastened together by the use of brads.

From the previous day's discussion she knows that the students are simply identifying the names of geometric shapes with a typical image. They are not considering the defining properties of a triangle, such as the fact that a triangle is any closed figure with three straight sides. So she gives each child three strips from the box, choosing three strips that she knows will make a triangle. She asks them to use the strips and the fasteners to create a triangle. By choosing the strips, she has made sure that all varieties of triangles—equilateral, isosceles, and scalene—will be produced by at least one or two students in the class.

After each child has made a triangle, Mrs. Sigler tapes them all to the front board. She then holds a large-group discussion about the triangles.

1. **Mrs. S:** Let's look at these. Does anybody notice anything about the shapes? Cecile?

2. **Cecile:** All of them are made from three strips.

3. **Mrs. S:** Craig, can you put what Cecile just said in your own words?

4. **Craig:** The triangles all have three pieces.

5. **Mrs. S:** Does anybody see a triangle that was made from *more* than three strips?

6. **Students:** No, no. They all have three.

7. **Mrs. S:** I notice that all of these triangles are not identical; they don't all look the same. How are they different? Pooja?

8. **Pooja:** Some of them are big and some are small.

9. **Mrs. S:** What makes a triangle big or small? See these two triangles? [Mrs. Sigler takes one large triangle and one small triangle and places them next to each other on the board.] What did someone do to make them different?

10. **Pooja:** You use long strips to make the big one and short strips to make the small one.

11. **Paul:** Mine is the big one and I used the really long strips.

12. **Mrs. S:** How many long strips did you use, Paul?

13. **Paul:** Three.

14. **Mrs. S:** Who else made a big triangle? [Points to a couple of triangles on the board that are large.] How many strips did you use?

15. **Cristobal:** I made that one over there. [Points to an isosceles triangle.] I used three strips.

16. **Mrs. S:** Who made a small triangle?

17. **Ben:** I did! I used three strips, too!

18. **Ali:** Me, too. My triangle took three strips.

19. **Mrs. S:** OK, so now let's use a word that people use to talk about some geometric shapes. We can use the word *side*. This triangle has three sides—one, two, three. [Mrs. S points to each side as she counts.] How many sides does Ali's triangle have? [Here Mrs. S points to Ali's triangle, a long and thin scalene triangle made with two longer strips and one short one.]

20. **Ali:** My triangle has three sides.

21. **Marsha:** But Mrs. Sigler, I don't know if that's a triangle. It doesn't look like the triangles from yesterday.

22. **Mrs. S:** That's an important question. Can somebody repeat for us what Marsha just said? Ali, can you repeat what Marsha just said?

23. **Ali:** She said that my triangle isn't really a triangle because it doesn't look like the ones we put in the triangle group yesterday.

24. **Mrs. S:** Marsha, is that what you said?

25. **Marsha:** Yes, but I didn't mean that Ali's triangle wasn't a triangle. I just meant that it didn't match the ones from yesterday in our group.

26. **Mrs. S:** OK, so Marsha has asked a really important question. Is this shape a triangle? And what about those triangles from yesterday? Remember yesterday, when we were sorting triangles? [General acknowledgment comes from the students.]

    Some of you thought that a shape like this [points to Ali's triangle] didn't belong in the same group with triangles that looked like this [points to an equilateral triangle on the board]. So we have a really important question here. [She pauses . . . all eyes are on Mrs. Sigler.] Just what *is* a triangle?

Recognizing and Understanding the Teacher's Moves in Mrs. Sigler's First-Grade Class

Mrs. Sigler has brought the discussion to a very important point: All of the children's attention is now focused on whether or not all of the shapes they have just constructed are triangles. She now has several choices.

(continued)

Mrs. Sigler's Choices at This Point in the Discussion

- She could tell the students that Ali's shape is a triangle and ask them to figure out why.
- She could ask the students what they think, and see where the discussion leads.
- She could provide some direct instruction about the properties of triangles, starting with the fact that they have three sides and are closed figures and then asking the students to check whether all the figures on the board meet those two conditions.

FOUR STEPS...

Step 1: Helping Individual Students Clarify and Share Their Own Thoughts

Step 2: Helping Students Orient to the Thinking of Others

Step 3: Helping Students Deepen Their Own Reasoning

Step 4: Helping Students Engage with the Reasoning of Others

Mrs. Sigler has succeeded in using classroom talk to bring these first graders to a point where they are *ready to engage with the idea* that triangles that are not equilateral triangles are also properly called triangles. Let's revisit the "Four Steps Toward Productive Talk." What steps did Mrs. Sigler accomplish by using the talk moves above with these first graders?

Notice that Mrs. Sigler asked many students to reiterate the idea that three strips are needed to make a triangle, even though everyone had agreed that all the shapes on the board had used three strips. By getting students to orient to one another's contributions (Step 2), she gave them more to work with. Students need time to generalize important ideas; in this case these first graders had to consider the fact that all of the different-looking shapes have three sides. Although this idea is less complex than those we describe in some other examples in this resource, it's an important idea for these first graders. They deserve the time it will take to make sure that everyone has seen the same generalization.

The slow and gentle nature of the talk in this first-grade classroom is also reflected in other ways. Mrs. Sigler lets these students spend time in their small groups working with an activity while she talks to the small groups. Then she moves the activity to a whole-class format, making sure that all students have had a chance to think about and talk about the material that will be discussed in the large group.

Notice that although Mrs. Sigler makes sure to give students time to consider the problem and to listen to one another, she does not shrink from difficult material. For example, Mrs. Sigler does not hesitate to introduce correct mathematical terminology. She uses the term *geometric shapes* and she directs the students to use the word *side* when talking about their triangles. She could have spent even more time with this, particularly if she had had many English language learners in the class.

Notice that although Mrs. Sigler makes sure to give students time to consider the problem and to listen to one another, she does not shrink from difficult material.

Finally, it is very important to note that even with these young children, Mrs. Sigler allowed the students to consider her questions for quite some time without providing them with answers. She could have started the first day by simply telling the students that they were wrong in their categorizations, that all three-sided closed figures are triangles. In some situations one might want to proceed in this way, and we would not rule it out as an option. But Mrs. Sigler chose the more indirect route, in the belief that letting students follow the ideas at their own pace and in their own way would more likely result in their being ready to face the question that Marsha brought up. Her ultimate aim is to use classroom talk to bring students to understand the criteria for what makes a shape a triangle, thereby moving them beyond their *Sesame Street* understanding of this geometric shape.

What Does Productive
Talk Look Like?

Ms. Stangle's Fifth-Grade Class:
Fraction Division (Peach Tarts)

See
Chapter 1. In Chapter 1 we used an example from Ms. D's third-grade classroom to introduce you to various talk moves. Following is an additional narrative example,
or case, that shows you how talk moves look in action in the classroom. This
example is a composite, constructed from a class we have observed. The case
begins with a brief description of the mathematical ideas or problems that are
central to the lesson, along with a description of what the class has done so far.
We then present the interaction in the form of a script, tracking the teacher's
and students' contributions to the conversation.

Episode 1: "So you drew a picture of the tarts?"

Ms. Stangle's fifth graders are focusing on a problem that is designed to give
them experience with fraction division:

Story Problem: Peach Tarts

Ms. Stangle wants to make peach tarts for her friends. She can either
use $\frac{1}{3}$ of a peach for each tart or $\frac{2}{3}$ of a peach for each tart. She has 10
peaches. What is the greatest number of tarts that she can make with
10 peaches if she uses $\frac{1}{3}$ peach per tart? If she
uses $\frac{2}{3}$ peach per tart?

    Ms. Stangle has the students work on the problem on their own for ten
minutes. At the end of the ten minutes she doesn't know what types of solutions students have come up with because she had an unexpected visitor to the
classroom and did not get a chance to circulate and look at their work. So she
is wading into murky waters. However, she does know that some students will

have difficulty setting up the problem, others will have difficulty representing the facts accurately, and still others will have difficulty with computation.

Teaching with the Common Core

5.NF Apply and extend previous understandings of multiplication and division to multiply and divide fractions.
5.NF Interpret division of a whole number by a unit fraction, and compute such quotients.

1. **Ms. S:** Who wants to present their solution? How about some hands here? OK, Marco.

2. **Marco:** Well, first I looked at them all and then I made lines on each one and then I counted.

3. **Ms. S:** Marco, I'm not really sure I follow you. It sounds like you drew a picture of the tarts and the peaches, is that right?

4. **Marco:** Well, yeah.

5. **Ms. S:** We can't really follow what you say about your solution unless we can see the picture in our minds. We have to be able to listen to you and really understand what you're describing. Would you like to tell us again about the details of what you drew?

6. **Marco:** Um, OK. I drew the ten peaches and then I cut each one into three parts. Then I counted all the parts. So it was thirty parts. You can use one or two of the parts for a tart.

7. **Ms. S:** Hold on, I'm getting lost again. I thought the problem said . . . well, wait. So you're saying that I can take either one or two parts of a peach and that will be enough for a tart? Is that what you're saying?

8. **Marco:** One or two of the three parts.

9. **Ms. S:** OK, so let me see if I can draw what you're describing. Here are my ten peaches [draws ten circles] and here I'm dividing each one into three parts [draws unequal partitions of each peach; see Figure 1.1 on the following page]. Did anyone else have a picture like this?

10. **Students:** [Several shifting restlessly] No! Not like that!

11. **Ms. S:** No? How come [innocently looking surprised]? What's wrong with this? I've cut each peach into three parts.

12. **Ginny:** No, it has to be equal or it won't be thirds.

13. **Ms. S:** Oh, so the problem says it has to be thirds? Is that right?

14. **Ginny:** Yes.

15. **Ms. S:** OK, so Marco, do you want to add to your statement of your solution?

Teaching with the Common Core

Practice Standard 6: Attend to precision.

16. **Marco:** OK. I drew ten peaches and I drew lines that cut them into *equal thirds*! And then I drew ten tarts and I matched them up.

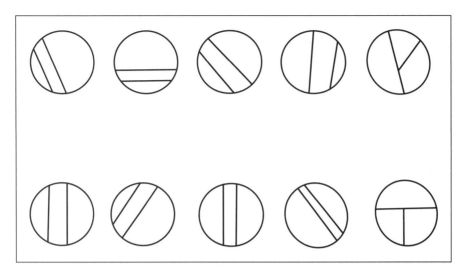

Figure 1.1 Ms. Stangle's representation of Marco's solution.

Episode 1: Recognizing and Understanding the Teacher's Moves in Ms. Stangle's Fifth-Grade Class

You might wonder why Ms. Stangle didn't just ask Marco to draw a picture on the board. After all, it's good mathematical practice to have students present their graphic representations to the class. What is Ms. Stangle trying to do here? Why is she subjecting the students to this ordeal of clarification? Why is she being so cautious in making sure that their meaning is absolutely clear? She could not be as obtuse as all that—surely she knew that Marco knew he was counting thirds, not just random parts of a peach.

In our work we have found that one of the most effective ways to increase students' attention to precise language is to engage in just such episodes as the fragment presented here. When the teacher sets a very

> When the teacher sets a very high criterion for clarity, when she herself "fails to understand" what the students are saying until they are utterly clear, she is modeling for them an attention to detail in language that will serve them in a variety of ways.

high criterion for clarity, when she herself "fails to understand" what the students are saying until they are utterly clear, she is modeling for them an attention to detail in language that will serve them in a variety of ways. Experiences like these will eventually lead students to use language more precisely, because it raises their level of awareness of the audience. They will also begin to scrutinize the language of others more carefully. We have seen that this kind of awareness leads to clear gains in reading comprehension, both in mathematics and in English language arts.

In this excerpt Ms. Stangle skillfully uses the technique of revoicing. She repeats what the student has said, clarifying, adding, or making more obvious some problematic feature of it. She then asks the student whether that is the correct interpretation. In the first few lines, she uses this talk move in order to get Marco to clarify his first statement from Line 2. Like many students, Marco is not particularly skilled at anticipating what his audience will need. An outsider to the classroom would not understand him when he says, "Well, first I looked at them all and then I made lines on each one and then I counted." Step 1 is to get students to say what they think clearly enough for others to understand. And although the other students have been working on the same problem, there is no guarantee that their solutions look the same. Therefore, Marco's description has to be clear enough for others to envision exactly what he has done, and to connect it to what they have done.

Ms. Stangle could have asked Marco to draw his picture on the board, and in fact she often does just that. But in this excerpt, she skillfully uses classroom discourse to get Marco to reach a higher level of verbal precision. This also supports Step 3, in that by getting students to clarify their thinking, they often gain a deeper understanding of what they are actually doing. In Line 9, she takes his words literally and draws a picture that matches what he has said (although it does not match his intentions). As other students see the discrepancy, they grow slightly anxious and want to correct it.

FOUR STEPS…
Step 1: Helping Individual Students Clarify and Share Their Own Thoughts
Step 2: Helping Students Orient to the Thinking of Others
Step 3: Helping Students Deepen Their Own Reasoning
Step 4: Helping Students Engage with the Reasoning of Others

Episode 2: "Thirds of tarts or thirds of peaches?"

17. **Ms. S:** Can somebody repeat what Marco did for his solution so far? Cheryl?

18. **Cheryl:** I think he said he drew a picture of the ten tarts, and then he, like, drew a picture of the ten peaches. Then he cut the tarts into three pieces each. And he drew, like, lines to the peaches.

19. **Ms. S:** OK, so does everyone agree with Cheryl's rendition of what Marco said? Was that what Marco said? Does anyone want to weigh in here? Ginny?

20. **Ginny:** Well, it was almost the same, but Cheryl said that Marco drew ten tarts and cut them into three pieces each. And I think he said that he drew ten *peaches* and cut them into three pieces, three *thirds*, each.

21. **Ms. S:** So Marco, would you clarify? Which one did you do? Did you cut the tarts into thirds in your picture or did you cut the peaches into thirds?

22. **Marco:** [Looks suspiciously at Ms. Stangle.] Umm, I'm not sure now.

23. **Ms. S:** OK, who can help out? Did anyone else have a picture where they divided either the tarts or the peaches into thirds? Tyavanna?

24. **Tyavanna:** I drew ten peaches? And . . . um . . . like . . . um, I think that's what you have to do because you have to show the thirds of the peaches? 'Cause that's what you have to figure out to make the tarts. Not the other way around.

25. **Ms. S:** OK, can somebody say again what Tyavanna just said? Kenny, can you say it in your own words?

26. **Kenny:** Well, I think she's saying that we have to draw pictures of the ten peaches so we can draw the thirds of each peach. She's saying we don't have to draw thirds of each tart. But I didn't draw the peaches at all.

27. **Ms. S:** OK, so you did it a different way? Will you tell us how you started out?

28. **Kenny:** I wrote the fraction *three-thirds* and I wrote it once for each peach. Then I added up all the three-thirds and I got thirty thirds. So then I knew how many thirds I had to work with. If each tart only takes a third of a peach, then I can make thirty tarts. But if each tart had to have two thirds . . . so I just divided two into thirty and so I got fifteen. So I knew there could be fifteen tarts for that one.

Episode 2: Recognizing and Understanding the Teacher's Moves in Ms. Stangle's Fifth-Grade Class

Notice how at the beginning of Episode 2, in Line 17, Ms. Stangle asks Cheryl to repeat what Marco said. This move quickly puts students on notice that they must listen to their classmates' contributions and cannot simply sit and wait for their turn. They must actively engage in trying to understand what others are saying. In fact, Cheryl incorrectly repeats what Marco said, perhaps because she does not understand or perhaps because she has made a simple speech error. We do not know which is the reason for her error, and neither does Ms. Stangle. Nevertheless, Ms. Stangle brings other students into the process of clarifying and correcting. As part of this process, she asks Tyavanna to explain her understanding, and Tyavanna is able to shed some light on the situation (Step 4).

Why does Ms. Stangle choose to ask Kenny to repeat what Tyavanna has said (Line 25)? Is it because she thinks he isn't listening and she wants to get his attention? Or is it because she wants to make sure that all students have heard and understood what Tyavanna has just said? Ms. Stangle could have both intentions: Her skillful use of this request for students to repeat could serve both functions simultaneously.

Some readers may comment that this set of moves—the questioning about details and the requests for repetition—is awfully time-consuming, and perhaps even annoying. How could one run every class this way? Who has the time? Doesn't this focus on precision drive people crazy?

Ms. Stangle does use these techniques with regularity, but there are many times during lessons when she does *not* require students to achieve the same degree of precision as in Episode 1. For example, when students encounter a new idea and are trying to come to grips with it, their language typically becomes imprecise and even incoherent. A moment's reflection reveals that this is true of adults as well—when we are dealing

(*continued*)

with new concepts and unfamiliar ideas, any of us may sound quite inarticulate! As the cognitive demands on us increase, our ability to talk precisely may deteriorate precipitously.

Knowing this, teachers like Ms. Stangle strike a delicate balance. She does *not* require absolute precision of students as they are working through *new ideas*. When they are engaged in the most demanding kinds of thinking, she is less stringent in her attention to clarity and precision. On the other hand, when students are more comfortable with the mathematical ideas, she can afford to emphasize the precision of their language. Her students encounter these demands for precision often, and thereby come to understand and accept the need for precision. They develop an appreciation for the effort we all must make to communicate clearly, in mathematics and elsewhere. And although at first some students do not like to have to repeat what other students have just said, over time they become remarkably attentive and skilled at keeping track of where the conversation is going. It is in just such settings that teachers are able to eventually achieve real advances in mathematical understanding through talk.

> Although at first some students do not like to have to repeat what other students have just said, over time they become remarkably attentive and skilled at keeping track of where the conversation is going.

Summary Tables of Productive Talk Moves (Including Video Clips)

Step 1. Helping Individual Students Clarify and Share Their Own Thoughts

The moves described here will serve you even *after* you have gotten most of your students to participate. It is *always* necessary to give students time to work through their thoughts, time to clarify, and time to expand. Your goal is to make each student's thinking visible, so that everyone can work with that thinking.

BEFORE YOU WATCH THE VIDEOS

To make the most productive use of the video clips, you and any colleagues you are working with should take time to read through the "Guidelines for Watching Videos of Teaching" (see page xxi).

Talk Move	Examples	Why Use It?	What Your Students Need to Know	Strategies for You	Video Clips
Wait Time	• In thirty seconds, I'm going to ask you for your definitions. Think quietly about what you want to say. • What operation did you use? [Wait ten seconds.]	Wait time is a subtle but critical aspect of productive classroom discussions. Your discussions will include questions that ask students to connect ideas, justify strategies, or defend a claim. These are complex mental operations, and students will need time to think before presenting their ideas to the entire class. Asking a conceptually rich question and then waiting only one or two seconds before calling on a student is likely to frustrate most participants. It will also diminish the productivity of the discussion since students will be called on to speak before having had the chance to gather their thoughts. And perhaps worst,	You might start by giving your students the reasoning behind your use of wait time. Of course, what you say will need to be appropriate for your students' age level but you should explain the purpose of wait time as a way to give students time to think. Below is one example of what you might say to students. "I want you to think about whether this has ever happened to you. Imagine a teacher asked a really difficult question and you start to think about that question so that you can answer it in front of the class. But before you can gather	Students who put their hands in the air immediately after the teacher asks a question and then wave it in the air during the entire period of wait time can distract other students who are trying to formulate an answer. Before you begin a whole-class discussion, remind your students that after you ask a question you will be waiting at least five seconds before you call on a student to respond. You may even wish to direct your students not to raise their hands until you signal them that five seconds have elapsed (e.g., "Let's sit and think about my question for a little while. I'll tell you when it's time to raise your hands."). You can also suggest to your students how they might channel their enthusiasm to speak in ways that are less distracting and more productive. Younger students can be advised to alert	 **1A** **Grade 3** **Hands down: let him think.** *In this clip, the teacher, Mrs. Foley, reinforces respectful behaviors in the midst of a problem-solving lesson.*

(Continued)

Talk Move	Examples	Why Use It?	What Your Students Need to Know	Strategies for You	Video Clips
Wait Time, continued		calling on students with no wait time will mean that you will be calling on those students who think most quickly and have their hands up right away, again undercutting your goals for equitable participation. However, research shows that increasing wait time can be a challenging endeavor for many classroom teachers. When we demonstrate a wait time of ten seconds in professional development settings, most teachers are shocked at just how long that wait time feels. For many classroom teachers, moving from short wait times of one or two seconds to longer ones of five or ten seconds marks a huge shift in their instructional practice. This change is likely to be noticed by the students as well. If you plan to use longer wait times during your discussions in math class (and we certainly suggest you should), it is important to talk with your students about why you are waiting for such a long time before selecting a speaker.	all of your thoughts, the teacher calls on someone else to answer it. Well, if that has happened to you, you know how frustrating it can be. "This year, I am going to try to avoid putting you in that kind of frustrating situation. One way I am going to do that is by giving you lots of time to think about your answers before I call on someone to share their thinking. One way I'm going to work on that goal is to count to at least five after I ask a question but before I call on someone. For example, I might say, 'What does it mean for a number to be even?' [Count under your breath—but loud enough for students to hear— "one Mississippi, two Mississippi, three Mississippi, four Mississippi, five Mississippi."] During that time, even if I see people have their hands up, I'm not going to call on anyone until the time is up."	the teacher that they are ready to talk with more subtle gestures like giving a thumbs up. Older students may want to use the time to jot down a few notes about what they will say if they are called upon to speak.	

50

Talk Move	Examples	Why Use It?	What Your Students Need to Know	Strategies for You	Video Clips
Turn and Talk	• Is 24 odd or even? Turn and talk with your partners about that. • Okay, Deva just shared with us her strategy. Turn and talk with your neighbors about it—why does it work? What questions do you have?	*Partner talk* or *turn and talk* or *think-pair-share* are all names for a very useful tool that gives students a brief time to focus and refine their thoughts with a partner. After a turn and talk, students are much more willing to put their ideas out into the open. As they talk with a partner, they can say aloud to one person what they might want to say to the whole group. Particularly for English learners and those students who might feel unsure about their thinking, a minute of partner talk is invaluable.	If your students are not familiar with this move, they need to understand that you will call for a turn and talk when you want them to think with a partner, or practice what they want to say. They need to know that both partners need a chance to talk, and both partners need to listen. They also need to know that turn and talks take only a minute or so. This is not a long discussion!	If you are already using this tool successfully, you will have figured out that it works well when you have asked a question and gotten only one or two raised hands. This is a perfect time to give students a chance to try out their thinking. If you have used it you will also know that it works best if used for *brief* periods of time. Sometimes teachers tell us that they don't use partner talk because students "get off topic." This is usually because these teachers are giving students too much time to talk to their partner. When you use it, try telling students to take *sixty seconds* to talk to their partner: "Time is short, so stay on task!" Then immediately bring them back to report their discussions. If you have students who are particularly hesitant to talk about their own ideas, here's a strategy that may help them contribute. When you ask students to turn and talk about a question, tell them that you will be asking them to report what their *partner* said. For some students, this is less threatening than reporting their own answers. It has the added advantage of encouraging all	 **1B** **Grade 3** **How many cans of grape juice?** *In this clip, Mrs. Foley's students are solving a complicated problem with two kinds of packs of juice cans.* **1C** **Grade 6** **How do we know those are greater than a whole?** *In this clip, the student, Jaehun, has just given his thinking about where $\frac{7}{6}$ and $\frac{13}{9}$ are on a number line. The teacher, Mrs. Rowan, realizes that this was a point of confusion during a previous lesson.*

(Continued)

Talk Move	Examples	Why Use It?	What Your Students Need to Know	Strategies for You	Video Clips
Turn and Talk, continued				students to pay attention to their partner's ideas. (This is particularly important for those students who usually want to talk only about their own ideas.) As you begin to incorporate this move in your instruction, you will want to provide students with an example of a successful turn and talk conversation. Pose a question to the class. Then say, "In a minute, I'm going to ask you to turn and talk about that question with a partner. But first, listen as I talk with my partner about that question." After you talk for thirty to sixty seconds, ask students what they noticed about your turn and talk.	 **1D** **Grade 6** **Can everyone turn . . . and repeat that idea?** *In this clip, the teacher, Ms. Fournier, asks all students to state an important idea about ratios.*
So Are You Saying . . . ? [Revoicing]	• Are you saying you think 24 is odd? Is that right? • So it sounds like you're agreeing with Beth that four-fifths is greater than five-eighths. Is that what you're saying?	Often students will produce a garbled utterance that is tough to understand, for you and for others. Many of us move on: We don't want to embarrass students who appear to be unable to say something clear. But this good intention may be misplaced: Often, an unclear or confusing utterance can be	One of the great things about revoicing is that it can be used anywhere, with no introduction. Your students don't even need to know that you are using a talk move. You simply try to repeat part or all of what they said, and ask them if that is correct. The rest happens naturally.	Some teachers, out of nervousness as they begin to run discussions, overuse revoicing. Everything any students says they may follow with "So you're saying . . . is that right?" This can get old for everyone. Try to use it when you are really struggling to understand what a student has said. Use it as a tool to help them get the time and space to clarify their thinking.	 **1E** **Grade 3** **So you're saying I can't buy one can . . . ?** *In this clip, the teacher, Mrs. Foley, asks a student what at least twenty-six cans means.*

Talk Move	Examples	Why Use It?	What Your Students Need to Know	Strategies for You	Video Clips
So Are You Say-ing . . . ? [Revoic-ing], continued		repaired with a little bit more time. When a student's reasoning is finally clarified, everyone can benefit. The revoicing move also gives you time to think as you say, "So . . . you're saying that . . . the denominator is bigger? Is that right?" Even if you are simply grasping at threads of what a student said, it gives you a place to start. In addition, sometimes a student says something really insightful, something that could move the classroom forward, but the student produced a long and complex utterance. This is *also* a good occasion for you to revoice what you understand. Again, it gives the student a chance to clarify, and it gives other students a chance to hear it again, perhaps in a clearer version.			 **1F** **Grade 5** **So you multiplied the length . . .?** *In this clip, Mrs. Foley's students are working on ways to find the volume of a rectangular prism.*

[*Continued*]

Talk Move	Examples	Why Use It?	What Your Students Need to Know	Strategies for You	Video Clips
Say More . . .	• So you decided to round both numbers. So go on, what did you do next? Tell us more. • I'm not sure I understand yet. I need you to say more.	As you begin using discussion, you will notice that many students respond to your questions with one- or two-word answers. You may wonder, *where are all the great responses I read in the examples in books about discussion?* Don't give up. Simply ask your students to say more: "Can you tell us more? Can you give an example?" There are many ways to get students to expand.	One of the great things about *Say more . . .* is that it can quickly become a natural part of any conversation. As your students get used to it, they will know that you truly want to understand them, and that will help them become better and more willing explainers! At first, however, they may react to your prompt by assuming that they must be wrong. Students are so used to the sequence "Teacher Question—Student Answer—Teacher Evaluation (good or not good)" that they get rattled when you depart from that. But when you explain that you really want to understand them, that asking them to say more doesn't mean they were wrong, they *will* try to explain. And when they start to get better at communicating their thinking, you often won't even have to prompt them!	This is one of the easiest talk moves to use. It is tough to misuse it. If you find yourself going too far afield as students begin to talk more, simply bring them back to the original question. From the beginning, just make sure to let them know that when you ask them to say more, it doesn't mean they were wrong. Remind them that it's tough to understand other people, and it's tough to explain what we really mean. It takes effort and persistence, and we're not going to give up! **If a student falters . . .** Communicating about one's reasoning takes both hard work and courage. Students may falter when asked to say more about their thinking in real time, in front of twenty-four sets of eyes and ears. If this happens, you can say, "Turn and talk with the person next to you about your classmate's thinking. What has she shared so far? What questions would you ask her?" While students are talking, work with the original speaker to help her expand on her initial explanation. Then, call on this student to share additional thoughts when the whole-class discussion resumes.	**1G** **Grade K** **Can you tell me what you did?** *In this clip, Mrs. Luizzi's students have just done a turn and talk. She asks one student to report what she and her partner talked about.* **1H** **Grade 3** **Tell me a little bit more.** *In this clip, the teacher, Mr. Danella, asks a student to give an argument as to why his [Mr. D's] claim is wrong. (This clip also provides a revoicing example.)*

Summary Tables of Productive Talk Moves (Including Video Clips)

Step 2. Helping Students Orient to the Thinking of Others

Many teachers have told us "My students have no trouble talking about their ideas—they just won't listen to others!" If a student is simply waiting to speak, and is not *listening* to others and *trying to understand them*, he or she will not be able to contribute to a real discussion. A discussion involves sharing ideas and reasoning, so it is important to steer students away from a series of individual, unrelated thoughts. If they can't listen to one another, and hear one another, they won't really be able to engage in productive talk.

BEFORE YOU WATCH THE VIDEOS

To make the most productive use of the video clips, you and any colleagues you are working with should take time to read through the "Guidelines for Watching Videos of Teaching" (see page xxi).

Talk Move	Examples	Why Use It?	What Your Students Need to Know	Strategies for You	Video Clips
Who Can Repeat?	• Who can say again what Juana just said? • Who can put what Tim said in their own words? • Could everyone please turn to the person next to you and repeat what Linh just said?	A discussion involves multiple thinkers talking about a set of common ideas. In order to talk about a set of ideas we all have to be able to hear them, understand them, and work with them. This talk move helps you get students to pick up and work with the ideas and reasoning that other students are producing. By asking them to repeat or put something into their own words, you	It is important to be clear with your students that repeating and rephrasing each other's ideas is one way that we can use talk to help us learn. When we repeat or rephrase each other's ideas, our brains have a chance to think about those ideas, connect them with our own, and begin to think about whether or not they make sense. You may also need to eradicate any misconceptions that students may have about this move. For example,	It's important not to use this talk move as a basis for punitive action. If you use it to catch those who aren't paying attention, this will undermine its real purpose. So as you begin to use this move, make sure to call on students who *want* to try to put another student's contribution in their own words. At the beginning of your efforts to use productive classroom talk moves, some students may resist repeating. It's important to get across that they are allowed to say "I didn't hear" or "I didn't	 **1I** **Kindergarten** **He's not all done yet.** *In this clip, Mrs. Hayward's students are working on circling groups of hearts on a card with seven hearts. One student circles only three of the hearts.*

(Continued)

Talk Move	Examples	Why Use It?	What Your Students Need to Know	Strategies for You	Video Clips
Who Can Repeat?, continued		are getting them to take an active stance toward the thinking of others. Over time, as they know you will ask this question, they will begin to orient toward what others say, seeing their own participation as normal. This also gets across the larger goal of giving students an understanding that communication is difficult, and we all have the right and the obligation to struggle with it.	assure students that if you ask someone to repeat their idea, it does not mean that their idea was confusing or unclear. In fact, it often means the opposite—the idea was so clear and important that you want to give other students a chance to think about it. Assure students that if you call on them to repeat, that does not mean that you think they weren't listening. Again, the opposite is probably true. You think they were listening and want to give their brains more time to process what was said. Students may feel taken aback being asked to repeat, at least at first, particularly if they have trouble putting other people's ideas into their own words. Be patient and let them know that this is not always easy. Accept any kind of repetition at first—even an incomplete one. If they can't do it, tell them you can come back to them later. They will start to listen more closely!	understand," but they must then ask the other student to repeat his or her point, and then you must follow up by asking them to repeat it. A good time to use this is when a student has said something interesting and important. Getting students to put the contribution into their own words helps them think about it more deeply. When a student says something complex—too complex to repeat—you can use this move to help them break it down. When another student tries to repeat and can't manage to reformulate the whole thing, you can go back and ask the first student to break it down a bit so that others can get it. After one or more students respond to the question "Who can say that again?," ask the original speaker, "Are we interpreting your reasoning correctly?" This question gives the original speaker an opportunity to clarify or amend any misinterpretations of the original remark and assures all students that when you use this move you will work hard to make sure that their ideas are taken seriously.	 **1J** **Grade 1** **She was counting by fives.** *In this clip, Mrs. Delaney's students are using a hundreds chart to explore counting patterns.* **1K** **Grade 5** **Finding the volume of a rectangular prism** *In this clip, a student gives his way of finding the volume of a rectangular prism. The teacher, Mrs. Foley, asks others to repeat.*

Talk Move	Examples	Why Use It?	What Your Students Need to Know	Strategies for You	Video Clips
Who Can Repeat?, continued				

1L
Grade 6
How did you know that seven-eighths was greater than three-fourths?

In this clip, a student explains her reasoning in deciding where to place fractions on a number line. The teacher, Mrs. Rowan, asks others to repeat.

1M
Grade 6
Which table is "the root beer drinkers?"

In this clip, the teacher, Ms. Fournier, asks a student to repeat another student's strategy for solving a ratio problem. |

(Continued)

Summary Tables of Productive Talk Moves (Including Video Clips)

Step 3. Helping Students Deepen Their Own Reasoning

Even if students express their thoughts and listen to others' ideas, the discussion can still fail to be academically productive if it does not include solid and sustained reasoning. Some classroom discussions are superficial—most students are not skilled at pushing to understand and to deepen their own reasoning. Therefore, the teacher's role includes continuous and skillful use of the tools that *keep the focus on reasoning.*

BEFORE YOU WATCH THE VIDEOS

To make the most productive use of the video clips, you and any colleagues you are working with should take time to read through the "Guidelines for Watching Videos of Teaching" (see page xxi).

Talk Move	Examples	Why Use It?	What Your Students Need to Know	Strategies for You	Video Clips
Press for Reasoning: Why Do You Think That?	• Why do you think that? • Can you prove it to us? • What's your evidence? • What convinced you that was the answer? • Why did you think that strategy would work?	At the heart of the Common Core is *reasoning.* Many students are not used to having discussions about their reasoning. But these are an important part of what students need to do to satisfy content standards and practice standards. By getting practice in explaining their thinking, and being encouraged to dig deeper, to push beyond the easy or obvious answer, your students will be engaging in exactly the kind of intellectual activity called for by the CCSS. As they	At first, when you ask students why they made a claim or gave a certain answer, they may assume that they must be wrong. Next, they may feel confused, not knowing what it means to provide a rationale for what they say. You will have to talk with them about the purpose of digging into their reasoning. In Chapter 8, we provide several lesson plans for introducing students of different ages to these tools.	Students often are unaware of what it means to provide justification for their statements. They may not be used to explaining their thinking in this way, and may at first be puzzled. T: Why did you choose that answer? S: I chose that because . . . like . . . it was the right answer? T: How did you know that was the answer? S: I just . . . I followed the directions. In cases like these, you will need to be persistent. When students get the hang of explaining their thinking, many of them start to do so spontaneously!	 **1N** **Grade 2** **Are you sure? How do you know?** *In this clip, the teacher, Ms. Powers, uses press for reasoning to help students make sense of a strategy for subtracting numbers.*

Talk Move	Examples	Why Use It?	What Your Students Need to Know	Strategies for You	Video Clips
Press for Reasoning: Why Do You Think That? continued		become used to you asking them for evidence, for reasoning, for a description of their thinking, they will become more adept at digging deeper themselves, without prompting.		Ask students guiding questions, such as "Is there a fact, or a connection, or a relationship that you used to get your answer?" and "How did you use that information?" Sometimes asking everyone to turn and talk about why a statement is true and then returning to the original speaker in the whole-class discussion can enhance the level of response for why a claim was made. We want to make it clear that the examples listed for this talk move are just a start. As you ask students to explain their thinking, you will be using lots of utterances that contain lots of mathematical examples, terms, and specific queries. The basic move *Why do you think that?* is just the first step!	 **10** **Grade 4** **Can you prove it?** *In this clip, Mrs. Burgess's students are solving a mystery number puzzle. She presses for reasoning several times.* **1P** **Grade 5** **Why does that work?** *In this clip, the teacher, Mrs. Foley, presses for reasoning in students' explanations of how they found the volume of a rectangular prism. You will see the talk move Who can repeat? mixed in with press for reasoning.*

[Continued]

Summary Tables of Productive Talk Moves

Step 4. Helping Students Engage with the Reasoning of Others (including Video Clips)

The final goal involves students actually absorbing the ideas and reasoning of other students and responding to them. This is when real discussion can take off, discussion that will support robust learning. It is also when you have everything in place to make real progress on the Common Core State Standards Mathematical Practice 3: *Construct viable arguments and critique the reasoning of others.*

BEFORE YOU WATCH THE VIDEOS
To make the most productive use of the video clips, you and any colleagues you are working with should take time to read through the "Guidelines for Watching Videos of Teaching" (see page xxi).

Talk Move	Examples	Why Use It?	What Your Students Need to Know	Strategies for You	Video Clips
What Do You Think About That? *or* **Do You Agree or Disagree . . . and Why?**	• Who agrees or disagrees with Natalia's conjecture? • What do you think about Davio's strategy? • Will it always work? • Did someone think about it in a different way?	After a student has put forward a claim or a reason or a solution method, and after it has been understood, you are ready to actually get other students to weigh in. This is what will give you material for a full-fledged productive discussion. Asking students whether they agree or disagree, and why, is perhaps the most powerful tool for focusing their attention on what another student has said. As they begin to take	As soon as you begin to ask students to directly comment on, to agree or disagree, and to assess what others have said, some students may feel insecure and worried about their own status. Other students may begin to tell others what they think in no uncertain terms, with no regard for others' feelings. What students need to know at this point concerns the norms for respectful and equitable discussion. These will have	Different versions of this talk move bring different challenges and benefits. Some versions are asking for divergence (Who disagrees? Did anyone do this a different way? Do you see it differently?). Other versions are asking for support and convergence (Who agrees? Do you want to add more evidence to her claim? Does that make sense to you? Why?). Often teachers simply ask for "thumbs up if you agree, thumbs down if you disagree."	 **1Q** **Grade 1** **Why do you agree with him?** *In this clip, Mrs. Delaney's students are explaining how they counted two nickels and five pennies. Mrs. Delaney asks one student whether he agrees or disagrees with what the previous student said.*

60

Talk Move	Examples	Why Use It?	What Your Students Need to Know	Strategies for You	Video Clips
What Do You Think About That? *or* **Do You Agree or Disagree... and Why?**, continued		a position on what another student has said, they begin to have a stake in the talk.	been introduced by you before this point, of course. (See Chapters 2 and 8 for detailed approaches to introducing both talk moves and discussion norms.) However, it is never a bad idea to revisit them. This will also be a powerful place for your students to begin to understand that your ultimate focus is on the mathematical truth and meaning of a statement or claim: It's not about *who* said something, it's about *what was said*.	While this can provide some useful information, it is usually not helpful in getting students to deeply engage with others' reasoning. It is crucial that you follow up with the question *"Why do you agree?"* or *"Why do you disagree?"* Otherwise, students may provide generic answers without really thinking through their position. Disagreement can bring conflict. In Chapter 2 we discuss how to work with this. On the other hand, many teachers start out by simply asking, "Does everyone agree?" A few minutes of reflection will reveal how this can undermine your goals for reasoning. Too many teacher questions asking only for agreement can signal to students that they *should* be agreeing, that you don't want them to diverge from the group in their reasoning.	 **1R** **Grade 3** **Do almost all of the people do their homework before dinner?** *In this clip, the teacher, Mrs. Schineller, asks her students to turn and talk about whether they agree with the claim that almost all of the thirty-eight people polled do their homework before dinner.* **1S** **Grade 3** **Not to be rude, but...** *In this clip, the teacher, Mr. Danella, asks students whether they agree or disagree with Jeda's claim about what numbers would solve their puzzle, and one student disagrees.*

61

(Continued)

Talk Move	Examples	Why Use It?	What Your Students Need to Know	Strategies for You	Video Clips
Who Can Add On?	• Rosalee got us started. Who can pick it up from there? • Who can predict what they think Wally did next? • Who has something to add?	Sometimes, as you discuss a topic, you find that few students seem willing to address the core question. Or maybe you are not able to come up with a specific question on the fly, but want to encourage students to continue interacting with one another's ideas. This very general talk move, which is simply asking others to respond to the recent contribution of one or more students, is a way of signaling that you are throwing open the doors and inviting everyone in.	This is another talk move that needs little introduction. All students need to know is that their contributions will be welcomed and treated with fairness and respect. By now they will know that they are obligated to work with you and others to clarify whatever their contributions will be.	You might think that students will become bored or uninterested when asked to "add on." However, in our experience, this has not been the case. Students' contributions tend to deepen and extend the conversation; this benefits the individual speaker but also the class as a whole. Thus, don't hesitate to ask a number of students to participate. Younger students do not always see the connections between the contributions so you may need to summarize them for the class.	 **1T** **Grade 1** **Would you like to add on to the beginning of her thinking?** *In this clip, Mrs. Delaney's students are discussing ways to add nickels and pennies. One student explains her approach but reaches an impasse. Mrs. Delaney asks for input from others.*

Talk Move	Examples	Why Use It?	What Your Students Need to Know	Strategies for You	Video Clips
Who Can Add On?, continued					**1U** **Grade 2** **Who can add on to that?** *In this clip, the teacher, Ms. Powers, uses the talk move Who can add on? to help her students reason about measurement concepts.* **1V** **Grade 5** **What is a rectangular prism?** *In this clip, the teacher, Mrs. Foley, asks her students to weigh in with their understandings of what a rectangular prism is.*

How Do We Begin? Classroom Norms for Productive Talk

How do we talk about math?

About This Chapter

See
Chapter 1.

To be successful implementing the talk moves introduced in Chapter 1, you first need to provide your students with a rationale about *why* you will be focusing so much on explanation and discussion. As part of this rationale, you can provide students with an overview of what math class will look and sound like this year. Second, you'll need to set the ground rules for how you will talk to each other in *respectful*, courteous ways. Third, you'll need to establish your expectation for *equitable* participation from all members of the class. In this chapter, we provide a number of ways to do this, and a number of ways to talk with your students about this new form of instruction. We also look briefly at two productive talk formats.

Explaining and Discussing New Forms of Talk

It is important to explain to students *why* you are focusing on student explanation and discussion in math class. Even at very young ages, students enter classrooms with beliefs and prior experiences that can affect the way they participate in classroom discussions.

Addressing Students' Beliefs About Mathematics

Students' beliefs about the subject of mathematics itself can affect how they participate in math discussions. If students think success in mathematics means saying the correct answers in the least amount of time, they will find discussion puzzling. If they think success in math means remembering and applying rules correctly, they may be reluctant to participate in forming conjectures or questioning claims. These students need to hear that mathematics focuses on *reasoning, problem solving,* and *sense making*—and that therefore, as a class, they will be spending time talking about their ideas, their problem-solving strategies, and their generalizations in order to become better mathematical thinkers.

> **If students think success in mathematics means saying the correct answers in the least amount of time, they will find discussion puzzling.**

Addressing Students' Social or Cultural Backgrounds

Students' social or cultural backgrounds may also affect how they participate in classroom discussions. It's very likely that there will be some students in your class who have lots of experience discussing their ideas with adults. Other students may believe that it's rude to disagree with a peer or adult—even in math class. For still other students, this form of activity will be completely new. Some students are from social or cultural backgrounds in which it's not typical for children to engage in talk on intellectual topics with adults. These children may be more used to listening attentively to what adults say, or to learning through careful observation. Furthermore, some immigrant students may come from countries where students are never allowed to talk in school and the very idea may be confusing and even upsetting. These students may need to hear that this type of talk is expected of them in their math class this year. Assure students that although this type of instruction is new to them, many students all over the world learn math this way because talking about ideas is one way mathematicians explore what is true and what is not true.

> Talking about ideas is one way mathematicians explore what is true and what is not true.

Clarifying Your Expectations

In addition to providing a rationale for whole-class discussions, you must also be explicit with your students about your expectations for their participation in your class discussions. Begin by addressing two overarching expectations—*that students will talk about their own reasoning and will respond to each other's ideas.*

At this time, you must also set up the norms—the ground rules—for respectful, courteous discourse. Neither students nor teachers will engage in productive talk about mathematics if they are afraid that they will be laughed at, "dissed," or somehow made to feel stupid. Therefore, it's important to emphasize the positive and forestall the negative. In addition, you must be clear with students that you expect *everyone* to participate in class discussions. It's important to acknowledge and discuss the reasons that students might not want to talk.

> You must be clear with students that you expect *everyone* to participate in class discussions. It's important to acknowledge and discuss the reasons that students might not want to talk.

As you build the classroom norms along with your students, they will begin to feel more confident of not risking being ridiculed or dismissed when they get the courage to talk. And while you acknowledge that participation may sometimes require a certain amount of courage, you can also emphasize that each of us has an obligation to participate. As each person contributes, we can all learn from one another's ideas.

Teacher Reflections: Modeling Respectful Talk

Mrs. Luizzi

Learning how to engage in respectful discussion is crucial; modeling and role playing are powerful ways to introduce and reinforce these skills. My assistant teacher and I often act out conversations and talk aloud about our thinking or decision making in order for students to internalize these behaviors. We also invite students to participate in dramatizations as a fun way for them to experience classroom discussions firsthand and improve upon their own skills.

Mrs. Hayward

When I ask, "How did you get your answer?," I think students' natural inclination is to say, "Well, I know it in my head" or "Because I just do." When I model what it means to explain and ask, "Show me how you know" or "How can you prove it to me?," my kindergarteners learn that they're expected to explain their reasoning.

The Two Major Goals of Setting Up Classroom Talk Norms

It's common knowledge that learning takes place most easily within an atmosphere of respect and support. We have all had the positive experience of learning in a supportive environment, and have seen what it can do for us. Conversely, we have all experienced the feeling of being silenced or shut down, of not wanting to speak up because we were afraid of ridicule or criticism. If students are afraid that their ideas will be ridiculed, they will not talk freely, no matter what inducements you offer. Even one hostile or disrespectful interchange can put a serious damper on students' willingness to talk openly about their ideas and thoughts. Therefore, it's important to put norms in place that support respectful discussion.

Equity is equally important. Students are quick to pick up implied messages that only the most academically successful students are expected to make real contributions. This has two negative consequences. First, students who do not think of themselves as star students will get the message that they are "off duty" and that their only obligation is occasionally to pretend to weigh in when asked to do so. This will seriously affect the success of your math discussions. Second, students who consider themselves on the top rung academically will not feel obligated to pay attention to the ideas of those they consider "less than." For both reasons, finding ways to support equitable participation is a key to success for your math discussions.

In this section we introduce ways to create norms that support respectful and equitable discussions.

The Two Major Goals of Setting Up Classroom Talk Norms

- *Respectful Discourse:* Talk is respectful when each person's ideas are taken seriously; no one is ridiculed or insulted, and no one is ignored or browbeaten.
- *Equitable Participation:* Participation is equitable when each person has a fair chance to ask questions, make statements, and express his or her ideas. Academically productive talk is not just for the most vocal or the most talented students.

Goal 1: Respectful Discourse

Most teachers already set norms for classroom behavior—respect, hard work, showing up—but the use of classroom talk and discussion require more specialized norms. The ground rules must focus on each student's obligation to treat what others say with respect. Specifically, you must make it abundantly clear to your students that no name-calling or derogatory noises or remarks are ever allowed; a student can't say, for example, "I was just joking" to excuse a disrespectful remark.

Students must know that you will hold them to a high standard. There must be clear consequences for violating this basic agreement; you can decide whether you want to set these consequences yourself or negotiate them with students. Either way, be sure to set consequences that you are prepared to follow consistently and fairly with all students.

Other dilemmas, perhaps much less egregious than name-calling or insults, can still discourage participation and should be addressed. Conduct a discussion with your students during which you identify scenarios that may prevent people from sharing their thoughts, including the more subtle situations that bother students, and then together brainstorm ways to address these problems. For example, you can ask, "What else might keep people from sharing a good idea or asking a question during class discussions? What can we do to resolve or even prevent these problems?" In addition, you may want to rely on the following list of common discussion dilemmas to address the importance of respectful, courteous discussions with your students.

Discussion Dilemmas

Directions: Once a week, choose one of the dilemmas below and post it where everyone can see it. Talk with your students about what they can do to not only *prevent* this problem from occurring but also *correct* it once it does occur.

- People are writing or talking while someone is speaking.
- A student interrupts the speaker in the middle of his or her explanation.
- Someone is complaining that he or she is the one who should be talking, not the speaker.
- A student offers an idea and immediately seven or eight students raise their hands shouting, "I disagree!"
- A student starts to give an explanation and several students yell, "You lost me!" and "I don't get that at all!"
- One student in a group of four takes credit for another student's clever idea.
- You have what you think is a very good idea but you were wrong already four or five times this week and are afraid to be wrong again.

Your ground rules for respectful and courteous talk must include a rule that obligates students to listen attentively as others talk. This is respectful behavior, but just as important, it is pragmatic behavior. It enables students to participate in the ongoing talk. If they do not know what was just said, they cannot possibly build on it.

Students' Rights and Obligations

You may need to remind students of the rules for respectful, courteous discussions every day until the rules become a routine part of your classroom culture. We recommend creating a poster of your rules for courteous and respectful discourse and prominently displaying it so that you and your students can refer to it when necessary. It is imperative that you consistently maintain the ground rules for respectful and courteous talk and that your students know there will be no exceptions. While establishing ground rules may sound difficult, many teachers have had success within the first few weeks or months of teaching this way.

> We recommend creating a poster of your rules for courteous and respectful discourse and prominently displaying it so that you and your students can refer to it when necessary.

In Project Challenge (see Appendix A: The Research: Project Challenge, page 319), we used the following list of students' rights and obligations to help make talk norms explicit: [See Appendix A.]

Project Challenge: Students' Rights and Obligations

Project Challenge Rights

- You have the right to make a contribution to an attentive, responsive audience.
- You have the right to ask questions.
- You have the right to be treated civilly.
- You have the right to have your *ideas* discussed, not *you*.

Project Challenge Obligations

- You are obligated to speak loudly enough for others to hear.
- You are obligated to listen for understanding.
- You are obligated to treat others civilly at all times.
- You are obligated to consider other people's ideas and to explain your agreement or disagreement with their ideas.

With upper elementary and middle school students, it works best to involve students in designing their own set of norms. You can then supplement students' suggestions for norms to make sure that all the important points are covered. In grades kindergarten through grade 2, you will need to adapt the rights and obligations for younger students. For example:

Grade 1: Students' Rights and Obligations

As speakers we will:

- Talk loud enough for others to hear.
- Turn to talk to the class.
- Share different ideas.
- Explain our ideas.
- Agree and disagree with ideas, not with each other.

As listeners we will:

- Ask speakers to speak up.
- Show speakers we are listening.
- Listen to understand.
- Ask questions to make sense of the idea.
- Think carefully about all speakers' ideas.

How might you introduce and use the idea of rights and obligations with your students? What rights and obligations would you add to the above lists?

Teacher Reflection: The Green Sheet

Mrs. Chapin

Our Project Challenge teachers used discussions about respectful discourse as an occasion to create a wall chart codifying the norms of respectful discourse and full participation. Teachers then distributed a version of this chart to all students to put in the front of their math notebook. It was printed on green paper and became known as simply "the green sheet." When teachers encountered a problem with compliance or disrespect, they would simply say, "Take out the green sheet. Let's go over it again." You might want to construct your own "green sheet," adding to these rights and obligations and emphasizing issues that are of importance to your class.

It is very important to put the goal of respectful discourse first. Even one hostile or disrespectful interchange can put a serious damper on students' willingness to talk openly about their ideas and thoughts. It is up to you to consistently maintain the ground rules for respectful and courteous talk, and it's important that your students know there will be no exceptions.

Goal 2: Equitable Participation

As you establish the conditions for respectful and courteous talk, you will also need to set the conditions for full and equitable participation: All students must have the *opportunity* to engage in productive talk about mathematics, not just those who are high in status or academically most able.

> All students must have the *opportunity* to engage in productive talk about mathematics, not just those who are high in status or academically most able.

Students need to know that our goal of talking about our mathematical thinking carries with it a very important obligation: Every student in the class must participate on a regular basis in our class discussions. This is critical, because students' past experiences may lead to different interpretations of what it means to *participate* in a discussion. For example, in past years, teachers may have told students that it was OK if they did not talk as long as they listened to other students' explanations and thought privately about whether they made sense. Or students may have been told that it was OK if they did not understand a classmate's idea as long as they listened respectfully to what that person said. Although we see the value and intent behind both of these positions, we recommend that teachers set up the expectation that all students must talk from time to time during class discussions.

We believe that equitable participation means all students *regularly* talk about their own ideas and actively respond to each other's contributions. This does not mean that each student must talk during every lesson or that a discussion must consist of every single student speaking in turn. In fact, this can actually diminish the quality of participation. However, it does mean that the teacher has an obligation to find ways for all students to participate in significant ways on an ongoing basis.

> How can we expect all students to participate when many classrooms include students with special learning needs or conditions that might make it difficult for them to join in discussions?

At this point, we know that many teachers will ask how they can expect all students to participate when many classrooms include students with special learning needs or conditions that might make it difficult for them to contribute to discussions. We have taught in or observed many classroom discussions in which students with Individualized Education Programs (IEPs) for a variety of learning or behavioral challenges have made important contributions to math discussions. In some cases these contributions were voiced for the student by a partner. In other cases they were contributed by the student him- or herself, with support from an in-class aide. We encourage you to persist in your efforts to find ways to include all your students in ongoing discussions of mathematical ideas.

"You're Picking on Me!"

Occasionally we have encountered a student who felt that by calling on him, we were picking on him and that we did not like him. Talking with the student, reassuring him that he is a valuable member of the class, and letting him know how much we want to hear his good ideas in our classroom, made a difference. We explained that we called on him and everyone else because our job as the teacher is to make sure everyone learns the math and we believe the best way to do so is by talking.

Standing up in front of your students and saying, "Everyone must talk," is unlikely to establish equitable participation in your classroom. Instead, equitable participation will depend on your instructional decisions—decisions that allow all students a chance to take the floor and that support students who have previously been reticent in class.

Practices to Improve Equitable Participation

In our work implementing classroom discussions, we have developed a list of strategies for working on equitable participation when things aren't going as well as they could. Not every classroom will need these. In some classes, use of the talk moves that we describe in Chapter 1 are enough to bring about equitable participation. However, if you have been working with those, and you still find that some students never participate, and others routinely monopolize

See Chapter 1.

the floor, you might want to try some of the techniques listed below. You can use them on an occasional basis, and set them aside when you feel that things are working more smoothly.

Practices to Improve Equitable Participation

- Give time to think.
- Give time to practice.
- Randomly assign speakers to report out for a group.
- Encourage students to self-monitor their participation.
- Offer a "token to talk."
- Use the technique "one of three."

Give Time to Think

In almost all of the math classes we have taught or observed, there have been several students who almost never raise their hands to speak during class discussions. In order to fulfil your expectations for equitable participation, you may need to speak with these students in private about how you can help them talk during class discussions. In the early elementary grades, see if you can reach an agreement with these students that you will use *turn and talk* to help them prepare responses that they can then share during whole-class discussions. In other words, reassure them that you will call on them in situations in which they will have time to prepare.

Give Time to Practice

Many students, especially English language learners, benefit from practicing what they will say prior to reporting out to the whole class. During small group or partner talk you can be lining up the next few speakers. Let the students know ahead of time what contribution you are hoping they will share. This enables them to prepare more completely and reduces anxiety. It also guarantees that a student will have a positive speaking experience that will help build confidence for future participation.

Randomly Assign Speakers to Report Out for a Group

Some teachers may notice that the same students always take on the role of reporting out for groups or in pair work. In classes that use a lot of discussion, students typically work on problems in pairs or small groups before discussing their solutions as a whole class, so if some students always take it upon themselves to speak for others, this can really undercut equitable participation.

As the class prepares to transition from partner talk or small group work time to whole-class discussion format, ask students to determine which student in their group will be the next to celebrate their birthday. (Any random selection process can be used—for example, when students put their names in alphabetical order, the speaker could be the third person in the list.) Explain that this student will speak for the group about the assigned task—presenting their solution strategy, stating a definition, justifying a conjecture—when you reconvene as a whole class. This same technique can also be used following a turn and talk to decide which of the two students will present what they talked about in pairs.

Encourage Students to Self-Monitor Their Participation

Relying on whole-class discussion in math classes may be a big adjustment for students who are used to doing the majority of talking in class. If you suddenly start inviting more students into your class discussions, you may find that your most vocal students are resentful or even angry about these changes. One way to address or even circumvent this problem is to remind your students about *why* you are calling on all students to speak during discussions. You can then explain to students that this means you can't always call on the same student multiple times during one discussion.

> When the same students raise their hands repeatedly throughout discussions, ask them to make decisions about when to raise their hands and when to "sit the question out."

Suggest to students who raise their hands repeatedly throughout discussions that they make decisions about when to raise their hands and when to *sit the question out*. You could talk with individual students outside of class and say something like, "If we're discussing a problem in class and you have lots to say about that problem and keep raising your hand over and over again, you know that I can't call on you every time I see your hand up. So here's something you can do to help me think about when I should call on you. If I ask a question or if one of your classmates says something that you want to respond to, think about whether that question or idea is something you really want to share or whether you would rather wait to talk about something else. Then, when I see your hand up, I'll know that it's something you really, really want to say."

Offer a "Token to Talk"

At the start of class, give each student a small object like a token or coin to help remind them to make at least one comment during the class discussion. Explain to students that this is their token to talk today, and ask them to turn in their tokens when they speak. If you have one or two students who monopolize the floor, others who don't talk at all, or when there is a lot of chaos and people talking over one another, you may even decide to tell students that no one can speak for a second time until everyone who wants to has spoken at least once. (If you choose this latter option, be sure to read about the popsicle-stick approach, below.)

Use the Technique "One of Three"

In upper elementary grades, with students who are fearful about participating, we have found it helpful to rely on a technique we call "one of three." During private conversations with students who struggle to participate on a regular basis, we ask them to do *at least one of three things per class*:

1. Volunteer a comment during a whole-class discussion.
2. Respond when called on at random to do so.
3. Ask a question during a whole-class discussion.

What About Choosing Names at Random? The Popsicle-Stick Approach

As a way to get students to know that they are always "on call," some people recommend choosing names at random, for example, by drawing names from a box or writing students' names on popsicle sticks. While this sometimes can be a helpful approach, it can in some cases lead you away from meaningful discussion. Why? In our view, an intellectually productive discussion will have a certain coherence: An idea brought up by one student will evoke a response in one or two other students. They will want to query one another and respond in what may be extended exchanges. If you have decided to draw names to choose students at random, you may sacrifice some really excellent and motivating discussions.

When might you use the popsicle-stick approach?
- At the start of your discussion, you ask a question (for example, "Is twenty-four odd or even?") and you see a sea of hands.

(continued)

If nearly everyone in the class wants to be the first to get the discussion started, the popsicle-stick approach can help you choose a speaker in a fair and unbiased way.

- A student has just raised a key point and you want to use the talk move *Who can say that again?* to give the student's idea more air time. In order to choose students to respond, you can use the popsicle-stick approach, which is particularly effective in this situation since it communicates to all students that you aren't using this move just to call on certain students—for example, those who tend not to pay attention or those who regularly need extra help. Instead, you are using this move, and so many of the other moves, because you expect all students to listen to each other's contributions and you want to give all students the chance to think more about key mathematical ideas.

When might it be best to avoid the popsicle-stick approach?

- If you see a particularly reticent student raise his or her hand and you want to give him or her a chance to participate.
- In the midst of a discussion or mathematical debate where important ideas are being discussed by many fully engaged students, and you want to preserve the coherence of the discussion.

We point out the popsicle-stick approach above to emphasize the fact that orchestrating math discussions is a complex undertaking. At each moment, you will have goals for content discussion, goals for respectful talk, and goals for equitable participation. When these goals come into conflict, you may feel stress. However, we want to encourage you to continue by reminding you that an academic year is a long ball game. Don't worry about making the perfect decision every time. Over the long run your efforts will pay off. Just keep at it!

Connecting Classroom Norms with the Talk Moves: Video Clips

See
Chapter 1.
As we mentioned in Chapter 1, academically productive classroom discourse is made up of specific talk moves and tools that you'll need to introduce to students and maintain just as you do more general norms. In the following examples, teachers address how to introduce specific talk moves and tools to students and to make sure that the enactment of these talk moves and tools proceeds in a civil and productive manner.

Video Clip 2A: Discussing *Fair Turns* and Repeating

In this clip, Mrs. Hayward is working with her kindergarten students to review what constitutes a *fair turn*—this is her term for a collection of positive behaviors that help students orient to each other's contributions. Watch the clip. What norms did you see evidence of? Was the focus on equitable participation, respectful discourse, or both?

Video Clip 2B: How Do We Agree and Disagree?

In this clip, Ms. Luipold discusses with her fourth-grade students how to disagree in a respectful, courteous manner. Watch the clip. What distinction is made between disagreeing with a person versus with his or her answer? How might you help your students make this distinction as you conduct your whole-class discussions?

Two Productive Talk Formats

Along with thinking about implementing classroom norms and talk moves to guide our students' learning, it is also useful to consider the talk *formats* we can use. Talk formats are different ways that teachers configure classroom interactions for instruction and are among the major tools that teachers use to accomplish their goals for student learning. For example, Ms. Davies uses the *whole-class discussion* talk format, having her entire class work together on mathematical thinking and reasoning. Every classroom teacher makes use of a variety of talk formats.

Each format has its own "rules for talk." Some of these rules are rarely discussed, but students know them, nevertheless. For example, in the traditional and familiar talk format that we might label *direct instruction* or, in the higher grades, *lecturing,* the rules go something like this: The teacher has the right to talk, and students must not talk unless the teacher calls out their names. *Quizzing* is another commonly used talk format in which the teacher asks questions for which he or she knows the answers and expects the students to know the answers as well; for example, the teacher calls on a student and evaluates his or her answer for correctness: "Jamie, how much is three times eight?" "Twenty-four?" "Good." In research on classroom talk this is called the IRE format, for *Initiation* (by the teacher), *Response* (by the student), and *Evaluation* (by the teacher). Other talk formats include *sharing time, group recitation,* and *student presentations.*

While there are many academic purposes that may be served by using these talk formats for mathematics instruction, in this resource we focus on two talk formats: whole-class discussion and small-group discussion. We have found these talk formats to be particularly supportive of maximizing opportunities for mathematical learning by all students.

Two Productive Talk Formats

1. Whole-Class Discussion
2. Small-Group Discussion

Talk Format 1: Whole-Class Discussion

The talk format that appears most prominently in *Classroom Discussions in Math* is whole-class discussion. In this talk format, the teacher is in charge of the class, just as in direct instruction. However, in whole-class discussion, the teacher is not primarily engaged in delivering information or quizzing. Rather, he or she is attempting to get students to share their thinking, explain the steps in their reasoning, and build on one another's contributions. These whole-class discussions give students the chance to engage in sustained reasoning. The teacher facilitates and guides quite actively, but does not focus on providing answers directly. Instead, the focus is on the students' thinking.

> In whole-class discussion, the teacher is not primarily engaged in delivering information or quizzing. Rather, he or she is attempting to get students to share their thinking, explain the steps in their reasoning, and build on one another's contributions.

It takes students a great deal of practice to become solid and confident mathematical thinkers, and the whole-class discussion talk format provides a space for that practice. In our model of whole-class discussion, the teacher often refrains from providing the correct answer immediately. She or he does not instantly reject incorrect reasoning, but instead attempts to get students to explore the steps in their reasoning, with the aim that they will gain practice in discovering where their thinking falls short. Invariably, these discussions reveal many examples of faulty reasoning, mistakes in computation, and misunderstandings. These flaws, however, are the raw material with which teachers can work to guide students' mathematical learning. And, in the process, students become more confident in their ability to stick with making sense of concepts, skills, and problems. They gradually lose some of the anxiety and avoidance that many students display when confronted with complex mathematical ideas.

Focus on the Correct Answer?

The purpose of whole-class discussion is to provide students with practice in mathematical reasoning that will further their mathematical learning. To accomplish this, the focus is on the students' ideas and the soundness of their reasoning, *not* on the correctness of their answers. This does not mean that we advise teachers to deemphasize correct answers and mathematical truth. In our view, the ultimate goal is for students to achieve mathematical power through precision, accuracy, insight, and reliable reasoning. However, we have found that it is important for students to have opportunities to *practice reasoning* in discussions without an immediate focus on correct answers.

> It is important for students to have opportunities to *practice reasoning* in discussions without an immediate focus on correct answers.

(continued)

Many people new to instructional discussions may ask, "How is students' learning of mathematics supported when teachers don't let them know right away when their thinking is misguided or an answer is incorrect? Aren't there times when it's better to tell students that their answer or idea is wrong?" To answer these questions, it's important to think about what learning of mathematics involves. More specifically, when confronted with any new mathematical concept or skill, it is important to consider where the source of the knowledge is for the student.

Sources of Knowledge External to Students

Sometimes the source of mathematical knowledge lies outside a student and the only way that a student can have access to that knowledge is from an external source, such as a book, a television program, the teacher, or another student. For example, the mathematical symbols we use to represent ideas are socially agreed-upon conventions, and the source of learning these symbols lies outside the student. There is no way for a student to "discover" the meaning of a plus sign—we show it to students and tell them what it means. The same is true for the operation signs for subtraction, multiplication, and division; for the relational symbols for equal, greater than, less than; even for the way we write the numerals. These symbols have no meanings that are inherent to them but rather are mathematical conventions that we all agree to use for ease of representing and communicating mathematical ideas. The same is true for the terminology we apply to mathematical ideas—*triangle, prime number, even, fraction,* and so on. When mathematical knowledge is linked to social conventions, direct instruction is appropriate for furthering students' learning.

> When mathematical knowledge is linked to social conventions, direct instruction is appropriate for furthering students' learning.

Sources of Knowledge Internal to Students

When mathematical concepts and skills are not linked to social conventions but rather have their own internal logic, the source of knowledge is not external to the student. Instead, students learn by processing information, applying reasoning, hearing ideas from others, and connecting new thinking to what they already know, all for the goal of making sense for themselves of new concepts and skills. The source of the knowledge, of creating new understanding, lies within the student, and making sense is the key.

For example, we can tell a student that the order of the numbers in a multiplication problem does not alter the answer—that 2 × 5, for example, produces the same product as 5 × 2. But this is an idea that students can figure out for themselves from experimenting with problems, thinking about what happens to the products when factors are reversed, and then talking about their ideas. (See Chapter 1, page 6, for an example from Mrs. Schuster's classroom.)

See Chapter 1.

Simply *telling* students through direct instruction is not sufficient for teaching ideas in which the source of the knowledge is inside the student. In order for children to learn, understand, and remember, they need experiences to interact with the idea, think about it in relation to what they already know, uncover its logic, and then apply their thinking to new ideas. Using talk in a whole-class discussion provides students with opportunities to *make sense of new ideas*. Such discussions may reveal students' confusion, partial understandings, and misconceptions, but these are also aspects of learning. Explaining their reasoning is important for all students as it helps them to cement and even extend their thinking. Over the long run, we have seen that asking, "Why do you think that?" has profound effects on students' mathematical thinking and on their "habits of mind" in general.

> Simply *telling* students through direct instruction is not sufficient for teaching ideas in which the source of the knowledge is inside the student.

Just as crucially, these discussions provide important information for teachers in planning instruction. Discussions provide many formative assessment opportunities regarding individual students and the class as a whole.

Talk Format 2: Small-Group Discussion

In *Classroom Discussions in Math* we make a distinction between whole-class discussion and small-group discussion. In the small-group discussion talk format, the teacher typically gives students a math problem or question to discuss among themselves in groups of two to four. Although the teacher can circulate and provide assistance as needed, he or she cannot possibly talk with all of the students in every group. Thus, what students accomplish as they work in small groups is highly variable. Students can spend time in off-task behavior, violate the norms of respectful discourse, and develop shallow or faulty understanding about the key ideas of the lesson.

> In the small-group discussion talk format, the teacher typically gives students a math problem or question to discuss among themselves in groups of two to four.

Small-group discussions can lay the foundation for a productive whole-class discussion.

Despite these shortcomings, teachers can use small-group discussions—specifically, the three small-group activities listed below—to lay the foundation for a productive whole-class discussion.

Small-Group Discussion Activities That Increase Whole-Class Discussion Productivity

Activity 1: Assist Students in Small Groups to Reach Lesson Goals

Activity 2: Observe Students in Small Groups to Gather Information for Whole-Class Discussion

Activity 3: Use Small-Group Work Time to Prepare Students to Speak During Whole-Class Discussion

---

Activity 1: Assist Students in Small Groups to Reach Lesson Goals

First, the teacher can *assist students in small groups to reach the goals of the lesson.* Working with a small group, the teacher can remind students of similar problems, activate prior knowledge, provide a counterexample for a faulty claim, and demonstrate key ideas with mathematical models. This type of activity not only helps individual students learn but also prepares students to talk about the mathematical goals of the lesson in accurate and robust ways when they talk as a whole class.

Activity 2: Observe Students in Small Groups to Gather Information for Whole-Class Discussion

Second, the teacher can *observe students in small groups, gathering information to set up the whole-class discussion.* Class discussions are productive only if they help students learn. As students work in small groups, the teacher can note which mathematical ideas, strategies, and skills they are already proficient with and which need further discussion. For example, if most students are using a particular strategy effectively, the teacher may decide that this strategy need not be discussed further as a whole class. By contrast, if the teacher notices that students are struggling to use a targeted strategy, he or she may decide to make that strategy a focus of the ensuing whole-class discussion. Or, if many students are converging on a wrong answer or faulty claim, the teacher can decide to address these particular errors or misconceptions during the whole-class discussion.

Activity 3: Use Small-Group Work Time to Prepare Students to Speak During Whole-Class Discussion

Finally, the teacher can *use small-group work time to prepare students to speak during whole-class discussion.* Specifically, if the teacher knows he or she is going to call on a particular student to talk about a certain strategy or claim, he or she can notify that student of this decision during small-group discussion time. This allows the student an opportunity to prepare a response before delivering it in front of the entire class. The teacher can also ask students to share questions they have about a particular problem, strategies they tried but ultimately abandoned, and other areas of confusion they have about the discussion topic.

It is important to note that we are not suggesting that teachers limit discussions to only the strategies and claims that they have observed during small-group work. Nor should teachers restrict student participation to a set of predetermined "reporters." Teachers should use talk moves such as *Who can repeat?* and *What do you think about that?* to bring other ideas and other students into the discussion. In fact, we believe that the discussion fomented by these moves offers the greatest potential for learning to occur. What we are suggesting, however, is that teachers use small-group work time to make key decisions about how to use whole-class discussion to develop student understanding.

Tips for Working with Small Groups

Use Your Judgment in Grouping Students

Many researchers have noted that the biggest threat posed by small-group work is that low-status students can be treated poorly by higher-status students and those seeking to dominate others. You know your students, and this is something important to guard against, so use your judgment in grouping students and in monitoring them.

Follow the Classroom Norms for Discussion

Make sure that the positive norms for discussion are followed in small groups as well as in whole-group discussions.

Don't Give *Too* Much Time

Another challenge of small-group work is the worry that students will stray off topic. Make sure you don't give groups *too* much time for the task at hand. Circulate and try to follow what is happening.

Consider Assigning Roles

Some teachers like to assign roles to students in small groups, for example, note taker, reporter, and so on. Assigning roles can work well as long as students in all roles are supported in thinking deeply and participating productively.

Discussion and Reflection

1. Ensuring equitable participation is not always easy. Discuss some of the major obstacles that you face in getting everyone to participate in your classroom, within your school. What kinds of practices or routines could help mitigate your particular set of obstacles?

2. If you are reading this resource, chances are that you have tried to use discussions in your classroom before this. Can you recall students who had trouble participating in the past? Discuss personal, cultural, social, psychological, or medical issues that might lead to some students not talking at all, or talking too much. Discuss your attitudes and feelings about these things. Identify one or two of the most difficult situations and think about ways to deal with them if they should arise.

3. We have stressed in this chapter that students must feel safe from ridicule or they will not participate. What if you begin to use classroom talk in the ways described here and some students do not cooperate? Do you and your school have a behavioral system in place that will support you in instituting a zero-tolerance policy for disrespectful behavior? What are the procedures? Is it clear how you would use them in your classroom?

4. It is sometimes more difficult to implement a change in your pedagogical practice if you do not have support from your fellow teachers. If more than one teacher at your school is working on using classroom talk to support math learning, how can you work together to support one another, given your time constraints and resources? What aspects of productive math discussions could you help one another implement? Can you involve your principal or department head in your efforts? How?

For professional development sessions and additional video clips that go with this chapter, see:

*Classroom Discussions in Math: A **Facilitator's Guide** to Support Professional Learning of Discourse and the Common Core* (Anderson, Chapin, and O'Connor 2011)

ISBN: 978-1-935099-12-3

The Mathematics
What Do We Talk About?

Section Overview

In this section, we address how to use discussion with important facets of mathematical learning, building each chapter around suggestions for what to talk about—and how to talk about it. Specifically, in Chapters 3 through 7, we

- provide examples, in many cases with accompanying video, of content-based discussions in math in grades K through 6 classrooms;
- break down important dimensions of mathematical knowledge—mathematical concepts; computational procedures; solution methods and problem-solving strategies; mathematical reasoning; and mathematical terminology, symbols, and definitions; and
- explore connections between the discussion examples and the Common Core State Standards for Mathematics.

Talking About Mathematical Concepts

About This Chapter

Knowledge of mathematics involves understanding relationships among ideas, also known as concepts. When students organize their knowledge around concepts, they remember them better. Knowledge of concepts also helps students to use what they know flexibly. Carefully guided classroom talk is an especially effective method for developing concepts and building connections among mathematical ideas. Subsequently in this chapter we address lessons that feature students talking about mathematical concepts.

> "Carefully guided classroom talk is an especially effective method for developing concepts and building connections among mathematical ideas."

What Is a Mathematical Concept?

Mathematical concepts are very important for students to understand. But what exactly is a mathematical concept? Most educators agree that a mathematical concept is an idea that is based on one or more relationships. For example, the concept of one-half is built around two ideas: first, that a whole unit can be partitioned into two equal-sized pieces, and second, if you take one of those pieces and compare it to the original whole unit, the quantity can be represented as $\frac{1}{2}$.

Since this concept is based on relationships between parts and wholes, halves are not all identical. One-half of a pizza is different from one-half of a line segment and that is different from one-half of a room; yet all of these one-halves represent the same relationship between the part and the whole.

As you might suspect, a concept can be recorded in a variety of ways—using symbols, pictures, models, graphs, and words. This can be confusing for students as they must learn that each representation reveals the same conceptual relationships but in a unique way.

Conceptual understanding is sometimes described in terms of how information is represented and structured in the mind of the student. When teachers indicate that students have *conceptual understanding*, they usually are referring to the fact that the students have an "integrated and functional grasp of a number of mathematical ideas" (National Research Council 2000). Their knowledge is "organized into a coherent whole which enables the students to learn new ideas by connecting them to what they already know."

When students understand a group of concepts related to one mathematical topic and see how these related concepts are connected, we say that they have *conceptual knowledge*. Conceptual knowledge consists of well-defined concepts, informal mathematical ideas, and relationships and connections among ideas, concepts, and skills. For example, conceptual knowledge of division includes knowledge of the relationships between division and multiplication, and division and subtraction. It involves information about the different representations for division, the uses of remainders, and how remainders are affected by the size of the divisor. It includes an understanding of mathematical properties such as associativity and commutativity, and knowledge of which properties hold true for division. When students have conceptual knowledge of division, they can talk or write about these relationships and can give examples of problems and tasks that could be solved using division.

Three Suggestions for Using Whole-Class Discussions on Concepts

As stated earlier, carefully guided classroom talk is an especially effective method for developing concepts and building connections among mathematical ideas. We offer three suggestions for facilitating whole-class discussions focused on helping students make sense of concepts.

Three Suggestions for Using Whole-Class Discussions on Concepts

1. Use whole-class discussion to explore a mathematical concept.
2. Use whole-class discussion to build connections among concepts.
3. Use whole-class discussion to uncover misconceptions and errors.

Suggestion 1: Use Whole-Class Discussion to Explore a Mathematical Concept

Many researchers argue that understanding of concepts occurs through the activity of *participating* in communities of learners who together become more and more competent in doing and making sense of mathematics. As students talk about their reasoning and what relationships they grasp, they externalize their understanding. This helps them build individual mental connections regarding concepts. Also, listening to students gives teachers a better grasp of what conceptual relationships individual students do and do not know.

As teachers, we sometimes take it for granted that students will understand concepts in the same ways that we do and will readily build relationships among different but related ideas. For example, the following lesson uses base ten blocks to develop the notions of grouping by ten. But a set of base ten blocks looks to many students just like any set of different-sized blocks. The materials do not automatically convey the structure of the base ten system. Even when students understand what the blocks are meant to indicate, classroom talk can help them interpret and link symbols, objects, and the linguistic expressions that describe them. Talk can be used productively to get students to ask questions about what these forms of representation mean, and how the meanings are connected.

Example 3.1.1 Use Whole-Class Discussion to Explore a Mathematical Concept

Working with Place Value (Mrs. Hollinger, Grade 2)

Place value involves many different concepts including the idea that we group objects into sets of ten and that we record these groupings symbolically in a very structured way. In September in a second-grade classroom, the teacher, Mrs. Hollinger, focuses her lesson on these concepts. She starts the class by asking students to work individually and use base ten blocks to show the number 37 in different ways. She also posts the directions:

Base Ten Blocks and the Number 37

Use your base ten blocks to show the number 37. Try to find more than one way to show the number with the blocks.

About half of the students represent 37 with three "ten" blocks and seven "one" blocks, whereas the other half use thirty-seven "one" blocks. One of the students uses one "ten" block and twenty-seven "one" blocks. Another student uses two "ten" blocks and seventeen "one" blocks. Mrs. Hollinger wants her students to understand that all of these groupings show the quantity 37. Of course she could *tell* her students that the four combinations of blocks are equivalent, but she thinks that if she asks students to talk about the different combinations possible they will gain insight into grouping by tens and ones.

Mrs. Hollinger knows that in anticipation of two-digit subtraction with regrouping, students will need to realize that three tens and seven ones is equivalent to two tens and seventeen ones. But in this lesson, she is focusing on the fact that three tens and seven ones uses the fewest blocks, is the most efficient grouping, and connects directly to the numeral that represents the quantity.

Small-Group Discussion

First, Mrs. Hollinger initiates small-group discussions, organizing students into groups of three to share what they have done individually. She then instructs them to work together to generate other combinations. She asks groups to try to show the quantity 37 in four different ways. After groups have had time to work, she calls the class to attention. She asks a student to bring one combination of blocks to the front of the room and place them so everyone in the class can see them. Then she asks other students to display different combinations, continuing until all four grouping combinations are displayed—three tens and seven ones, two tens and seventeen ones, one ten and twenty-seven ones, and thirty-seven ones. Mrs. Hollinger next asks the class, "How can we be sure that each of these four different combinations of base ten blocks equals thirty-seven?"

> **MATH TALK TIP**
>
> **Small-Group Discussions**
>
> Use small-group discussions to lay the foundation for a productive whole-class discussion. Groups of two or three work best as every student will have an opportunity to participate within the small-group discussion.

Mrs. Hollinger is not sure that all students agree that the different groupings are equivalent, so she decides to ask students to count the value of each pile of blocks displayed. Two students count by tens and ones, and the other two count just by ones, but all four verify that each combination of blocks is equal to thirty-seven. (See Figure 3.1 on the following page.)

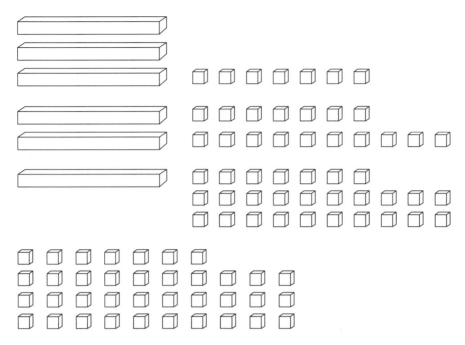

Figure 3.1 Different representations of 37 using base ten blocks.

Whole-Class Discussion

After students have counted all of the piles, one student states, "The piles look different but they are the same amount." Another student adds, "The three tens and seven ones pile uses the smallest number of blocks." Let's join Mrs. Hollinger as she starts a whole-class discussion where she asks students to explain how they decided on their combination of blocks. The following vignette provides a composite example of the types of insights students might have regarding concepts and the decisions the teacher makes to highlight the relationships inherent in all concepts.

1. **Mrs. H:** Liana, can you explain one way you used blocks to show thirty-seven?

2. **Liana:** I used three tens and seven ones since you can count like ten, twenty, thirty. Then I had to use ones to get to thirty-seven.

3. **Mrs. H:** How is your combination the same or different from one of the others?

4. **Liana:** I used tens and I took a tens block for each ten. But the people who used thirty-seven ones didn't use any tens blocks.

5. **Mrs. H:** So you used all the tens you could, right? [Liana nods.] Peter, can you explain another way, a different way?

6. **Peter:** I counted out thirty-seven ones. Then I took one ten and put away ten ones. So I counted the rest. I have one ten [points to one ten] and twenty-seven ones.

7. **Mrs. H:** Could you have divided the other twenty-seven ones into groups of ten the way Liana did?

8. **Peter:** Mine is sort of like Liana's but I have lots of ones left. I could have made more tens but I didn't.

9. **Mrs. H:** Deacon, could you tell us in your own words how Peter showed thirty-seven using tens and ones?

10. **Deacon:** He made a ten from the thirty-seven ones. Then he had lots of ones left. [He starts counting the ones and Mrs. Hollinger waits.] Twenty-seven ones.

11. **Dave:** I think you could make what Deacon has into two tens by taking some from the ones.

12. **Mrs. H:** Are you saying that another way to show thirty-seven is to use two tens?

13. **Dave:** Yup. Here, I'll show everyone. [Dave takes the thirty-seven one blocks, counts out ten ones, and trades them for one ten. He does this again, and holds up two tens.] Here are two tens and there are still more ones left, seventeen ones left.

> **FOUR STEPS...**
>
> Asking students to restate or repeat each other's ideas supports Step 4: Helping Students Engage with the Reasoning of Others (see "Four Steps Toward Productive Talk," Chapter 1, page 10).

> **FOUR STEPS...**
>
> Revoicing a student's contribution supports Step 1: Helping Individual Students Clarify and Share Their Own Thoughts (see "Four Steps Toward Productive Talk," Chapter 1, page 10).

Each time that a student contributes or weighs in with his or her thoughts, it provides them with more to work with as they consider the different ways 37 can be represented. Notice how Mrs. Hollinger revoiced Dave's comment to focus on the key point of using two tens.

14. **Mrs. H:** OK, so Liana used three tens, and Peter used one ten, and Dave used two tens. What else can we say about the different number of tens and the number of ones we can use to show thirty-seven? Crystal?

15. **Crystal:** You can have one, two, or three tens.

16. **Luis:** Can't you also have zero tens?

17. **Mrs. H:** Hmm. That's an interesting idea. Can you have zero tens? Let's think about this. Do you agree or disagree with the idea that we can show thirty-seven using zero, one, two, or three tens? Turn and talk to your partner.

MATH TALK TIP

Turn and Talk

If students need more time to grapple with a concept, consider doing the talk move *turn and talk*. In this example, turn and talk is an effective method for getting every student involved and helps Mrs. Hollinger's second graders practice stating their ideas (these second graders are at the beginning stages of being proficient at talking productively!).

Mrs. Hollinger now has the class at a point where all options for the number of tens have been stated. You might think she would want to move to a new topic. However, this idea that a number can be represented using different numbers of tens and ones is quite complex. Students need more time than the short exchange here to grapple with the concept. So Mrs. Hollinger poses the question again and asks everyone to talk about it. She walks around listening to the students discuss the question and then states, "I would like Crystal, then Leonard, Simi, and finally Brian to share."

18. **Crystal:** Yes, you can have zero tens. Like the one that uses thirty-seven ones blocks.

19. **Leonard:** You can show thirty-seven in all of these ways. See, you just keep trading ones for tens. Zero tens, then one ten, then two tens, and three tens. [Leonard moves blocks around to show trading ten ones for one ten.]

20. **Simi:** We [Simi and her partner] didn't know this but I see now how you can trade. Ten ones is the same as one ten.

21. **Brian:** I think there's a problem. If you have one ten and twenty-seven ones, is that the number one-two-seven? Thirty-seven and one-two-seven aren't the same.

22. **Mrs. H:** Brian, are you saying that you can make thirty-seven using one ten block and twenty-seven ones blocks but wonder about writing that as one-two-seven?

23. **Brian:** Yeah. What do we call one ten and twenty-seven ones?

24. **Students:** One ten twenty-seven ones! Another name for thirty-seven. . . . One-two-seven. . . . I'm not sure.

25. **Mrs. H:** So let me ask you this. Everybody agrees that we can use zero, one, two, or three tens to show thirty-seven with base ten blocks, right? But most of the time we think of thirty-seven being made with three tens and seven ones. So why do we do that? Think about how we write

it as thirty-seven, not one ten and twenty-seven ones. Turn and talk to your partner for a minute and then be ready to share your ideas with the class.

Mrs. Hollinger had not expected the question from Brian about how to record these representations. One of the benefits of talking about mathematics is that students' questions can help us as teachers realize what students find most confusing. After two minutes of partner talk, the discussion in Mrs. Hollinger's class continued

> One of the benefits of talking about mathematics is that students' questions can help us as teachers realize what students find most confusing.

as students shared their ideas about how grouping by tens is related to the symbols we use to represent the quantities. Mrs. Hollinger was able to have students articulate how grouping a quantity into the greatest number of tens possible was important for writing the number.

What did Mrs. Hollinger do to facilitate a productive discussion? First, Mrs. Hollinger asked many students to explain the grouping methods they used. Occasionally Mrs. Hollinger revoiced the students' explanations, to make sure that everyone heard or to emphasize a point such as the number of tens. Third, Mrs. Hollinger used a variation of the *Do you agree or disagree . . . and why?* talk move in order to get students to apply their own reasoning to others' contributions by reflecting on a grouping method different from their own. Finally, Mrs. Hollinger used the whole-class discussion format to make sure that everyone was exposed to the important concept that a number such as 37 can be represented in multiple ways.

Try It Out!

LESSON: Working with Place Value

You might want to try the above lesson with your own students. The idea of grouping by tens is important to place value. Just as important is the concept that we use the most efficient grouping to represent quantities numerically. Focus the discussion on the equivalent relationship between ten ones and one group of ten, and the combination that is most closely linked to the numeral 37. One way to do this is to ask students to explain the reasoning of others who have articulated the relationship between tens and ones. In addition, ask students to describe how their arrangement differs from those already described.

Teaching with the Common Core

2.NBT Understand place value.
2.NBT Use place value understanding and properties of operations to add and subtract.

Example 3.1.2 Use Whole-Class Discussion to Explore a Mathematical Concept

Counting and Place Value (Mrs. Delaney, Grade 1)

In this next example, let's observe a first-grade teacher, Mrs. Delaney, facilitate a discussion focused on counting. There are many important concepts associated with primary students' counting abilities and knowledge of counting patterns. One key concept is the idea of counting by a unit larger than one to reach a particular number. Being able to use a unit of ten to count to a certain number is a milestone in the primary grades. We can't overestimate the importance of grouping by tens to place value understanding. Yet students need practice applying this counting pattern to reach different target numbers. They also need practice applying counting patterns to sequences that begin with a variety of starting numbers. For instance, students who can count by tens starting at zero may struggle to count by tens when the starting number changes to nine or eleven since they can't simply memorize the pattern—they must understand the relationship between the starting number and how to use skip counting (and eventually groups of ten) to find subsequent numbers.

In the following lesson excerpt from *Number Patterns on the Hundreds Chart*, first graders practice counting using the hundreds chart. They first count to one hundred by ones and then use a variety of counting patterns such as fives, tens, and twenty-fives. The hundreds chart is a mathematical model that helps students count by providing a visual of the actual numerals and enables students to think about the next counting jump from a geometric perspective. It also visually shows how the digit in the tens place changes as we count by tens (for example, 8, 18, 28, 38, 48, 58, . . .). Mrs. Delaney knows that counting forms the basis of number operations; students with strong counting skills can use these skills to make sense of quantities.

Try It Out!

See the lesson plan *Number Patterns on the Hundreds Chart (Grade 1)* in Appendix B.

LESSON: Number Patterns on the Hundreds Chart

If you plan to use the lesson you just watched with your own students, first have students practice counting by ones to one hundred, starting at any number. Then introduce the hundreds chart to count by ones and have students talk about the many different number patterns they notice (for example, patterns involving the tens or the ones in each row and each column). Use talk moves such as *Who can repeat?* and *Who can say that in their own words?* to bring many students into the conversation. Use some of the lesson time to work on counting by tens, demonstrating how a jump of ten from any number can be found by counting ten ones. Many teachers ask students to predict, when counting by tens, what number they will land on and have them articulate any counting patterns they notice. The goal is that students will understand the concept that counting by tens is equivalent to making jumps of ten (or adding ten), and they will start to realize that with each jump of ten, the digit in the tens place changes.

Teaching with the Common Core

1.NBT Extend the counting sequence.
1.NBT Understand place value.

Video Clip 3A: Number Patterns on the Hundreds Chart
(Mrs. Delaney, Grade 1)

As you watch the video clip, consider:

1. Which talk moves does Mrs. Delaney use in this clip? What has she done to help her young students remember the talk moves? How do students respond?
2. How does the hundreds chart support the talk about the different number patterns?
3. Some students are grappling with counting by tens starting at a number other than ten. How does this type of activity coupled with talking about counting help them learn to count by tens starting at any number?

For more videos from Mrs. Delaney's number patterns on the hundreds chart lesson, as well as an additional lesson, *Counting Money Using Nickels and Pennies*, see the companion resource *Classroom Discussions in Math: A **Facilitator's Guide** to Support Professional Learning of Discourse and the Common Core.*

BEFORE YOU WATCH THE VIDEO

To make the most productive use of the video clips, you and any colleagues you are working with should take time to read through the "Guidelines for Watching Videos of Teaching" (see page xxi). For demographics, see page xliv.

Suggestion 2: Use Whole-Class Discussion to Build Connections Among Ideas

The role of *connections* in understanding is considered central by the vast majority of psychologists and educators. When students are able to connect ideas and concepts to procedures and

> **MATH TALK TIP**
>
> ### The Use of Models in Discussions
> The use of models such as the hundreds chart or a number line can facilitate classroom discussions because these tools help students visualize a pattern or computation. Be sure that any visual is large enough for students to see from all parts of the classroom.

> One of the things we want to talk about in mathematics class is how concepts and relationships among concepts are connected and how these ideas connect to what students already know.

representations, learning is especially robust. Thus, one of the things we want to talk about in mathematics class is how concepts and relationships among concepts are connected and how these ideas connect to what students already know. Let's examine how talk can be used to assist students in organizing what they already know into larger and more powerful conceptual structures—the "big ideas" of mathematics.

Example 3.2.1 Use Whole-Class Discussion to Build Connections Among Ideas

Area of a Parallelogram, $A = bh$ (Ms. Sanchez, Grade 6)

Ms. Sanchez regularly uses discussion in her sixth-grade classroom to help students build relationships. One of the concepts she is responsible for teaching is *area*. She wants her students to understand that area is a measure of how much surface is covered; it is not a length. Within this big topic, there are many relationships. For example, when measuring area, the size of a unit and the number of units needed to cover a surface are inversely proportional. If you measure the area of a rug with square meters you will need fewer units than if you measured the same rug using square centimeters.

Ms. Sanchez's students have already engaged in many activities and discussions about area concepts. They have decomposed a shape into two or more parts, found the areas of the parts by counting or multiplying, and then recombined the parts to determine the area of the original figure. They have generated a formula for finding the area of rectangles and triangles and now can apply the formula in many situations. Students also have learned to use the terms *base* and *height* to label the dimensions of rectangles and triangles.

In this next vignette, Ms. Sanchez first asked her students to follow the steps shown in a worksheet (see Figure 3.2). She wanted her students to justify some of their observations about dimensions and areas of parallelograms that are formed into rectangles. Let's join the class discussion that followed the investigation.

Make two copies of parallelograms A, B, and C below. Cut out both sets of parallelograms. On one set, draw in a segment to show the height. Cut along the height to form two pieces. Reshape the pieces into a rectangle.

a) What are the bases and heights of the rectangles formed using parallelograms A, B, and C?
b) What are the base and height of parallelograms A, B, and C?
c) Why are the dimensions of the parallelograms and their corresponding rectangles the same?
d) Use what you know about the area of a rectangle to determine the areas of parallelograms A, B, and C.
e) What generalizations can you make about the area of a parallelogram?

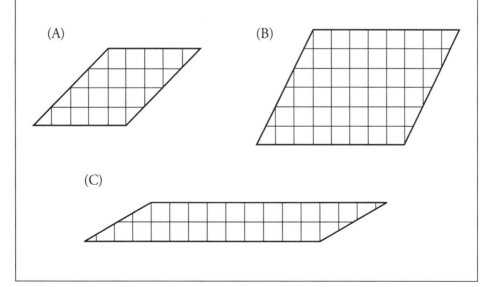

(A)

(B)

(C)

Figure 3.2 Student parallelogram worksheet.

1. **Ms. S:** Let's talk about the first parallelogram and the questions you answered about it. [Ms. Sanchez waits for students to look at their answers before calling on Ben.]

2. **Ben:** For the first parallelogram, the base is five and the height is four. I made the cut along this line. [Ben points to the height.] And the area is twenty.

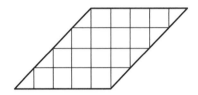

3. **Ms. S:** You gave us some numbers but I'm not sure what they stand for. Could you give us some more information?

4. **Ben:** Um. The five and four are just units. And the area is twenty.

5. **Ms. S:** Roberta, could you please say again what Ben just said?

6. **Roberta:** The base is five centimeters and the height is four centimeters and the area is twenty.

7. **Ms. S:** I heard Ben describe the dimensions using units and Roberta used centimeters. How do we decide on the labels for the dimensions? Why can't we just say five and four? Talk to your partner.

> ### MATH TALK TIP
>
> #### Adding On
> Sometimes when students are asked to restate or repeat the contributions of another student, they add additional information that enhances everyone's understanding of the topic. This also regularly occurs when you use the talk move *Who can add on?*

Determining what units to use to measure an attribute is an essential component of the measurement process. Often diagrams do not include labels, so students must interpret the numbers and apply their own labels. Ms. Sanchez thought she would be able to immediately start talking about area, but she notices that students are not paying attention to labels and interpreting dimensions, so she decides to slow down.

MATH TALK TIP

Organizing Partners

When asking students to turn and talk to a partner, it is important to consider who should work together. Many teachers try to match students first by considering social issues; they partner students together who will have a good working relationship but are not best friends. Next, consider academic issues: Sometimes putting two high-achieving students together works well as they can be pushed to consider the ideas more deeply. In general, however, putting two low-achieving students together is not productive. It is better to match a low-achieving student with an average-achieving student so they can make progress on the questions under discussion. Explain to students that your job is to match them with a partner who helps them learn, and you will change the partner grouping if you notice that it isn't the best match for either student.

8. **Eileen:** I measured the picture. Those little squares are half a centimeter long, not a centimeter, so I don't think we should say five and four centimeters.

9. **Janet:** They aren't inches either.

10. **Ms. S:** Would everyone measure and confirm that the little squares are not one centimeter on a side. [Students measure and find the units are each 0.5 cm.]

11. **Ryota:** Ms. Sanchez, can we say the base is five half-centimeters?

12. **Ms. S:** Yes, we can. But it is more common that the label describe a whole unit such as centimeters, rather than a fraction of a unit such as half-centimeters. Sometimes, though, the actual unit is not a whole unit measure such as one inch, yard, centimeter, millimeter, or meter. Ben?

13. **Ben:** That's why I just used the word *units*. There are five units along the base. The word *units* can stand for anything.

14. **Ms. S:** Yes, we need labels so we know what the numbers represent. When we aren't sure of the labels, such as in this case, we can use the general term *units*. Units here can stand for measures such as half-centimeters.

This short interchange has been helpful in its focus on units, but Ms. Sanchez feels that she needs to make a decision. Where is this discussion going? Should she continue to discuss units? There are no predetermined guidelines as to how to facilitate a discussion or when to continue or when to redirect. In this case, Ms. Sanchez really wants her students to talk about area, so she makes an instructional choice, one that all teachers must make daily, and refocuses the class.

15. **Ms. S:** OK, so let's label these dimensions using the term *units*. But what does the twenty represent? Twenty units?

16. **Andrei:** Twenty squares, I mean twenty square units. It's like what we talked about a while ago. We have to cover the surface so you use something that covers it.

17. **Sabra:** I agree with Andrei. He said twenty square units and that's how many I got when I counted.

18. **Ms. S:** Alright. So the dimensions of this parallelogram are five units for the base and four units for the height. It has an area of twenty square units. Next, you cut this parallelogram and made it into a rectangle. Janet, what is the area of the rectangle? What are its dimensions?

19. **Janet:** They are all the same. Twenty and five and four.

20. **Ms. S:** Twenty what? Five what? Four what?

21. **Janet:** [Laughing] Twenty square units, five units, and four units.

22. **Ms. S:** Here's the important question. Why are the areas of the parallelogram and the rectangle the same? Turn and talk to your partner for a minute about this.

Ms. Sanchez walks around the room, listening in to the partner talk. She is listening with a purpose—who to select to talk about why the areas and dimensions are the same. She wants to give students who have not talked a chance to speak, and she wants to make sure she selects some students who have a solid explanation and some who don't.

Why choose students who are inarticulate or unclear on the reasoning? By forcing the whole class to try to make sense of an answer—or to clarify the reasoning—Ms. Sanchez is going to ensure that more students are engaged with the ideas. Learning can occur only if her students are truly pondering the relationships. To facilitate the discussion, Ms. Sanchez in advance cut out multiple copies of each parallelogram from a transparency. Now she asks students to cut one of the transparency copies in the same way as they cut the

> **MATH TALK TIP**
>
> **Listening to Partner Talk**
>
> During a turn and talk, circulate and listen to partners talk. Decide who will share his or her explanations during the whole-class discussion. Consider giving students who have not talked a chance to speak, and select some students who have a solid explanation and some who don't.

parallelogram from the worksheet and to show on the overhead projector how they adjusted their cut pieces.

23. **Leland:** I cut the parallelogram along the line and moved the piece like this. [Leland shows how he moved the piece to make a rectangle.]

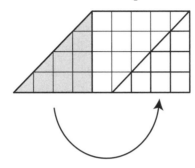

24. **Ms. S:** First, what's that line called that you cut along?

25. **Leland:** Umm, a diagonal?

26. **Ms. S:** OK. [pointing to the height of the parallelogram] We call this the *height* because it is the distance straight up from the base. It is *perpendicular* to the base. Who can remind us what the term *perpendicular* means? Kay.

27. **Kay:** *Perpendicular* means that two lines intersect at a 90-degree angle. So the height comes straight down to the base and forms a right angle.

28. **Ms. S:** OK, Leland. Now can you please restate what you did using the words *height* and *perpendicular*?

> ## MATH TALK TIP
>
> ### Encourage Use of Mathematical Vocabulary
>
> Consistently require students to use mathematical vocabulary. Doing so will encourage students to start using these words more regularly on their own. One way to support students is to post vocabulary words on the board at the start of the lesson and to refer to the correct terms during the discussion.

In order to build vocabulary, students need to use mathematical words. Ms. Sanchez regularly corrects students as in this exchange. Furthermore, she always requires the student to then use the words or phrase in context. When teachers consistently require students to use mathematical vocabulary, the students start using these words more regularly on their own. However, don't correct every incident or you will interfere with the flow of the discussion and the exchange of ideas.

29. **Leland**: I cut the parallelogram here along the height which is a segment that is perpendicular to the base, and then I took this piece and moved it here to form a rectangle. The base is the same.

30. **Ms. S**: And why is the base the same?

31. **Leland**: This part of the base was on this side, and I just moved it over. But I didn't make it longer or shorter, I just moved it.

32. **Ms. S**: How about the height? Did the height stay the same when the parallelogram was transformed?

33. **Deval**: The height also stays the same. See. This piece is slided over but the height hasn't been changed in any way.

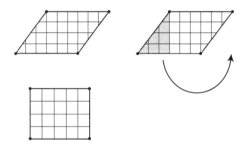

34. **Lily**: And the area is the same too. We didn't take away or add square units. We just moved them around a bit.

35. **Ms. S**: Lesley, could you say again what Lily just said?

36. **Lesley**: The area is the same because you just move a piece but you don't take anything away.

37. **Sabra**: There are still twenty square units. The pieces have just been put together in a different order.

38. **Ms. S**: So let's summarize what we found with the first parallelogram. When we cut it along a height and rearranged the two pieces into a rectangle, the base lengths of the two shapes were the same, the heights of the two shapes were the same, and the areas were the same. Let's examine the next two parallelograms. What did you find?

Mrs. Sanchez has used this discussion to help students develop some understanding of the relationship between the areas of a parallelogram and a rectangle with the same base and height. She will continue to ask students to notice that when the dimensions are the same, the areas are equal. Talking about these ideas helps students *generalize*. She

Talking about these ideas helps students *generalize*.

wants them to generalize that to find the area of any parallelogram they multiply the base by the height ($A = bh$). Whole-class discussions also assist students in connecting this new information to what they previously have learned and understood—the formula for the area of a rectangle.

Try It Out!

LESSON: Area of a Parallelogram, $A = bh$

If you try this lesson, focus your discussion on generating and explaining the area formula for a parallelogram. The formula is often simply memorized by students. Yet students benefit from understanding why area formulas work—this knowledge deepens their conceptual understanding of the topic. Furthermore, understanding is generative; it enables us to learn new related material and helps us remember and apply knowledge more accurately. You may wish to ask students to "add on," "restate what others have said," and "explain why the area of the parallelogram can be found by multiplying the length of the base by the length of the height." Do not assume that just because one student can explain the formula, all students completely understand why the formula works.

See the lesson plan *Area of a Parallelogram, A = bh (Grade 6)* in Appendix B.

Teaching with the Common Core

6.G Find the area of right triangles, other triangles, special quadrilaterals, and polygons by composing into rectangles or decomposing into triangles and other shapes.

Practice Standard 5: Use appropriate tools strategically.

Practice Standard 6: Attend to precision.

Example 3.2.2 Use Whole-Class Discussion to Build Connections Among Ideas

Perimeters of Rectangles with a Fixed Area (Ms. Luipold, Grade 4)

In this lesson, Ms. Luipold's fourth graders find the dimensions of all possible rectangles with an area of 20 square inches and then determine the perimeter of each. Students discover that there are three distinct rectangles: 1 in. by 20 in. (P = 42 inches), 2 in. by 10 in. (P = 24 inches), and 4 in. by 5 in. (P = 18 inches). They realize that rectangles with a fixed area of 20 square inches do not have to have the same perimeter. They also conclude that long, thin rectangles have a greater perimeter than rectangles that are more square-like. Yet, explaining what happens to the perimeter when a 1-by-20 rectangle is transformed into a 2-by-10 rectangle is challenging. Much of this whole-class discussion is spent explaining what the students understand about the connection between area and perimeter.

Video Clip 3B: *Examining Area and Perimeter*
(Ms. Luipold, Grade 4)

As you watch the video clip, consider:

1. During a discussion, many students work together to articulate solid meaning for concepts. What talk moves does Ms. Luipold use to help students build off of each other's comments?
2. How does Ms. Luipold use the interactive whiteboard to support the discussion?
3. At the end of the lesson, Ms. Luipold asks students to summarize key ideas. What are the benefits of asking students to reflect on their learning?

For more videos from Ms. Luipold's area and perimeter lesson, see the companion resource *Classroom Discussions in Math: A **Facilitator's Guide** to Support Professional Learning of Discourse and the Common Core.*

BEFORE YOU WATCH THE VIDEO

To make the most productive use of the video clips, you and any colleagues you are working with should take time to read through the "Guidelines for Watching Videos of Teaching" (see page xxi). For demographics, see page xliv.

It Out!

LESSON: Perimeters of Rectangles with a Fixed Area

If you plan to use this lesson with your own students, first have them determine the dimensions of rectangles with an area of 20 square units. Then have students talk about the rectangles' different perimeters and why they are not identical. Think about how you can help students clarify and share their own thoughts by using talk moves such as *turn and talk* and *Say more.* . . . Also, remember to keep the focus on helping students orient to the thinking of others. Use talk moves such as *Who can repeat?* and *Who can say that in their own words?* to bring many students into the conversation. The goal is for students to realize that a fixed area of 20 square inches can be transformed into different-sized rectangles with different perimeters.

> See the lesson plan *Perimeters of Rectangles with a Fixed Area (Grade 4)* in Appendix B.

Teaching with the Common Core

3.MD Recognize perimeter as an attribute of plane figures and distinguish between linear and area measures.

3.MD Solve real world and mathematical problems involving perimeters of polygons, including finding the perimeter given the side lengths, finding an unknown side length, and exhibiting rectangles with the same perimeter and different areas or with the same area and different perimeters.

4.MD Apply the area and perimeter formulas for rectangles in real world and mathematical problems.

Practice Standard 7: Look for and make use of structure.

Practice Standard 8: Look for and express regularity in repeated reasoning.

Suggestion 3: Use Whole-Class Discussion to Uncover Misconceptions and Errors

Classroom talk not only helps students develop conceptual understanding, but also is effective for revealing and clarifying students' partial understandings and misconceptions. In the process of making sense of experiences, students often generalize ideas in incomplete ways. For example, as seen in Chapter 1 ("Case 1: What Does Productive Talk Look Like? Mrs. Sigler's First-Grade Class: Experiences with Triangles"), if young students' experiences with triangles involve only viewing pictures of equilateral triangles oriented along a base, their generalization of the concept *triangle* may be very limited—they might conclude that scalene triangles are not triangles or that a triangle that is resting on a vertex is not a triangle. Talk is a powerful tool for revealing students' partial understandings of a concept or their misconceptions about that concept.

> See Chapter 1.

> **Talk is a powerful tool for revealing students' partial understandings of a concept or their misconceptions about that concept.**

Example 3.3.1 Use Whole-Class Discussion to Uncover Misconceptions and Errors

Operations with Decimals (Mr. Lyman, Grade 5)

Mr. Lyman uses talk to learn about his fifth-grade students' generalizations and misconceptions. One topic that Mr. Lyman felt was not too difficult for his students was decimal addition and subtraction. Yet he noticed that when he didn't list the numbers vertically, one under the other with the decimal points lined up, many students made errors. Because of comments by a few students, he began to suspect that their understanding of decimals was procedural and not very complete. One day, when students were working in small groups on decimal word problems, he noticed that one group of four students incorrectly solved the computation 25 – 17.7 by setting up the exercise with the 2 and 5 underneath the two 7s:

```
 17.7
– 2 5
```

Mr. Lyman decided to probe the understanding of the students in the small group.

1. **Mr. L:** I noticed that you've been adding and subtracting decimal numbers to solve these word problems. How are decimals the same or different from whole numbers? How is adding and subtracting decimals the same or different from adding and subtracting whole numbers? Take a minute to think about what you know about decimal numbers and how we add and subtract them. Then I'll talk with your group about this.

After giving them a couple of minutes to talk among themselves, Mr. Lyman listened carefully to his students' ideas. At first he allowed them to make their points without much commentary from him, but then he began to ask clarifying questions as alternative understandings emerged.

2. **Sarah:** Decimals are like regular numbers; you just line them up and add them.

3. **Corey:** Yeah, it's easy because we all know how to add and subtract.

4. **Kei:** Decimals are numbers with a dot in them.

5. **Mr. L:** Sarah, what do you mean by "like regular numbers"?

6. **Sarah:** You know, like the numbers we use to count with—tens, hundreds, thousands.

7. **Mr. L:** So decimals are exactly the same as the counting numbers?

8. **Sarah:** Yes.

9. **Mr. L:** What do other people think? Are decimals the same or different from our regular counting numbers?

10. **Kei:** They're the same. You just line everything up on the right side and then add or subtract.

11. **Mr. L:** Could you give us an example, Kei?

12. **Kei:** Sure. Eight point two plus seven point nine. [Kei records and solves the addition problem correctly.] I lined up the two and the nine on the right and then just added. You bring the decimal point straight down.

$$
\begin{array}{r}
8.2 \\
+7.9 \\
\hline
16.1
\end{array}
$$

13. **Bob:** I think you have to line up the decimal points.

14. **Mr. L:** What do you mean?

15. **Bob:** Well, if the problem was eight point twenty-five plus seven point nine, you don't line up the five and the nine. [Bob writes the following on his paper as he speaks to the group.]

$$
\begin{array}{r}
8.25 \\
+7.9 \\
\hline
\end{array}
$$

16. **Mr. L:** Bob, would you please say those numbers again but read them so we hear the place values?

17. **Bob:** Sure. Let's add eight and twenty-five hundredths and seven and nine tenths. I think we should line up the decimal points, not the last two numbers. It should look like this. [Bob records the addition on his paper.]

$$
\begin{array}{r}
8.25 \\
+7.9 \\
\hline
\end{array}
$$

Teachers regularly must decide how to respond to an interaction similar to this one. One response is to tell students how to line up the numbers and to offer some explanation as to why this is the case. Another possible teacher response is to ask Bob to explain his reasoning in order to establish for the group the correct procedure. This has the benefit of another student providing the justification for the choice.

We have found that a third alternative that uses talk productively is for the teacher to give no indication of the right or wrong answer—in this case how to line up the decimal numbers—and instead to send the question back to the students.

> ## MATH TALK TIP
>
> ### Is the Answer Right or Wrong?
>
> One way to use talk productively is to give no indication of the right or wrong answer—and instead send the question back to your students. By forcing them to engage with the ideas, you prompt students to think more deeply about the mathematics.

18. **Mr. L:** Would you all discuss what Bob just said? Do we line up decimal numbers using the last digit or the decimal point? Also be ready to explain why you think your choice is correct.

Why use talk in this way? What are the benefits? Both the teacher and Bob understand the mathematics in this situation. But it is unclear exactly what the other three students in the group do and don't understand. By forcing them to engage with the ideas—namely, to take a position on how to line up the numbers—the teacher has prompted them to think more deeply about the mathematics. They will be listening more closely to each other now to see if their ideas are the same. They will be working to come up with a way to explain why their response is correct. If the reasoning behind their ideas is faulty (line up the last number on the right), other students will usually offer explanations, evidence, or counterexamples in their own words, words that often resonate more effectively with the other students. Bob will be able to add his ideas to the group in response to the other students, which will help move them all forward to understanding they need to line up the decimal points. But the main advantage of talking in this way is that the three students who will benefit the most mathematically from the exchange are being forced to talk and reason about the ideas.

19. **Sarah:** I don't think it matters which way you do it.

20. **Corey:** Let's use one of the word problems to see if it makes a difference. [She reads] "Gus put four gallons of gasoline into the gas can. He kept filling and adding another seven-tenths of a gallon. How much gas is now in the can?"

21. **Kei:** I think maybe Bob is right. I thought you just lined up the numbers but if you add four and point seven like this [Kei writes the problem down], the answer is wrong; it's too small. Like four gallons of gas plus seven-tenths more is more than four.

> **FOUR STEPS...**
>
> Asking students to justify their strategies and solutions supports Step 4: Helping Students Engage with the Reasoning of Others (see "Four Steps Toward Productive Talk," Chapter 1, page 10).

$$\begin{array}{r} 4 \\ + \ 0.7 \\ \hline \end{array}$$

22. **Bob:** I think it is because the four is four whole gallons but the seven-tenths is a part of one gallon. We have to add the same things—like we add hundreds and hundreds with big numbers so now we have to add tenths and tenths or ones and ones.

23. **Corey:** But where are the tenths in four? It kinda makes sense but not completely.

Mr. Lyman has already learned a lot using the small-group format for this short discussion. First, three of the students in the group did not think there was a difference between whole numbers and decimal numbers. He will need to probe further to really understand what they think. However, he doubts that many students in his class think of a decimal number as the sum of a whole number and a part of a whole. He now suspects that many students' conceptions of decimals are unrelated to quantity and that they instead think that a decimal is a number with a "dot" in it. When adding decimals, they do not consider the size of the numbers or the place values of the digits.

By listening to students as they discussed their ideas in a small-group format, Mr. Lyman was able to hear from each student and learn about his or her superficial understanding. Sometimes talking with a small group can clarify and extend concepts for students; however, in this case, Mr. Lyman realized that small-group talk was not enough and additional instruction would be necessary. Mr. Lyman used productive talk to get mathematical ideas and

> " Sometimes talking with a small group can clarify and extend concepts for students; however, in this case, Mr. Lyman realized that small-group talk was not enough and additional instruction would be necessary. "

concepts visibly out on the table. Both he and the students benefited from this interaction; Mr. Lyman gained valuable information on which to build future lessons, and these students had an opportunity to start making sense of the addition algorithm for decimals.

Try It Out!

LESSON: Operations with Decimals

You may wish to use this lesson to assess your own students' understanding of relationships between whole numbers and decimal numbers. You can begin just like Mr. Lyman did by posing two discussion questions: How are decimals the same or different from whole numbers? How is adding and subtracting decimals the same or different from adding and subtracting whole numbers? Ask students to talk about these questions in small groups or with partners. As they talk, listen in on their conversations to help you determine the focus of the ensuing whole-class discussion. For example, if students classify decimal numbers as "numbers with a dot in them," you may wish to use the discussion to help students develop a deeper conceptual understanding of decimal numbers. Or, if students say that adding whole numbers and adding decimal numbers are exactly the same, encourage them to be more specific about their comparisons so that they focus on important ideas related to place value and the base ten number system.

> **CCSS**
>
> **Teaching with the Common Core**
>
> 5.NBT Perform operations with multidigit whole numbers and with decimals to hundredths.
> Practice Standard 2: Reason abstractly and quantitatively.

Discussion and Reflection

1. In this chapter, we examined the complexities of talking about mathematical concepts. What is a math concept? How are concepts different from skills? For each of the teacher/student vignettes and videos, make a list of the concepts discussed.

2. One of the benefits of talking about concepts is that students' misconceptions or confusions often are revealed. Describe some examples from your own teaching experiences in which you learned about a student's misconception. For one example, give suggestions on how talk might be used to help the student address his or her misconception.

3. Pictures and models can help students build relationships as long as the salient features of the picture or model are clearly understood by students. How did Ms. Sanchez (page 102) use classroom discussions to help students understand the pictures of the parallelograms and the relationships between the dimensions and area?

For professional development sessions and additional video clips that go with this chapter, see:

*Classroom Discussions in Math: A **Facilitator's Guide** to Support Professional Learning of Discourse and the Common Core* (Anderson, Chapin, and O'Connor 2011)

ISBN: 978-1-935099-12-3

Talking About Computational Procedures

About This Chapter

Performing computations with whole numbers and rational numbers is a capstone of elementary mathematics instruction. Whole-class discussions can help students use computational procedures in accurate and efficient ways. Discussion can also help students build connections between those procedures and their underlying concepts. Learning based solely on memorization is often forgotten and is not readily transferred. However, when students use computational procedures that are connected to concepts (see Chapter 3, "Talking About Mathematical Concepts"), they develop more flexibility with their skills and they rarely provide answers that are unreasonable. Classroom discussions can also help students think of computational skills as tools that can be used to solve a wide variety of problems. Subsequently, in this chapter, we address lessons that feature classroom discussions in which students learn about a new computational strategy, connect an algorithm to the underlying concepts, or develop important number sense skills.

See Chapter 3.

What Is a Computational Procedure?

Much of the work students do in the elementary grades is focused on learning how to compute with numbers. Students' earliest experiences with computation begin in the primary grades when they compute with objects such as blocks and pictures. They next learn to use the counting sequence of whole numbers to compute the results of simple problems. As the numbers in these computations get larger in size, students discover a need for more sophisticated strategies to perform calculations. Instead of relying on blocks, pictures, or counting, they learn to use computational procedures to calculate.

Two Categories of Computational Procedures

A computational procedure is often categorized as either an *algorithm* or *strategy*. A *computational algorithm* describes a generalized set of steps used to perform computations of a particular class. Algorithms are efficient, produce accurate results, and can be used to perform many computations using the same process. A *computational strategy* is a method where the numbers in the computation are manipulated in order to create an equivalent but easier computation. There are many different strategies. Some involve partitioning numbers into tens and ones, others use relational thinking or compensation. Computational strategies differ from algorithms; the steps involved in enacting the strategy change depending on the specific numbers involved. Just like algorithms, however, computational strategies offer efficient and accurate ways to compute.

Two Categories of Computational Procedures

Computational Algorithms: a generalized set of steps used to perform computations of a particular class

Computational Strategies: a method where the numbers in a computation are manipulated in order to create an equivalent but easier computation

Can talk be used to assist students in obtaining computational proficiency? Absolutely! Classroom discussions are powerful tools for developing students' knowledge and skills. It is through whole-class discussions that students often learn about a new computational strategy or connect an algorithm to the underlying concepts upon which it is based.

> It is through whole-class discussions that students often learn about a new computational strategy or connect an algorithm to the underlying concepts upon which it is based.

Three Suggestions for Whole-Class Discussions on Computational Procedures

In this chapter we offer three suggestions for how to facilitate discussions that focus on using computational algorithms and strategies correctly, connect procedures to underlying concepts, and develop students' important number sense skills.

Three Suggestions for Whole-Class Discussions on Computational Procedures

1. Use whole-class discussion to teach computational procedures.
2. Use whole-class discussion to connect computational procedures to concepts.
3. Use whole-class discussion to build number sense skills.

> **Connecting computational procedures to concepts is the most important goal to remember; all of the examples in this chapter illustrate how this can be done.**

Whereas we have divided this chapter into three sections, we want to highlight the second suggestion. Connecting computational procedures to concepts is the most important goal to remember; all of the examples in this chapter illustrate how this can be done. For example, if students are to learn a new computational strategy or build number sense, they need to make sense of the underlying concepts that support the steps in a procedure or help them become more flexible with numbers such as benchmark values, place values, decomposition, and mathematical properties.

Suggestion 1: Use Whole-Class Discussion to Teach Computational Procedures

A major goal of elementary mathematics instruction is creating students who are computationally proficient. By the time they enter middle school, students should be able to use common computational procedures to operate on whole and rational numbers with both accuracy and efficiency. Students can develop proficiency using computational strategies and algorithms by participating in discussions about those procedures. As students talk about their own procedures and respond to the explanations of their classmates, they can develop deeper understanding of the ins and outs of those procedures and become more adept at using those procedures accurately and efficiently.

While classroom discussions can be an effective method for helping all students learn to compute accurately and efficiently, it is important that these discussions consist of more than just a series of presentations where students

> **Classroom discussions should center on student *explanations* about the ins and outs of computational procedures including *why* mathematically they can perform certain steps.**

stand in front of the class and tell the steps they followed to compute a particular sum, difference, product, or quotient. Instead, classroom discussions should center on student *explanations* about the ins and outs of computational procedures including *why* mathematically they can perform certain steps. Questions about computational procedures and strategies should align closely with the instructional goals. In addition, the students who are listening to those explanations must be called upon to respond to their classmates' explanations so that they too have the opportunity to use talk to develop their own computational proficiency.

Example 4.1.1 Use Whole-Class Discussion to Teach Computational Procedures

Teaching Addition Strategies (Ms. Moylan, Grade 1)

Let's first observe first-grade students using counting strategies to find the sum of three one-digit numbers. Students' strategies include counting on, skip-counting, doubles, doubles plus one, and doubles minus one. The teacher, Ms. Moylan, designed an *Adding Three Numbers* lesson where students first worked with their partners to find the sum of three one-digit numbers before sharing their strategies in a whole-class discussion. Ms. Moylan planned to use the whole-class discussion to help students learn particular computational strategies including "doubles plus or minus one." With this strategy, students use the sum of a double (for example, 4 + 4) to compute a sum with an addend that is one more or one less than the addends in the related "double."

As students worked in pairs, Ms. Moylan overheard one student talk about how she used the double 4 plus 4 to find the sum of 3 + 4. Ms. Moylan asked this student if she would be willing to share her thinking with the class during the ensuing whole-class discussion. In the following video clip, we see how Ms. Moylan manages the whole-class discussion about this student's strategy. As you watch the clip, notice how Ms. Moylan uses the talk move *Who can repeat?* to focus students' attention on the strategy of using the sum of 4 + 4 to compute 3 + 4. Specifically, Ms. Moylan uses this talk move to focus students' attention on the idea that the number 3 can also be thought of as one less than four. She also uses this talk move to help students recognize sums of doubles as a powerful tool for computing other unknown sums.

> **FOUR STEPS...**
> Asking students to restate or repeat each other's ideas supports Step 2: Helping Students Orient to the Thinking of Others (see "Four Steps Toward Productive Talk," Chapter 1, page 10).

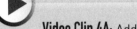

Video Clip 4A: Adding Three Numbers

As you watch the video clip, consider:

1. Describe Imogene's strategy for adding 3 + 4 + 2.

2. Why might Ms. Moylan choose to spend so much class time
   discussing this particular strategy for adding 3 + 4 + 2?

3. Describe Ms. Moylan's use of *Who can repeat?* during the whole-class
   discussion. How does she decide who will repeat a student's
   statement? Why might she use the move in these ways?

For more videos from Ms. Moylan's *Adding Three Numbers* lesson, see the
companion resource *Classroom Discussions in Math: A **Facilitator's Guide**
to Support Professional Learning of Discourse and the Common Core.*

Try It Out!

LESSON: Adding Three Numbers

The next time you conduct a lesson that focuses on computational
strategies, you may wish to incorporate more student talk in
your instruction by following a routine similar to what you saw in
Ms. Moylan's class. The following guidelines may be helpful as you
plan for and manage your discussions.

See the
lesson plan
*Adding
Three
Numbers
(Grade 1)* in
Appendix B.

- *Begin with small group or partner work time.* Students should
  take turns explaining their strategies to their partners. In
  turn, partners should provide feedback following a classmate's explanation, ask questions, offer suggestions, and give
  assistance as needed.

**Teaching with
the Common Core**

1.OA Understand
and apply
properties of
operations and
the relationship
between addition
and subtraction.

1.OA Add and
subtract within 20.

- *Use partner work time to prepare for the whole-class discussion.* As students are working, look and listen for students who are using strategies that are efficient and effective but currently unfamiliar to many students in the class. Ask these students to share their thinking during the whole-class discussion. Sometimes teachers introduce an especially effective strategy themselves, mentioning that they saw a student perform it at another time.

- *Use talk moves to focus student thinking on targeted strategies.* During the whole-class discussion, call on the students who you had previously asked to speak.

Use talk moves such as *Who can repeat?* and *turn and talk* to encourage the other students to actively engage with their classmates' reasoning.

> **MATH TALK TIP**
>
> **Using a New Strategy**
>
> After a student talks about how she solved a particular computation, post a similar computation where everyone can see it and ask the entire class to perform the computation using their classmate's strategy. Call on a student to talk about his thinking and then revisit with the original speaker to see if that student followed the strategy correctly.

Example 4.1.2 Use Whole-Class Discussion to Teach Computational Procedures

Teaching Subtraction Strategies (Ms. Powers, Grade 2)

A key idea that undergirds many computational procedures is the idea that any number can be rewritten as the sum of two other numbers. This concept—often referred to as *decomposition*—provides the foundation for many computational procedures in the elementary grades including ones that involve the addition and subtraction of whole numbers. For example, one way to compute $23 - 5$ is to decompose 5 into 3 and 2, subtract 3 from 23 to get 20 and then subtract 2 from 20 to get the final difference of 18. Subtracting numbers via decomposition is an effective strategy for primary students because it allows them to rely on "friendly" or "landmark" numbers to compute more challenging differences.

Ms. Powers wanted her second-grade students to become proficient with decomposition as a strategy for subtracting whole numbers. After practicing this strategy in class, Ms. Powers collected a set of student papers and

> ### MATH TALK TIP
>
> **Review Student Work**
> Reviewing student work can help you identify what students might benefit in having a whole-class discussion around.

noticed that many students were unable to use this strategy to compute differences with accuracy. She noticed that many students seemed to be struggling with one particular step. Although students could subtract a part of the subtrahend to reach a friendly number, many could not figure out what number to subtract next.

For example, to compute 26 − 8, most students took the first step of subtracting 6 from 26 to get 20. After reaching 20, however, many students were stymied. They did not seem to understand that since the subtrahend, 8, had been decomposed into 6 and 2, they needed to subtract 2 in order to reach the final dif-

> **Ms. Powers knew that understanding decomposition was the key factor in overcoming this confusion. She decided to use whole-class discussion to address students' difficulties.**

ference. Or perhaps they were not able to manage this three-step process and would benefit from a discussion that would make the steps more salient and memorable. Ms. Powers knew that understanding decomposition was the key factor in overcoming this confusion. She decided to use a whole-class discussion to address students' difficulties.

Ms. Powers begins the whole-class discussion by posting a number line to model the subtraction 26 − 8. The number line that is posted shows how to find this difference by first subtracting 6 from 26 to reach 20.

26 − 8

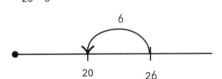

She asks students to turn and talk with their partners about whether they agree or disagree that beginning the subtraction in this way is a good idea. Students agree that this is a good decision because twenty-six minus six results in a "round" number. (Students' use of the word *round* here is equivalent to calling 20 a friendly or landmark number.) Ms. Powers then asks the students to turn and talk with their partners about what they would do next. During this time, she listens to Teddy who explains that "minus two" should be the next step since six plus two equals eight. Ms. Powers tells Teddy that she will call on him to speak when the whole-class discussion resumes and she suggests that he practice what he is going to say with his partner.

When the whole-class discussion resumes, Ms. Powers calls on Teddy to share his thinking. She asks, "Who can say that again?" to orient students toward Teddy's thinking. After providing a visual model of Teddy's idea on the interactive whiteboard, Ms. Powers once again uses turn and talk to give everyone a chance to think about this important and challenging step in the computational strategy. Ms. Powers concludes the discussion by asking students how they know that they have taken away eight—the value of the subtrahend in the original computation. This question helps students justify the validity of the solution strategy by recomposing six plus two as eight.

> ## MATH TALK TIP
> ### Will You Share That With the Class?
> In a turn and talk, a student's idea might form the basis for a productive discussion. It is helpful to let the student know that you would like him or her to share the idea in a whole-class discussion. When you pose the question to the whole class again, you can call on that student to speak.

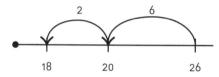

Video Clip 4B: Subtracting on the Number Line

As you watch the video clip, consider:

1. When Ms. Powers asks students to turn and talk with their partners about the next step in the computational procedure, many immediately call out "Minus two!" Yet some students in the clip struggle to explain why this step makes sense. What might this indicate about their understanding of subtraction and decomposition?

2. Pick a student to watch throughout the video clip. What clues are given that enable you to decide if he or she understands the strategy or is confused by the strategy?

> ### BEFORE YOU WATCH THE VIDEO
> To make the most productive use of the video clips, you and any colleagues you are working with should take time to read through the "Guidelines for Watching Videos of Teaching" (see page xxi). For demographics, see page xliv.

Try It Out!

See the
lesson plan
*Teaching
Subtraction
Strategies
(Grade 2)* in
Appendix B.

LESSON: Teaching Subtraction Strategies

You may also find that your students' ability to use decomposition as a subtraction strategy is tenuous. Talk can be used to help those students build connections to the concept that every number can be decomposed into two or more addends. Choose problems that lend themselves to using this strategy (for example, 45 – 8 or 45 – 18) and plan a whole-class discussion that aims to address and remediate students' difficulties. Post an example of student work on a number line that is partially completed with the targeted computational strategy. The posted work should show the steps of the procedure but stop right before the step that is particularly problematic for your students. During the discussion, focus the student talk on the step of the procedure that is often misunderstood. Ask students, "What do you think we should do next?" Use press for reasoning to help students connect the steps of the strategy to the concept of decomposition. Specifically, students should explain the total amount subtracted in all of the steps should add up to the value of the original subtrahend.

**Teaching with
the Common Core**

2.NBT Use place value understanding and properties of operations to add and subtract.

2.NBT Explain why addition and subtraction strategies work, using place value and the properties of operations.

Example 4.1.3 Use Whole-Class Discussion to Teach Computational Procedures

Teaching Division Strategies (Mr. Canavan, Grade 5 Inclusion Class)

Whole-class discussions help students develop computational proficiency by developing students' awareness of their own understandings and misunderstandings. It is very easy for a student to listen to a classmate talk about a particular computational procedure and think, "Oh, I get it." But oftentimes, students who think they understand a particular approach ultimately struggle to explain why that strategy works or how it can be used to solve a related computation. The good news is that these difficulties can serve as the catalyst for knowledge growth. When students realize that they don't understand as much as they thought they did, they can begin the work of seeking out key concepts, developing new skills, or forging new connections between ideas.

> It is very easy for a student to listen to a classmate talk about a particular computational procedure and think, "Oh, I get it." But oftentimes, students who think they understand a particular approach ultimately struggle to explain why that strategy works or how it can be used to solve a related computation.

Mr. Canavan uses strings of related computations to help his students learn how to use computational procedures. Recently he has begun to incorporate more student discussion during these instructional episodes. He made this shift after noticing a discrepancy between students' class participation and their work on written assignments. During instructional episodes when some students talked about how to perform a given procedure, the rest of the students in the class not only appeared to be listening but also typically indicated that they were following along by giving a thumbs-up signal following a classmate's presentation. Yet, when students completed written independent work following these episodes, many struggled to use the same strategies that were presented in class just moments earlier.

Mr. Canavan began to doubt whether simply listening to their classmates' explanations was an effective way for students to use each other's computational strategies independently. He decided to focus more heavily on talk moves such as *turn and talk* and *Who can say that again?* to encourage students to actively engage with each other's reasoning and become more aware of their own understandings and misunderstandings.

During one recent lesson, Mr. Canavan used a string of related computations to help his students learn how to use partial quotients to divide whole numbers. He posted the following three computations to help his students learn how to compute 624 ÷ 6 using easier and related computations. For example, students could reason that when you take 600 and divide it among 6 groups, there is 100 in each group. Next, when 24 is shared among 6 groups, there is 4 in each group. So, when 624 is shared equally among 6 groups, there is a total of 104 in each of the 6 groups. He planned to use a whole-class discussion to focus on this particular strategy.

600 ÷ 6
24 ÷ 6
624 ÷ 6

1. **Mr. C:** Who can tell me the value of the quotient of six hundred divided by six? Abigail?
2. **Abigail:** Ten.
3. **Mr. C:** OK, who can tell me the value of the quotient of twenty-four divided by six? Tim?
4. **Tim:** Four.
5. **Mr. C:** OK, how about this one: six hundred twenty-four divided by six? Before you find the value of the quotient, first discuss with your partner the two different meanings of division.

As students are talking in pairs, Mr. Canavan overhears Sarah explain that one way to think of division is as a way to divide an amount into an equal number of groups. She mentions that 624 can be shared equally among 6 groups. He calls on her when the whole-class discussion resumes.

6. **Mr. C:** Sarah, what did you and your partner discuss?

7. **Sarah:** I think of it as how much is in each group when six hundred twenty-four is divided into six equal groups.

8. **Mr. C:** Who can say again what Sarah said? Jacob?

9. **Jacob:** She said it can mean how much is in each group when six hundred twenty-four is shared equally among six groups.

10. **Mr. C:** And you are right, Sarah—that is one way to interpret division. What I want to ask you now is, how can we use that interpretation and the other two computations posted on the board already to compute six hundred twenty-four divided by six? Think quietly for ten seconds about that. [Ten seconds pass.] OK, turn and talk to your partner about your thinking. [Students talk for sixty seconds. Mr. Canavan overhears Sebastian giving an accurate and insightful explanation. He asks him if he would be willing to share his thinking with the group. He agrees.]

11. **Mr. C:** OK, Sebastian, what did you and your partner discuss?

12. **Sebastian:** You can think of six hundred twenty-four as six hundred plus twenty-four. When you take six hundred and divide it among six groups, there is hundred in each group. Then if you take twenty-four and share it among six groups, there is four in a group. So the answer is one hundred four.

13. **Mr. C:** Sebastian, is what I wrote here an accurate description of what you said? [Sebastian nods.]

$$624 = 600 + 24$$
$$600 \div 6 = 100$$
$$24 \div 6 = 4$$
$$100 + 4 = 104$$

14. **Mr. C:** Who else thought about the problem like Sebastian did and can put what he said in his or her own words? Helena?

15. **Helena:** Yeah, so he did six hundred plus twenty-four and then he divided six hundred by six because that's easier and also because there

are six groups—no, groups of six. Wait. Why is that twenty four there? [Long pause.] Can you come back to me?

16. **Mr. C:** Sure. Latisha?

17. **Latisha:** He broke the six hundred twenty-four into six hundred and then twenty-four, since those are easy to work with. When six hundred is shared by six groups, each group gets hundred. When twenty four is shared by six groups, each group gets four. So if you put those together, you get one hundred four.

18. **Mr. C:** How about now, Helena? Can you try explaining that?

19. **Helena:** Um, yeah. [Long pause.] Actually, I'm still not sure why he added one hundred plus four even though we are talking about six groups. I don't get that.

20. **Mr. C:** OK, who else thinks they can explain what Sebastian did? In fact, you know what? There's a lot going on here. So, let's have Sebastian talk us through his method again. Then, we'll all turn and talk with our partners about his process.

MATH TALK TIP

Use That Talk Move Later . . .

When using strings of related computations to teach a computational strategy, remember that you don't need to discuss each and every computation. Save talk moves such as *How do you know?* and *Who can repeat?* for the more difficult computations in the string.

Mr. Canavan realizes that recasting a classmate's explanation of a computational procedure often gives the other students a chance to think about the meaning behind individual steps and connect those steps to underlying concepts. It can also reveal misconceptions and holes in students' understanding. In this particular episode, thinking about the computation in terms of decomposition ($624 = 600 + 24$) and using the equal grouping interpretation of division are key to understanding Sebastian's partial quotient procedure. Helena appears to struggle with both of these concepts. Now that she is aware of what confuses her, she can work with her math partner and Mr. Canavan to find the information that will help her talk about Sebastian's procedure and, more importantly, use it to solve other division computations.

Try It Out!

LESSON: Teaching Division Strategies

If you try using this string of division computations with your own students, you may wish to begin by reviewing different interpretations of the operation of division. You can post a computation such as 24 ÷ 6 = 4 and ask students to interpret the equation. It is particularly important that students can read the equation as both equal grouping (in other words, if twenty-four is shared equally among six groups, there are four in each group) as well as repeated subtraction (in other words, if six is repeatedly subtracted from twenty-four to make make groups, there are four groups). Once you review these concepts, you can begin talking about the equations in the string.

See the lesson plan *Teaching Division Strategies (Grade 5)* in Appendix B.

CCS

Teaching with the Common Core

5.NBT Find whole-number quotients of whole numbers ... using strategies based on place value, the properties of operations, and/or the relationship between multiplication and division.

Suggestion 2: Use Whole-Class Discussion to Connect Computational Procedures to Concepts

Students who understand why a computational procedure works are more likely to remember how to use that procedure correctly and apply it to appropriate classes of problems. Whole-class discussions are an effective way to develop students' understanding of the mathematical principles and concepts that give important computational procedures their meaning.

Talking about computational procedures can do more than clarify students' understanding of the ins and outs of those procedures. It may actually promote a more profound understanding of the numbers, properties, and concepts at the heart of those procedures. In other words, at the same time that talk is building facility with procedures, it is deepening conceptual knowledge as well.

Understanding why computational procedures make sense is a key component of students' computational proficiency. Students who understand the purpose of each step in a procedure are more likely to be able to recover those steps if they lose their automaticity. Understanding prevents students from making systematic errors that derive from applying a procedure by rote. Finally, understanding why computational procedures make sense reinforces the idea that arithmetic consists of logical and connected ideas and not just a set of meaningless rules and procedures that must be memorized and repeated by rote.

One way to strengthen students' understanding of computational procedures is to talk about how two procedures for the same computation are related. Younger elementary students often characterize their computational strategies using the models they used to represent their thinking. They may say, "I found the difference using a number line." Or, "I drew a picture to find the sum." Furthermore, asking students to talk about how different representations of the same computational procedure are related refocuses their attention on the important mathematical ideas that give the procedure and its various representations their meaning.

> One way to strengthen students' understanding of computational procedures is to talk about how two procedures for the same computation are related.

Example 4.2.1 Use Whole-Class Discussion to Connect Computational Procedures to Concepts

Comparing Subtraction Strategies (Ms. Powers, Grade 2)

Let's revisit Ms. Powers's second-grade class (first observed on page 125). The lesson on subtraction strategies that use the concept of decomposition continued with a discussion of a related problem. Students used two different models to help them make sense of the computation: a number line or pictures of tens and ones. In each case, they used their model to show how to decompose the subtrahend into smaller parts. For example, to compute $34 - 6$ on a number line, a student started at 34, jumped four spaces left to land on 30, and then jumped two more spaces left to land on 28. Another student drew pictures of three groups of ten and four ones. After crossing out the four ones, he drew two units inside of the first ten, crossed these out and counted the remaining ones and tens blocks to find the difference of twenty-eight.

$34 - 6 = 28$

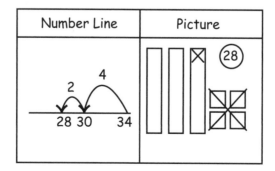

> **Ms. Powers uses a whole-class discussion to compare the two models that were used to show the decomposition strategy.**

Ms. Powers uses a whole-class discussion to compare the two models that were used to show the decomposition strategy. By connecting representations, Ms. Powers hopes to deepen her students' understanding of subtraction. She knows that the more her students understand about the decomposition strategy, the greater the chance that they will use it effectively. She posts the student work on the interactive whiteboard. Let's join her as she facilitates the discussion about students' ideas.

Video Clip 4C: Comparing Subtraction Strategies

As you watch the video clip, consider:

1. As Ms. Powers talks with Bryn, she presses him for reasoning to help him clarify his thinking. What do we learn about Bryn's understanding of decomposition and subtraction as a result of Ms. Powers's questions?

2. When does Ms. Powers use turn and talk? Which of the four steps toward productive talk does this talk move support in this discussion?

BEFORE YOU WATCH THE VIDEO

To make the most productive use of the video clips, you and any colleagues you are working with should take time to read through the "Guidelines for Watching Videos of Teaching" (see page xxi). For demographics, see page xliv.

FOUR STEPS...

Step 1: Helping Individual Students Clarify and Share Their Own Thoughts

Step 2: Helping Students Orient to the Thinking of Others

Step 3: Helping Students Deepen Their Own Reasoning

Step 4: Helping Students Engage with the Reasoning of Others

LESSON: Connecting Subtraction Strategies and Concepts

If you plan to use this or a similar lesson with your own students, focus your whole-class discussion on connecting the computational strategy or procedure with underlying concepts. For example, you might select two different samples of student work that use decomposition but represent this strategy in different ways. Keep the discussion focused on similarities, not differences. Ask questions such as "How are these two approaches similar?" or "What do they have in common?" Use the talk moves *Who can repeat?* and *turn and talk* to give many students the opportunity to articulate how both models show how to decompose a subtrahend into two parts and then subtract each of the two parts separately.

See the lesson plan *Teaching Subtraction Strategies (Grade 2)* in Appendix B.

CCSS
Teaching with the Common Core

2.NBT Use place value understanding and properties of operations to add and subtract.
2.NBT Explain why addition and subtraction strategies work, using place value and the properties of operations.

Example 4.2.2 Use Whole-Class Discussion to Connect Computational Procedures to Concepts

Connecting Multiplication Strategies and Concepts (Mrs. DeFreitas, Grade 4)

Talking about students' invented computational procedures is another way to help students identify the concepts that give those procedures their meaning. Mrs. DeFreitas's fourth-grade students have been exploring different ways to solve multidigit multiplication problems. Some students use repeated addition, some use partial products, and some use the standard multiplication algorithm. As they apply strategies for multiplying, they also must justify their steps, thus reinforcing the idea that mathematics makes sense. In the following example, one student in Mrs. DeFreitas's class uses a particularly efficient mental procedure to solve the problem 19 × 12, based on the distributive property. Mrs. DeFreitas asks this student to explain his method to the class.

FOUR STEPS...

It is important to help students get better at saying what they are thinking in ways that can be understood. Asking a student to talk through his or her thinking again supports Step 1: Helping Individual Students Clarify and Share Their Own Thoughts (see "Four Steps Toward Productive Talk," Chapter 1, page 10).

1. **Kim Lee:** I wanted to solve nineteen times twelve. This looked hard to me. So, instead I first did twenty times twelve because that's easier. It's two times twelve, which is twenty-four with a zero—two hundred forty. Then I did two hundred forty minus twelve, which is two hundred twenty-eight.

2. **Mrs. D:** Kim Lee, I want your classmates to really understand your procedure because I think they will want to use it themselves. Can you talk us through it again, this time a little more slowly?

3. **Kim Lee:** OK. Nineteen times twelve would be tough for me. Nineteen is close to twenty and twenty times twelve is easier because we know a shortcut for multiplying numbers that end in zero.

4. **Mrs. D:** Let me stop you for a minute. What's one way to interpret nineteen times twelve? Fran?

5. **Fran:** Nineteen groups of twelve.

6. **Mrs. D:** Then, twenty times twelve means twenty groups of twelve. Keep going, Kim Lee.

7. **Kim Lee:** Yeah, so once I figured out that twenty times twelve was two hundred forty, I subtracted twelve.

8. **Mrs. D:** Who thinks they can explain why Kim Lee subtracted twelve? Talk to the person next to you for a moment about this. [Partners talk for about one minute.] Go ahead, Felicita.

9. **Felicita:** The number *two hundred forty* is from twenty groups of twelve. We only want nineteen groups of twelve, so we have to get rid of one group of twelve.

10. **Mrs. D:** Is that why you subtracted, Kim Lee? [He nods.] Kim, as you talk us through your procedure, tell me what number sentences to write.

11. **Kim Lee:** OK, it's nineteen groups of twelve, which is close to twenty groups of twelve, so write *twenty times twelve*. [Mrs. D writes *20 × 12*.] But now I take away one group of twelve, since I only want nineteen groups, so write *minus twelve*. [She writes *20 × 12 – 12*.] The answer is two hundred twenty-eight.

12. **Mrs. D:** We can use parentheses to show what operation we do first. [She writes on the board $(20 \times 12) - 12 = 228$ and $19 \times 12 = (20 \times 12) - 12$.] Talk to your partner about these equations. Are these equations equivalent? Why or why not?

Mrs. DeFreitas doesn't spend a lot of time having students discuss the equations, but she wants to make sure that students understand that the equations are equivalent. She rewrites the second equation so that it starts with the expression $(20 \times 12) - 12$.

$$(20 \times 12) - 12 = 228$$
$$(20 \times 12) - 12 = 19 \times 12$$

After a number of students have explained why they are equivalent, Mrs. DeFreitas writes one more equation and asks students to think about what it is saying mathematically, $(20 - 1) \times 12 = (20 \times 12) - (1 \times 12)$.

Next, Mrs. DeFreitas asks everyone to solve another problem.

13. **Mrs. D:** Let's try Kim Lee's procedure for eighteen times thirteen. Work with the person next to you.

One reason that Mrs. DeFreitas asks everyone to try Kim Lee's procedure is that she suspects that students are confused about which number to round, what to round it to, and how much to subtract. While students work she circulates among them, noting who is applying Kim Lee's method correctly and who is not. She notices that Jonathan's answer is correct while Sierra and Beatriz and Felicita have made different types of errors. She plans on using their errors in the discussion to help students better understand Kim Lee's method. Prior to the whole-class discussion, she mentions to each of these students that she will be calling on them to explain their thinking. This enables the students to prepare their thoughts.

14. **Mrs. D:** OK, now that you've had a chance to try Kim Lee's procedure, who would like to explain to us what you did? Beatriz?

15. **Beatriz:** Me and Felicita did twenty times thirteen to get two hundred sixty, because thirteen times two is twenty-six and then add a zero.

16. **Mrs. D:** What do you mean "add a zero"?

17. **Beatriz:** It's not thirteen times two, it's thirteen times twenty, so you need to put a zero down.

> **FOUR STEPS...**
> Asking students if they will share specific ideas later on in a class discussion supports Step 1: Helping Individual Students Clarify and Share Their Own Thoughts (see "Four Steps Toward Productive Talk," Chapter 1, page 10).

18. **Mrs. D:** Why?

19. **Felicita:** It's like the two is really a twenty but you pretend it's a two since that's easier and then put the zero back when you're done.

20. **Mrs. D:** Who can explain why they rounded eighteen to twenty?

21. **Richard:** Kim Lee's method works with friendly numbers, like ones that end in zero. So you look for a close number that ends in zero. Eighteen is close to twenty.

22. **Mrs. D:** Is that why you did it? [The girls nod.] Who thinks they can predict what we have to do next?

23. **Jonathan:** I think we do two hundred sixty minus twenty-six. The twenty times thirteen means twenty groups of thirteen but we only really want eighteen groups, so we need to take away two groups of thirteen, which is twenty-six.

24. **Mrs. D:** Does anyone else have a different prediction?

25. **Sierra:** I think it is two hundred sixty minus eighteen because you have to take away eighteen.

26. **Mrs. D:** Does anyone else have a prediction? OK, Felicita and Beatriz, tell us what you did.

27. **Beatriz:** We subtracted thirteen because that's what Kim Lee did in his problem. The answer is two hundred forty-seven.

MATH TALK TIP

Slow It Down . . .

If a discussion seems to be getting confusing or may be confusing to some students, consider slowing it down and summarizing the main points made thus far before continuing.

Mrs. DeFreitas realizes that this discussion may be confusing to many in her class. She decides that she needs to slow everything down even further and summarize the main points students have made. Since there are a number of suggestions for what to subtract from two hundred sixty, she decides to recap them and then restart the discussion.

28. **Mrs. D:** OK. So we have several different predictions here, and several different answers have been mentioned. So let's take stock here. What do we agree on? So far, to solve eighteen times thirteen we all agree that you can multiply twenty times thirteen, which equals two hundred sixty. This is part of Kim Lee's method to work first with friendly

numbers. But it is not clear what number should be subtracted from two hundred sixty. We have three predictions. The first prediction, I'll call it A, suggests that we should subtract twenty-six. The second prediction, called B, is that we should subtract eighteen. And prediction C is that we should subtract thirteen. I am going to write the number sentences on the board while everyone talks to their partner about the three predictions. Which of the predictions do you agree with and why? [Mrs. DeFreitas writes the following predictions on the board and gives students about two and a half minutes to discuss them.]

$18 \times 13 = ?$
Step 1: Multiply 20×13 $20 \times 13 = 260$
Step 2: Predictions
A: $(20 \times 13) - 26$
B: $(20 \times 13) - 18$
C: $(20 \times 13) - 13$

29. **Mrs. D:** OK, which prediction did you and your partner decide upon? Lindsey?

30. **Lindsey:** We got rid of prediction B because it's eighteen groups of thirteen changed to twenty groups of thirteen.

31. **Mrs. D:** Would you elaborate a bit more for us? I agree it is twenty groups of thirteen, but why is that important?

32. **Lindsey:** Since it's groups of thirteen, we think you subtract groups of thirteen, not a group of eighteen.

33. **Kim Lee:** I agree with Lindsey. I would subtract twenty-six since twenty times thirteen is over by two groups. You need to take away those two groups of thirteen, which is twenty-six. The answer should be two hundred thirty-four. I checked with the calculator and that's right.

34. **Mrs. D:** Peter, do you think you could explain in your own words what Lindsey and Kim Lee said?

35. **Peter:** They said that prediction B is wrong because twenty is too many groups of thirteen, so you have to subtract groups of thirteen, not eighteen.

36. **Mrs. D:** OK, let's look at the third prediction. Can someone explain why you think prediction C is either right or wrong?

37. **Jonathan**: It only takes away one group of thirteen, not two, like Kim Lee said.

38. **Mrs. D**: Beatriz, what do you think of what Jonathan and Kim Lee both said?

39. **Beatriz**: I think I get it. You don't always take away the number. You have to think about how much you rounded up and then take that many groups. We rounded up two so we have to subtract two groups.

Mrs. DeFreitas's class then used Kim Lee's procedure to multiply other numbers. They discussed the reasoning behind each step, especially how much to subtract and why. As they became more comfortable with the method, they discussed different number sentences they could write. Mrs. DeFreitas chose not to formally introduce the distributive property at this time because the class was still grappling with making sense of the idea of rounding up and subtracting. However, she would return to the topic and focus exclusively on the distributive property in a future lesson.

<table>
<tr><td>

FOUR STEPS...

Asking students to try out a classmate's solution strategy supports Step 4: Helping Students Engage with the Reasoning of Others (see "Four Steps Toward Productive Talk," Chapter 1, page 10).

</td></tr>
</table>

Did you notice how Mrs. DeFreitas asked more than one student to suggest what number should be subtracted from 20 × 13? Jonathan gave a correct answer, but Mrs. DeFreitas knew that not everyone in her class could immediately make sense of his reasoning. Thus, she called on two students she suspected might have incorrect predictions. This allowed the students time to really think about which number to subtract and to discuss their reasoning.

One effective talk strategy that assists students in reasoning about a particular answer is to set up a discussion around different positions. Instead of telling students that Jonathan's method to subtract twenty-six from two hundred sixty was correct, Mrs. DeFreitas summarized the three possible answers students had suggested. Discussing a variety of possible answers to a calculation can help students make sense of the numbers used.

> **Teachers sometimes wonder if discussing wrong answers is in students' best interest. We have found that students learn more when they consider incorrect options and then reject them based on reasoning rather than on the basis of an authority's decision.**

Teachers sometimes wonder if discussing wrong answers is in students' best interest. We have found that students learn more when they consider incorrect options and then reject them based on reasoning rather than on the basis of an authority's decision. When students make sense of a situation, they deepen their understanding of procedures and calculations. Also, as they align themselves with one position or another, their stake in the outcome increases their interest and attention.

Recall that Mrs. DeFreitas did not identify any prediction with a particular student's name but instead labeled the predictions in an impersonal way with letters. Sometimes teachers want to focus the discussion on the mathematics, rather than on the person who gave the response, so that incorrect responses are not associated with individuals. Other times teachers want to identify a procedure or conjecture with a particular student's name as a way to recognize that student's contributions.

> **MATH TALK TIP**
>
> **Naming a Student's Contribution**
> When a student "discovers" a new and efficient computational procedure, you may want to identify that procedure by the student's name as a way to recognize his or her contribution. In other discussions, however, you may instead want to focus on the mathematics, rather than the student.

It's important that students understand the computational procedures they use, rather than just applying them in a rote fashion. When students are learning a computational procedure, understanding why it works will help them commit it to memory. One of the best ways to assist students in understanding and remembering procedures is to talk with them about the procedures. Talking about the math we are doing slows down and clarifies processes so that more students can understand them. Additionally, many students are motivated to compare their own ways of solving a problem with those of other students, which teaches them new computational procedures and strengthens their understanding of the workings of procedures they are more familiar with. Furthermore, by listening to students talk, teachers can gain insights into their understanding of procedures as well as into their misconceptions and mistaken ideas about computation. Fluency, however, requires practice, so teachers should be sure that students have ample opportunities to practice a procedure or skill once they have talked it through.

Try It Out!

LESSON: Connecting Multiplication Strategies and Concepts

Learning to perform multidigit multiplication accurately is a focus of the Common Core State Standards in Mathematics at grade 4. One way to assist students in learning to multiply accurately is to use whole-class discussions to explore the connections to properties and place-value concepts. If you try this lesson, consider asking students to predict the next step in a computation as Mrs. DeFreitas did. This can be an effective way for students to focus on the conceptual underpinnings of the procedure. Notice how Mrs. DeFreitas provided structure and information to the students that kept the focus on the distributive property. In addition, she introduced the correct way to represent the steps using equations in order to provide visual support of the method and regularly asked students to explain their ideas.

Teaching with the Common Core

4.NBT Use place value understanding and properties of operations to perform multidigit arithmetic.

Suggestion 3: Use Whole-Class Discussion to Build Number Sense Skills

No computational procedure offers a one-size-fits-all approach for any given operation. Students need to develop the number sense skills that enable them to look at a computation and choose a procedure that will give them the correct answer in an efficient amount of time. Classroom discussions that focus on making decisions about computational procedures are a particularly effective way to develop these important skills.

The overarching goal of arithmetic instruction is for students to use computational procedures as problem-solving tools. No computational procedure offers a one-size-fits-all approach for any given operation. For example, it makes sense to use the standard algorithm for subtraction to compute $87 - 13$ but not $1000 - 1$. And although the standard algorithm for multiplication will derive the correct product of 0.5×4.8, there are faster and easier ways to reach the same result. Students must be able to look at a computation and choose a procedure from their arithmetical tool kit that is likely to give them the correct answer in an efficient amount of time. The ability to make sound decisions about computational procedures is often

> The ability to make sound decisions about computational procedures is often referred to as a student's *number sense*. We have found classroom discussions to be an effective format for developing students' number sense.

referred to as a student's *number sense*. We have found classroom discussions to be an effective format for developing students' number sense. In the section that follows, we present classroom examples of teachers and students working on this important arithmetical endeavour.

Example 4.3.1 Use Whole-Class Discussion to Build Number Sense Skills

Developing Fraction Sense (Ms. Castro, Grade 4)

Ms. Castro's fourth-grade class has been learning how to add fractions with like denominators. So far, the class has developed two strategies that they have titled "break apart" and "add fractions, then wholes." In the first strategy, "break apart," the students decompose one or both numbers in the computation to create more manageable partial sums. For example, to find the sum of $4\frac{2}{3} + 5\frac{2}{3}$ one can break apart $5\frac{2}{3}$ into $5\frac{1}{3} + \frac{1}{3}$, add $\frac{1}{3}$ to $4\frac{2}{3}$ to get 5 and then add $5\frac{1}{3}$ to reach the final sum of $10\frac{1}{3}$.

$$4\frac{2}{3} + 5\frac{2}{3}$$

$$5\frac{2}{3} = 5\frac{1}{3} + \frac{1}{3}$$

$$4\frac{2}{3} + \frac{1}{3} = 5$$

$$5 + 5\frac{1}{3} = 10\frac{1}{3}$$

With the second strategy, "add fractions, then wholes," students compute sums of mixed numbers by finding the sum of the fractions and then the sum of the whole numbers. Students regroup as needed if the sum of the fractions is greater than or equal to one. To compute $4\frac{2}{3} + 5\frac{2}{3}$ using this strategy, one can add the fractions $\frac{2}{3}$ and $\frac{2}{3}$ to get $\frac{4}{3}$ and then add 4 plus 5 to get 9. After regrouping the $\frac{3}{3}$ within $\frac{4}{3}$ as 1, the final sum is $10\frac{1}{3}$.

Ms. Castro's students have been practicing using two these strategies to compute sums of mixed numbers for several weeks. Ms. Castro wants her students to think more deeply about the kinds of computations that lend themselves to each strategy. After all, Ms. Castro knows that the goal of computation is to be able to look at a computation and choose a strategy that will lead to the correct answer in the least amount of steps. She planned a whole-class discussion that focused on the following question: When you see a mixed number addition computation, how do you decide which strategy to use? She posted the following three computations on the board and said to her students, "Here are three mixed number addition computations. So far, we have learned two strategies for computing these sums: 'break apart' and 'add fractions, then wholes'. Which strategy would you use for each of these computations? Tell us why you think so. Take sixty seconds and think about that on your own. Then talk to your partner."

$$3\frac{3}{5} + 4\frac{3}{5}$$

$$3\frac{3}{5} + 8\frac{1}{5}$$

$$4\frac{5}{8} + 5\frac{7}{8}$$

As students were talking with their partners, Ms. Castro heard Maria explain to her partner Tim that she would use the break-apart strategy for the first computation since she knew $\frac{3}{5}$ plus $\frac{2}{5}$ was equal to one. Ms. Castro asked Maria if she would be willing to share her thinking with the entire class.

1. **Ms. C.:** When Maria was talking to her partner, I heard her explain that she would find the sum of $3\frac{3}{5} + 4\frac{3}{5}$ using our break-apart strategy. Maria, tell us a little more about your thinking.

2. **Maria:** Well, the first number is $3\frac{3}{5}$. So I thought about trying to see if I could get another $\frac{2}{5}$ to get to 4. And I could do that if I took the $\frac{2}{5}$ out of the $\frac{3}{5}$.

3. **Ms. C:** Say a little bit more about that.

4. **Maria:** OK, I left $3\frac{3}{5}$ alone. And I thought about maybe getting to 4. So I broke apart $4\frac{3}{5}$ so it was $4\frac{1}{5}$ plus another $\frac{2}{5}$. I added the $\frac{2}{5}$ to $3\frac{3}{5}$ to get 4 and then I added 4 plus $4\frac{1}{5}$ to get $8\frac{1}{5}$.

5. **Ms. C.** Is this what you did? [See below.]

$$3\frac{3}{5} + 4\frac{3}{5}$$

$$4\frac{3}{5} = 4\frac{1}{5} + \frac{2}{5}$$

$$3\frac{3}{5} + \frac{2}{5} = 4$$

$$4 + 4\frac{1}{5} = 8\frac{1}{5}$$

6. **Maria:** Yes.

7. **Ms. C:** OK, so why did you use the break-apart strategy?

8. **Maria:** Because of the numbers.

9. **Ms. C:** Can you be more specific? What is it about the numbers in this computation that made you choose our break-apart strategy?

10. **Maria:** Well, the two fractions are both fifths. So I looked to see if there was something in the second number that I could add to the first to get a whole number of fifths or five-fifths, 'cause whole numbers are really easy to work with.

11. **Ms. C:** OK, that's a really key idea. Can everyone turn to the person next to them and say again what Maria just said?

> **FOUR STEPS...**
>
> Asking students to justify why they chose a particular computational strategy supports Step 3: Helping Students Deepen Their Own Reasoning (see "Four Steps Toward Productive Talk," Chapter 1, page 10).

Notice how Ms. Castro uses press for reasoning to help Maria identify the characteristics of the addition computation that helped her choose the computational strategy based on decomposition. Ms. Castro wants Maria and all of her students to recognize that this strategy is appropriate when one of the addends can be decomposed into two parts such that one part can be added on to the other addend to create a whole-number partial sum. Once this idea is brought to the surface, Ms. Castro then uses turn and talk to give everyone a chance to think about that idea further.

Try It Out!

LESSON: Developing Fraction Sense

You may want to plan your own whole-class discussion that focuses on choosing a computational procedure for a particular computation. The goal is for students to share their reasoning about how they decide which procedure to use. It is important that students understand that the numbers involved in any computation guide the decision-making process. Students will reveal their understanding (or lack thereof) of benchmarks and what are sometimes called "friendly numbers." Keep the following guidelines in mind as you plan for and manage your discussions.

Teaching with the Common Core

4.NF Build fractions from unit fractions by applying and extending previous understandings of operations on whole numbers.

- *Develop a list of computational procedures.* Choose strategies and algorithms that your students have been practicing and label them with names that are familiar to your students.

- *Post a set of three or four computations.* Be sure the list includes at least one computation that lends itself to each strategy posted.

(Continued)

- *Ask students the following question:* Which of our strategies would you use to perform each of these computations? Why?
- *Ask students to discuss these questions with a partner.* As students are talking with their partners, listen for students who talk about using the numbers in a computation to determine which strategy to use. Ask these students to share their ideas later in the whole-class discussion.
- *Begin the whole-class discussion by calling on the students you had previously asked to speak.* Use press for reasoning talk moves to focus the discussion on the importance of choosing a strategy based on the numbers in the computation.
- *Use talk moves such as* Who can repeat? *and* turn and talk *to give other students the opportunity to think about these key ideas.* Then ask, "What do other people think about that?" to open the floor to discussion about alternate strategies.

Example 4.3.2 Use Whole-Class Discussion to Build Number Sense Skills

Placing Fractions on a Number Line (Mrs. Rowan, Grade 6)

As students move into upper elementary grades, their mathematical horizon extends beyond the set of whole numbers to the set of rational numbers. Arithmetic becomes focused on computing and solving problems about fractions, decimals, and percents. Like whole numbers, rational numbers can be represented in many different ways. Although students often think of rational numbers—particularly fractions—as parts of wholes, it is also important that they learn to represent these numbers in other ways too. The number line model, in particular, is a representation of fractions that often receives less attention than other models. Yet, it is important that students make sense of fractions as numbers on a number line and think about moving flexibly between this model and other representations of rational numbers. Students also need to learn that the strategies they use to compare parts of wholes or sets can also be used to locate rational numbers on a number line.

It is also important that students learn to move flexibly between different forms of rational numbers. Rational numbers can be expressed using different notation systems. A rational number—which is defined as a ratio of two integers, a and b, where $b \neq 0$—can be written using fraction notation as $\frac{a}{b}$. Any rational number written in fraction notation also can be rewritten using decimal notation by computing a ÷ b. Finally, rational numbers can be written as percents which are defined as comparisons to one hundred. For example, $\frac{1}{4}$, 0.25, and 25% all represent the same rational number.

Rather than simply converting between forms of rational numbers by rote, students should understand that different forms of rational numbers are better for performing certain comparisons or calculations. Percents may offer an easier way to compare two rational numbers because all percents are comparisons to one hundred. If two or more fractions are rewritten in percent form, students need only compare the values of the percents to determine the greater number. Rewriting fractions as percents, however, is only an effective strategy if students can make the conversions easily. Classroom discussions can be an effective way to develop students' proficiency in moving between these forms of rational numbers.

In one classroom, Mrs. Rowan and her sixth-grade students talk about ways to solve the following number line task.

Which is a better choice, $\frac{3}{5}$ or $\frac{7}{8}$, for the location marked A on the number line?

The first solution method they discuss focuses on using equivalent fractions and fraction comparison strategies to find the label of the unknown location. The second solution strategy focuses on converting fractions to percents. Prior to teaching the lesson, Mrs. Rowan and her students had talked in the past about how to use well-known percents to derive other fraction relationships. For example, students had talked about how to use the equivalent relationship between $\frac{1}{4}$ and 25 percent and the relationship between $\frac{1}{8}$ and $\frac{1}{4}$ to reason that $\frac{1}{8} = 12.5$ percent. She was hoping that students could use these relationships to find the percent equivalent of $\frac{7}{8}$. As students solved the number line task during partner work time, Mrs. Rowan heard several students talking about exactly these types of strategies. She decided to ask these students to articulate their reasoning during the whole-class discussion as a way to help all students develop facility in moving between forms of rational numbers.

Video Clip 4D: Fraction Number Line

1. What fraction skills and strategies do students use to complete this fraction number line task?

2. Describe the strategies that the students use to convert seven-eighths to a percent. What can you glean about their number sense of rational numbers from listening to their explanations?

3. Mrs. Rowan calls on Jaehun to repeat Milo's explanation of how he converted seven-eighths to a percent. Compare Jaehun 's repetition with Milo's original explanation. What do you notice? How might Jaehun's repetition help other students make sense of Milo's thinking?

For more videos from Mrs. Rowan's *Placing Fractions on a Number Line* lesson, see the companion resource *Classroom Discussions in Math: A **Facilitator's Guide** to Support Professional Learning of Discourse and the Common Core.*

BEFORE YOU WATCH THE VIDEO

To make the most productive use of the video clips, you and any colleagues you are working with should take time to read through the "Guidelines for Watching Videos of Teaching" (see page xxi). For demographics, see page xliv.

Try It Out!

LESSON: Placing Fractions on a Number Line

If you try the fraction number line task with your own students, first have students complete the task with a partner. A stumbling block encountered by students is where on the number line to place the number one. Do not show students the location, but instead ask questions such as "If one-fourth is here on the number line, how can you determine where two-fourths or three-fourths or four-fourths should be placed?"

Select students who have used "number sense" to present their strategies for solving the problem. The talk move *Do you agree or disagree . . . and why?* is an especially important one to keep the focus on reasoning.

See the lesson plan *Placing Fractions on a Number Line (Grade 6)* in Appendix B.

Teaching with the Common Core

6.NS Understand a rational number as a point on the number line. Find and position integers and other rational numbers on a number line diagram.

6.NS Apply and extend previous understandings of numbers to the system of rational numbers.

Discussion and Reflection

1. Reread the section on Mrs. DeFreitas's fourth-grade class discussion about the three possible answers to the multiplication problem 18 × 13. She chooses to post the three possible answers using letters. It is also possible to set up a discussion using the student names associated with claims or predictions. Can you think of occasions on which one approach might have clear advantages? When might that approach have disadvantages? How do you decide which one to use?

2. In Suggestion 2 for using whole-class discussion, we made the following claim: "Talking about computational procedures can do more than clarify students' understanding of the ins and outs of those procedures. It may actually promote a more profound understanding of the numbers, properties, and concepts at the heart of those procedures. In other words, at the same time that talk is building facility with procedures, it may deepen conceptual knowledge as well." Consider Ms. Powers's discussion, or others in this chapter. Do you see evidence for our claim? Explain.

3. Sometimes teachers do not want students to discuss errors or misconceptions. What types of errors or misconceptions would you want students to discuss? Why? What type of errors or misconceptions would you rather not discuss? Why?

For professional development sessions and additional
video clips that go with this chapter, see:

*Classroom Discussions in Math: A **Facilitator's Guide**
to Support Professional Learning of Discourse and the
Common Core* (Anderson, Chapin, and O'Connor 2011).

ISBN: 978-1-935099-12-3

About This Chapter

In this chapter we explore the purposes and benefits of talking about solution methods and problem-solving strategies. There are many mathematical situations and questions for which there is not an apparent algorithm or immediate solution; these are referred to as *problems*. When solving problems, students must first make sure they understand the problem situation, then they must develop a plan for the solution process. Next they carry out their plan, and finally they reflect on the solution to make sure it makes sense in terms of the initial question or situation. Talking about the different stages of the problem-solving process can help students understand and solve a wide range of problems. Talking also builds students' confidence in their abilities to approach a new situation and apply what they know to find the solution. The examples in this chapter focus on how talk can be used to assist students in understanding the information in multistep problems, finding solutions to these problems, and expanding students' knowledge of solution methods.

> Talking about the different stages of the problem-solving process can help students understand and solve a wide range of problems.

Why Solution Methods and Problem-Solving Strategies?

Solution methods and problem-solving strategies are good topics for discussions in mathematics classes. To most educators, a "problem" in mathematics is a puzzling yet intriguing situation for which there is no immediate, apparent solution. In other words, when faced with a problem, a student can't immediately call upon a procedure or an algorithm to find the answer. In solving a problem, the solver makes a plan for reaching the solution and then carries out the plan. Talk about solution methods and problem-solving strategies can reveal shallow understanding or holes in previously learned concepts, as well as misconceptions and overgeneralizations that may impede current and future learning. Once these issues are revealed, teachers can make instructional decisions, both immediate and long term, based on students' needs.

> Talk about solution methods and problem-solving strategies can reveal shallow understanding or holes in previously learned concepts, as well as misconceptions and overgeneralizations that may impede current and future learning.

Four Suggestions for Using Whole-Class Discussions in Problem Solving

So how exactly do we use talk to assist students in becoming better problem solvers? Let's say you have this great math problem you want to use in class but are unclear on how to get started. The four suggestions in this chapter give you guidance for what to do in order to facilitate productive whole-class discussions that help students problem solve and grow mathematically.

Four Suggestions for Using Whole-Class Discussions in Problem Solving

1. Use whole-class discussion to understand a problem.
2. Use whole-class discussion to explain one solution method.
3. Use whole-class discussion to extend students' knowledge of problem-solving strategies.
4. Use whole-class discussion to compare solution methods and generalize.

Suggestion 1: Use Whole-Class Discussion to Understand a Problem

Problems pose challenges to students for many different reasons. However, if a student does not understand the information provided, it is extremely difficult to come up with a solution plan. Many novice problem solvers spend little to no time on this critical aspect. Discussions about the givens in a problem can be extremely effective in developing students' abilities to read carefully, to identify the important information in the problem, and to formulate a plan for solving.

Research on problem solving has revealed that good problem solvers spend a lot of time trying to understand a problem and all the relevant relationships, while novices rush to try a plan without really thinking through the plan's effectiveness. Good problem solvers ask themselves key questions about

> Talking about the facts in a problem broadens students' knowledge base, helps them recognize the important information, and is a form of scaffolding for problem solving.

the given and unknown information in the problem. Talking about the facts in a problem broadens students' knowledge base, helps them recognize the important information, and is a form of scaffolding for problem solving. Many students give up early in the problem-solving process because they do not understand the mathematical relationships inherent in the words.

We recommend that at the start of the school year, teachers begin each problem-solving session by conducting a discussion about the givens in the problem. Sometimes this will be a lengthy discussion due to there being complex vocabulary or hard-to-understand relationships in the problem statement. As the year progresses, however, teachers may find that they do not need to discuss the givens in all problems; students' abilities to monitor this stage of the problem-solving process will have improved!

Example 5.1.1 Use Whole-Class Discussion to Understand a Problem

The Pencil Problem (Ms. Dunbar, Grade 4)

Multistep problems can be hard for students! Let's look at how Ms. Dunbar, a fourth-grade teacher, uses discussion to help her students understand the given information in a complicated problem scenario involving multiplication and division. Ms. Dunbar has learned that students often have difficulty identifying the facts and at times cannot even determine the question that is being asked. She has found that the time she has them spend on making sense of the language and constraints in the problem is well worth the investment. With experiences that require them to grapple with problems, students improve their ability to interpret complex texts and ideas.

Let's join Ms. Dunbar in her mathematics class after she posted *The Pencil Problem* (written below) on the board. The following vignette provides a composite example of some of the issues that arise when students talk about a problem's givens, constraints, and goals.

The Pencil Problem

Mrs. Smith has to order pencils for all of the fourth-grade classrooms in the Miller School. Pencils come in packages of 48 pencils each. Mrs. Smith ordered 25 packages. Each of the 6 fourth-grade classes will get the same number of pencils. How many pencils will each class receive? Write a number sentence that represents this problem.

Ms. Dunbar asks students to read the problem silently to themselves, to jot down some of the important facts, and then to talk about what they read with a partner. She tells the class that before they can begin to solve the problem, they first have to make sure that everyone understands the information in the problem and what the question is asking. Following partner talk, Ms. Dunbar initiates a discussion.

1. **Ms. D:** OK. Who can tell us some information about this problem? Missy?

2. **Missy:** This problem is about pencils.

3. **Kenley:** And figuring out how many pencils to give each class.

4. **Ms. D:** What else? Mohammed?

5. **Mohammed:** We have to figure out how many pencils there are altogether. You add or maybe multiply all the numbers.

6. **Ms. D:** I'm not ready yet to figure out what to do to solve the problem. I want to understand all the facts and ideas in the problem first. Can you give me a fact, Mohammed?

7. **Mohammed:** Mrs. Smith has to order pencils for all of the fourth grades in the school.

8. **Ms. D:** Yes, that is a fact. Who can give me another fact? Ellen?

9. **Ellen:** There are forty-eight pencils in one package of pencils.

10. **Ms. D:** Where did you get that information, Ellen? Would you please show us? [Ellen goes to the board and underlines the sentence *Pencils come in packages of 48 pencils each.*] Now everyone turn to your partner and share another fact from the problem.

Ms. Dunbar goes on to elicit information from the students, and she records the relevant facts

> ## MATH TALK TIP
> ### State in Your Own Words
> When starting to discuss a problem, first ask five or so different students to state in their own words what the problem is all about and what question(s) they are trying to answer. Taking the time to do this ensures that everyone understands the relationships inherent in the problem statement and the question being asked; students will then be better prepared to choose a method for solving the problem.

on the board. Once the facts are established—twenty-five packages of pencils ordered, forty-eight pencils per package, six fourth-grade classrooms—Ms. Dunbar asks different students to state in their own words what question they are trying to answer. Why do this? If she takes the time to make sure everyone understands the relationships and the question, she knows that students will be better prepared to choose a method for solving the problem. Likewise, the ensuing discussions will be more valuable since everyone will be on the same page. It also will be easier for her students to represent the problem using a number sentence. Ms. Dunbar first calls on a student she thinks will be able to restate the question correctly, but then she calls on students who she knows are likely to still be confused.

MATH TALK TIP

When a Student Needs Help Answering a Question

Sometimes students are not able to answer a question. What do we do? In Ms. Dunbar's case, she has established a routine that when a student is confused or unable to answer a question for any reason, he or she simply asks for someone to repeat the question, repeat an answer, or repeat some information.

11. **Lily:** We have to figure out how many pencils to give each of the fourth-grade classes.

12. **Ms. D:** Josh, what's this problem asking us to find?

13. **Josh:** I'm not sure.

14. **Ms. D:** OK. What can you do when you're not sure?

15. **Josh:** Ask someone? [Ms. Dunbar nods.] Lily, would you repeat what you just said?

16. **Lily:** We have to figure out how many pencils Mrs. Smith is buying, and then we have to give those pencils out to the fourth-grade classes. It's a bit confusing because there are packages of pencils and these have forty-eight pencils in them. Then we need to find out how many pencils to give to each class. Does that make sense? [Josh nods.]

17. **Ms. D:** Can you put that in your own words, Josh?

18. **Josh:** Mrs. Smith is buying a lot of pencils and we have to find the number. But then the pencils are going to be shared by the fourth-grade classes, so we have to figure out how many each class gets.

19. **Ms. D:** I agree. Andy, will you please underline the words in the problem that tell us one of the facts Josh just shared?

This type of interaction seen in lines 14 through 18 is common in many classrooms that use talk extensively. When students are unclear of how to respond they can ask another student for assistance. This is not looked upon in a negative way; it is simply one of the classroom routines that allows everyone to get some form of support when needed. The important mathematical information is out in the public arena where students can hear it again. Notice that Ms. Dunbar does not chastise Josh for not knowing. Most students are legitimately confused when they say they don't know. They welcome a safe environment where there are ways to get information without feeling inadequate. But in order to use this interchange to help Josh learn, it is important that Ms. Dunbar immediately return to him after he has listened to Lily and ask him to repeat what Lily said. When students know that their teacher will always return to them after a similar exchange, they really concentrate and work hard to understand the material.

> ## MATH TALK TIP
> ### Make Sense of the Problem First
> When having discussions about the givens of a problem, don't be afraid to interrupt students who want to use this time to talk about the solution. Remind them that good problem solvers spend a lot of time making sense of the problem before trying to find its solution, and that you will call on them later when everyone is ready to discuss the solution. Also use the text of the problem to highlight what words and phrases provide important information about the givens and goal.

Try It Out!

LESSON: The Pencil Problem

If you plan to use *The Pencil Problem* with your own students, consider starting your discussion the same way that Ms. Dunbar did. What talk moves will you use to emphasize the relationship between a package of pencils and the number of pencils? What will you do when a student can't answer a question in the discussion?

Teaching with the Common Core

4.OA Use the four operations with whole numbers to solve problems.

Practice 1: Make sense of problems and persevere in solving them.

Example 5.1.2 Use Whole-Class Discussion to Understand a Problem

The Birthday Party Problem (Mrs. Foley, Grade 3)

Let's now examine how another teacher, Mrs. Foley, facilitates a discussion with her third-grade students focused on understanding the givens in a problem. *The Birthday Party Problem* is a multistep problem that involves multiplication and addition with multiple solutions and complex language.

The Birthday Party Problem

Mrs. Foley needs to buy drinks for her daughter's birthday party. She wants to buy both apple juice and grape juice. Cans of apple juice are sold in 6-packs. Cans of grape juice are sold in 4-packs. Mrs. Foley needs to buy at least 26 but no more than 30 cans of juice. How many packs of apple juice might she buy? How many packs of grape juice might she buy? Show or explain how you got your answer.

Did you notice how the problem mentions that apple juice is sold in six-packs? Students need to understand that when they buy apple juice they can buy six cans or multiples of six, but they cannot buy one can of apple juice. Likewise, grape juice is sold in four-packs and can only be purchased in multiples of four. Another feature of this word problem that makes it difficult is the language of *at least twenty-six but no more than thirty cans of juice*. The relationships inherent in this one sentence are complex. It is not obvious to students that the phrase *at least 26* implies 26 cans or more than 26 cans. Many students jump to the conclusion that they can buy 26 or 30 cans. Thus, in the discussion Mrs. Foley is hoping to help students understand that these phrases, in combination, mean that 26, 27, 28, 29, or 30 cans of juice may be purchased.

Take a minute to solve the problem yourself prior to watching the video. Think about which statements and facts from the problem are most important for making sense of the problem. Which relationships are most likely to be overlooked by students? Why?

Video Clip 5A: Solving a Multistep Word Problem, Part 1
(Mrs. Foley, Grade 3)

As you watch the video clip, consider:

1. Which talk moves does Mrs. Foley use to help students understand the statements and facts from the problem?

2. How does Mrs. Foley make sure that students focus on understanding the problem rather than solving the problem?

3. Earlier in the lesson, these students were introduced to using classroom discussions. What norms are already established? What norms would you want to address in future mathematics lessons?

For more videos from Mrs. Foley's *Solving Multistep Word Problems* lesson, see the companion resource *Classroom Discussions in Math: A **Facilitator's Guide** to Support Professional Learning of Discourse and the Common Core.*

BEFORE YOU WATCH THE VIDEO

To make the most productive use of the video clips, you and any colleagues you are working with should take time to read through the "Guidelines for Watching Videos of Teaching" (see page xxi). For demographics, see page xliv.

Try It Out!

LESSON: The Birthday Party Problem

See the lesson plan *The Birthday Party Problem (Grade 3)* in Appendix B.

If you plan to use *The Birthday Party Problem* with your own students, make sure you have first established norms for respectful discourse. Otherwise, you will find it difficult to get students to share when they are confused.

The language used in this problem offers rich fodder for whole-class discussion. For instance, students must pick up the difference between working with packs of juice (six packs

(Continued)

Teaching with the Common Core

3.OA Solve problems involving the four operations, and identify and explain patterns in arithmetic.

and four packs) but at the same time, determine the total number of cans of juice purchased. Use talk moves such as *Who can repeat?* and *What do you think about that?* to give many students the opportunity to talk themselves and hear what others have to say about these ideas. Likewise, *turn and talk* is an effective tool for students to practice their newfound understanding; they can explain the meaning of the different phrases to each other.

Suggestion 2: Use Whole-Class Discussion to Explain One Solution Method

Once students understand the problem, the next part of the discussion may go in a number of directions. For example, if during small-group work as you monitor the groups it becomes clear that most students are not making much headway or could only solve a portion of the problem, then you may want to have a whole-class discussion that focuses on one solution method or strategy. The goal in this case is to help all students understand one solution method and to connect the solution and method to specific mathematical concepts from the problem.

Once the problem solver understands the givens in a problem, the next step is to select a plan for solving the problem. While a plan can draw from many possible strategies, commonly used problem-solving strategies include guessing and checking, looking for a pattern or mathematical structure, using an algorithm, making a list or table, modeling the situation, making a drawing, writing an equation, and solving a simpler problem.

Commonly Used Problem-Solving Strategies

- guessing and checking
- looking for a pattern or mathematical structure
- using an algorithm
- making a list or table
- modeling the situation
- making a drawing
- writing an equation
- solving a simpler problem

Example 5.2.1 Use Whole-Class Discussion to Explain One Solution Method

The Pencil Problem (Ms. Dunbar, Grade 4) (Revisited from 5.1.1)

Now that you have viewed some video footage on using talk to support students' understanding of the givens in a problem, let's revisit Ms. Dunbar's class as she facilitates the next stage of her discussion (Ms. Dunbar's lesson is first introduced on page 154). Having now engaged the class in a common and accurate interpretation of the problem, she is ready to have students implement their strategies. She asks students to work in pairs to solve the problem, and then plans to conduct a whole-class discussion. Her goal is to focus on one solution method that links the number sentence to the operations used. Why focus on only one method? Sometimes it is important to help students connect the constraints in a problem to particular operations. Ms. Dunbar wants her students to be able to explain how they knew to use multiplication and division to solve *The Pencil Problem*. The Common Core State Standards for Mathematics also highlight the importance of helping students connect operations to solution methods when solving problems. "The overwhelming focus of the CCSS in the early grades is arithmetic . . . that includes the concepts underlying arithmetic, the skills of arithmetic computation, and the ability to apply arithmetic to solve problems . . . (K–8 Publishers' Criteria for the Common Core State Standards for Mathematics, 3). Talking about one solution method can assist students in gaining insights into specific mathematical relationships.

> **MATH TALK TIP**
>
> ### Focusing on One Method
>
> Why focus on one method? Sometimes it is important to help students connect the constraints in a problem to particular operations. The Common Core State Standards for Mathematics also highlight the importance of helping students connect operations to solutions methods when solving problems.

Since there are 25 packages of pencils and each package holds 48 pencils, one solution method involves first multiplying 25 by 48 to determine that there are 1200 pencils available for the 6 fourth-grade classes to share equally. Then to find out how many pencils each class receives, the total number of pencils (1200) must be divided by 6.

$$25 \times 48 \div 6 = 200 \qquad \text{Each class will get 200 pencils.}$$

Ms. Dunbar monitors the small-group work and works with Missy and Mel who are confused and will most likely need even more scaffolding in

> **Ms. Dunbar plans to focus the discussion on one solution method and on having students articulate why the solution involves multiplication and division.**

order to understand the solution. She notices that a few pairs, such as Sam and Amanda, solve the problem by multiplying first, then dividing, but are not representing their solution method with an equation. Other pairs are not clear on what operation to use. Since only one pair of students solves the pencil problem by dividing 48 by 6 (to find the number of pencils each class gets from one package) and then multiplying the answer, 8, by 25, for a total of 200 pencils per class, Ms. Dunbar decides not to discuss this method at this point. Instead, she plans to focus the discussion on one solution method and on having students articulate why the solution involves multiplication and division.

Before Ms. Dunbar starts the whole-class discussion, she decides that she will call on Sam and Amanda first since she thinks their method affords most students access to understanding the solution. She plans to call on Missy and Mel to engage them in the solution process. She also hopes to have the class talk about how the equation $(48 \times 25) \div 6 = N$ represents the solution method. Let's join Ms. Dunbar during part of this whole-class discussion.

20. **Ms. D:** Sam and Amanda, could you please explain the method you used to solve the problem?

21. **Amanda:** Sure. First we wanted to find out how many pencils Mrs. Smith ordered. We did twenty-five times forty-eight and got one thousand two hundred.

22. **Ms. D:** What made you decide to multiply twenty-five times forty-eight?

23. **Sam:** Because there are forty-eight pencils in each package and twenty-five packages in all.

24. **Ms. D:** Missy and Mel, can you explain why your classmates multiplied twenty-five times forty-eight?

25. **Missy:** I'm not sure. Can you repeat what you said?

26. **Sam:** It's a faster way to add forty-eight plus forty-eight plus forty-eight twenty-five times.

27. **Amanda:** And multiplication is like taking groups of things. There are twenty-five groups of forty-eight pencils each.

28. **Ms. D:** Missy, would you repeat what Sam or Amanda said?

29. **Missy**: Amanda said that there are groups of forty-eight pencils. Twenty-five groups.

30. **Ms. D**: Missy, what are the groups?

31. **Missy**: The twenty-five packages?

32. **Ms. D**: So Mel, what are in each of these twenty-five groups or packages?

33. **Mel**: Oh, I get it. There are forty-eight pencils in one package and you have twenty-five packages, so you need to multiply.

34. **Ms. D**: [Writes on the board, *25 packages with 48 pencils in each package. 25 × 48.*] Please do the multiplication on your own.

35. **Ms. D**: Josh, what did you get for the answer?

36. **Josh**: One thousand two hundred.

37. **Ms. D**: So now that they know there are one thousand two hundred pencils, who can predict what Sam and Amanda did next? Raphael?

38. **Raphael**: I bet they divided one thousand two hundred by six to get two hundred because we're splitting the pencils equally among six classes.

39. **Ms. D**: Is that what you did? [Sam and Amanda nod.] Yah, we got 200 as the answer. Alex, why do you think Sam and Amanda decided to use division?

40. **Alex**: *Divides* means *sharing*, and that's what we want to do with the pencils: take all those pencils and split or share them between the classes. Each class will get 200.

41. **Ms. D**: Is that how you knew? [Sam and Amanda nod.] Missy, can you repeat what Alex said in your own words?

42. **Missy**: He said that they divided since we're sharing the pencils equally.

43. **Ms. D**: Good. So can anyone write on the board the number sentence that shows the steps we took? Leiha? [Leiha writes *25 × 48 ÷ 6* on the board.]

44. **Ms. D**: Turn to your partner and explain to each other what the numbers twenty-five, forty-eight, and six stand for in the problem. Then explain why we multiplied twenty-five and forty-eight and then divided by six. [Students share with each other for two or three minutes while Ms. Dunbar listens in on many of the conversations.]

45. **Ms. D**: OK, Carla, I heard you and your partner describing very clearly how the numbers and operations connect to the words in the problem. Would you share it with us?

> **FOUR STEPS...**
>
> Asking students to restate or repeat each other's ideas supports Step 2: Helping Students Orient to the Thinking of Others (see "Four Steps Toward Productive Talk," Chapter 1, page 10).

In this part of the whole-class discussion, Ms. Dunbar uses talk moves to help students orient toward and engage with each other's reasoning. Notice that Ms. Dunbar asks students who are confused to restate and explain other students' explanations of their effective method. She also asks students to explain the meaning of the two operations. Her hope is that they will connect grouping with multiplication and equal sharing with division.

Ms. Dunbar also asked students to predict what came next in solving the problem. When she did this, she checked back with the original speakers to see whether the prediction was accurate. As a result, many students who had not solved the problem or who had made mistakes were able to make progress in their understanding of the problem and this first solution method. Finally, Ms. Dunbar made sure every student in the classroom had an opportunity to articulate how the words and numbers were connected, as they reviewed one last time the first solution method. Ms. Dunbar's next step will be to call on Robin and Keisha to explain their method of determining the number of pencils per class since they divided first ($48 \div 6 \times 25$).

Try It Out!

LESSON: The Pencil Problem

If you use this problem with your students, monitor the small-group work so you are aware of the different strategies. Consider only discussing one strategy and connecting the strategy to specific operations and the symbols that represent those operations. If your students are ready to discuss a variety of approaches, consider the order of presentations—who will you have share first, second, and so on.

Partner talk is a powerful way for every student in your class to summarize a solution method or strategy. Ask students, as Ms. Dunbar did, to explain the solution to each other, connect symbols and words, and to help each other use correct vocabulary.

Teaching with the Common Core

Practice 3: Construct viable arguments and critique the reasoning of others.

Example 5.2.2 Use Whole-Class Discussion to Explain One Solution Method

The Birthday Party Problem (Mrs. Foley, Grade 3) (Revisited from 5.1.2)

When conducting a discussion about one student's solution method, manage the discussion so that it helps other students engage with their classmate's reasoning. The *Who can say that again?* and *turn and talk* moves are very effective. It is particularly important that you use these moves to help students link the solution method to the underlying concepts. For instance, in Mrs. Foley's class during *The Birthday Party Problem* (see page 158), the teacher used talk moves to focus students' attention on the relationship between the multiplication equations in the solution method to the concept of putting equal groups of juice together. In other words, the point of all of the repeating is for students to think, "Oh, I get it. I can use multiplication to figure out the number of cans of each type of juice."

Let's revisit Mrs. Foley's class to see how they are doing with *The Birthday Party Problem.* When we rejoin the lesson, students are sharing their solution methods. There are six possible solutions to this problem:

> ## MATH TALK TIP
> ### Engage Everyone!
> When conducting a discussion about one student's solution method, manage the discussion so that it helps other students engage with their classmate's reasoning. Sometimes teachers ask everyone to turn and talk and explain, in their own words, the reasoning of another student who just presented. Have the original student be a "helper" to pairs that express confusion about the solution method.

1.

Apple	Grape
1 pack	6 packs
6 cans	24 cans
Total: 30 cans	

2.

Apple	Grape
1 pack	5 packs
6 cans	20 cans
Total: 26 cans	

3.

Apple	Grape
2 packs	4 packs
12 cans	16 cans
Total: 28 cans	

4.

Apple	Grape
3 packs	2 packs
18 cans	8 cans
Total: 26 cans	

5.

Apple	Grape
3 packs	3 packs
18 cans	12 cans
Total: 30 cans	

6.

Apple	Grape
4 packs	1 pack
24 cans	4 cans
Total: 28 cans	

In the video clip, Mrs. Foley is working on having students explain one solution and how they calculated that specific answer. She does not attempt to get all possible solutions on the table at this stage nor is she interested in having students discuss how they know they have all of the solutions. These are important goals for another class once everyone understands the problem. In this clip, Mrs. Foley wants students to be able to articulate why it makes sense to use multiplication and addition to solve it—using one solution.

How does Mrs. Foley keep the focus on these relationships? Her third graders are bound to use a range of methods—some more sophisticated than others. For example, you will see how one student (Alexia) explains she calculated $(10 \times 2) + 6 + 4$. Her strategy works because she put one pack of apple juice and one pack of grape juice together for a total of ten cans. She then doubles this number and continues to add six (pack of apple juice) and four (pack of grape juice) until she has thirty cans (which fits the restrictions of the problem). Mrs. Foley does not explore this method in this video clip but makes a mental note to return to it later. Instead she consistently asks students to repeat the parts of a solution where they must think about the packs versus the cans of juice to highlight the role of multiplication. Namely, if they have three packs of apple juice there are eighteen cans (3×6), but if they have three packs of grape juice there are only twelve cans (3×4).

Video Clip 5B: Solving a Multistep Word Problem, Part 2

As you watch the video clip, consider:

1. When a student is unable to repeat another student's idea, Mrs. Foley asks the first student to repeat his idea again in smaller parts. She then asks the other student to repeat each part. Why do this? What is the second student able to do at the end of the interchange?

2. How does Mrs. Foley make sure that students are differentiating between the number of packs and number of cans? What talk moves does she use?

3. When in the video clip does Mrs. Foley ask students to turn and talk to their partners? For what purpose is Mrs. Foley using this talk move?

For more videos from Mrs. Foley's *Solving Multistep Word Problems* lesson, see the companion resource *Classroom Discussions in Math: A **Facilitator's Guide** to Support Professional Learning of Discourse and the Common Core.*

BEFORE YOU WATCH THE VIDEO

To make the most productive use of the video clips, you and any colleagues you are working with should take time to read through the "Guidelines for Watching Videos of Teaching" (see page xxi). For demographics, see page xliv.

MATH TALK TIP

Adding On

The talk move *Who can add on?* can be used to include more students in the conversation. When asked to add on, students sometimes explain in more detail a relationship or calculation. Other times they use different words and phrases to explain the same procedure. The retelling of key points helps the speaker clarify his or her understanding of the solution method and often resonates with other students who need to hear the explanation more than once. This talk move supports Step 4: Helping Students Engage with the Reasoning of Others (see "Four Steps Toward Productive Talk," Chapter 1, page 10).

Try It Out!

LESSON: The Birthday Party Problem

See the lesson plan *The Birthday Party Problem* (Grade 3) in Appendix B.

Depending on the prior knowledge of your students, you too might want to focus the discussion of *The Birthday Party Problem* on one solution and how multiplication is used to find that solution. Remember to ask students how they used the facts in the problem to determine the number of cans. If you wish to have students find all six solutions, plan on taking two class periods for the discussion. The second class period can look more broadly at determining if all solutions have been found. This second discussion might begin by systematically assigning a number of packs of apple juice (for example, one, two, three, or four) and then seeing what options for grape juice fit the criteria.

Teaching with the Common Core

Practice 1: Make sense of problems and persevere in solving them.

Practice 2: Reason abstractly and quantitatively.

Practice 3: Construct viable arguments and critique the reasoning of others.

Suggestion 3: Use Whole-Class Discussion to Extend Students' Knowledge of Problem-Solving Strategies

Often students solve problems in ways that do not use the mathematics that you as the teacher hoped would be the focus of the discussion. For example, young students often persist in using addition when a problem could be solved using multiplication. Or students use very informal counting methods

> While informal strategies are important starting points for making sense of a problem, one of the responsibilities of a teacher is to support students in learning and then using more sophisticated strategies.

instead of computations. While informal strategies are important starting points for making sense of a problem, one of the responsibilities of a teacher is to support students in learning and then using more sophisticated strategies. One way to accomplish this goal is to use a whole-class discussion to introduce and explore a more sophisticated approach. Students can then be asked to practice the strategy by applying it to a similar problem. A discussion about more advanced or abstract approaches often follows a discussion about a particular solution strategy.

Learning about different problem-solving strategies has the potential to extend students' knowledge and understanding. Sharing strategies during a discussion, however, is only the start. In order for students to make a new or more sophisticated strategy their own, they have to understand it and practice it.

Example 5.3.1 Use Whole-Class Discussion to Extend Students' Knowledge of Problem-Solving Strategies

The Coin Problem (Mr. Cooper, Grade 3)

Mr. Cooper, a third-grade teacher, passed out the following problem:

The Coin Problem

The juice machine only takes quarters, dimes, and nickels. List all possible coin combinations you can use to buy a box of juice that costs 35¢.

Mr. Cooper gave the students time to work on the problem individually, and then he had them work with a partner to compare combinations. For some students he reduced the complexity of the problem by asking them to list all the combinations that make twenty-five cents (there are fewer combinations of quarters, dimes, and nickels that can be used to make twenty-five cents). One strategy that can be used to solve this problem is to make an organized list of possibilities. However, Mr. Cooper doesn't show the students how to organize the data. He wants them to come up with a way to organize their lists, regardless of the number of cents being explored. Finally, he pulls the class together to talk as a group about their solutions. We are entering the discussion toward the end. Many students have been posting possible combinations that total twenty-five cents on the board. One student, Jaire, has found some possible answers but is missing many.

1. **Mr. C:** Jaire, could you tell us how you solved this problem?

2. **Jaire:** I wrote things here on my paper. I know that a quarter and a dime is thirty-five cents, then three dimes and a nickel is thirty-five cents, then you can also get it with seven nickels. [Mr. C writes the combinations on the board.]

Combinations that add to 35 cents

25 + 10

10 + 10 + 10 + 5

5 + 5 + 5 + 5 + 5 + 5 + 5

3. **Mr. C:** We've talked a lot about how important it is to look back at your work when you think you have found a solution. How did you check your work?

4. **Jaire:** I checked and each one added to thirty-five cents. So I knew I got it right.

5. **Mr. C:** Jaire has a list of some different coin combinations. He has checked to make sure that each one adds to thirty-five cents. Who would like to respond to Jaire's work? Rebecca?

6. **Rebecca:** I have three that aren't on your list.

7. **Mr. C:** Rebecca, can you give some advice to Jaire on what he can do to find these other combinations?

8. **Rebecca:** Well, I wrote at the top of the page twenty-five cents, ten cents, and five cents. Then I put a one under twenty-five and a one under the ten. Then I wrote all of the ones that used dimes next. That way I wouldn't skip any.

9. **Mr. C:** Rebecca, can you put your work under the document camera for us all to see? Would you point to the places where you organized the information? [Rebecca shares her chart and what the numbers mean.]

25¢	10¢	5¢
1	1	
1		2
	3	1
	2	3

FOUR STEPS...

Asking students to explain their thinking aloud and pressing them to provide evidence supports Step 1: Helping Individual Students Clarify and Share Their Own Thoughts and Step 3: Helping Students Deepen Their Own Reasoning (see "Four Steps Toward Productive Talk," Chapter 1, page 10).

10. **Mr. C:** I see you started with a quarter. But how do you know you have all of the combinations of coins that go with the quarter?

11. **Rebecca:** I used one quarter so that leaves ten cents. So then I said, "How can I get ten cents?" See here it is one dime, and here it is two nickels.

12. **Mr. C:** So then what did you do?

13. **Rebecca:** See here is dimes. I can have three dimes and one nickel or two dimes and three nickels . . . .

14. **Mr. C:** Does anyone else have advice for Jaire? Louie?

15. **Louie:** Well, it's still a T-chart and it kind of goes in order like Rebecca's, but I started with the way to use the smallest number of coins, which was one quarter and one dime. Then I kept the quarter and changed the dime to two nickels. I kept doing that, changing from only a few coins to more. See [points to his sheet], I got the nickel here.

16. **Mr. C:** Louie, come show us your work. Talk us through this idea of changing to more coins.

17. **Louie:** [Louie talks through his list of possibilities.]

18. **Mr. C:** How many people think they have every single possible combination? OK, I can see that most people think they might have missed a few. Let's see if we can make our T-charts more complete. Everyone work with your partner to use one of the methods to find all the combinations. Let's practice being systematic, listing all the possibilities. Jaire, which suggestion of your classmates do you plan to try?

19. **Jaire:** I'll try the one that starts with a quarter.

> As students talk about solving problems, they become more aware of their own understanding and can better monitor their own strategies and solutions. This kind of self-monitoring is sometimes referred to as a *metacognitive* activity.

As students talk about solving problems, they become more aware of their own understanding and can better monitor their own strategies and solutions. Monitoring your understanding of a topic calls for reflecting on what you do and do not understand. This kind of self-monitoring is sometimes referred to as a *metacognitive* activity. We have found that the process of explaining one's thinking aloud assists students in clarifying their own ideas and can help them correct their own mistakes, especially when teachers and classmates ask probing questions. The goal is for students eventually to monitor their own comprehension and ask themselves questions that will help them modify and refine their thinking. However, for many students, this is a learned behavior. Talk provides one methodology to support the development of a reflective response to problem solving.

Instead of using the discussion to reveal to Jaire the missing coin combinations, Mr. Cooper used it to support thoughtful reflection about the overall process. He knew that many students, like Jaire, probably had missed some combinations through lack of a systematic strategy. Therefore, he took the time to have two students talk through their systematic approach for finding all the combinations. But the more important instructional decision was in line 18. Here Mr. Cooper asks students to go back to the problem and solve it using the organizational methods suggested by Rebecca and Louie. As a result, Jaire and others are getting practice in systematic listing. Mr. Cooper plans to ask everyone to solve a similar problem of finding combinations of dimes, nickels, and pennies to make twenty cents. He is going to require everyone to fill in a chart labeled with ten cents, five cents, and one cent. We believe that students improve their ability to choose an appropriate strategy after they have had opportunities to learn about and practice new strategies. Mr. Cooper consistently asks his students the following questions.

Questions to Support the Learning of New Strategies

- Why did you choose this strategy or representation?
- Did you consider any others? Which ones?
- Why did you consider those?
- How can you show the relationships in the problem?
- When have we used this strategy before?
- Why does it make sense to use the same strategy on these problems?
- Can you think of other problems where using this strategy would be appropriate?
- Can you represent the problem in a different way?
- Does your answer make sense? Does it answer the question?

Try It Out!

LESSON: The Coin Problem

If you try *The Coin Problem* with your students, give them time to work in small groups before discussing their strategies as a class. Observe the strategies they are using to solve the problem and use this information to decide who you will call on during the whole-class discussion. After students talk about their strategies as a whole class, use the small-group format again so that students can try out and learn from each other's strategies.

Teaching with the Common Core

3.OA Represent and solve problems involving multiplication and division.

Suggestion 4: Use Whole-Class Discussion to Compare Solution Methods and Generalize

In some discussions, you want to focus on helping students connect solution methods so that certain key ideas get "lifted out" of all of the methods. The goal is for students to generalize these big ideas and articulate how they are manifested in a variety of representations such as pictures, equations, and tables. For instance, if most students agree upon the correct answer, there is limited value in discussing "OK, how did you get your answer?" Instead, a whole-class discussion that focuses on how various solution methods are alike and how they are different can support students in reflecting on the different approaches and help them to generalize about the overarching concepts.

> **MATH TALK TIP**
>
> **Equivalent Expressions**
> Some teachers find it is useful to make a chart on the board to record similarities and differences between methods. It is especially important to show symbolically the equivalent expressions, and with older students, how mathematically one expression is equal to another.

Many problem-solving methods involve representing a mathematical idea or relationship in a different form. Representations are tools that help us record and work with our mathematical ideas, communicate our thoughts to others, and clarify our own understanding. Students in the elementary and middle grades use a variety of forms of representation to record and communicate their solution methods: symbols, drawings and pictures, tables and charts, physical materials, graphs, models, and oral and written language. Some representations are conventions that are well known and accepted throughout the mathematics community such as the addition, subtraction, multiplication, and division symbols we use to represent arithmetic operations (for example, +, -, ×, and ÷). Students should be able to understand these and connect them to other conventional representations. For example, students might explain the multiplication 3×4 using an array, a number line, or repeated addition. Likewise, a division equation such as $8 \div 2$ can be represented with fractional notation ($\frac{8}{2}$), with a picture of eight objects partitioned into two groups, and with a story problem about distributing eight cookies equally into two bags.

One of the reasons it is important to talk about representations is that the same problem-solving method can be represented in more than one way. For example, adding two-digit numbers by counting groups of tens and then ones can be shown using an equation, groups of base ten blocks, and a drawing of "sticks" and ones. As students try to make sense of problems, concepts, and procedures, some may use representations that are idiosyncratic. These may be temporary processes that a student abandons over time. Thus, it is not essential for everyone in the class to discuss or experience these kinds of representations. In fact, these are the representations *not* to discuss since they rarely help students generalize the important ideas. For example, Doug, a second grader, adds a column of two-digit numbers using a method of counting tens and then counting ones. He represents his method by first looking at the tens column and recording one X on his paper for each group of ten. He then counts the number of Xs and records that numeral in the tens column. He next makes checkmarks for the ones and counts them before recording the numeral. Sometimes he has to adjust the numeral he writes in the tens column if there are enough ones to make another ten. Doug's use of Xs and checkmarks is a nonstandard way to keep track of the number of tens and ones.

$$\begin{array}{r} 23 \\ 14 \\ +31 \\ \hline 68 \end{array} \qquad \begin{array}{l} X\ X\ X\ X\ X\ X \\ \checkmark\ \checkmark\ \checkmark\ \checkmark\ \checkmark\ \checkmark\ \checkmark \end{array}$$

While this notation is helpful to Doug, it creates an unnecessary extra step for other students. While Doug's teacher wants him to rely on the method of adding by counting tens and then counting ones, she would like to help him move away from representing this method using Xs and checkmarks. She asks

> Teachers must consider which methods and representations are worth sharing with the whole class, and in what order they should be shared during problem-solving discussions. Not all methods are created equal!

> We want students to be able to understand and explain the connections among methods that use a variety of representations. This is a key component of becoming mathematically proficient as outlined by the *Common Core State Standards for Mathematics*.

students who are solving problems using groups of tens and ones to share how they are using these ideas. In summary, teachers must consider which methods and representations are worth sharing with the whole class, and in what order they should be shared during problem-solving discussions. Not all methods are created equal!

Since it is likely that students will use a variety of methods in any problem-solving situation, it's important for teachers to maintain a consistent focus on the meaning of what they did and how they represented the ideas. Our goal is for students to be able to understand and explain the mathematical meaning of each part of different symbolic, graphic, or language-based representations of a problem. Furthermore, we want students to be able to understand and explain the connections among methods that use a variety of representations. This is a key component of becoming mathematically proficient as outlined by the Common Core State Standards for Mathematics:

Mathematically proficient students can explain correspondences between equations, verbal descriptions, tables, and graphs or draw diagrams of important features and relationships, graph data, and search for regularity or trends. Younger students might rely on using concrete objects or pictures to help conceptualize and solve a problem. Mathematically proficient students check their answers to problems using a different method, and they continually ask themselves, "Does this make sense?" They can understand the approaches of others to solving complex problems and identify correspondences between different approaches. (CCSS, 6)

The CCSS highlight the need for students to communicate what they understand about the relationships inherent in problems and how different methods are connected. In kindergarten, this might involve a student being able to explain that each dot in a diagram stands for one piece of candy that the children in a math problem got from their parents, and that the number 4 stands for four dots, which indicates four pieces of candy. In the sixth grade, this might involve students being able to explain that a ratio of two portions of lemon juice to one portion of sugar in a lemonade concentrate can be symbolized as 2:1, or $\frac{2}{1}$, and can be shown using a bar diagram where one bar is twice as long as the other.

Sometimes during discussions, teachers ask many students to share their solution methods and representations. The focus is simply on reporting what one did to solve a problem and sharing as many different methods as possible. In general, this emphasis rarely leads to deeper understanding unless the discussion directly connects the methods and highlights the underlying mathematical ideas. Often students do not grasp how different methods are similar; they do not see the connections on their own. Connecting methods and helping students generalize, however, is not simple. For one, students do not always understand various forms of representation used by their classmates. For example, even though one student uses base ten blocks to solve a problem, we should not assume that all students firmly grasp the structure of the base-ten system from the materials and follow the solution method. Second, students sometimes focus on the surface features of representations (for example, pictures look different than numbers) and ignore their conceptual underpinnings. Classroom talk can help students transform their understanding of that representation and see its potential in the solution but this requires the teacher to ask questions such as, "How are the groups of tens shown with the blocks? What happens when you have more than ten groups of ten?" and to directly connect the blocks to symbols, "How is what Peggy did to add using the base ten blocks shown with numbers? Let's look at the computation on the board." Even when students understand what blocks or other representations are meant to indicate, it takes a long time for students to learn to interpret and link the symbols, pictures, models, and the linguistic expressions that describe them. Here, talk can be used productively to get students to ask questions about what these forms of representation mean, and how their meanings are connected.

> Sometimes during discussions, teachers ask many students to share their solution methods and representations. The focus is simply on reporting what one did to solve a problem and sharing as many different methods as possible. In general, this emphasis rarely leads to deeper understanding unless the discussion directly connects the methods and highlights the underlying mathematical ideas.

> Talk can be used productively to get students to ask questions about what these forms of representation mean, and how their meanings are connected.

Example 5.4.1 Use Whole-Class Discussion to Compare Solution Methods and Generalize

The Field Trip Problem (Mr. Evans, Grade 1)

Let's examine how a teacher can use a discussion about a problem on addends to compare students' solution methods and help students link different representations to number concepts. Mr. Evans is a first-grade teacher. His students have been working on adding and subtracting within twenty. One purpose of his lesson is to examine the different addends that make ten. But it is also to help students generalize how they can use a drawing to solve addition problems. Mr. Evans wants to start building common knowledge of this strategy so that in the future, when a student says, "I drew a picture," the other students know that this is an accepted strategy. A final goal for the lesson is to assist students in understanding how relationships can be represented in drawings and tables. He wants to connect the different representations in the hopes of deepening their understanding of addends. Learning how to make sense of different representations will support students' understanding and is an important CCSS mathematical practice. Mr. Evans knows that this is just the introduction to this practice; he will repeatedly need to ask students to talk about how they interpret different representations.

To start the lesson, Mr. Evans reads *The Field Trip Problem* to his students. He passes out paper and pencils to the students and reminds them that they can also use materials from the classroom's math center (for example, teddy bear counters) to solve the problem. He first asks students to solve the problem with their math partners and then he conducts a whole-class discussion of students' solutions.

The Field Trip Problem

Ten students are going to the zoo with Mr. Evans and Ms. Zito, another teacher. The children have to be with one of the teachers at all times. How many children can be in each of the two groups?

1. **Mr. E:** Who would like to tell us how they solved this problem? Robin? What did you and your partner, David, do?
2. **Robin:** We drew a picture. [Robin holds up her picture for others to see (see Figure 5.1).] This one shows five and five [points to the two equal

groups], and here is one student and the other nine [points to the second grouping]. This one has six friends together and one, two, three, four, four in this group. Here is three and seven, and over here is a group with eight kids and another one with two kids. There are a lot of ways to put the children.

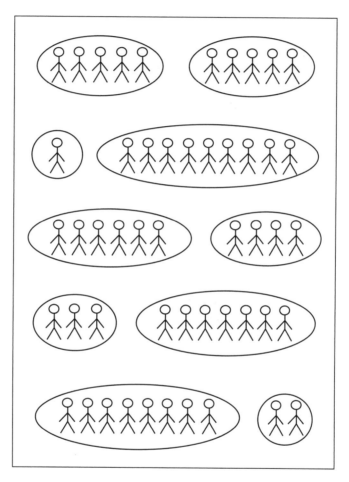

Figure 1.1 Robin's drawing of the different ways in which ten friends can be configured into two groups.

3. **David:** I think we forgot one. Everybody could be in Mr. Evans's group and no one could go with Ms. Zito.

4. **Mr. E:** Drawing a picture is a good problem-solving strategy. Talk to your partner about what Robin and David's picture means. Then in

a few minutes I'd like Pedro and Briana and Suman and Josh to come up together and tell us in their own words about Robin and David's drawing.

5. **Pedro and Briana:** This circle is one kid—see how it looks like a person? And this circle is for nine kids. That doesn't seem very fair. The nine kids are really squashed. Our picture is different. We didn't put arms and legs on people, just heads.

6. **Suman and Josh:** Each of these [points to one of the circles of students on Robin's paper] is the students that go with one teacher, and these are the circles that go with the other teacher. There are eight students here and two students here. That makes ten.

7. **Mr. E:** How do you know which circles go together to make ten?

8. **David:** Ours are next to each other.

9. **Josh:** See we have lines connecting them [holds up his and Suman's picture].

10. **Pedro:** I can't tell. Let me count.

11. **Briana:** No, don't do that. Remember we put *E* for Mr. Evans and *Z* for Ms. Zito. See here. [Briana points to one circle with three marks and an *E* and another circle with five marks and a *Z*. She does not seem to recognize that these two circles don't account for all ten students.]

Mr. Evans next asks other students to comment on what the pictures show or to share their own pictures. He is using the talk move of adding on to further participation in the discussion because young children need to share their unique experiences. But at the same time, Mr. Evans is also trying to help them generalize about how pictures can be used to solve problems and that everyone's pictures do not need to be identical. He holds off talking about the addends until he feels that everyone in his class understands the pictures.

12. **Mr. E:** So one way to decide how to put the students with the two teachers is to arrange the students in a drawing. Now let's use the pictures to help us write down the number of students that will go with each teacher. [Mr. Evans draws and labels a T-chart on the board.]

Mr. Evans's group   Ms. Zito's group

13. **Robin:** We started by putting five in one group and five in another. Then we did it again.

14. **Mr. E:** I'm going to record five in each group on the board. But I'm not sure what you mean by "did it again." David, can you tell us more about that?

FOUR STEPS...

Students often clarify their statements when asked to "tell us more." This supports Step 1: Helping Individual Students Clarify and Share Their Own Thoughts (see "Four Steps Toward Productive Talk," Chapter 1, page 10).

Mr. Evans's group	Ms. Zito's group
5	5

15. **David:** Like, we made a circle with one person and the other group with nine. We just kept thinking about how to put the students with the teachers. We got six and four, three and seven, and eight and two. [Mr. Evans records the numbers.]

Mr. Evans's group	Ms. Zito's group
5	5
1	9
6	4
3	7
8	2

16. **Mr. E:** How did you know when you had found all of the different ways to place the ten students into two groups?

17. **Robin:** We just thought we were done.

18. **Mr. E:** Everyone who drew a picture, please look at it. Are there other ways to arrange the ten students into the two teacher groups?

Mr. Evans continued to collect data from the students. Some students mentioned number pairs that were already recorded, but others noticed that some of the pairs could be turned around. For example, Mr. Evans could have two students and Ms. Zito could have eight students. When no one mentions zero, Mr. Evans asks, "What if no one was in my group? How many students would be in Ms. Zito's group?" He plays an informal game with the class, picking one number in a row (for example, three) and asking what number goes with it to make ten (for example, seven).

Earlier, Mr. Evans noticed that Anthony and Nina made an organized list of addends. So he asks them to explain their strategy to the class.

19. **Mr. E:** Anthony and Nina, would you tell us how you solved this problem?

20. **Anthony:** We just wrote numbers. I wrote one and nine, then two and eight, three and seven, and I saw a pattern. One line was going up and

the other was going down. [Mr. Evans makes a new T-chart on the board next to the other one and fills it in systematically.]

Mr. Evans's group	Ms. Zito's group
1	9
2	8
3	7
4	6
5	5
6	4
7	3
8	2
9	1
10	0

21. **Mr. E:** Am I filling in this chart so it looks like how you wrote the numbers? [Anthony and Nina nod.]

22. **Mr. E:** Let's look at this chart. Who thinks they can explain what Anthony means when he says that one line is going up and the other is going down? Lindsey?

23. **Lindsey:** He means, like, in the picture, every time another person gets taken out, the other group gets one more and the other group is one less.

24. **Byran:** One number is counting up, and the other number is counting backward—nine, eight, seven, six, five, four, three, two, one, zero, blast off!

25. **Mr. E:** Anthony, is that what you mean? [Anthony nods.] So Nina, how does this pattern help you figure out how to arrange the ten students into the two teacher groups?

26. **Nina:** We just followed the pattern. After five and five then comes six and four and then seven and three.

27. **Mr. E:** Does this table show the same information as the pictures?

28. **Karla:** Yes. Like with my picture. One goes with nine, two goes with eight, three goes with seven. [Karla holds her picture up and points where she has groups of 1 and 9 and 2 and 8.]

29. **Mr. E:** I'm a little confused by how these can be the same. Turn and talk to your partner about how the table and the pictures show the same information. [Two minute elapse.]

30. **Mr. E:** OK, I need a pair to share with us.

Did you notice how Mr. Evans deliberately asked students to connect the picture and the table? Because this is an important idea, he asked everyone to talk about it to his or her partner. By listening to the conversations, Mr. Evans will have a better sense of how many students see the connection between the representations.

You might wonder why Mr. Evans did not pursue Robin's statement that "we just thought we were done" in response to his question about knowing when she had all of the pairs. Or why he didn't pursue the fact that Anthony and Nina missed forming a pair with zero and ten. There is a lot going on in every discussion. It is not easy in the middle of a discussion to respond to all comments. But because the discussion occurred, Mr. Evans knows that students need more experiences with zero and organizing data. He will be able to return to these ideas in future lessons.

MATH TALK TIP

Turn and Talk

Use the *turn and talk* talk move to support students in making sense of the material. This move helps keep all students engaged, not just the brightest ones. As students work, make note of students' solution methods and decide which you will ask students to share with the class. One approach is to choose one or two methods that use different representations that you think are most important for all students to master (like Mr. Evans did with the pictures and the table). If the representation is new to students, be sure to ask many students to explain the drawings, models, or symbols and what the representation tells them. Then be sure to ask questions that require students to try to understand the other method/representation and how that method also shows or explains the mathematics.

Try It Out!

LESSON: The Field Trip Problem

Use ideas from *The Field Trip Problem* vignette to help you plan a whole-class discussion on helping students' understand how different representations can show the same information. Connecting methods and generalizing the important ideas should be your goal.

When solving problems on their own, students do not always think about the givens in the problem as they carry out the problem-solving process. Instead they think that getting an answer, any answer, is the primary goal! Working with students to develop their abilities to reflect on the problem-solving process and to think about the reasonableness of their answers takes time. Students may

(Continued)

Teaching with the Common Core

1.OA Represent and solve problems using addition and subtraction.

1.OA Add and subtract within 20.

Practice 5: Use appropriate tools strategically.

not be aware of the mathematical connections among problems. When asked to consider such connections, however, students can do this well.

> Having the chance to generalize solution methods and problem-solving strategies, and to discuss connections among problems, helps students avoid using a method or strategy when it is not appropriate.

The implications for learning can be profound. Generalizing about a specific approach enables students to figure out whether this approach is appropriate when presented with a new problem. Having the chance to generalize solution methods and problem-solving strategies, and to discuss connections among problems, helps students avoid using a method or strategy when it is not appropriate. When students are taught to use a method or strategy without discussing why and when to use it, they may be less successful in applying that tool in sensible ways when confronted with new problems.

Example 5.4.2 Use Whole-Class Discussion to Compare Solution Methods and Generalize

The Newspaper Club Problem (Ms. Fournier, Grade 6)

Let's examine how Ms. Fournier uses discussion to help her students generalize about the solutions of missing value ratio problems. Ms. Fournier posted the following problem on the board. She asked students to solve the problem in groups of three to four before conducting a whole-class discussion of their ideas.

The Newspaper Club Problem

The ratio of boys to girls in a school newspaper club is 1 to 3. There are 5 boys in the newspaper club. How many girls are there? Solve this problem in two different ways.

For more information about using math talk to help students make sense of ratio, see Chapter 7.

Prior to this lesson, students in Ms. Fournier's class had talked about ratio as a comparison of two quantities. They talked about the similarities and differences between part-to-part and part-to-whole ratios and practiced using the language of ratios to read and interpret a variety of examples.

Ms. Fournier planned to focus her instruction next on solving missing value ratio problems. In these problems, students are presented with two quantities that together form one ratio. They are also given the value of one quantity in an equivalent ratio and asked to find the value of the missing quantity that would make the two ratios equivalent. A key idea that students must consider when they solve these kinds of problems is that both quantities in a ratio must be multiplied by the same factor in order to create an equivalent ratio.

As she planned her lesson on *The Newspaper Club Problem*, Ms. Fournier thought about the different ways that the students in her class might solve this problem. These strategies included using pictures, diagrams, and equations to represent the multiplicative relationships in the problem and find the missing value. As students worked in groups, Ms. Fournier looked for students who were using each of these strategies. Ms. Fournier also noticed that most of the students in the class were successful using at least one of these strategies to solve the problem and she asked several students to post their strategies on the board. But as she called the students back together for a whole-class discussion, she decided not to focus this discussion on each individual solution strategy. Instead, she chose to discuss what all three strategies had in common in order to help her students generalize about characteristics of equivalent ratios. Namely, she wanted students to focus on the idea that both quantities in a ratio must be multiplied by the same factor in order to create an equivalent ratio. In the first part of the whole-class discussion, she focuses students' attention on the fact that all three strategies make use of the operation of multiplication. Then, she asks all students to turn and talk with the people at their tables to explore this idea in greater depth. When the whole-class discussion resumes, the discussion focuses on the idea that since one number in the ratio has been multiplied by five, the other number in the ratio must also be multiplied by five.

> " Ms. Fournier chose to discuss what all three strategies had in common in order to help her students generalize about characteristics of equivalent ratios. "

MATH TALK TIP

Using Student Work in Whole-Class Discussions

Asking students to post their work before the whole-class discussion begins not only saves valuable class time but also uses students' own ideas as models that can generate new understandings for the entire class. An alternative strategy is to choose the student work you will post before the lesson begins. Examine a set of homework or class work papers, looking for examples of strategies, concepts, or solution methods that you want to discuss. Depending on the goals and needs of your students, you may decide to post an exact replica of a piece of student work or a re-creation of it. If you choose to make a re-creation, don't be afraid to enlarge or refine drawings, number lines, or equations so that the work is clear enough for the other students to follow.

Video Clip 5C: The Newspaper Club Problem

As you watch the clip, consider:

1. Which talk moves does Ms. Fournier use to help students connect the three strategies for solving the ratio problem?

2. Describe Ms. Fournier's use of *turn and talk* in this clip. Which of the four goals of productive math talk might she be working toward when she uses this move?

Try It Out!

LESSON: The Newspaper Club Problem

If you plan to use *The Newspaper Club Problem* with your own students, consider managing your discussion the same way that Ms. Fournier did. Begin by asking students to solve this problem in small groups. As they work, make note of students who are using different types of strategies. Ask these students to post their work where everyone can see it. Focus on the whole-class discussion of the question, "What do all of the strategies have in common?"

CCSS

Teaching with the Common Core

6.RP Understand ratio concepts and use ratio reasoning to solve problems.

Discussion and Reflection

1. Make a list of some problem-solving strategies you think are most important for students at your grade level to be able to use (for example, draw a picture, use a table, use an equation, model with real objects, guess and check). Write or find a mathematics problem that uses the math you are currently teaching and can be solved using more than one strategy. Design a talk lesson around this problem. See Chapter 8 for planning suggestions.

2. Classroom discussions can be formulated around the four types of discussions presented at the beginning of this chapter. Do you think the emphasis of discussions should equally address all four types? How do you decide what type of problem-solving discussion to facilitate? What might affect the emphasis?

3. In Suggestion 4 in this chapter, we examined how representations can be powerful tools for mathematical thinking. Give an example from your own teaching or this chapter in which a representation (for example, a picture, manipulative material, graph, equation, or word problem) clearly helped a learner understand a relationship or mathematical idea. How can talk be used to extend an individual student's insights to other members of the class?

For professional development sessions and additional video clips that go with this chapter, see:

*Classroom Discussions in Math: A **Facilitator's Guide** to Support Professional Learning of Discourse and the Common Core* (Anderson, Chapin, and O'Connor 2011).

ISBN: 978-1-935099-12-3

Talking About Mathematical Reasoning

About This Chapter

Reasoning stands at the center of mathematics learning. The mathematical practices in the Common Core State Standards for Mathematics highlight the importance of reasoning and argumentation. Teachers can use classroom talk to engage students in developing their own reasoning abilities and responding to the reasoning of others. In this chapter we consider examples of mathematical tasks that require deductive, inductive, and algebraic reasoning.

What Is Reasoning?

Many educators agree that reasoning involves the development, justification, and generalization of mathematical ideas. Reasoning is an integral part of doing mathematics. We reason when we examine patterns and detect regularities, generalize relationships, make conjectures, and evaluate or construct an argument. These activities are fundamental to making sense of concepts and understanding skills.

In addition, there are many general reasoning tools and skills that well-educated students should have available for use in mathematics, the sciences, social studies, and the humanities. For example, it's important for students to gain experience using the processes of deduction and induction. These forms of reasoning play a role in many content areas. Each type of reasoning has characteristics or components that are specific to its type, and productive classroom talk is an especially effective way for teachers to help students master the complexities of logical thinking in all areas.

One of the most important and difficult parts of trying to improve students' abilities to reason mathematically involves helping them extend their knowledge about reasoning to new problems. Often when students encounter a new strategy or tool that helps them reason through a particular problem, they seem to understand it well. However, their understanding may be limited to the context of that particular problem. Teachers sometimes watch in frustration as students fail to see how to apply or extend the strategy to solve a slightly different problem. We have found that talking about the reasoning involved in a problem helps students generalize problem types and solution strategies and apply them to new situations. To help them in this process, it's important to encourage students to look beyond the specific details of problems to the underlying mathematical

> We have found that talking about the reasoning involved in a problem helps students generalize problem types and solution strategies and apply them to new situations.

relationships, to talk about the similarities and differences among problems, and to reflect aloud on how what they learned from other problems can be used in the solution process.

Three Suggestions for Using Whole-Class Discussions to Help Students Reason

Students need practice with reasoning, and classroom discussions provide a method for sharing their understanding of this important process. We offer three suggestions for what to do to help students develop specific types of reasoning.

> **Three Suggestions for Using Whole-Class Discussions to Help Students Reason**
>
> 1. Use whole-class discussion to help students reason deductively.
> 2. Use whole-class discussion to help students reason inductively.
> 3. Use whole-class discussion to help students reason algebraically.

Suggestion 1: Use Whole-Class Discussion to Help Students Reason Deductively

Deduction involves reasoning logically from general statements or premises to conclusions about particular cases. How do we help students learn to reason deductively? One way is to regularly ask students to provide evidence for their claims regardless of the mathematical topic. This can be accomplished in almost all discussions, using one of the talk moves described in Chapter 1—asking students *why* they agree or disagree with someone else's reasoning—and pushing them to give examples that support their position. Another way is to provide instruction and practice

> *Deduction* involves reasoning logically from general statements or premises to conclusions about particular cases.

See Chapter 1.

focused specifically on the processes of deduction. Deductive statements can be especially confusing to students because of the language involved. Deductive statements often use negations and logical connectives (for example, *and, or, if–then,* and *if and only if*). Discussing the interpretation of a negation or the inferences that can and cannot be made from particular statements helps students become skillful in drawing defensible conclusions.

Example 6.1.1 Use Whole-Class Discussion to Help Students Reason Deductively

The Baseball Logic Problem (Mrs. Wolfe, Grade 4)

Mrs. Wolfe started using logic problems a few years ago as a way to teach about deduction and has been pleased with the results. Every Tuesday at the start of their math period, she asks her fourth-grade students to talk about their reasoning when solving one matrix logic problem. Her students like these problems and look forward to Tuesdays! She has found that students at first do not know what type of conclusions can reasonably be made from given statements. However, by the end of the year, her students have improved in their ability to make inferences and reason deductively. Mrs. Wolfe thinks that talking about these types of problems in a very purposeful way has been a key ingredient in their success.

In the following vignette Mrs. Wolfe uses discussion to introduce the process of elimination—drawing a conclusion based on the fact that all other options have been eliminated. In addition, she shows students how they can use an array or matrix, a table of rows and columns, to organize the information and draw conclusions. Mrs. Wolfe writes the following problem where everyone can see it. It is typical of the problems she uses every Tuesday to help students learn to reason deductively.

The Baseball Logic Problem

Art, Bill, and Debby play first base, second base, and third base on their school's baseball team, but not necessarily in that order. Art and the third baseman went with Debby to the movies yesterday. Art does not play first base. Who's on first?

Mrs. Wolfe does not give the students time to work on the problem on their own, but instead asks them to read the problem three times before initiating a class discussion.

1. **Mrs. W:** This logic problem requires us to reason from the statements that are given in the problem. Who can read us one of the statements and then tell us what conclusion you made from that statement? Jason?

2. **Jason:** I know that Art is not the first baseman because it says that Art does not play first base.

3. **Mrs. W:** I noticed that the statement you used to draw that conclusion is not the first statement in the problem. Is this OK to do?

4. **Jason:** I think so. I looked for a fact.

5. **Mrs. W:** In most logic problems it's OK to take statements out of order. What else can we conclude? Zach?

6. **Zach:** I think Art plays second base. It says that Art and the third baseman went with Debby to the movies, so Art is a different person from the third baseman.

MATH TALK TIP

Adding On

The talk move *Who can add on?* can be used to include more students in the conversation. When asked to "add on," students sometimes explain in more detail; they use different words and phrases to explain similar reasoning. The retelling of key points helps the speaker clarify his or her understanding of the solution method and often resonates with other students who need to hear the explanation more than once. This talk move supports Step 4: Helping Students Engage with the Reasoning of Others (see "Four Steps Toward Productive Talk," Chapter 1, page 10).

---

7. **Mrs. W:** OK, so Zach thinks that Art plays second base. Do people agree, disagree, have questions? Yuree.

8. **Yuree:** I don't understand why you think that Art plays second base.

9. **Zach:** We know that Art doesn't play first from what Jason said. Then this other sentence says that Art went with the third baseman to the movies, so that just leaves second base, because Art and the third baseman are two different people. So Art can't play third base. Do you see what I'm saying?

10. **Mrs. W:** Caroline? Do you want to add on to this?

11. **Caroline:** I made a list, like first base, second base, and third base, and put the name next to the right place.

12. **Yuree:** But how did you know Art goes next to second base?

Mrs. Wolfe recognizes that Caroline's explanation is not helping Yuree and others follow the logic of the situation. While she could continue the discussion using talk moves such as *revoicing* and *Who can repeat?*, she decides that this is the time to introduce a matrix as a way of organizing what is known. The matrix will enable students to keep track of their deductions by providing a record of the conclusions at each step. Mrs. Wolfe had previously prepared a worksheet with a labeled four-by-four matrix on it and hopes to talk with her students about how one can deduce something using the process of elimination.

13. **Mrs. W:** This is a bit confusing, isn't it? Let me show you a method that might help you keep track of the facts. [As she is talking, Mrs. Wolfe draws a matrix on the board.] First, I make a rectangular array showing rows and columns. We've used arrays when talking about multiplication and division but we're going to use one here in a different way and call it a *matrix*. I label each column with the names of the people because I am trying to match them up with the bases. [Mrs. Wolfe writes the names of the students above each column.] Where do you think I put the bases? Louise?

> **MATH TALK TIP**
>
> **Tools for Thinking**
>
> During a classroom discussion, it is important to provide students with "tools for thinking"—namely, tools that help them organize their thoughts and information. The matrix in this problem will enable students to keep track of their deductions by providing a record of the conclusions at each step—and students can use it to construct additional relationships.

	Art	Bill	Debby

14. **Louise:** Maybe on the other side? On the rows?

15. **Mrs. W:** Right! [She writes a base next to each row.] Now each of these small inside rectangles matches a name with a base. This rectangle [points] is where second base and Debby meet, so I could put a YES or a NO in it to show that Debby plays second base or she doesn't play second base. Look at the matrix on the worksheet [passes them out] and explain to your partner how it was made. Can you find the rectangle that stands for Bill and second base? Debby and third base? Which rectangles stand for Art? Which rectangles stand for first base?

	Art	Bill	Debby
1st base			
2nd base			
3rd base			

Mrs. Wolfe checks in with different groups of students, asking them to explain to each other how the matrix is structured and what the different rectangles, sometimes called *cells*, represent. She reviews the terms *rows* and *columns*, which the class used previously when describing arrays. She does not bother to talk as a class about the design of the matrix because she finds that all of her students during small-group talk can explain how it is like an array and what the different cells represent.

MATH TALK TIP

When to Use Math Talk . . .

As the teacher, you will have to make decisions about what to have students talk about. The problem is that it is not always obvious when to spend more time discussing a topic and when to move on. In general, if it appears that the majority of the students understand, move on. You can always pull a small group of students or an individual and review a term or idea with them separately. Also, don't discuss every single problem in your curriculum. Select an example that is meaty and spend whole-class time discussing it—using the other problems for practice.

16. **Mrs. W:** Now that we understand how to read a matrix, let's put some information into it. Remember how one of the statements was that Art doesn't play first base? Ken, explain to us how you showed this in your matrix.

17. **Ken:** I put an X in the box. The problem says Art doesn't play first base, so I put an X in that cell.

	Art	Bill	Debby
1st base	X		
2nd base			
3rd base			

18. **Caroline:** I put a NO in the box for Art and first base. Is that OK too? [Mrs. Wolfe nods.]

19. **Mrs. W:** Alright. We have a couple of ways to show that Art doesn't play first base. Look at the problem again. Do we know anything else about Art? Zach?

20. **Zach:** I think we can put an X next to third base, too, because it says that Art and the third baseman went to the movies so Art can't be the third-base person.

	Art	Bill	Debby
1st base	X		
2nd base			
3rd base	X		

21. **Mrs. W:** Juan, can you put this into your own words? How do we know that Art doesn't play third base?

22. **Juan:** Art and the third-base player went to the movies together, so they have to be different people. We can put a NO next to Art and third base.

23. **Mrs. W:** Notice how the column for Art has two Xs in it. Art does not play first base or third base. There is only one base left, second base. So Art must be the second baseman. Let's put a check or a YES in that cell.

	Art	Bill	Debby
1st base	X		
2nd base	✓		
3rd base	X		

We've just used the "process of elimination." We decided that Art plays second base not from a direct clue but because we eliminated the other options. The only base left for Art to play is second base. Turn and talk to your partner and explain how we used the process of elimination to conclude that Art is the second baseman.

MATH TALK TIP

Turn and Talk

When new material is presented to students, no matter how clear and organized the presentation, many miss the salient points. By asking everyone to turn and talk, students must engage and consider the ideas.

Notice how Mrs. Wolfe stops and uses the turn and talk move to make sure that every student engages with this idea of using elimination to draw a conclusion. When teachers present new material to students, no matter how clear and organized the presentation, many miss the salient points. However, by asking everyone to talk, Mrs. Wolfe forces them to consider the ideas. She calls on Yuree, who earlier in the conversation was confused by this idea, to explain how we know Art plays second base.

24. **Yuree:** The chart really helps see that all that is left for Art to play is second base. The other bases got eliminated earlier so this is the only thing left for Art to play.

25. **Mrs. W:** Here is another nice thing about using a matrix and the process of elimination. If Art plays second base, can Bill or Debby play second base? [Students respond no.] OK, so we can eliminate them and put Xs or NOs along the row of second base. [Mrs. Wolfe fills in the chart on the board.] Fill in your chart like I have.

	Art	Bill	Debby
1st base	X		
2nd base	✓	X	X
3rd base	X		

26. **Mrs. W:** Now we are ready to go back to the problem and find other information. Who can read another fact? Elise?

27. **Elise:** "Art and the third baseman went with Debby to the movies yesterday." This is like before. If Debby went with the third baseman, she can't be the third baseman.

28. **Mrs. W:** Talk with your partner and put this information into your matrix. Use the process of elimination when possible.

	Art	Bill	Debby
1st base	X		
2nd base	✓	X	X
3rd base	X		X

This discussion continued, with the class coming to the conclusion that Debby was the first-base player. Then Mrs. Wolfe asked many students to explain how they eliminated certain options and used this process of elimination to come to the conclusion that Bill played third base.

Notice how Mrs. Wolfe used a variety of talk moves to make sense of the logic statements. In Line 7 she asked students if they agreed or disagreed with Zach. When Yuree indicated that she was confused by Zach's statement, Mrs. Wolfe had Zach repeat it. Then in Line 10, Mrs. Wolfe asked Caroline to add her own ideas to Zach's comments. Throughout the discussion, Mrs. Wolfe asked students to explain the ideas under discussion to someone else during partner talk (Lines 15, 23, and 28). Finally, this vignette illustrates how teachers might use discourse to help students better understand content that they are introducing. Mrs. Wolfe was teaching students about a matrix and the process of elimination using direct instruction and talk. The discussions were all geared toward providing students with multiple opportunities to understand what inferences might be made from the statements.

One final note about this vignette: In the next chapter, we will discuss ways to use talk to develop definitions of words and symbols. However, in this case we see the teacher introduce a phrase that is important but very difficult to define in isolation: *process of elimination*. If Mrs. Wolfe had started out the lesson trying to define this term, she would have run into problems, and most students would not have followed her definition. But by having students engage in the procedures that actually constitute the process of elimination, and using the phrase again and again as they became more experienced with those procedures, Mrs. Wolfe built the experiential base they will need to eventually reflect on the meaning of the phrase and add it to their vocabulary.

Try It Out!

LESSON: The Baseball Logic Problem

If you try this lesson with your students, we suggest you follow Mrs. Wolfe's plan and introduce students to how to use a matrix. Use the small-group talk format to make sure that all students understand the structure of this tool. When discussing the statements in the problem, be sure to provide plenty of time for partner talk so that every student can articulate the relationships that enable him or her to draw certain conclusions. If this is your first time discussing a logic problem, be aware that students need practice in reasoning deductively. Integrate similar problems into your instruction over the next few months and discuss them as a class.

> **Teaching with the Common Core**
>
> Practice 2: Reason abstractly and quantitatively.
> Practice 3: Construct viable arguments and critique the reasoning of others.
> Practice 5: Use appropriate tools strategically.

Example 6.1.2 Use Whole-Class Discussion to Help Students Reason Deductively

Four Strikes and You're Out (Mr. Danella, Grade 3)

Mr. Danella uses the game *Four Strikes and You're Out* to help his third-grade students develop deductive reasoning skills. In the game, players (or teams) take turns trying to determine the numerals used in a two-digit plus two-digit addition computation. One player or team makes up a computation and solves it. The opposing player or team tries to identify all of the missing digits in the numbers in the computation before getting four strikes. (Note: Each correct guess is recorded in all of the appropriate place-value holders in the computation and every incorrect guess is recorded as a "strike.")

The game *Four Strikes and You're Out* can help students develop deductive reasoning skills because in order to make a good guess a player should use information about digits already filled in or incorrect guesses. You may want to take a minute and play one round of the game prior to watching the video. Think about how you used deduction to inform some of your choices.

Unfortunately, students can play the game without using any deductive reasoning at all. They can just guess digits at random and hope they make lucky guesses. One way that teachers can help students develop deductive

Four Strikes and You're Out

You need: a partner, a pencil, and a piece of paper

Directions:

1. Player A thinks of a two-digit plus two-digit addition computation and hides it from Player B. (Don't forget to find the sum!)
2. Player A creates a game board that looks like the one below.

Game Board

____ ____ + ____ ____ = ____ ____ ____   <u>*Strikes*</u>

0   1   2   3   4   5   6   7   8   9

3. Player B begins to guess the digits in the computation.
4. Player A fills in the game board when Player B's guesses are correct. Each guess is recorded in every appropriate place-value holder. If Player B's guess is not correct, Player A marks a strike.
5. Player B tries to fill in all of the digits in the entire computation before getting four strikes.

reasoning skills is by playing practice games and discussing what would and would not make good guesses and why. Pressing students to reason about their choices by using the facts in front of them (what has and has not been eliminated) is essential.

In this lesson excerpt, Mr. Danella first posted the practice game below and asked students to analyze the game as it has been played so far.

$$\underline{\quad} \; \underline{0} \; + \; \underline{\quad} \; \underline{1} \; = \; 81 \qquad \underline{strikes}$$
$$\cancel{0}\,\cancel{1}\,2\,\cancel{3}\,4\,5\,6\,\cancel{7}\,\cancel{8}\,9 \qquad\qquad XX$$

> **FOUR STEPS…**
>
> Pressing students to explain their reasoning supports Step 3: Helping Students Deepen Their Own Reasoning (see "Four Steps Toward Productive Talk," Chapter 1, page 10).

He then asks students to talk about what would not make a good next guess before going on to discuss what would.

MATH TALK TIP

Errors

In this video clip, Mr. Danella did not correct a student's error when speaking, as it appeared that he understood the concept. When students talk, they tend to inadvertently misspeak. Sometimes what they say is wrong, but it is clear from their other utterances that they understand what is going on. Students may also self-correct their errors as they continue to explain their reasoning. Consider this before stopping a student's explanation to make a correction.

BEFORE YOU WATCH THE VIDEO

To make the most productive use of the video clips, you and any colleagues you are working with should take time to read through the *Guidelines for Watching Videos of Teaching*, page xxi. For demographics, see page xliv.

Video Clip 6A: Finding Missing Digits (Mr. Danella, Grade 3)

As you watch the video clip, consider:

1. How does Mr. Danella use turn and talk during this lesson excerpt? How does it help students make deductions?
2. What other talk moves does Mr. Danella use in this lesson excerpt? How do they help students make deductions?
3. Listen for how students talk to each other. What norms are in place in this class?

For more videos from Mr. Danella's *Four Strikes and You're Out* lesson, see the companion resource *Classroom Discussions in Math: A **Facilitator's Guide** to Support Professional Learning of Discourse and the Common Core.*

Try It Out!

See the lesson plan *Four Strikes and You're Out (Grade 3)* in Appendix B.

LESSON: Four Strikes and You're Out

Your students will enjoy this game! You can use any operation and make it more or less complex (more or fewer digits) depending on the grade level and knowledge of your students. During the discussion, push students to provide their reasoning for why they are making a particular guess. They may need to practice sharing their thoughts first with a partner and then with the whole class.

The lesson *Four Strikes and You're Out* is based on *Teaching Arithmetic: Lessons for Addition and Subtraction, Grades 2–3* by Bonnie Tank and Lynne Zolli (Math Solutions 2001).

Teaching with the Common Core

3.NBT Fluently add and subtract within 1000 using strategies and algorithms based on place value, properties of operations, and/or the relationship between addition and subtraction.

Practice 2: Reason abstractly and quantitatively.

Practice 3: Construct viable arguments and critique the reasoning of others.

Suggestion 2: Use Whole-Class Discussion to Help Students Reason Inductively

Talk can help students develop their inductive reasoning abilities. *Induction* involves examining specific cases, identifying relationships among the cases, and generalizing the relationship. Many problems require students to find generalizations that hold for many different examples. Yet it's sometimes hard for students to recognize patterns when the examples are presented in different representational formats. Students may have trouble seeing the commonalities among examples presented in words, symbols, tables, pictures, and graphs. Extended discussion can help students come to understand that relationships among mathematical entities can be expressed in more than one form. Talk also provides ways to explore the limitations of inductive reasoning—sometimes a pattern does not generalize in a way that was expected, and students need models for how to reassess the situation.

> Talk can help students develop their inductive reasoning abilities. *Induction* involves examining specific cases, identifying relationships among the cases, and generalizing the relationship.

Example 6.2.1 Use Whole-Class Discussion to Help Students Reason Inductively

What's the Same? (Mr. Khoury, Kindergarten)

Mr. Khoury is a kindergarten teacher who regularly presents problems using induction. He has his students play a version of the game "one of these things is not like the other." He presents many different examples that represent a rule, and then he asks his students how the examples are the same and what the rule might be.

1. **Mr. K:** Look at these funny dolls. They live in a land where all the dolls have agreed to rules about some of the things they will wear. Let's see if we can find something that is the same for all of them.

A   B   C   D

So let's look at these four funny dolls. What do we see here? What are they wearing that's the same for all of them?

2. **Giselle:** Hats. They have hats!

3. **Mr. K:** OK, Giselle says they have hats. Thanks, Giselle. David, will you show us what Giselle means? Can you come up and point to what she's talking about and tell us in your own words?

> ## MATH TALK TIP
>
> ### Tell Us in Your Own Words
> By asking students to repeat or put something into their own words, you are getting them to take an *active* stance toward the thinking of others. Over time, as they know you will ask this question, they will begin to orient toward what others say, seeing their own participation as normal. This also gets across the larger goal of giving students an understanding that communication is not always easy, and we all have the obligation to improve our skill in making ourselves understood.

4. **David:** [Pointing] This one has a hat, and this one has a hat, and this one has a hat, and this one doesn't have hats.

5. **Mr. K:** OK, thanks David. Giselle, is that what you were saying?

6. **Giselle:** Umm, I thought they all had hats, but that one [A] just has something else in her hair.

7. **Mr. K:** Oh, OK, so this one [A] has something else in her hair?

8. **David:** Yeah, a bow tie.

9. **Mr. K:** OK, so remember that in the land our dolls are from, they all agree to wear something that is the same. We're trying to find out what is the same for these four dolls. Ahmad, do you have an idea about something that's the same for all four dolls up here?

10. **Ahmad:** Their shoes! They all have the same shoes!

11. **Mr. K:** Sandy, do you agree or disagree with what Ahmad said?

12. **Sandy:** Umm . . . [Fifteen seconds go by.]

13. **Mr. K:** Who can repeat what Ahmad thinks about all the dolls? Katrina?

14. **Katrina:** I think he said they all have shoes.

15. **Mr. K:** OK, Ahmad, is that right?

16. **Ahmad:** Umm, I said they all had the *same* shoes! I think they all agreed to wear the *same* shoes on their planet.

> **MATH TALK TIP**
>
> **Do You Agree or Disagree . . . and Why?**
> Asking students whether they agree or disagree, and why, is perhaps the most powerful tool for focusing their attention on what another student has said. As they begin to take a position on what another student has said, they begin to have a stake in the talk.

17. **Mr. K:** Oh, OK. So who agrees or disagrees, with what Ahmad just said? Tell us whether you agree or disagree, and why. Kylie?

18. **Kylie:** I think I agree? They all have shoes.

19. **Mr. K:** OK, let's look. [Points to all four in turn.] This one has shoes, this one has shoes, this one has shoes, and this one has shoes. But do they all have the *same* shoes? Remember, in their land the dolls all agreed to wear some things that are the same. Did they agree to wear the same shoes? James?

20. **James:** Yes, the shoes are the same. And, I noticed another thing that's the same. Three buttons.

21. **Mr. K:** Wow. Another thing that's the *same* for *all four* of the dolls up here? Who can show us what James means?

For teachers in higher grades, this conversation may seem a bit laborious, but there is important progress being made here. Mr. Khoury is working with ideas, phrases, and words that are important for inductive reasoning: *all, the same, all four,* and so on. It is not enough to notice properties of one or two or even three of the set of four dolls. By using the talk moves that are now familiar, Mr. Khoury is helping these kindergarten students focus their attention in ways that will support inductive reasoning. Once the students have identified a number of similar characteristics, Mr. Khoury will have them draw another doll from this planet, showing what is the same among all.

Try It Out!

LESSON: What's the Same?

If you try a similar lesson with your own primary grades students, you may wish to begin with a set of only three items. Ask students to find something that's the same about only two of the three items. Students may struggle to talk in precise ways about what they notice. If so, you may wish to revoice their contributions to help them articulate their thinking. For example, if a student says, "There is a bow here and here," you can say, "So you notice that only two of the three dolls have bows in their hair? Is that what you said?" After you revoice a student's contribution, use the talk move *Who can repeat?* to give other students a chance to think about their classmate's idea. You can then open the floor up for more discussion by asking students whether they agree that their classmate has found something in common to only two of the three items.

ccss

Teaching with the Common Core

K.MD Classify objects and count the number of objects in each category.

Example 6.2.2 Use Whole-Class Discussion to Help Students Reason Inductively

Volume of Rectangular Prisms (Mrs. Foley, Grade 5)

FOUR STEPS...

Asking students to evaluate and revise each other's methods supports Step 4: Helping Students Engage with the Reasoning of Others (see "Four Steps Toward Productive Talk," Chapter 1, page 10).

In mid-October, fifth graders are generating a method for finding the volume of any rectangular prism. In order to support her students' understanding of volume of rectangular prisms, Mrs. Foley in earlier lessons had them build prisms out of cubes, determine volume by counting cubes, and identify patterns. In this lesson, she has them develop methods for finding volume. Two of the suggested methods are *multiply length times width times height* and *break it into layers and add up the amount in each layer*. Mrs. Foley asks students to evaluate and revise all suggested methods within their small groups. Then the class discusses those methods that appear to work for all rectangular prisms. The teacher helps the students focus on the method of stacking layers of cubes and connecting this method to multiplication.

Video Clip 6B: Developing Methods for Volume of Rectangular Prisms

As you watch the video clip, consider:

1. Describe how the teacher, Mrs. Foley, reacts to Alex's statement. How does her reaction help students describe an accurate and general strategy for finding the volume of a rectangular prism?
2. Student talk focuses on comparing two particular methods. What role does generalization play in comparing these two methods?
3. At many points during the lesson, Mrs. Foley asks students to talk about ideas that she could state herself quite succinctly and coherently. Based on what you see in this video clip, what do students appear to gain as a result of Mrs. Foley's decision to use student discourse to generalize methods for finding the volume of a rectangular prism?

For more videos from Mrs. Foley's *Developing Methods for Volume of Rectangular Prisms* lesson, see the companion resource *Classroom Discussions in Math: A **Facilitator's Guide** to Support Professional Learning of Discourse and the Common Core.*

BEFORE YOU WATCH THE VIDEO

To make the most productive use of the video clips, you and any colleagues you are working with should take time to read through the "Guidelines for Watching Videos of Teaching" (see page xxi). For demographics, see page xliv.

Try It Out!

LESSON: Volume of Rectangular Prisms

When teaching this lesson, give students plenty of time in their small groups to come up with methods to determine the volume of any rectangular prism. Notice that Mrs. Foley had cubes on the table so that students could test out their ideas. Don't be surprised that many of the methods do not work for all prisms! Part of the process of generalization is experimenting with different ideas and sorting them into categories—in this case, those methods that work to determine

See the lesson plan *Volume of Rectangular Prisms (Grade 5)* in Appendix B.

Teaching with the Common Core

5.MD Geometric measurement: understand concepts of volume and relate volume to multiplication and to addition.

Practice 2: Reason abstractly and quantitatively.

Practice 3: Construct viable arguments and critique the reasoning of others.

(*Continued*)

volume of all rectangular prisms and those that do not. Use the revoicing and restating talk moves to highlight important ideas or generalizations. Keep your focus on the key idea of building layers of cubes, that the dimensions of one layer are the length and width, and then connecting the height of the prism to the number of layers that are stacked.

> **MATH TALK TIP**
>
> ### Revoicing
>
> When a student says something really insightful, something that could move his or her classmates forward, this is a good occasion for you to revoice what you understand. It gives the student a chance to clarify, and it gives other students a chance to hear it again, perhaps in a clearer version.

Suggestion 3: Use Whole-Class Discussion to Help Students Reason Algebraically

It's generally assumed that all students will formally study algebra in middle school or high school. Algebra is considered a pivotal course in a student's education because students must make sense of algebra if they are to be successful in many other mathematics courses. Lack of success in algebra sometimes translates into lack of opportunity for future schooling and careers. But how do we help elementary students prepare to be successful in future algebra courses? One way is to provide them with opportunities to use arithmetic to reason algebraically. Reasoning that involves topics such as variables, equations, and functions is often referred to as *algebraic reasoning*. Activities and discussions that revolve around patterns, equality, properties, generalizations, and symbolism are the precursors to the formal study of algebra. When we have students talk about these topics and how they make sense of problems, we help them develop an understanding of algebra.

> Activities and discussions that revolve around patterns, equality, properties, generalizations, and symbolism are the precursors to the formal study of algebra. When we have students talk about these topics and how they make sense of problems, we help them develop an understanding of algebra.

Mrs. Malloy is currently teaching sixth grade but has also taught algebra to eighth-grade students. She knows that her students often have difficulty making sense of the concept of equivalence. She remembers that many of her eighth-grade students could solve equations for unknowns by memorizing rules, but they didn't understand what they were doing or why they were doing it. Mrs. Malloy's goal this year is for her sixth graders to solve problems that involve unknowns in ways that make sense to them, by *reasoning* rather than following rules. She wants them to realize that in some situations there is only one value for a specific unknown, but in other situations a variable can represent a set of numbers. She also wants to help students gain a deeper understanding of equality so that they don't interpret the equal sign as a "do an operation" cue.

Example 6.3.1 Use Whole-Class Discussion to Help Students Reason Algebraically

Weighing Fruit (Mrs. Malloy, Grade 6)

Mrs. Malloy has been using balance-scale problems as a means for reasoning about variables and equality. At the time of the following discussion, students have learned that in order for a scale to balance, the objects in each pan must weigh the same amount. They have had experience drawing balance scales to represent equivalent quantities. Mrs. Malloy wrote the following problem on the board and gave the students about ten minutes to work on it with a partner.

Weighing Fruit

Three apples weigh the same as 1 orange and 2 plums. One orange weighs the same as 4 plums. How many plums equal the weight of 1 apple?

---

1. **Mrs. M:** Andrea, would you share with us your solution process?
2. **Andrea:** First, I drew two scales to show the information. On the first scale, three apples weigh the same as an orange and two plums. Then on the second scale I put an orange on one side and four plums on the other. [See Figure 6.1.]

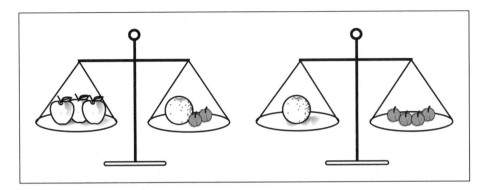

Figure 6.1 Andrea's balance-scale illustration.

3. **Mrs. M:** I'm going to interrupt you for a minute, Andrea. Did anyone show the relationships between the weights of the fruit in a different way? Amira?

4. **Amira:** I drew pictures of the fruit and used arrows. I remembered that the equal sign is used with numbers. [See Figure 6.2.]

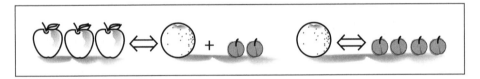

Figure 6.2 Amira's representation of the balance problem.

5. **Mrs. M:** Are both of these representations OK? Does the balance scale and the picture show the same relationships between the weight of the fruit? Talk to your partner about these questions. [A minute elapses.] OK, Vicky?

6. **Vicky:** Yes, I think both are the same. When a balance scale is level or balanced it shows that the objects weigh the same. I think you can show that they weigh the same with a picture and arrows, too.

7. **Mrs. M:** Good. When we have numbers, we also can use an equal sign to show that weights are the same. An equal sign also implies balance, like eight equals six plus two. Is that clear?

8. **Students:** Yes. Uh huh.

9. **Mrs. M:** OK, Andrea, go ahead. Please continue with your solution.

10. **Andrea:** On the first scale I took two apples away from one side and two plums away from the other side. I also took two plums away from the second scale. So we now have one apple and three plums left, so one apple is equal to three plums. [See Figure 6.3.]

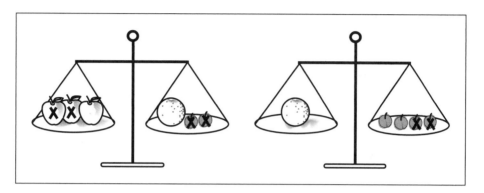

Figure 6.3 Andrea's attempt to solve the problem using her illustration.

Mrs. Malloy knows that Andrea's answer isn't correct, and she isn't sure how Andrea arrived at this incorrect solution. In addition, Mrs. Malloy is unsure if she should correct Andrea or not. To give herself some time, she might revoice Andrea's statement and then ask her to elaborate. Another tool Mrs. Malloy might use is to set up a discussion in which she presents two or three possible answers, not indicating acceptance or rejection of any. The subsequent discussion of the solutions would require students to reason about the statements their peers have made. Mrs. Malloy decides to use this approach.

11. **Mrs. M:** So here is one solution. Andrea is saying that the weight of one apple is equal to the weight of three plums. Does anyone else have a different solution? Ben?

12. **Ben:** That second scale says that the weight of one orange equals the weight of four plums, right? So I can use that to say that three apples equal six plums.

13. **Mrs. M:** Remember, we are talking about the weights of the fruit. Who can explain where the plums fit in?

14. **Ben:** [Ben comes the to the board and draws pictures to illustrate his explanation.] Three apples weigh the same as one orange and two plums. But one orange weighs the same as four plums so the three apples have the same weight as six plums. [See Figure 6.4.]

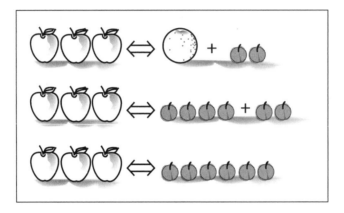

Figure 6.4   Ben's representation of the balance problem.

15. **Mrs. M:** Then what?

16. **Ben:** I just divided each side of the balance scale by three, and then I know that the weight of one apple equals the weight of two plums.

17. **Mrs. M:** OK, so we have two different solutions here. One is that three plums weigh the same as one apple and another is that two plums weigh the same as one apple. Which is correct? Discuss these two solutions with your partner. [Three minutes elapse, and Mrs. Malloy resumes the discussion by calling on the partner team of Nick and Elizabeth.]

> **MATH TALK TIP**
>
> ### More Than One Answer
>
> Set up a discussion in which two or three possible answers are presented; do not indicate acceptance or rejection of any. The subsequent discussion of the solutions requires students to reason about the statements their peers have made.

18. **Elizabeth:** Nick and I think that two plums equal the weight of one apple because you can't just cross off apples and plums—maybe they don't weigh the same amount.

19. **Brian:** I agree with Elizabeth. You can't cross off plums and apples because we don't know if the objects weigh the same.

20. **Carlos:** My partner and I think the second method makes sense. We think one apple equals the weight of two plums. Because you trade the orange for four plums so that makes six plums.

21. **Mrs. M:** A number of you are using a technique in algebra called *substitution*, where you substitute one value for another. Since one orange weighs the same as four plums, we can substitute the value of one orange by crossing it out and writing four plums. Talk to your partner about this. Does this make sense?

Students in Mrs. Malloy's class are starting to reason algebraically. Some of them are realizing they can use substitution to find the number of plums that equal the weight of three apples. Others do not yet realize that they can't remove unlike objects from both sides of the equal sign or balance scale. Talk, however, makes students' reasoning visible and helps Mrs. Malloy assist everyone in interpreting and solving problems. As the students share their insights and misconceptions, she is able to make instructional decisions to further their learning. In addition, talk helps students sort through multiple interpretations of algebraic situations and settle on common ground.

> As the students share their insights and misconceptions, Mrs. Malloy is able to make instructional decisions to further their learning.

When Andrea presents her solution strategy in Line 10, a teacher or other listener might have an immediate sense of confusion. How did Andrea get there? Could that method possibly be right? Should we take the time to work through her reasoning? Here the teacher chooses to focus on Andrea's solution rather than her reasoning, first eliciting another solution path from Ben and then letting students talk about the two possible answers. She could also have chosen to go into more detail with Andrea's reasoning, asking her to spell out her thinking in more detail. Notice that Mrs. Malloy presented the two solutions devoid of the students who presented them. She wanted her class to consider the mathematical validity of each method, unconnected to individual students. When using classroom talk to deepen mathematical reasoning, teachers frequently encounter puzzling or incoherent contributions from students. Many decisions about how to proceed must be made. We return to this issue in Chapter 9.

Try It Out!

LESSON: Weighing Fruit

If you plan to try this lesson, consider your students' prior understanding of balance scales and equations. If they have limited experiences, you may need to spend more time discussing the model and how it shows equality. Whereas Mrs. Malloy had her students solve the problem with a partner, you may want to have students work independently. Partner talk is especially effective when content is new for students. Ask a number of students to share their solution methods and ask the class to discuss how the methods are similar and how they are different.

Teaching with the Common Core

6.EE Apply and extend previous understandings of arithmetic to algebraic expressions.

Practice 2: Reason abstractly and quantitatively.

Practice 3: Construct viable arguments and critique the reasoning of others.

Discussion and Reflection

1. Why talk about reasoning? Can students in grades K–2 reason about mathematical ideas? Explain.

2. Mrs. Wolfe spent a lot of discussion time analyzing the matrix. What are the benefits of spending time discussing representations?

3. Students often have difficulty understanding negations. Find another matrix logic problem in which some clues involve negations (for example, the use of the words *none, no, not,* and so on). Describe the problem as if you were running a class discussion with students. What should you tell students? What should they figure out on their own?

4. National organizations and reports have highlighted the importance of algebra and algebraic reasoning. In the last vignette in this chapter, what did Mrs. Malloy do to focus the discussion on important algebraic concepts and skills?

For professional development sessions and additional video clips that go with this chapter, see:

*Classroom Discussions in Math: A **Facilitator's Guide** to Support Professional Learning of Discourse and the Common Core* (Anderson, Chapin, and O'Connor 2011)

ISBN: 978-1-935099-12-3

Talking About Mathematical Terminology, Symbols, and Definitions

(Continued)

About This Chapter

If students are to become competent mathematical thinkers, able to work with and communicate about mathematical ideas, they must become familiar with mathematical words and symbols, such as *multiply, perimeter, =, square unit, prime number*, and so on. In our work, we have learned that simply providing students with a definition for a mathematical term or symbol doesn't result in students gaining a deep understanding of that term or symbol. Understanding a term or symbol entails understanding the concept or action that term or symbol refers to, and the relationships that exist between that concept and related concepts and ideas.

Carefully guided talk—multiple opportunities to discuss aspects of the meaning of words and symbols—can help students develop this kind of understanding and can also provide them needed practice in using terminology precisely and effectively. As we guide students in talking— clarifying and discussing the complexities associated with the appropriate words, phrases, and symbols—we are helping them clarify their own thoughts and understandings.

> **CC₅Ꞩ**
> **Teaching with the Common Core**
> Practice 6: Attend to precision. "Mathematically proficient students try to communicate precisely with others."

In this chapter we discuss the difficulties inherent in helping students understand their mathematical vocabulary and use that vocabulary in context. We focus on the complexities of certain words and constructions. We think about the challenges that come along with teaching mathematical definitions. We aim to deepen your awareness of how talk can support the learning of complex ideas by tying together words, graphic representations, and symbolic representations. Finally, we explore ways to help students become more precise and accurate.

How Do We Learn Mathematical Terms?

For some mathematical terms, like *rectangle*, learning the definition is more complex than learning the definitions for everyday words that name concrete objects. Consider first how as children we learned the meaning of words that name ordinary objects, such as *chair*. Most of this learning takes place as we encounter instances of the category, gradually learning which things other humans label as *chairs*, and making inferences about what kinds of objects the label *chair* might refer to.

Now consider how we learn the meaning of a word like *rectangle*. First we encounter examples of rectangles and learn to recognize and label them, in part by paying attention to which things other humans label as *rectangles*. But even once we can recognize examples, our work is not over. To really understand what the term means in mathematics, we must know that it names a closed figure with two sets of parallel, congruent sides, and four internal ninety-degree angles. In other words, understanding the concept *rectangle* means understanding its formal definition.

This second stage of learning is difficult for students. If we ask elementary students to identify a rectangle, most of them will pick out the shape of a typical rectangle. When asked to provide a definition of rectangles, however, very few will list all of the criteria that define what a rectangle is. Furthermore, they may be unclear on why a rectangle can also be defined as a parallelogram with four right angles. Only by explicitly talking about the formal definition of a rectangle can we get at the real nature of the mathematical concept.

In general, words and symbols used in mathematics tend to have stricter or more precisely stated definitions than everyday words. If someone says, "Bring me a chair; I need to sit down," you are unlikely to be considered a failure if you bring them a stool or a bench. But if you are asked to construct a rectangle, you will fail unless it meets the criteria listed here. Mathematical terms carry "high stakes" definitions; there is less room for interpretation.

> Mathematical terms carry "high stakes" definitions; there is less room for interpretation.

As your students go on in school they will encounter such precisely stated "technical terms" in a wide range of content areas. The precise use of technical terms is difficult for many students, because it departs from their ordinary ways of using language. Talk about the exact meanings of mathematical terms can help them make the transition. Their discussions of definitions in your classroom may be their first encounter with the very important academic practice of using technical terms.

Four Suggestions for Using Whole-Class Discussions Related to Mathematical Terminology, Symbols, and Definitions

We offer four suggestions for using talk to help students begin this process of learning the meanings of words and symbols through discussion, even in kindergarten or pre-K settings. And at higher grade levels, we will see that students continue to benefit from talking about definitions, symbols, and other conventional kinds of representations.

Four Suggestions for Using Whole-Class Discussions Related to Mathematical Terminology, Symbols, and Definitions

1. Use whole-class discussion to sort out different word meanings.
2. Use whole-class discussion to extend students' knowledge.
3. Use whole-class discussion to build and monitor common understandings.
4. Use whole-class discussion to develop the meaning of symbols.

Suggestion 1: Use Whole-Class Discussion to Sort Out Different Word Meanings

Why is it important to talk about definitions of words, phrases, and symbols? One aspect of being an educated person is having a broad vocabulary and being able to choose words that exactly express what you are trying to say. And one of our jobs as teachers is to help students learn to use correct vocabulary to express themselves clearly and articulately. In the past, many teachers felt that it was not necessary to worry about language arts issues in mathematics class. Yet it is clear that if we want students to use specific words and phrases correctly, they must have opportunities to discuss word meanings and to practice correct word usage.

MATH TALK TIP

Mathematical and Nonmathematical Meanings

It is important to help students sort through mathematical and nonmathematical (or everyday) meanings of key terms. For example, the word *difference* can be interpreted mathematically as meaning the value we get when one number is subtracted from another number. But *difference* has nonmathematical meanings as well, such as *dissimilarity*, *disagreement in opinion*, and *distinction*. Students must be aware of the various meanings of words in order to decide which meaning makes most sense in a specific context. They must also be able to choose the word they want to use so as to achieve clear communication. Classroom discussion can help develop students' awareness of the meanings of mathematical terms, symbols, and definitions.

Example 7.1.1 Use Whole-Class Discussion to Sort Out Different Word Meanings

Making Sense of Scale (Ms. Lee, Grade 6)

Ms. Lee, a sixth-grade teacher of many English language learners, often uses homework assignments to begin the study of mathematics vocabulary. Before starting a lesson on scale drawings, her homework assignment was for students to write down as many definitions as they could find for the word *scale* and then to consider what a scale drawing might entail. The next day during the mathematics lesson, Ms. Lee posed the following question, "What does the term *scale* mean? Which meanings are related to mathematics and scale drawings?"

Ms. Lee often relies on the technique of calling attention to the many meanings of a word and contrasting them with the mathematical ones by writing two columns of examples—mathematical and nonmathematical—where everyone can see them. This type of careful consideration of vocabulary not only helps students heighten their awareness of the differences between technical terms and everyday language but also helps them broaden and deepen their understanding of concepts like *scale* and *scale factor*. In effect, she is using the everyday meaning of a word—something most students will know—as a tool in helping students focus and reflect on the distinctive mathematical meanings, which may be new for many students. Furthermore, in cases like this one where there are a number of mathematical meanings for the word *scale*, it enables her to differentiate among the meanings.

As we join the conversation, students offered definitions and Ms. Lee recorded them on the board as *mathematical* or *nonmathematical*. One student stated, "A scale is on a graph, like the numbers on the *x*- and *y*-axes but you also have a scale on a map." Not sure what the student really understood about both of these uses of *scale*, Ms. Lee responded, "Could you give us an example of each one and how they're different?" The student's response indicated her partial

> **MATH TALK TIP**
>
> **Using Everyday Meanings**
>
> Use the everyday meaning of a word—something most students will know—as a tool in helping students focus and reflect on the distinctive mathematical meanings, which may be new for many students. In cases where there are a number of mathematical meanings for the word, doing this helps differentiate among the meanings.

understanding. "Well, a scale on a graph can go up by ones or twos or tens. The scale is just the interval that the numbers jump each time on the axis. On a map there is usually something that says *scale* but I'm not sure what it tells us. Maybe it is whether the distances go by ones or fives or one hundred miles."

Notice that this student has incorrectly connected the meaning of the scale used to number an axis on a line graph to the scale of a map. However, the student is not completely incorrect; in both cases the scale uses the concept of ratio. For example, the scale used on a graph starts at zero and increases by set intervals (for example, a scale might go from 0 to 20, by twos). In this case, the ratio of 1 to 2 (one interval for every two numbers) is being used. On the other hand, the scale on a map indicates the ratio of a distance on the scale drawing to the actual distance (for example, one inch is equivalent to two hundred miles). This is a case where because there is more than one mathematical meaning of the word, it is easy to get them confused. Furthermore, because there is a connection, though subtle, between the two meanings, it may contribute to student confusion.

To push the student's thinking, Ms. Lee made two sketches where everyone could see them, one an *x–y* line graph and the other showing a map scale where she indicates the scale. She explained to the students that a map is an example of a scale drawing.

(i)

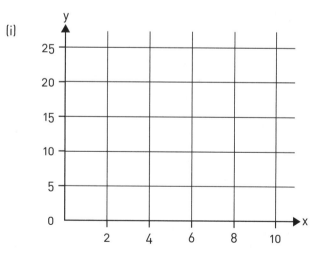

(ii)

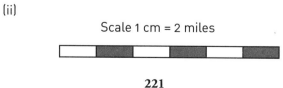

Scale 1 cm = 2 miles

Then Ms. Lee redirected the question to the entire class: "How are the scales on a line graph and on a map different?"

As students contributed to the discussion, some agreeing and others disagreeing that the scales were different. Ms. Lee required the class as a whole to reflect on these two meanings of the word *scale*. Many students added on and gave examples of scale drawings that also showed a scale similar to the one on the map. Guided by Ms. Lee, the differences were highlighted.

The discussion then returned to the task of determining a definition of the phrase, *scale drawing*. One student stated, "A scale drawing has a scale like the map." Another student added, "And a scale drawing is a drawing that shows a real thing, just smaller." In order to further assist students in understanding the relationship between a *scale* and a *ratio*, Ms. Lee directly addressed it by asking, "How is *ratio* used in the scale of a scale drawing?" She had students turn and talk with their partners, then asked the student pairs to record their responses where everyone could see them. The class then reviewed all of their conclusions, highlighting that a ratio was used to compare measurements on a scale drawing to real-life measurements.

Try It Out!

LESSON: Making Sense of Scale

You may wish to hold a similar discussion about the word *scale* when your students are studying the concepts of ratios and proportions. Begin this discussion by asking students to describe mathematical and nonmathematical meanings of the word *scale*. Then, post an *x–y* line graph and a map with a legend that shows its scale. Say to students that the word *scale* is often used to describe both of these representations. Ask them to compare and contrast the meanings of the word *scale* as it is used to describe the two representations. Scribe students' ideas as they share them. As this is a rich and complex topic, you may want to revisit this discussion during additional lessons. As your students learn more about proportional relationships, they will benefit from talking more about the different meanings of the word *scale* and how the term is related to the concept of ratio.

CCSS

Teaching with the Common Core

6.RP Understand the concept of a ratio and use ratio language to describe a ratio relationship between two quantities.

Example 7.1.2 Use Whole-Class Discussion to Sort Out Different Word Meanings

Making Sense of One-Half (Ms. Powers, Grade 2)

Some mathematical terms derive their meaning from the context in which they are situated. These terms are often called *relational words* because they bring along with them the context that is needed to understand them. One key example of a relational word is *half*. In this case, understanding the word *half* requires more than simply understanding a single word. If someone asks us to consider *half*, we are missing crucial information: Half of what? If instead, we are asked to consider half of a dollar, our understanding of the term becomes much clearer. Yet there is still more to unpack. Because meanings of relational terms are embedded in their contexts, young students need to understand that the meaning of a word like *half* shifts depending on the *of* phrase that follows it—the phrase that tells you what set or object the half is taken from.

> Some mathematical terms derive their meaning from the context in which they are situated. These terms are often called *relational words.*

Let's join another teacher, Ms. Powers, and her second graders as they talk about why half of a dollar is not thirty cents even though half of an hour is thirty minutes.

Video Clip 7A: Making Sense of One-Half

As you watch the video clip, consider:

1. Ms. Powers uses small-group work to get most students talking about halves. What confuses these second graders?
2. Ms. Powers asks her students to explain why thirty cents is not half of a dollar. What are some of their responses?

BEFORE YOU WATCH THE VIDEO

To make the most productive use of the video clips, you and any colleagues you are working with should take time to read through the "Guidelines for Watching Videos of Teaching" (see page xxi). For demographics, see page xliv.

Try It Out!

See the
lesson plan
*Making
Sense of
One-Half
(Grade 2)* in
Appendix B.

LESSON: Making Sense of One-Half

If you try this lesson, make sure that students have had prior experiences with the concept of one-half; they need to understand that halves divide an amount into two equal pieces. Listen in to small-group discussions in order to decide which students to call on to share and in what order, during the whole-class discussion. The idea that the size of one-half is related to the size of the whole is complex, so don't be surprised if students struggle to fully understand why thirty cents isn't half of one dollar. Ms. Powers revisited this topic during another class period to enable students to engage with the ideas again and reflect on others' comments.

Teaching with the Common Core

2.MD Work with time and money.
Practice 6: Attend to precision.

Example 7.1.3 Use Whole-Class Discussion to Sort Out Different Word Meanings

Making Sense of Quarter (Ms. Bajwa, Grade 2)

In another second-grade classroom the teacher, Ms. Bajwa, asked her students to write down the numerical expressions for different times of day. For the time *quarter past ten*, a number of students wrote *10:25*. At first, Ms. Bajwa thought that the students did not know how to tell time. She asked the students to tell her the meaning of *quarter*. One student replied,

> Since a quarter has a value of twenty-five cents, the students had assumed that a quarter past ten was twenty-five minutes past ten.

"Twenty five of something." When she probed further, asking other students for meanings of the word *quarter*, several gave the definition "a piece of money that is twenty-five cents." Since a quarter has a value of twenty-five cents, the students had assumed that a quarter past ten was twenty-five minutes past ten.

This is a common misunderstanding, particularly in the lower elementary grades. For many children, the first meaning of *quarter* they encounter is the meaning related to money. Once students learn about fractional parts of a whole, they can start the process of connecting the facts they know into a more coherent conceptual understanding. The word *quarter* is another example of a relational word where the context influences meaning. A student with a full understanding of the word *quarter* will know that the quantity it names depends on the quantity of the whole: A quarter of one hundred is twenty-five, but a quarter of sixty is fifteen. Ms. Bajwa's students, like others you may have encountered, thought it referred to a specific quantity rather than a fraction of a whole.

Getting students to understand the fractional meaning of *a quarter* is not easy; it takes time. Teachers who have already introduced concepts like one-half and one-fourth might schedule a discussion in which they talk about how *one-fourth* and *one-quarter* are two ways of saying the same thing. In this context, discussion of the meaning of *quarter* in the case of money versus time can move students closer to this understanding. If you, like Ms. Bajwa, are not ready to enter into a discussion of fractional parts of a whole, you can nevertheless be prepared for misunderstandings based on some students' limited understanding of the word *quarter* as a name for the quantity twenty-five.

> **"Teachers who have already introduced concepts like one-half and one-fourth might schedule a discussion in which they talk about how *one-fourth* and *one-quarter* are two ways of saying the same thing."**

Try It Out!

LESSON: Making Sense of Quarter

If you try this lesson, you may wish to start by talking about the terms *one-fourth* and *one-quarter* so that students recognize these terms as two ways of saying the same thing. To help students understand that the quantity named by the word *quarter* depends on the quantity of the whole, ask students a question that encourages them to think about the meaning of the word in two different contexts. For example, you can ask, "If a quarter of a dollar is twenty-five cents, is a quarter of an hour equal to twenty-five minutes? Why or why not?" Even if students quickly reject the validity of this statement, the experience of justifying their position will help them understand *quarter* as a relational word. For example, students can argue that a quarter of an hour is not equal to twenty-five minutes by thinking about the size of one hour as compared to the size of one dollar. Since an hour is sixty minutes and four groups of twenty-five is one hundred minutes, a quarter of an hour cannot be equal to twenty-five minutes.

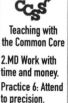

Teaching with the Common Core

2.MD Work with time and money.

Practice 6: Attend to precision.

Suggestion 2: Use Whole-Class Discussion to Extend Students' Knowledge

Another reason to talk about definitions of words and phrases is to extend students' knowledge. Connections between related terms naturally arise during discussions. Definitions can play an important part in extending students' general knowledge when discussions about definitions require students to think about networks of underlying concepts. In Ms. Lee's classroom (page 220), the discussion about the word *scale* led to another discussion about ratios.

Sometimes teachers must also monitor students' understanding of non-mathematical terms! When students do not know the meanings of words and phrases in a problem, they may have difficulty making sense of the content under discussion. For example, in the case in Chapter 1, page 42 in which the fifth-grade class was working on a problem about the number of peach tarts that could be made using a set number of peaches, a few students did not know what a peach tart was. They mistakenly confused it with the popular breakfast food Pop-Tarts. This confusion, though minor, made it difficult for them to follow other students' explanations of their solution processes. The students wondered why their classmates were representing the peach tarts with round circles since Pop-Tarts are rectangular. Unfortunately, students often focus on irrelevant features of problems, in part because they are trying to make sense of those features they find confusing. By discussing vocabulary and phrases, and by providing background information, teachers can help students understand the context of a problem (which will improve problem solving), and they can also extend students' overall knowledge of the world.

See Chapter 1.

Students often focus on irrelevant features of problems, in part because they are trying to make sense of those features they find confusing.

Example 7.2.1 Use Whole-Class Discussion to Extend Students' Knowledge

Using the Words *More* and *Less* (Mrs. Luizzi, Kindergarten)

Classroom discussions can help students learn to use words and phrases to develop understanding of important mathematical relationships. As students progress through the grades, they learn how to compare numbers in a variety of ways. In the primary grades, these comparisons focus on the operations of addition and subtraction and use the phrases *more than* and *less than* (for example, six is more than three). But students must learn to do more than just recognize the greater of two given numbers. They need to be able to express mathematical relationships that are situated in a variety of contexts using these statements.

In this lesson, students are comparing categorical data represented in a bar graph. Students need to use the concept of cardinality to compare categories numerically but they also need to express those comparisons in words (for example, "More students want pizza for lunch than tacos."). Even if students can look at a bar graph and identify the category that has more entries, they may still be unable to formulate clear and accurate statements about the comparisons and relationships they see. Thus, it is important that primary grade teachers provide time in a lesson for both types of activities.

> Even if students can look at a bar graph and identify the category that has more entries, they may still be unable to formulate clear and accurate statements about the comparisons and relationships they see.

Prior to the taping of this video clip in mid-October, kindergarten students collected data to find out the number of children whose shoes did or did not have shoelaces. They made two different representations of the data set. The first representation is a two-column chart that shows the number of students in each of the two possible categories. They also made two towers of interlocking cubes to show the number in each category. The teacher, Mrs. Luizzi, uses whole-class discussion to help her students use the words *more* or *less* to describe the quantities. She also helps students connect the idea that the longer tower also reveals the category that has more people in it. In other words, she tries to help students reason that since the tower that represents the number of people who are wearing shoes with laces is taller than the other tower, that tells us the number of students who are wearing shoelaces is *more than* the number who are not.

MATH TALK TIP

Modeling

Modeling is an effective way to help students learn how to use *turn and talk* in ways that support learning. Before she began the whole-class discussion, Mrs. Luizzi modeled turn and talk with one student. Following, she asked the students what they noticed each person did (and did not do) during the turn and talk. Mrs. Luizzi then asked everyone to turn and talk so that all students might practice. You can watch this model turn and talk by viewing Video Clip 8A.

BEFORE YOU WATCH THE VIDEO

To make the most productive use of the video clips, you and any colleagues you are working with should take time to read through the "Guidelines for Watching Videos of Teaching" (see page xxi). For demographics, see page xliv.

Video Clip 7B: Using the Words *More* and *Less*
(Mrs. Luizzi, Kindergarten)

As you watch the video clip, consider the following:

1. Students struggle to use the words *more* or *less* to describe the results of the survey question. What do you think accounts for their struggles?

2. Irene, the first student to speak, said that less people were wearing shoelaces. Why might Irene have said this?

3. What did Zean's turn reveal about his understanding of how the phrases *more than* and *less than* could be used to compare these data?

For more videos from Mrs. Luizzi's *Using the Words* More *and* Less lesson, see the companion resource *Classroom Discussions in Math: A **Facilitator's Guide** to Support Professional Learning of Discourse and the Common Core.*

Try It Out!

LESSON: Using the Words *More* and *Less*

You may wish to try this activity with your kindergarten or first-grade class. After students record their names in the graph, focus students' attention on describing the data. Ask students, "Is the number of people who are wearing shoes with laces *more than* or *less than* the number of people who are not wearing shoes with laces? How do you know?" Students may easily be able to conclude that one category has more people than the other and still struggle to use *more than* and *less than* to describe the data set. You can support them in using these vocabulary terms to describe data by discussing similar survey questions throughout the year.

See the lesson plan *Using More and Less to Describe the Data in a Graph (Kindergarten)* in Appendix B.

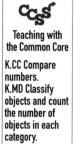

Teaching with the Common Core

K.CC Compare numbers.
K.MD Classify objects and count the number of objects in each category.

Example 7.2.2 Use Whole-Class Discussion to Extend Students' Knowledge

Connecting Factors and Multiples (Mrs. Burgess, Grade 4)

As they work to develop proficiency with the operations of multiplication and division, upper elementary students must also develop understanding about factors and multiples. In this grade span, students investigate factors pairs as a pair of whole numbers that produce a given product. They identify whether a given two-digit number is a multiple of a one-digit number. Students must also work to make connections between factors and multiples. One important connection that students should make is the idea that every number, n, is both a factor of itself and a multiple of itself.

In this clip, recorded in mid-October, Mrs. Burgess and her fourth-grade students discuss whether the number 28 is both a factor of and a multiple of 28. Some students justify that 28 is a factor of 28 by noting that 1 times 28 is 28. Some students justify that 28 is a multiple of 28 by stating that "you say twenty-eight when you skip-count by twenty-eight." But some students also justify that 28 is a multiple of 28 by saying that "you say twenty-eight when you skip-count by four." Mrs. Burgess uses a whole-class discussion to help students develop an accurate justification for why 28 is both a factor of and a multiple of 28.

Video Clip 7C: Connecting Factors and Multiples
(Mrs. Burgess, Grade 4)

As you watch the video clip, consider:

1. How do students justify that 28 is both a factor of and a multiple of 28? Which of their methods of justification are accurate? Which are misguided?

2. What definition of *multiple* are students working with? What are the advantages and disadvantages of this definition?

3. Describe how Mrs. Burgess uses the *Who can repeat?* talk move in this clip. How might her use of this talk move help students understand that 28 is a factor of and a multiple of 28?

For more videos from Mrs. Burgess's *Connecting Factors and Multiples* lesson, see the companion resource *Classroom Discussions in Math: A **Facilitator's Guide** to Support Professional Learning of Discourse and the Common Core*.

BEFORE YOU WATCH THE VIDEO

To make the most productive use of the video clips, you and any colleagues you are working with should take time to read through the "Guidelines for Watching Videos of Teaching" (see page xxi). For demographics, see page xliv.

Try It Out!

See the lesson plan *Reasoning About Factors and Multiples (Grade 4)* in Appendix B.

LESSON: Connecting Factors and Multiples

Prior to trying this lesson, have students explore these two concepts (for example, factors and multiples) separately. Understanding how factors and multiples are related is difficult for students and discussion can be used to effectively connect the concepts. However, be prepared for confusion! It may help to use a variety of examples and to ask students repeatedly to turn and talk with their partners in order to let them practice articulating the relationships.

Teaching with the Common Core

4.OA Gain familiarity with factors and multiples.

Suggestion 3: Use Whole-Class Discussion to Build and Monitor Common Understandings

Whenever talk is used as an instructional tool in the classroom, it's important for students and the teacher to be in agreement on definitions. They must work at maintaining what is sometimes referred to as "shared meaning" or "common ground" so that everyone can follow a discussion as it develops. Central to the use of mathematical discourse is the premise that students and the teacher will work toward common understandings that are satisfactory to all. The greatest value of this practice becomes apparent after a short time: When all students and the teacher have explicitly agreed-upon facts, definitions, and procedures, this shared understanding becomes part of the ongoing discourse and helps move the whole class forward. Time invested in building a solid common ground of understanding pays off in multiple ways.

> Central to the use of mathematical discourse is the premise that students and the teacher will work toward common understandings that are satisfactory to all.

Example 7.3.1 Use Whole-Class Discussion to Build and Monitor Common Understandings

Sorting: Attributes of Shapes (Mr. Radulfo, Grade 3)

What do shared understandings look like in practice? Not surprisingly, they take time to build. Mr. Radulfo asked his third graders to sort into two groups a variety of solid figures—pyramids, cones, cylinders, rectangular prisms, triangular prisms, spheres, and cubes. Then he held a class discussion regarding the sorting characteristics that students used. Here are a few student responses:

- My group sorted them [solids] by looking at how all of these are flat [points to flat faces of prisms, cubes, and pyramids] and all of these are curved [points to curved surfaces of cones, cylinders, and spheres].

- We used the flat sides too, but we sorted them by a flat base or not a flat base.

- I separated the blocks by the roundness or flatness of the faces.

Students used a variety of words to describe the same idea—*side, face, base, flat surface*—but because they were able to point to a physical feature on the actual blocks, everyone was able to make sense of each individual student's contributions. If there had been confusion about the different terms for the side of a prism, Mr. Radulfo would have needed to shift the discussion in order to clarify the meaning of each word. Note that this discussion was not intended as a discussion of vocabulary. Students were describing the basis for their sorting of shapes. The teacher intended to address solid geometry vocabulary *after* the students were familiar with the solids and their characteristics. Nevertheless, he had to carefully follow the words that students used, in order to make sure that everyone was following the meaning of the discussion. He also had to monitor whether all students had access to what those words referred to. In this case, he had to ascertain whether all students could see what the speaker was pointing to when using a word like *side* or *face*.

When the discussion is not about common physical objects, this monitoring process can get more challenging, but it becomes even more important. In some cases, teachers have to stop a discussion briefly in order to make sure that everyone agrees on the meaning of a word or phrase. During the discussion in Mr. Radulfo's class, one boy, Armin, kept calling a *cube* a *square*. Pointing to a collection of cubes, Armin said, "These squares are all different sizes." Mr. Radulfo decided to call attention to this in a sympathetic way.

1. **Mr. R:** Let's slow down right here. It's hard to follow sometimes when people talk about these shapes. Let's take a moment to talk about the terms we're using. I noticed that sometimes we are calling these shapes *squares*. Why might there be a problem calling these solids *squares*? Donna?

> **MATH TALK TIP**
>
> **Monitoring a Discussion**
> As part of monitoring a discussion, don't be afraid to briefly stop a discussion in order to make sure that everyone agrees on the meaning of a word or phrase.

2. **Donna:** Well, I was calling them *cubes*. But I don't know. . . .

3. **Mr. R:** Go on. Why is a cube [holds up a cube] sometimes mistakenly called a *square*?

4. **Donna:** I think people might call them a square because they're square.

5. **Mr. R:** Tell us what you mean when you say they're square.

6. **Donna:** Well, I mean the sides are squares. See? [She picks up a cube and points to a face.]

7. **Mr. R:** Does someone remember another word we used for *sides* here?

8. **Felicia:** *Faces.* We said faces are square. So a cube has square faces.

9. **Mr. R:** OK, so there's an interesting thing here: We said that these solid shapes are three-dimensional, right? And we talked about

> **MATH TALK TIP**
>
> **Partner Talk**
>
> *Partner talk*, also called *turn and talk*, can be used to give extra time to students who are still grappling with making connections. After partner talk, consider calling on students with weaker understanding and giving them a chance to demonstrate their knowledge.

two-dimensional shapes, right? So let's think about the words *square* and *cube*. Who can tell me which is a name for a three-dimensional object, and which is a name for a two-dimensional object? Talk to your partner for one minute.

As he walked around listening to the partner talk sessions, Mr. Radulfo saw that virtually all the students were able to make the connection between three dimensions and *cube* and two dimensions and *square*. By using partner talk, he had given extra time to the few students who were still trying to make this connection. In the discussion that followed, he called on those students with weaker understanding and gave them a chance to demonstrate their knowledge of the difference between names for two- and three-dimensional shapes in this case. He then decided to extend the discussion to cylinders, another case where students often use the more common two-dimensional term *circle* instead of the infrequent term *cylinder*. In that discussion, he learned that some students did not have a firm grasp of the term *cylinder* in the first place, calling it a *cyndaler* and *a silo shape*. After using the discussion and the interactive whiteboard to make sure that everyone knew how to say and spell *cylinder*, Mr. Radulfo returned to the confusion that had started the whole discussion.

1. **Mr. R:** [Holding up a cylinder] So we just said this is a three-dimensional object, right? And that its mathematical name is a *cylinder*. But let's say we heard someone calling it a *circle*. Why do you think they might be saying that?

2. **Ben:** I think somebody might say that because the ends of the cylinder are circles. Like the sides of the cube are squares.

MATH TALK TIP

Why Do You Think That?

By getting practice in explaining their thinking, and being encouraged to dig deeper, to push beyond the easy or obvious answer, your students will be engaging in exactly the kind of intellectual activity called for by the Common Core State Standards for Mathematics. As students become used to you asking them "Why do you think that?," they will become more adept at digging deeper themselves without prompting.

Mr. Radulfo was able to use this discussion of names for shapes and solids to go beyond the original misunderstanding in a way that strengthened all students' understanding of two and three dimensions, and that helped them see that language is part of what makes math complicated and sometimes difficult, but interesting! It is worth giving some time and attention to the words and expressions we use, discussing them in their own right. The words and expressions often provide the perfect entry point into better understanding of the concepts themselves.

Try It Out!

LESSON: Sorting: Attributes of Shapes

You may wish to try this lesson with your students. You will need a variety of solid figures—pyramids, cones, cylinders, rectangular prisms, triangular prisms, spheres, and cubes. First, ask students to describe the characteristics of the shapes. Make a list of important vocabulary terms as they arise (for example, *cube*, *pyramid*, *flat*, *circular*, *base*). Following, give each pair or small group of students their own set of solids. Ask them to work together to sort the solids into two groups based on a certain "rule" or set of sorting characteristics. In other words, all of the shapes in one pile must have the same set of sorting characteristics while all of the shapes in the other do not. (You may need to model this activity for the students.) After students work on this task in their groups, ask each group to show their shapes to the class and explain the "rule" or sorting characteristics they used to form their two groups. You can conclude the lesson with the game *Guess My Rule* by placing a set of solids into two groups and asking students to figure out the "rule" or sorting characteristics that you used to sort the shapes. Ask students to justify their proposed rules and ask other students to respond to their classmates' ideas.

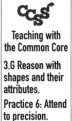

Teaching with
the Common Core

3.G Reason with shapes and their attributes.
Practice 6: Attend to precision.

Example 7.3.2 Use Whole-Class Discussion to Build and Monitor Common Understandings

Guess My Object: **Attributes of Shapes (Mrs. Johnson, Kindergarten)**

Mrs. Johnson introduced a classification game to her kindergarten: *Guess My Object*. In this game, sets of objects with different properties—colors, shapes, sizes—are set out on the floor in the middle of the rug. The teacher selects one object and puts it behind her back. She then calls on students to ask her a question, such as, "Do you have a blue circle?" If the teacher says no, she is not hiding a blue circle, the students can take all the blue circles and remove them from the pile. Mrs. Johnson first introduces the students to the objects. She makes sure that everyone can label each object in the same way, including its color, shape, and size.

1. **Mrs. J:** So who can tell me what we call this? [Holds up a red circle.]

2. **Students:** It's a circle! A circle. A circle!

3. **Mrs. J:** I heard people say "a circle." Can someone find another one like it? Jeremy? Can you find another circle?

4. **Jeremy:** [Picks a large blue circle out of the pile.] This one.

5. **Mrs. J:** OK, Sandra, do you agree with Jeremy that that's a circle?

6. **Sandra:** [Says nothing.]

7. **Mrs. J:** [Waits for fifteen seconds.] Jeremy, hold up the shape you picked again. OK, Sandra, here's Jeremy's and here's mine. Do you think we can call them both circles?

8. **Sandra:** Jeremy's is blue and yours is red. His is big.

9. **Mrs. J:** Good observation! Do other people agree? Who agrees that Jeremy's is big and blue and mine is red?

10. **Karen:** I agree. But yours is a circle and his is a circle too.

11. **Mrs. J:** OK, let's see how we can tell that each one is a circle. Mine is round. Is Jeremy's shape round? Mina?

12. **Mina:** Yes but it is big.

13. **Mrs. J:** OK, good. So Jeremy's is round and mine is round. Jeremy's is a big, round circle and mine is a small, round circle. Should we call them both circles because they are both round?

14. **Tony:** A red round circle and a blue round circle!

15. **Mrs. J:** OK, let's call this a small red circle and this a big blue circle OK, everybody say those together. [Holds up red circle as all repeat: "Small red circle!" Holds up blue circle as all repeat: "Big blue circle!"] Great! Now can somebody find another circle in the pile?

After the students have spent several minutes finding red circles and blue circles, Mrs. Johnson invites them to notice the different sizes of the circles. There are large, medium, and small circles. Next she invites the students to consider the other shapes, which are all triangles, blue and red, large and small. A similar discussion ensues. When she is finally ready to begin the game, the students are well practiced in referring to the classes of objects in a common fashion.

MATH TALK TIP

Math Games

Math games provide a wonderful format for using mathematical terms and phrases in precise and meaningful ways. But in the midst of a playing a math game, students may be so focused on winning that they forget to use precise mathematical language. One way to address this issue is to hold discussions about mathematical language either before or after students have had a chance to play the game.

This kind of game, and the preparatory discussion, may look very different from those we describe in higher grades, but the principle is the same. Mathematical thinking and learning require students to use language in precise and coordinated ways. This is somewhat different from their everyday language use, so we can help them get used to it by gently engaging in discussion in ways that help them practice these things.

Try It Out!

LESSON: *Guess My Object:* **Attributes of Shapes**

You may wish to play this game with your primary grade students. You will need a set of objects with different properties—colors, shapes, sizes—that are set out on the floor in the middle of the rug. Select one object (while no students are watching) and put it behind your back. Call on students to ask a question about the hidden object, such as, "Do you have a blue circle?" If this is not

Teaching with the Common Core

K.G Analyze and compare shapes.

the hidden shape, ask the students to identify the shapes that can be removed from the pile in front of them. Some students may think that all circles should be removed from the pile. If this misconception arises, it provides a wonderful opportunity to talk about the difference between the attributes of color and shape. Students can continue to ask questions until the mystery shape is revealed. You may also want to periodically ask students to justify the question they have posed (for example, "Tim, you want to know if I have a red square behind my back. What is it about the shapes in the pile that makes you think that that might be the hidden object?").

Example 7.3.3 Use Whole-Class Discussion to Build and Monitor Common Understandings

Differentiating Between Squares and Cubes (Mrs. Foley, Grade 5)

Let's observe fifth graders working together to define volume. Their teacher, Mrs. Foley, assists them in defining volume as the amount of space an object takes up. In the discussion of this definition, it is revealed that some students think that volume is measured in square inches. Mrs. Foley uses whole-class discussion to investigate whether this misconception is isolated to just a few students or is much more widespread.

Students' understanding of measurement can be strengthened if they clearly grasp the units that are used to measure specific attributes. For example, cubic units are used to measure volume because cubes take up or fill space (which is the attribute volume is measuring). On the other hand, square units are used to measure area since area is involved with covering a two-dimensional surface. We suggest that when teaching geometric measurement topics such as perimeter, area, and volume, you incorporate time into your lessons to discuss the units used and why they are suited to measuring the particular attribute.

Video Clip 7D: Defining the Word *Volume* (Mrs. Foley, Grade 5)

As you watch the video clip, consider:

1. Why is it important that students identify units when calculating measurements?

2. Why might students confuse cubes and squares? What other units are easily confused?

3. One student mentions that squares are too small (thin) to use to measure volume as it will take too long. What might this statement reveal about this student's thinking about squares as a geometric object?

For more videos from Mrs. Foley's *Volume of Rectangular Prisms* lesson, see the companion resource *Classroom Discussions in Math: A **Facilitator's Guide** to Support Professional Learning of Discourse and the Common Core.*

BEFORE YOU WATCH THE VIDEO

To make the most productive use of the video clips, you and any colleagues you are working with should take time to read through the "Guidelines for Watching Videos of Teaching." page xxi. For demographics, see page xliv.

Try It Out!

LESSON: Volume of Rectangular Prisms

If you try this lesson with your students, encourage them to identify the units of measure when talking about the different attributes of rectangular prisms. Keep in mind that this can be a challenging endeavor. For example, each dimension of a rectangular prism is measured in units, the area of the base is measured in square units, and the volume is measured in cubic units. If you notice that students are struggling to identify the correct unit of measure for a given attribute, hold a brief discussion to address and remediate this confusion.

See the lesson plan *Volume of Rectangular Prisms (Grade 5)* in Appendix B.

Teaching with the Common Core

5.MD Understand the concept of volume.

Example 7.3.4 Use Whole-Class Discussion to Build and Monitor Common Understandings

Talking About Ratios (Ms. Fournier, Grade 6)

The topic of ratio and proportion is considered by many to be the bridge that connects primary to secondary mathematics study. As students move from the lower to upper elementary grades, the focus of their work shifts from reasoning additively about quantities to reasoning multiplicatively. Furthermore, ratios involve two numbers that are being compared and *both* of these two numbers change multiplicatively as we scale the ratio up or down (for example, 3:5 is equivalent to 6:10 but not to 6:5). When students begin their formal work within the topic of ratio and proportion, there is sometimes a rush to develop their procedural knowledge. But before students learn computational procedures for solving proportions, it is important that they first explore the concept of ratio itself and the role of multiplicative reasoning. One way they can do this is by practicing the language associated with this concept.

> Before students learn computational procedures for solving proportions, it is important that they first explore the concept of ratio itself and the role of multiplicative reasoning. One way they can do this is by practicing the language associated with this concept.

Some of the language associated with proportionality involves phrases used to express the multiplicative relationship between the two numbers in a ratio. Such phrases include *for every*, *for each*, *per*, and *compared to*. Talking about these phrases can also help students deepen their understanding of ratios as comparisons. For example, some students read the expression *four pennies:three nickels* using the word *and*—in other words, *four pennies and three nickels*. Instead, the expression should be read using a term or phrase that conveys its proportional relationship—in other words, *four pennies for every three nickels*. Although on the surface this may seem like a minor linguistic difference, it is important that students use appropriate terms to describe ratios so that they do not confound additive and multiplicative relationships.

When students are presented with a statement about a ratio, one goal is for them to be able to reformulate that statement to create different but equivalent multiplicative statements. For example, the following three statements all express the same relationship between the quantities of boys and girls:

a. The ratio of boys to girls in the school newspaper club is two to three.

b. Two-fifths of the students in the school newspaper club are boys.

c. The number of girls in the newspaper club is one and a half times the number of boys.

Talking about the language of ratios and the meaning of each of these statements can help students make sense of them, move flexibly between part-to-part and part-to-whole comparisons, and connect ratios with expressions using fractions and decimals.

Let's examine how Ms. Fournier facilitated a discussion about reading and interpreting ratio statements in her sixth-grade class. At the beginning of the school year, Ms. Fournier and her sixth-grade students began their unit on ratio by focusing on the symbols and language associated with this mathematical topic. Ms. Fournier defined a ratio as a comparison of two quantities, and she presented her students with a list of common symbols and terms used to describe ratios. But before she continued on to the next major objective within the unit—solving problems about ratios—Ms. Fournier focused her instruction on having students practice using key terms and phrases to describe a variety of situations. We join the class just after she has posed the following task:

Task

Use the language of ratios to rewrite the sentence below in two other ways:

Sixth-grade students prefer plain to pepperoni pizza in the ratio of 2 to 1.

Students worked in small groups to create statements and then practiced stating their statements. Then Ms. Fournier conducted a whole-class discussion about their statements.

MATH TALK TIP

Using Precise Language

While teachers often incorporate precise language into their discussions about solution strategies, computational procedures, and concepts, it's also helpful to conduct discussions where using precise language is itself the goal of instruction. *Turn and talk* can be an especially effective talk move for helping students use precise language. When a student uses a certain term to convey an idea or gives a particularly precise definition, ask everyone in the class to turn to their partners and repeat the contribution.

Video Clip 7E: Talking About Ratios (Ms. Fournier, Grade 6)

As you watch the video clip, consider:

1. Describe what you see in this clip about students' abilities to talk about the given ratio using precise mathematical language. Describe their successes, challenges, and struggles.

2. Describe how Ms. Fournier uses *revoicing* after students read their statements out loud. Why do you think she chose to use that talk move?

3. Ms. Fournier asks students to talk more about only one of three statements that were posted on the board. This statement reads, "The ratio of the students who prefer pepperoni to plain is 1 to 2." Why might she have chosen to focus students' attention on this particular statement?

BEFORE YOU WATCH THE VIDEO

To make the most productive use of the video clips, you and any colleagues you are working with should take time to read through the "Guidelines for Watching Videos of Teaching," page xxi. For demographics, see page xliv.

Try It Out!

LESSON: Talking About Ratios

You may wish to try this lesson with your own students. Like Ms. Fournier did, use talk formats and talk moves that give lots of students the opportunity to practice talking about ratios using precise mathematical language. Don't be surprised if students have difficulty representing the relationship using fractions and decimals. Statements about ratios and other multiplicative comparisons are inherently very complex and students need repeated experiences in order to talk about them in articulate and meaningful ways. You may also wish to use the discussion to address common misconceptions about interpreting ratio statements. One common misconception students might have is that the order of the quantities in a ratio cannot be changed. For example, students might reject the notion that the following two statements express the same relationship:

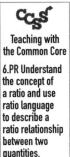

Teaching with the Common Core

6.PR Understand the concept of a ratio and use ratio language to describe a ratio relationship between two quantities.

a. Sixth-grade students prefer pepperoni to plain pizza in the ratio of one to two.
b. Sixth-grade students prefer plain to pepperoni pizza in the ratio of two to one.

Suggestion 4: Use Whole-Class Discussion to Develop the Meaning of Symbols

> Symbols can be misunderstood and used incorrectly, especially by young learners, just as words can. As a result, we also need to talk about the meanings and uses of a variety of symbols.

Mathematics is sometimes referred to as a language, partially because of its symbolic notation. Symbols enable us to express ideas unambiguously and to form precise statements about quantitative relationships. But symbols can be misunderstood and used incorrectly, especially by young learners, just as words can. As a result, we also need to talk about the meanings and uses of a variety of symbols.

One of the most important symbols students encounter is often misunderstood. Researchers have shown that many students do not see the equal sign (=) as a statement of equivalence. Instead they interpret this symbol as a signal to "write the answer." When students rely on this interpretation of the equal sign, they might respond to the following equation, $12 + 8 = \underline{\quad} + 12$, by replacing the blank with 20 instead of 8.

Further evidence of this misunderstanding of the meaning of the equal sign is seen in the common practice of writing a chain of partial calculations that are connected by the equal sign. For example, the expression $1 + 6 = 7 \times 4 = 28 \div 2 = 14$ may be written by a student as a "running record" of thinking: First add 6 to 1, then multiply the sum by 4, and finally divide by 2. However, as an expression out of context, it's incorrect and misleading because it implies that $1 + 6 = 7 \times 4$ and that $7 \times 4 = 28 \div 2$.

Just as words take on different meanings in different contexts, so do symbols. For example, a fraction bar can be interpreted in a number of ways. It can indicate a fraction ($\frac{2}{3}$—two parts out of three parts), a division ($\frac{2}{3}$—two divided by three), or a ratio ($\frac{2}{3}$—two items compared to three items). We need to find out what preconceived notions students have about symbols and orchestrate discussions that build on students' *current* understanding as we introduce them to *new* interpretations.

One practice we recommend is to call students' attention to the multiple meanings of a symbol or word. When we introduce a new meaning for a symbol, we explicitly ask students first to put into words their understandings of that symbol. Just as Ms. Lee did in the example concerning the term *scale* (see page 220), we can ask students to give us examples of the meaning of the symbol they are already familiar with. We might ask them to remember a previous lesson in which it was used in the way they are familiar with. The class can organize these examples on the board into one coherent meaning for the symbol. The teacher can then introduce the new meaning in explicit contrast to the old meanings. Even young students are able to accept that there can be more than one meaning for a word. They are also able to accept that there can be more than one meaning for a symbol. But in order to do this, they need time to work through the meanings explicitly. Group discussion, conducted using the talk moves we describe, is an effective way to help students work through different meanings for words or symbols.

> When we introduce a new meaning for a symbol, we explicitly ask students first to put into words their understandings of that symbol.

> Group discussion, conducted using the talk moves we describe, is an effective way to help students work through different meanings for words or symbols.

Sometimes teachers avoid introducing extra discussion of multiple meanings of words or symbols in mathematics, thinking it will only confuse their students. In fact, we have found that discussion of the kind we describe in this resource actually reduces confusion and supports more robust understanding. Only after students have discussed and solidified their current understandings do we introduce the new meaning. Over time, we have seen real improvement in students' ability to monitor their own use of symbols and words. Their written and spoken expression becomes more precise, and they are more mindful of how they formulate their ideas in words. They also become more willing to exert effort to understand how others are using words or symbols!

> Over time, we have seen real improvement in students' ability to monitor their own use of symbols and words. Their written and spoken expression becomes more precise, and they are more mindful of how they formulate their ideas in words.

Even young children can benefit from participating as active "meaning makers" in discussions of symbol meaning. Young children are just learning about using symbols as a form of representation. They often know less about the symbols used to represent a computational procedure than the actions associated with the procedure. Teachers can use young students' knowledge of the actions involved in a procedure to strengthen their understanding of the symbols. They may know, for example, that Julia has eight candies in all if she had five and her friend gave her three more, but they may not know that this situation can be represented with symbols as $5 + 3 = 8$. This should not be surprising—there is no intrinsic quality of symbols that signals their meaning. They are social conventions that children become familiar with over time and with much experience. Discussion, however, can help link young children's understanding of a computational procedure and the symbols used to represent it.

Example 7.4.1 Use Whole-Class Discussion to Develop the Meaning of Symbols

Decomposing the Number Seven: How Many Groups? How Many Hearts? (Mrs. Hayward, Kindergarten)

In this lesson excerpt recorded in mid-October, kindergartners work with their teacher, Mrs. Hayward, to find *groups* of different sizes on a large sheet of chart paper with a picture of a 7 of hearts playing card.

In order to complete this task, students must count and work with more than one group and think both about the quantity of groups and about the quantity of elements. Students are learning how to connect physical representations of groups and their elements to numeric representations, including number sentences. They are learning which symbols in a number sentence correspond to the number of groups and which correspond to the number of elements *in* each group.

For example, imagine that one student circles one group of two hearts, one group of three hearts, and two groups of one heart each. The number sentence $2 + 3 + 1 + 1 = 7$ can be used to represent this model. Students need to learn that the numbers in the number sentence reveal the number of hearts in each group. In addition, the sum of the *addends* represents the total number of *hearts* in the drawing. Mrs. Hayward uses whole-class discussion to help students work toward these goals.

MATH TALK TIP

Use a Common Set of Words

Sometimes teachers of kindergarten and pre-K students feel that an extended discussion might be too much for their students. We think that it's a good idea to start gradually, but you may be surprised at how well your kindergarteners respond. One good place to start is by focusing on getting students to use a common set of words to refer to the same things. This helps very young students develop their ability to pay attention to the words used for different objects, actions, and concepts.

BEFORE YOU WATCH THE VIDEO

To make the most productive use of the video clips, you and any colleagues you are working with should take time to read through the "Guidelines for Watching Videos of Teaching" (see page xxi). For demographics, see page xliv.

Video Clip 7F: How Many Groups? How Many Hearts?
(Mrs. Hayward, Kindergarten)

As you watch the clip, consider the following:

1. How did Mrs. Hayward connect the words and the graphic representation of the number of hearts to mathematical symbols?

2. When Mrs. Hayward asks her students to count the number of groups that their classmate circled, some students can be heard counting, "one, two, three, four, five, . . ." What might this reveal about their understanding of counting groups?

For more videos from Mrs. Hayward's *Decomposing the Number Seven* lesson, see the companion resource *Classroom Discussions in Math: A **Facilitator's Guide** to Support Professional Learning of Discourse and the Common Core.*

Try It Out!

See the lesson plan *Decomposing the Number Seven* *(Kindergarten)* in Appendix B.

LESSON: Decomposing the Number Seven: How Many Groups? How Many Hearts?

You may wish to try this lesson with your kindergarten or first-grade students. (You will need several copies of a large picture of the 7 of hearts card from a deck of playing cards.) Begin by asking students if they see any smaller groups of hearts within the 7. Call on a volunteer to come up and circle the groups they see. Ask each volunteer to describe what he or she circled. Record a number sentence for what the student saw. Ask students to talk about how each part of the number sentence relates to the drawing. Don't be surprised if students struggle to link the addends with the size of each group and the number of addends to the number of groups; differentiating between the quantity of groups and the quantity of elements is a challenge for many students at this grade level.

This lesson is adapted from *Teaching Number Sense: Kindergarten* by Chris Confer (Math Solutions 2005).

CCSS

Teaching with the Common Core

K.OA Decompose numbers less than or equal to 10 into pairs in more than one way, for example, by using objects or drawings, and record each decomposition by a drawing or equation (for example, $5 = 2 + 3$ and $5 = 4 + 1$).

Example 7.4.2 Use Whole-Class Discussion to Develop the Meaning of Symbols

Making Sense of Subtraction Symbols (Mrs. Hartwig, Grade 1)

When students talk about word problems, teachers have an opportunity to extend their understanding of how mathematical symbols can be used to represent their solution strategies. In this example, we see how a first-grade teacher uses a whole-class discussion to extend her students' understanding of the various interpretations of the symbol for subtraction (in other words, the minus sign, −). Prior to this lesson, Mrs. Hartwig mainly has had students solve problems that used a take-away model for subtraction. However, in this lesson she presented a comparison problem.

The Stickers Problem

Julia has 6 stickers. Raphael has 10 stickers. How many more stickers does Raphael have compared to Julia?

Mrs. Hartwig gave the children the chance to work on the problem individually and encouraged them to record their work in any way that made sense to them. Some students used manipulative materials such as teddy bear counters to solve the problem. A few students used a number sentence. After students worked with partners, Mrs. Hartwig conducted a whole-class discussion of their solution strategies. As soon as the discussion began, Mrs. Hartwig realized that many students' limited understanding of subtraction was impeding their ability to model the problem using symbols.

1. **Mrs. H:** Who wants to tell us how they figured out the answer? Tim?

2. **Tim:** It's four because I did ten minus six equals four.

3. **Mrs. H:** Is this what you wrote? [Teacher writes $10 - 6 = 4$. Tim nods.] What do other people think about Tim's answer? Meli?

4. **Meli:** I don't think that's right. You can't do ten minus six here. Minus means take away but this is not a take-away problem.

5. **Mrs. H:** Interesting, Meli. Nanette do you agree or disagree with Meli's idea? Do you think we can use subtraction to solve this problem?

6. **Nanette:** No, we can't. I used teddy bear counters.

7. **Mrs. H:** OK, hold that thought for a moment. Give me a thumbs up if you agree with Meli's thinking that we cannot use ten minus six to solve this problem. [Approximately twelve students give a thumbs-up signal.] OK,

MATH TALK TIP

Thumbs Up If You Agree

Asking students to respond to a classmate's idea with "thumbs up if you agree" can be an effective strategy when the idea includes an error or misconception. Counting the number of thumbs in the air can help the teacher decide whether the error or misconception warrants further discussion by the whole class or individual remediation with individual students.

MATH TALK TIP

Translating Mathematical Symbols into Words

Asking everyone to turn to a partner and repeat a particular statement can be an effective strategy for helping students translate mathematical symbols into words. This can also be an effective strategy when the statement contains a new vocabulary term or a familiar vocabulary term that is being used in a new context.

let's talk about this a little bit more. I need to give you some more information about the subtraction isymbol. This sign [points to – sign in the equation 10 – 6 = 4] can mean *take away*. But it can mean other things too. For example, it can also mean *difference*. So we can read something like ten minus six as "the difference between ten and six." [Teacher writes on the board, *10 – 6 can be read as the difference between 10 and 6.*] Let's take three seconds and have everyone practice saying "the difference between ten and six" with the person next to you. [Students turn and talk.]

Young students sometimes connect a symbol to only one meaning. Yet expanding their understanding of arithmetic symbols and their interpreta-tions is crucial to success with computation. In this discussion, Mrs. Hartwig's use of the question "What do you think about that?" helped her realize that most students did not know there were other ways to think about subtraction. When it appeared that many students in her class thought that the subtraction sign only models take away situations, Mrs. Hartwig decided to address this issue with the whole class by providing additional information about this symbol to her students. She told the students that the symbol for subtraction can be interpreted in

MATH TALK TIP

Direct Instruction

When student talk reveals that students do not yet have the prior knowledge needed to form new understandings, continuing to ask questions such as, "What do you think about that?" is unlikely to create new insights. Instead, when faced with such impasses, teachers may wish to embed direct instruction within the class discussion. Stepping in to describe a concept, demonstrate a skill, or provide a definition and then giving students opportunities to talk about those ideas is an effective way to get the discussion moving forward again.

terms of both "take away" and as an expression of a difference. She followed this by giving all students the opportunity to practice interpreting a subtraction expression using the term *difference*.

Try It Out!

LESSON: Making Sense of Subtraction Symbols

You may wish to try this lesson with your own students as you explore addition and subtraction story problems. If none of your students introduce a subtraction sentence as a way to represent and solve the problem, you may decide to bring this solution strategy up yourself. Hold a position-driven discussion where students must take and defend a position on whether the equation makes sense for the story problem. If necessary, introduce the word *difference* to help students justify the equation as an appropriate solution strategy.

Teaching with the Common Core

1.0A Represent and solve problems involving addition and subtraction.

Example 7.4.3 Use Whole-Class Discussion to Develop the Meaning of Symbols

Interpreting Numerical Expressions (Mr. Acevedo, Grade 5)

Whole-class discussions can also help students interpret mathematical symbols in ways that help them notice key characteristics about the underlying structures. Mr. Acevedo and his students have been using the distributive property informally to multiply mentally. Now he wanted to emphasize how to show the distributive property symbolically and how to read expressions with parentheses using the phrase *the quantity of*. For example, he taught his students to read the expression $2(4 + 6)$ as *two times the quantity of four plus six*. One day, Mr. Acevedo was startled to find that despite his attention to this language, students' abilities to analyze and compare expressions that included parentheses appeared to be shaky. Mr. Acevedo posted the following task for everyone to see.

> Mr. Acevedo was startled to find that despite his attention to this language, students' abilities to analyze and compare expressions that included parentheses appeared to be shaky.

Numerical Expressions

Compare expressions A and B below. How do we read each expression? What is true about their values?

Expression A

Expression B

$2(431 + 529)$

$(2 \times 431) + (2 \times 529)$

Mr. Acevedo asked his students to take a couple of minutes to write out each expression in words. Next he asked them to compare the values of A and B and then check their values by computing. He decided to use a short whole-class discussion to help his students use the structure of the expressions to recognize that their values are equivalent.

1. **Mr. A:** How do we interpret expression A?

2. **Students:** Two times the quantity four hundred thirty one plus five hundred twenty-nine. [Almost all students call out in unison.]

> **MATH TALK TIP**
>
> **Turn and Talk**
>
> Use *turn and talk* to identify a student who has an idea that can be used as a springboard for discussion with the entire class.

3. **Mr. A:** Yes, that's true. Do you think expression A is more than, less than, or equal to expression B? Turn and talk with your partner about that. [Students talk for thirty seconds. Mr. Acevedo overhears Ziv telling his partner that both expressions have the same numbers but B has an extra two. He reconvenes the whole-class discussion by calling on Ziv to share his idea.] As you were working, I heard Ziv say something interesting. Ziv, can you repeat what I heard you say right now to the whole class?

4. **Ziv:** I looked at expressions A and B and I noticed that they both have the same things inside the parentheses but there is an extra two in expression B.

5. **Mr. A:** So I heard you say that both expressions A and B have the same numbers: four hundred thirty one and five hundred twenty-nine, but expression B has an extra two. Is that what you said?

6. **Ziv:** Yes.

7. **Mr. A:** OK, who can add on to that? How does that help us compare the two expressions?

8. **Jenny:** Well it isn't exactly the same things inside the parentheses. In B each part of the sum is multiplied by two: two times four hundred thirty-one and two times five hundred twenty-nine [points to each part of expression B]. That helps us because once you see that they have the same numbers, you can see that expression A is adding first and then multiplying but in expression B you multiply first. But they both have the same value.

9. **Mr. A:** How do we know A is going to have the same value as B, Ken?

10. **Ken:** It's like when we drew rectangles. We can add first and then multiply or multiply each part and then add them together. A is easier to do in your head.

11. **Mr. A:** Ken, would you come and draw the rectangles you mentioned on the board? [Ken produces the following.]

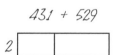

12. **Mr. A:** Ziv, can you read expression B for us?

13. **Ziv:** The quantity *two times four hundred thirty-one* added to the quantity *two times five hundred twenty-nine*. I agree they are the same. I can first add four hundred thirty-one and five hundred twenty-nine and multiply that sum by two. Or I can take each part and multiply by two first. I like doing A.

14. **Mr. A:** Could everyone turn and talk with their partner about what these expressions are telling us? Do you agree or disagree that they have the same value? Be ready to tell us why you think so.

> ## MATH TALK TIP
>
> ### Adding On
>
> Use *Who can add on?* to encourage other students to fill in the next steps in a justification. As students "add on" to each other's contributions, use the whiteboard to keep a record of their contributions. Once the entire justification has been revealed, you may wish to use *turn and talk* to give students a chance to talk about the justification in its entirety.

FOUR STEPS...

Asking, "How do you know . . . ?" gives students practice in explaining their thinking and supports Step 3: Helping Students Deepen Their Own Reasoning (see "Four Steps Toward Productive Talk," Chapter 1, page 10).

In this example, we see Mr. Acevedo using whole-class discussion to attend closely to the structure of a numerical expression. Mr. Acevedo first uses small-group work time to assess his students' understanding of reading and interpreting numerical expressions. Following, he uses *turn and talk* to encourage his students to think more deeply about the two given expressions.

Mr. Acevedo also uses the talk move *Who can add on?* to identify a student who has an idea that can be used to deepen the discussion with the entire class. Jenny's explanation in line 8 may direct all students' attention toward the structural similarities of both expressions. But her observation only provides a tentative first step in formulating a complete and convincing interpretation of the symbols. In line 9, Mr. Acevedo asks

MATH TALK TIP

Attending to the Structure of a Numerical Expression

Attending to the structure of a numerical expression or equation is an overarching goal of the Common Core State Standards for Mathematics in the elementary grades. Whole-class discussion is a particularly effective way to help students become proficient with this mathematical practice.

students to make their reasoning more explicit for why expression A and B represent the same quantity. Finally, Mr. Acevedo uses *turn and talk* to give everyone a chance to think about the expressions again.

Try It Out!

LESSON: Interpreting Numerical Expressions

If you try this lesson with your own students, you may wish to begin just as Mr. Acevedo did. First, ask students to compare the expressions without calculating or evaluating. As they work, notice how many students are able to conclude that the two expressions represent the same numerical value by attending to their structure. Later, when you discuss the question as a whole class, insist that students explain why the two expressions represent the same value. As seen in the vignette, geometric models can be a powerful way to show that this relationship is true.

CCSS

Teaching with the Common Core

5.OA Write and interpret numerical expressions.

Discussion and Reflection

1. Can you recall examples from your own teaching where the everyday meaning of a word seemed to cause difficulties with students acquiring the mathematical meaning of the word? Describe one example that comes to mind.

2. Can you recall examples where student knowledge of the everyday meaning of a word *helped* them understand the mathematical meaning of a word? Describe one example that comes to mind.

3. Consider the meaning of the equal sign in mathematics. How might you define *equal* for students at your grade level? What will your students say the symbol means? Are there particular problem contexts in which we use the term *equal* but perhaps shouldn't? If there are potential confusions at your grade level, how could you plan a discussion that might clarify these?

4. Reread the vignette on page 231 about Mr. Radulfo's class discussing two-dimensional and three-dimensional shape names. Imagine that the class continued talking about cylinders and a student asked, "How many faces does a cylinder have?" Mr. Radulfo suddenly realizes that he does not know how many faces a cylinder has! Is it the two ends only, or does the surface of the curved part count as a face? Math discussions sometimes lead to territory where the teacher is not sure of the correct answer. What could the teacher do in this case? What would you do?

For professional development sessions and additional video clips that go with this chapter, see:

*Classroom Discussions in Math: A **Facilitator's Guide** to Support Professional Learning of Discourse and the Common Core* (Anderson, Chapin, and O'Connor 2011).

ISBN: 978-1-935099-12-3

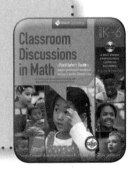

Implementing
Classroom Discussions

Section Overview

In Chapter 8, we focus on planning lessons with an explicit focus on student talk. We provide two lesson plans that teachers can use to introduce their students to the goals, talk moves, and norms of productive math talk. We also present the components of a talk-based lesson plan and share a classroom video case of a teacher enacting a lesson plan that includes these components.

In Chapter 9, we address many frequently asked questions that may arise as you begin to incorporate talk in your instruction.

Planning Talk-Based Lessons

How do we create lesson plans that focus explicitly on student discourse?

About This Chapter

Now that you are thinking about how to use productive classroom talk in mathematics, you probably have lots of practical questions about how to get started. For example, you may be wondering how to introduce these new forms of talk to your students. Another big question you may have is how to plan lessons that will keep the student talk focused on the mathematical goals of the lesson. In this chapter, we provide guidance about these questions and many others. In the first part of the chapter, we present two lesson plans that you can use to introduce your students to discussion-centered mathematics instruction. In the second part of the chapter, we describe the components of a lesson plan that focuses explicitly on student discourse. Following, we share a lesson plan that includes these components along with video clips showing what occurred when the lesson plan was enacted in an actual elementary classroom.

Lesson Plans for Introducing Your Students to Math Talk

In this section we present two lesson plans that you can use to introduce your students to discussion-centered mathematics instruction. Both of these lesson plans are derived from our own classroom experiences as well as those of other experienced classroom teachers. The first lesson plan is intended for teachers and students in the lower primary grades and the second is for students and teachers in the upper elementary grades. You may decide to use these lesson plans as a script that you follow very closely, adapting it to your students' needs, or you may instead decide to use them as a rough guide or template to develop your own lesson that introduces students to mathematical discourse.

Each of these lesson plans is built around two big questions:

1. *Why* do we talk about our own and other people's reasoning in math?
2. *How* do we talk about our own and other people's reasoning in math?

You can decide to work through each lesson plan at your own pace. For example, you can break up the plans into smaller minilessons that you conduct over the course of several days or weeks. Use your own judgment about how things are going in your class. You don't have to rush: Let your students get used to talking about their own thinking if this is something they haven't done before.

Introducing Your Students to Math Talk in Grades K–2: Lesson Plan

For grades K through 2, we recommend that you bring another teacher or aide into the classroom to help you in introducing math talk. Following is the plan divided into six key parts; each part of the lesson plan is intended to take approximately ten to fifteen minutes of instructional time. You can present each part of the plan over a series of days or weeks depending on the ages, backgrounds, and needs of your students. For example, if your students are very young or inexperienced with discussion, you may wish to take it very slowly, presenting each new part of the plan as students begin to acclimate toward this new form of talk.

MATH TALK TIP

Looking Back . . .

We highly recommend that before you use these lesson plans with your students, you first become familiar with the components of productive math talk that are described in this resource. In particular, we suggest that you read (or reread) the following excerpts very carefully before you introduce your students to math talk:

Why Use Talk in Mathematics Classrooms? (see the Frontmatter, page xv)
Four Steps Toward Productive Talk (see Chapter 1, page 10)
Summary of Productive Talk Moves (see Chapter 1, page 28)
The Two Major Goals of Setting Up Classroom Talk Norms (see Chapter 2, page 68)

Six Key Parts to the Introductory Lesson Plan

1. We're going to be talking in math class this year . . .
2. What do we mean by talking in math class?
3. Why should we talk about math in this way?
4. Some useful words: *explain, explanation, reasoning*
5. How do we talk about our own thinking in math?
6. How do we talk about each other's ideas this year?

Part 1: We're going to be talking in math class this year . . .

1. Ask students, "When we work on math, what are we learning to do?" Students will offer ideas such as working with numbers, adding and subtracting, perhaps "solving problems" and "getting the right answer."

2. List these ideas where everyone can see them and respond that these are important parts of math. Emphasize that doing math is also about a *new way of thinking*. It's about making sense of confusing situations. It's about figuring things out together. It's about getting confused but not giving up!

> One way to get better at thinking mathematically is *talking about what we're thinking.* So this year we're going to be doing a lot of talking in math class.

3. Segue into talk. Say, "Learning how to think in this way is challenging, but there are lots of ways to get better. One way to get better at thinking mathematically is *talking about what we're thinking.* So this year we're going to be doing a lot of talking in math class."

Part 2: What do we mean by talking in math class?

4. At this point consider modeling for students how to talk your way through a confusing problem. Say, "I'm going to show you what I mean by talking about our own thinking."

5. Post a problem where everyone can see it. Make sure that it is appropriate for your students and contains something that your students may have struggled with, but have come to understand. In other words, choose something that they *have* learned. This will make it possible for them to follow what is being said without being confused by the math.

6. Ask your collaborating teacher or aide to play the role of the teacher; you will play the role of a student. The "teacher" starts by asking you to solve the problem. Look at the problem and don't say anything. Look confused. When the teacher asks you, "What is the answer?" say "I don't know." (Feel free to look dejected!)

7. Then have your "teacher" (who is your collaborating teacher or aide) ask questions about how you tried to solve the problem. Talk about your thinking as you work through it.

8. After the role-play, say to students, "You just heard me talk about my thinking with the help of my 'teacher.' Describe something you saw or heard in our role-play." Call on students to talk about their ideas. You may even decide to make a list of important norms and expectations as students suggest them.

9. Summarize by explaining to students that one goal of doing all of this talk-ing is to learn more math. As they just saw, talking with another person can help us get to that "Oh, I get it!" moment.

Video Clip 8A: Turn-and-Talk Modeling (Mrs. Luizzi, Kindergarten)

In this clip, Mrs. Luizzi is working on making turn and talk a productive practice for her kindergarten class. She decides to model a turn and talk with one of the students and discusses it with the rest of the class.

As you watch the video clip, consider:

1. How might the turn and talk modeling in this clip help Mrs. Luizzi's students use this talk tool in productive ways? How might you enact a similar role-play in your classroom?

2. Modeling is a very effective way to introduce your students to the com-ponents of productive math talk. What other talk moves, formats, or norms could you model for your students?

BEFORE YOU WATCH THE VIDEO

To make the most productive use of the video clips, you and any colleagues you are working with should take time to read through the "Guidelines for Watching Videos of Teaching" (see page xxi). For demographics, see page xliv.

Part 3: Why should we talk about math in this way?

10. Revisit the role-play and reiterate for the students how you talked out loud about what you were thinking. Ask them: "Do you think this is a good way to learn? How does it help?"

11. Students may mention that they could tell what you were thinking, or that the teacher could understand what you were having problems with. You can reinforce that "We can't see inside each others' heads, so we need to use our words to help people understand what is going on inside our minds."

> We can't see inside each others' heads, so we need to use our words to help people understand what is going on inside our minds.

12. Add that when you talked out loud about what you were doing, you felt less confused because you could understand your own thinking better.

13. Tell students that the teacher's help in solving the problem helped you think about it better—so thinking together about math can help us all understand math better.

Part 4: Some useful words: *explain, explanation, reasoning*

Many students in grades K through 3 will not know the words *explain, explanation,* or *reasoning*. Consider proceeding in your lesson by holding a vocabulary discussion about these words.

14. Use the context of the role-play you did. Reenact the teacher asking you to "Explain what you are thinking when you work on the problem."

15. Provide a student-friendly definition of *explain*, such as "when we explain, we make ideas clear by talking about them. That is *explaining our thinking*. In this class, we'll be *explaining* our thinking a lot this year."

16. Do the same for *explanation* and *reasoning*.

Part 5: How do we talk about our own thinking in math?

17. Ask students, "Let's suppose we are working on solving an addition problem and I call on you to explain how you got your answer. What are some things you should try to do or say during your explanation?"

18. Listen to students' ideas. You may even decide to make a list of their ideas that can be revisited and modified throughout the year. If students do not mention important norms and expectations (for example, speaking in a loud voice), offer these ideas yourself.

19. Ask students, "If one of your classmates is giving an explanation and you are in the audience listening, what should you be doing or not doing?" Listen to students' ideas. Add their ideas to the list you created earlier. If students do not bring up the following, offer these suggestions yourself: When someone is speaking, it is important to quietly look at and listen to the speaker. It is also important to ask questions if you don't understand what that person is saying.

20. Say to students, "Sometimes when people talk about their thinking, you might hear them explain their strategy and it sounds exactly like what you did to solve the problem. You might say to yourself, 'Ugh. They took

my answer!' But in this class, I don't want you to be upset if this happens. Instead, you can to raise your hand and say, 'I did it the same way,' and then tell us what you did in your own words."

21. Offer another way to handle the above situation. Point out that as the teacher you might say, "Who else solved the problem the same way and wants to tell us what they did?" Explain that when more than just one person talks about their thinking, that's how we learn because we all get lots of time to think about important ideas.

22. Ask students if they have any questions about your expectations for talking and listening in math class. Tell students that talking in math discussions takes a lot of courage and that you are going to work really hard this year to help them use their words and those of their classmates to understand math better.

Part 6: How do we talk about each other's ideas this year?

23. Remind students that you are focusing on *thinking* and *reasoning* in math, not just right answers.

24. Ask students, "Does everyone solve every math problem the same way?" You might give them a problem to solve that will invite different solution paths. Work through all the different ones that emerge. Ask students if they can think of others.

25. When students see that the answer to your question, "Does everyone solve every math problem the same way?" is *no*, emphasize that this is a good thing! Having lots of ideas helps us see different ways to solve problems.

Teacher Reflection: Setting Expectations for Math Talk

Ms. Moylan

The most challenging aspect of implementing classroom discussions has been the time it takes—especially in the first two months of school—to set up the expectations for how to talk and how to listen in first grade. It takes patience from the teacher. It takes patience from the students. And it takes a lot of explaining why we need to talk and listen in math class. The biggest challenge is finding the time to do all of this. But when you take the time to do it, and model the expectations for how to talk and listen, the payback is well worth the investment.

Introducing Your Students to Math Talk in Grades 3–6: Lesson Plan

Following are four key steps for introducing math talk to students in grades 3 through 6.

Four Key Parts to the Introductory Lesson Plan

1. We're going to be talking in math class this year . . .
2. Why should we talk about math in this way?
3. We're going to be talking about *each other's* ideas . . .
4. What is expected from each of us in our math discussions . . .

Part 1: We're going to be talking in math class this year . . .

Convey something like this to your students, using your own words: "You may be used to the kind of math class where the teacher asks the questions, you give the answers, and then the teacher tells you if you're right or wrong. If you're right, your turn is over. If you're wrong, the teacher then explains to you what the right answer is. This math class is going to be different.

> You may be used to the kind of math class where the teacher asks the questions, you give the answers, and then the teacher tells you if you're right or wrong. This math class is going to be different.

I'm still going to ask you questions, and when you give me an answer sometimes I will tell you whether it is right or wrong. Other times, however, I won't say one way or another that your answer is right or wrong. Instead, I will say, 'Keep going. Tell us more about your thinking.' Or, I may ask, 'Why do you think it's correct? Can you convince us that's true?'"

Part 2: Why should we talk about math in this way?

Provide your students with a rationale for talking in math class. Consider the following ideas.

Talking Allows Us to Share Our Thoughts

- Thinking usually seems to go on inside a person's head. But since we can't hear or see what's going on inside other people's minds, we have to rely on talking to share our thinking with one another.

Talking About Our Own Ideas Can Help Us Learn

- Talking through our thinking can also help us clarify our own thoughts. If we try to communicate clearly, our thinking may get better as a result of our efforts.

Talking Helps Us Figure Out What We Do and Do Not Understand

- When you see how to do something in math like follow a rule to add a string of numbers, you might say, "Oh that's easy." But then when you are asked to explain it to someone else or talk about why it works, you realize that you aren't completely sure what to do or say. Once you know what's confusing you, you can get the help you need by asking someone else to talk with you about it.

We Can Learn By Listening to Each Other's Ideas

- Thinking together about math can help us all understand math better. We can all learn new ways of thinking about mathematics from listening to how others think.

Talking Together Prepares Us for the Future

- Talking together in math class will help you get better at giving mathematical explanations. One day, you'll each have a career where you'll be asked to solve problems; maybe they'll be math or science problems; maybe they'll be other kinds of problems. You'll be asked to present your solutions in ways that convince others that your solutions make sense and work. You can't just say, "Trust me, the answer's four. I can't explain how I got it, you just have to believe me." So it is important that we are able to explain our thinking.

Part 3: We're going to be talking about *each other's* ideas . . .

Say, "In addition to asking you to talk about your own ideas, I'm also going to ask you to respond to each other's ideas too. I might ask you to repeat what someone has said, add on to a classmate's explanation, or explain whether or not you agree with what they said. And here are some reasons why I'm going to ask you to do those things." Go through the following reasons:

Repeating

- Repeating or rephrasing someone's idea gives our brains a chance to think about it. Have you ever had that experience of listening to a person explain an idea and being confused? But then when you heard the idea repeated or said it over again yourself, you said, "Oh! I get that!" Well, that's another reason why I'm going to ask you to repeat each other's ideas or put those ideas in your own words—to give everyone a chance to think about the ideas and really understand them.

Thinking Together

- Difficult problems often require more than one person to solve them. Each one of us alone may not be able to give a complete explanation to a complex problem but together, if we talk about individual steps and link them together, we may be able to accomplish this task.

Debating Ideas

- All good mathematicians talk to each other about their ideas. When they have an idea, they use their words to convince each other why that idea makes sense. When they hear an error in someone else's explanation, they address that error and talk to that person about why it doesn't make sense and how it can be corrected. So, in this class, we'll have debates about each other's ideas because we are mathematicians-in-training and debating is exactly the kind of work mathematicians do.

> **MATH TALK TIP**
>
> **Modify Your Introduction So That It Addresses Your Students' Needs**
>
> Keep in mind that students in grades 3 through 6 vary greatly in their ability to take in complex explanations for instructional practices. Rely on your own judgment in using and sequencing these suggestions. Remember to be explicit in your explanations and leave time for discussion and clarification of the ideas you discuss.

Part 4: What is expected from each of us in our math discussions . . .

Post the list of expectations shown on the next page. Say to students, "Talking in math class takes both courage and hard work. We'll use this list of expectations so that we all know what is expected from each of us in our math discussions this year."

Discussion Expectations

1. Treat each other with kindness and respect at all times.
2. Participate in the discussion.
3. Speak loudly enough for others to hear.
4. Repeat a speaker's idea.
5. Respond to a speaker's idea.

For other examples of discussion rights and obligations that teachers have used in their classrooms, see Chapter 2.

Assign each pair of students one statement from the list. Ask each pair to read and interpret their assigned statement and explain *why* that expectation is important for productive and respectful class discussions. Then conduct a whole-class discussion, encouraging students' reflections about your discussion expectations.

Video Clip 8B: If I Call on You . . . (Ms. Fournier, Grade 6)

In this clip, Ms. Fournier explains to her students what they might do if she calls on them to speak and they are not ready to respond.

As you watch the video clip, consider:

1. How might the strategies that Ms. Fournier offers her students help her improve equitable participation during class discussions? What other norms and expectations do they address?

2. What other strategies might you suggest to your own students if you call on them to speak and they are not ready to respond?

BEFORE YOU WATCH THE VIDEO

To make the most productive use of the video clips, you and any colleagues you are working with should take time to read through the "Guidelines for Watching Videos of Teaching" (see page xxi). For demographics, see page xliv.

Four Steps for Planning Talk-Based Lessons

See Chapters 1–7.

Once you introduce your students to math talk, you are ready to focus on planning lessons that incorporate the goals, formats, and moves of productive classroom discussions. After reading Chapters 1 through 7 of this resource, you probably have lots of practical questions about incorporating talk into your lessons. Do some of the following questions sound familiar?

MATH TALK TIP

Carefully Planned Lessons Create Productive Class Discussions

It is easy to get caught up in a discussion that sounds great and then realize at the end of the class that students probably did not learn any new mathematical content. Thoughtful lesson planning will enable you to keep the discussion focused on students' understanding of the mathematics that you want them to learn.

Which talk formats should I plan to use at various stages in the lesson?

Should I plan to use specific talk moves in advance or make those decisions during the actual lesson, depending on what students say?

How do I plan lessons that will keep student talk focused on the goals of the lesson?

Implementing lessons that focus explicitly on student discussion follows a three-part cycle. First, you must plan ahead and project what will happen. We do this by analyzing the mathematics in the lesson, anticipating confusion with the mathematics, and then asking questions that will lead to either clarity or new, deeper questions about the material. Second, teachers must be willing to make changes to lessons as they respond to what students know and don't know. They may have to improvise, slow down, change gears, or regroup. Finally, teachers need to reflect on their lessons so that what was gleaned from the student talk in one lesson becomes a powerful tool in planning for future instruction.

We suggest you use the following four steps as you write your talk-based math lessons.

A reproducible master of this lesson planning template is available in Appendix C.

Four Steps for Planning Talk-Based Lessons

1. Identifying the mathematical goals
2. Anticipating confusion
3. Asking questions
4. Planning the implementation

Step 1: Identifying the Mathematical Goals

In this part of your lesson plan you need to identify the mathematics that will be the focus of instruction. Chapters 3 through 7 describe the different components of mathematics that compose mathematical proficiency: mathematical concepts; computational procedures; solution methods and problem-solving strategies; mathematical reasoning; and mathematical terminology, symbols, and definitions. You may wish to refer back to these chapters when writing your lesson plan, but keep in mind that any one lesson rarely includes all components.

In order to maximize students' understanding, you have to be extremely clear about what mathematics you will stress or highlight during discussions. It helps to list ahead of time the key concepts, problem-solving strategies, vocabulary, forms of representations, reasoning, and computational procedures that are at the heart of the topic.

> ### MATH TALK TIP
> #### Time, Materials, and Vocabulary
> As you plan your lessons, you will also want to think about the possible duration of the lesson, the materials needed to complete the assigned tasks, and the vocabulary that will help students express their ideas. You might find it helpful to fill in these parts of the lesson plan after you think about the goals, anticipated confusions, key questions, and sequence of the instruction.

Step 2: Anticipating Confusion

In this step of your lesson planning you list the particular aspects of the mathematical content that may be potentially confusing or misconstrued by students. It helps to identify possible incorrect notions as well as common errors that might occur. By highlighting in your lesson plan the mathematics that may be problematic for students, you are more likely to make sure that students think carefully about these ideas and procedures during whole-class discussions.

Step 3: Asking Questions

At the heart of using productive talk in instruction are the questions we pose. Our questions are the catalyst for students' thinking and talking. So how do you come up with questions that further students' mathematical knowledge? Consider the following strategies.

Refer to the Mathematical Goals and Anticipated Confusions

As you write questions for each lesson, you should refer back to the mathematical goals you have defined. Avoid questions that can be answered by "yes" or "no" and instead ask questions that require students to analyze a computational procedure or problem-solving strategy, connect skills to the underlying conceptual ideas, generalize patterns and relationships, and/or link new understanding to previous knowledge. You may also wish to plan questions that will reveal students' misconceptions. Sometimes teachers write what they think some of their students' likely responses will be so that they can have additional questions and counterexamples ready for use.

Make Use of Curriculum Materials

Some curriculum materials do not provide any guidance for using discussion to help students understand key ideas. However, other curriculum materials state the mathematics in the lesson and provide questions to ask students. This is a great starting place, and we suggest you use these prepared questions. However, we also have found that even excellent curricula do not provide all the questions that you will want your students to consider. In many cases the questions provided are low-level, single-response questions rather than questions that encourage students to analyze, synthesize, or generalize. Furthermore, you have worked with the individuals in your class and are aware of your students' knowledge of related topics and their strengths and weaknesses. Thus, you can pose pertinent questions for your students.

Focus on High-Level, Cognitively Demanding Questions

Almost every question-categorization scheme that exists, starting with Bloom's famous taxonomy, makes a distinction between low-level, cognitively undemanding questions, and high-level, cognitively challenging questions. The simplest, lowest-level questions ask students to recall knowledge that they already know. The most challenging questions ask students to explain a complex situation, evaluate the usefulness of a method, or synthesize a set of findings. At the far ends of the spectrum, it is fairly easy to tell the low-level question from the high-level question. For example, everyone knows that "yes/no" questions are less challenging in general than more open-ended "why" questions. There are many kinds of questions, however, where it is not so easy to tell what the "level" of the question really is.

Mary Kay Stein and Margaret Smith have spent many years thinking about the cognitive demands of tasks in mathematics instruction—what makes a low-level versus a high-level task. After many years of working with mathematics teachers, they have concluded that it is not always easy to tell how a question or task will pan out. Will it evoke high-level intellectual activity, a good discussion, or a conceptual breakthrough? Or will it devolve into a routine and unexciting activity? The answer depends upon the task, the teacher, and the students. If you are interested in thoughtful discussion on this matter, we recommend reading *Implementing Standards-Based Mathematics Instruction* (Stein et al. 2000).

In the meantime, though, we can suggest a strategy: *Plan for high-level questions—the low-level questions tend to take care of themselves.* In other words, as you plan your lesson, try to come up with several big questions that will move students' thinking forward, questions that will require them to explain, synthesize, and make connections. You may not get all of these questions answered in one lesson, but at least they will help you define the trajectory you want to be on. The low-level questions that you must ask to check whether students remember, comprehend, or follow the discussion will emerge naturally as you pursue your larger, more complex questions.

MATH TALK TIP

Extend Low-Level Questions to Generate More Math Talk

If you do ask a low-level question, consider how you can extend it so it has more than one purpose. As we will see in Mrs. Schineller's lesson later in this chapter, a discussion about a part-to-whole comparison can start with a very straightforward question such as, "Who can talk about the data using the phrase *more than half*?" But by asking students to justify how they know this conclusion is true, Mrs. Schineller moved the instruction to a higher level of cognitive challenge.

MATH TALK TIP

Keep a Record of Engaging, Higher-Level Questions

When you hit upon a higher-level question that really stimulates productive talk—talk that results in student advances in mathematical thinking—write it down! Share it with your colleagues! Tell your colleagues how the discussion proceeded after you introduced the question. These questions are among the valuable tools you will discover as you become more adept at using this type of instruction.

Step 4: Planning the Implementation

In this final step of your lesson planning, outline the sequence and content of the activities that you will use to help students make sense of the mathematics. It is important to think about which talk formats you will use and when, which steps of productive math talk you will work toward, and which talk moves you will rely on to reach these goals. It is also important to think about how you will summarize key points of the discussion at the end of the lesson.

See Chapters 1 and 2.

As we explained in Chapters 1 and 2, you have a choice of talk moves and formats to use during instruction. Thinking about which moves and formats to use, and when to use them, saves valuable time during class and strengthens the productivity of the talk. When making decisions about how to incorporate these key components of productive math talk in your instruction, we recommend you keep in mind the following.

Link Talk Moves to the Four Steps of Productive Math Talk

Although it is not necessary to plan, in advance, every talk move you will ask, thinking ahead about how to incorporate these moves in your instruction can increase the productivity of your class discussions. When planning which talk moves to use during a lesson, we suggest that you keep in mind the four steps toward productive math talk as well as the mathematical goals of instruction. As you think about the sequence of the lesson (for example, the introduction, exploration, and summary of the assigned tasks), you will begin to get a sense of how the big ideas of the lesson will develop. Make note in your lesson plan of when you might use specific talk moves to support students' learning. For instance, think about when you will use *Say more* . . . to help bring key ideas to the surface. Or, consider when the *press for reasoning* move may be used to help students deepen their understanding of the mathematics at the heart of the lesson. You may also want to identify the places in the lesson where talk moves that prompt students to respond to each other's ideas (for example, *Do you agree or disagree . . . and why?*) are likely to deepen students' understanding of the topic.

For more information on the four steps of productive math talk and an explanation of talk moves, see Chapter 1.

Choose Talk Formats That Support the Development of the Lesson

When planning a lesson, many teachers wonder about which talk formats they should use. They often ask, "When is small-group work time most productive?" Or, "When should the whole-class discussion take place during a lesson?" As you think about which talk formats to use, you may want to keep in mind the following.

Small-Group Discussion

We have found small-group discussion to be effective when the problems or tasks presented to students are particularly difficult. The benefit of four minds instead of two focused on one problem cannot be underestimated! Also, tasks that lend themselves to a division of labor are also good for small groups because students can share the results of their individual subtasks. And small-group talk can be used when students need to practice talking and listening to each other. If you use small-group discussion in your lesson, think in advance about how you will use that format to prepare students to speak during the ensuing whole-class discussion.

See Chapter 2 for additional suggestions on the talk formats and how to maximize the effectiveness of small-group discussions.

Whole-Class Discussion

Whole-class discussion can be used at the beginning of a lesson to set the stage for what is to come and to clarify the parameters of the instructional task. Whole-class discussion can also be used during the last third of the lesson as a forum for students to develop the ideas they have discovered in their small groups as well as summarize and generalize the important ideas. Sometimes a full math class is spent discussing one question! One reason that whole-class discussion is used regularly is that it allows all students the opportunity to consider everyone's ideas and thoughts about the mathematics. Specifically, by listening and contributing, students are building their own understanding. The class as a whole is also developing shared meaning for whatever ideas are under consideration. Finally, whole-class discussion provides the teacher with a way to assess student understanding by asking specific students to repeat a statement or opinion, react to another student's contribution, or provide their own solution methods.

Summarize the Big Ideas from the Lesson

In the planning the summary part of a lesson, you'll likely have questions such as, "How do I bring the whole-class discussion to a close? What kinds of summary statements should I make? What should I do about unresolved issues?"

As the discussion draws to a close, ideally the teacher or the students should summarize what occurred during the lesson. Remember that many discussions

MATH TALK TIP

What We Know for Sure and What We Still Need to Think More About

In summarizing a talk-based lesson, some teachers like to present two lists to their students. The first is called, "What we know for sure," and includes information and ideas that are accepted as true by the members of the class. The second list is entitled, "What we still need to think more about," and includes questions that remain unresolved. This kind of summarization is an effective way to help students monitor their own learning. For example, if there is an idea listed under "What we know for sure" that a student finds quite confusing, he or she knows to seek help. Conversely, if students are leaving the lesson scratching their heads about an idea that appears on the latter of these two lists, they can be reassured that their confusion is shared by many and will be addressed in upcoming lessons.

include contributions that are either inarticulate or unrelated to the instructional goals of the lesson. One job that the teacher has is to sort out the productive comments (those that will help students make sense of the content) from all that was said during the discussion. Teachers often need to solidify what has been discussed in the lesson by clearly summarizing key points. Sometimes this happens in the middle of a class, sometimes it happens at the end of the class period, and sometimes it occurs first thing the next day. When lessons take two or three days, a summary might not occur until the lesson is brought to closure. Part of the summary should also acknowledge the big ideas, generalizations, or strategies that are still "works in progress."

The importance of summary cannot be overestimated. It is through this process that conclusions are drawn and shared meaning among the students is developed.

Exploring a Sample Talk-Based Lesson Plan: Analyzing Data from a Bar Graph

In this next section we examine a lesson plan that could be used with third- or fourth-grade students; it focuses on analyzing data from a bar graph. This lesson plan incorporates all four planning steps mentioned earlier. It aims to provide readers with a detailed example of how teachers can plan instruction that attends carefully to student discussion as a mechanism for developing mathematical understanding.

At the start of the second month of their school year, Mrs. Schineller's students began a unit on graphing. Mrs. Schineller's goals for instruction were to help students create bar graphs with scales that used intervals greater than 1 and to write conclusions about the data. The lesson described here used data from a survey question about homework (see below). The data were displayed in a bar graph and the students were to write conclusions about the data using terms and phrases from the following list: *more, less, more than half, less than half,* x *times as many, almost all, almost none.*

Teaching with the Common Core

3.MD and 4.MD Represent and interpret data.

Making Sense of the Lesson as Readers

Before we examine Mrs. Schineller's lesson plan and video clips, let's first focus on Step 1 of the lesson planning process—the mathematics at the focus of the instructional episode. To make sense of the choices that Mrs. Schineller made for her students, we suggest you examine the data from the homework survey that are summarized in the bar graph below and then complete the tasks that follow.

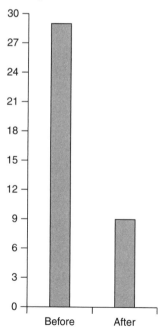

Do you prefer to do your homework before or after dinner?

1. Write three conclusions about the homework data set as it is displayed in the bar graph. Use the following terms or phrases in your conclusions: *more, less, more than half, less than half,* x *times as many, almost all, almost none.*

2. Examine the following three conclusions:
   A. More students prefer to do their homework before dinner.
   B. More than half of the students prefer to do their homework before dinner.
   C. About three times as many students prefer to do their homework before dinner compared to after dinner.
      a. How are the conclusions similar mathematically?
      b. How are the conclusions different?
      c. Why is it important for third-grade students to be able to state and explain each conclusion?

Following is how we've thought about and answered the above questions.

Statement A

Statement A above uses addition to compare the data in the two categories. Though this conclusion is accurate, it is not particularly informative since it does not give any indication of the magnitude of the difference between the data in the two categories. The number of students who chose *before dinner* is described without relating it to the number who chose *after dinner* or to the total number of students surveyed.

Statement B

Statement B compares the data in the two categories by expressing the number of students who chose *before dinner* as a fraction of the total number of students surveyed. In a data set with just two categories, this conclusion does not reveal any more information than the prior conclusion that uses only the word *more*. In other words, if there are just two categories, the category with more people also has more than half of the data. This connection, however, is not obvious to students. While they may be quite proficient stating and justifying statements that use the word *more*, they need lots of experiences using the data and the graph to form and justify statements that use the phrase *more than half*. In addition, talking about statements that use the phrase *more than half* to describe a data set with two categories will help students learn how to use fractions to describe data sets with three or more categories, which is a focal point in the Common Core State Standards for Mathematics in the upper elementary grades.

Statement C

Statement C uses multiplication to compare the data. A comparison that is expressed using multiplication enables us to better understand the relationship between the two quantities: One is about three times as great as the other. It also enables us to compare the number who prefer doing their homework before dinner to the total number of surveyed students: About three-fourths of the students surveyed prefer to do their homework before dinner rather than after dinner. Using the operation of multiplication to analyze data sets is a target area of the Common Core State Standards for Mathematics beginning in grade 3.

Examining the Lesson Plan

Now that we have explored the mathematics of the lesson, we are ready to examine Mrs. Schineller's lesson plan.

Grade 3 Lesson Plan: Analyzing Data from a Bar Graph

IDENTIFYING THE MATHEMATICAL GOALS

- Students will interpret data presented in a bar graph.
- Students will write comparison statements about these data.
- Students will justify their statements.
- Vocabulary: Students will use the following words or phrases to make comparisons: *more, less, more than half, less than half,* x *times as many, almost all, almost none.*

ANTICIPATING CONFUSION

- Students may not use the total number of students to justify the statement that more than half of the students prefer to do their homework before dinner.
- Students may think that twenty times as many students prefer to do their homework before dinner than after, because the difference between the data in two categories is twenty.
- Students may think that only three people said they prefer to do their homework after dinner.

(Continued)

- Students may not be able to write a *times as many* statement because twenty-nine is not a multiple of nine.

Asking Questions

- How do you know your conclusion is true?
- How can we use the height of the bars to help us write a *more than half* statement? How high would each bar be if half of the students chose *before* and half of the students chose *after* dinner?
- How does finding the total number of students surveyed help us write a statement that uses the phrase *more than half*?
- How can we use the height of the bars to help us write a *times as many* statement? How can we use multiplication to help us write this statement?
- Do you agree or disagree that only three students prefer to do their homework after dinner? Why?

Planning the Implementation

1. Post the graph of the data:

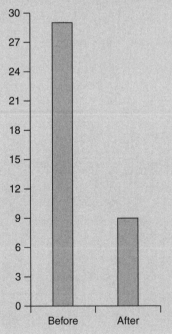

Do you prefer to do your homework before or after dinner?

2. Ask students to work with a partner to write at least three statements about the data using the following terms or phrases: *more, less, more than half, less than half, times as many, almost all, almost none.*

3. As students work with their partners, provide assistance as needed. Also during partner work time, prepare for the whole-class discussion by asking students to share particular conclusions. For example, identify students who will share statements that include the phrase *more than half* or *less than half* as well as those that include *times as many.*

4. Conduct a whole-class discussion. Focus on the *more than half* and *times as many* statements, since these may be difficult for students to state and justify. First, give students many experiences to practice saying each conclusion by asking them to repeat each statement. Then, ask students to justify why each statement is true. Following a student's justification, ask other students whether they agree or disagree with their classmate's reasoning, and why.

5. Ask students if they would like to share and justify other conclusions. One conclusion that may generate a lot of rich discussion is: *Almost all of the students prefer to do their homework before dinner.* Ask students to explain why they agree or disagree that that statement describes the data.

6. End the lesson by reviewing the conclusions that use the phrases *more than half* and *times as many.* Explain to students that in future lessons they will learn how to use these terms to describe data sets with more than two categories.

Taking a Closer Look at the Lesson Plan

Let's examine the kinds of things Mrs. Schineller was thinking about when she wrote this lesson plan. We will take a particularly close look at the role of student discussion in each component of her plan.

Step 1: Identifying the Mathematical Goals

In the "Identifying the Mathematical Goals" section, Mrs. Schineller lists the concepts and vocabulary that she wants students to develop during the lesson.

Mrs. Schineller had initially planned to have students make a bar graph and write the conclusions in one lesson. She changed her plan, however, after reflecting on the time needed for both instructional activities. She realized that if even if she succeeded in addressing both tasks in one class period, there would not be time for students to talk about the mathematics in depth. One of Mrs. Schineller's professional goals is to plan lessons that give students time to talk about fewer mathematical ideas in depth rather than many ideas on a superficial level.

Step 2: Anticipating Confusion

In the "Anticipating Confusion" section, Mrs. Schineller predicted that her students would have difficulty writing conclusions that use the phrases *times as many* and *more than half* (or *less than half*). She used this section of her lesson plan to explicitly address the nature of their difficulties and misconceptions so that she would be prepared to react to them during the discussion. Mrs. Schineller relies on a number of resources to help her write this section of her lesson plan. First, she uses her experience as a classroom teacher to reflect on difficulties students in prior years had with the topic. She also examines her teacher's manual and other resource books for information about possible errors or misconceptions. Finally, Mrs. Schineller works with her school's mathematics coach to gain insight into students' learning progressions in order to budget enough instructional time on topics.

Step 3: Asking Questions

Mrs. Schineller looks back at the first two components of her lesson plan when writing the "Asking Questions" section. First, she writes comprehension-type questions that she thinks might reveal students' knowledge, misconceptions, or confusion about the mathematics. Second, she writes questions related to the mathematical objectives she identified. For example, Mrs. Schineller knows that writing comparison statements that use the phrase *times as many* and *more than half* will be very challenging for many students. So, she plans in advance what questions she can ask to help students formulate these comparisons in meaningful and accurate ways (for example, "How does finding the total number of students surveyed help us write a statement that uses the phrase *more than half*?"). Third, she writes questions that might cause students some cognitive conflict—ones that she thinks will force them to reconsider any incorrect, preconceived notions (for example, "Do you agree or disagree that only three students prefer to do their homework after dinner? Why?").

Step 4: Planning the Implementation

In the "Planning the Implementation" section, Mrs. Schineller outlines the sequence of the lesson. She uses partner work time so that students can develop their comparison statements about the data with the help of another; she also knows that this time will help prepare the students for the whole-class discussion. In particular, she makes a note to identify students who are ready to talk about the phrases *more than half* and *times as many*. This strategy ensures that the whole-class discussion will begin with students who are already prepared to talk about targeted mathematical ideas. Mrs. Schineller thinks about how she will manage the whole-class discussion in ways that address each of the four steps of productive math talk (see Chapter 1, page 10). Mrs. Schineller plans to ask students to share their conclusions and then ask other students to repeat or rephrase each other's contributions. In addition, she will ask students to justify their own conclusions before asking other students whether they agree or disagree with their classmates' reasoning. Finally, she plans to leave some time at the end of the class period so that she can summarize the key points made in the lesson.

See Chapter 1.

Seeing the Lesson Plan in Action

Now that we have reviewed Mrs. Schineller's lesson plan, let's examine footage from her actual lesson. How did the lesson play out in comparison to Mrs. Schineller's lesson plan? As you know, sometimes lessons don't go according to plan. In addition, the following three video clips can be used to reflect on Mrs. Schineller's responses to students' unexpected questions and contributions!

Video Clip 8C: Analyzing Data from a Bar Graph, Part A
(Mrs. Schineller, Grade 3)

BEFORE YOU WATCH THE VIDEO

To make the most productive use of the video clips, you and any colleagues you are working with should take time to read through the "Guidelines for Watching Videos of Teaching" (see page xxi). For demographics, see page xliv.

In this first of three video clips from Mrs. Schineller's lesson, Mrs. Schineller introduces the lesson to the whole class and then students work in pairs to write their comparison statements about the data set using the bar graph. During this clip, you will see Mrs. Schineller enact the part of her lesson plan where she planned to use small-group work time to prepare for the whole-class discussion (see step 3 under "Planning the Implementation" in the lesson plan, page 279). Specifically, observe when she uses small-group work time to do the following:

Answer questions and provide assistance

Mrs. Schineller uses small-group work time to provide assistance and remediate misconceptions. Just as Mrs. Schineller had anticipated in her plan, at least one student, Sophia, has mixed up additive and multiplicative comparisons. Sophia reports that the comparison between the two categories is "twenty times as many" instead of "twenty more" or "three times as many." Mrs. Schineller works with Sophia to help her distinguish between these two comparisons. She shows Sophia how to use spatial reasoning to reason that the taller bar is about three times as long as the shorter bar. (In a later clip, we will see that Mrs. Schineller calls on Sophia to talk about the multiplicative comparison in front of the entire class.)

FOUR STEPS...

Asking students to practice saying their contributions with a partner supports Step 1: Helping Individual Students Clarify and Share Their Own Thoughts (see "Four Steps Toward Productive Talk," Chapter 1, page 10).

Create confident and prepared speakers

At the end of the small-group work time, Mrs. Schineller asks students to choose one conclusion that they would like to share and to practice stating that conclusion with their partners. This strategy may encourage more students to talk in front of the whole class after having practiced what they are going to say with their partners. It is also a way to save valuable class time that is often lost when students search through their papers trying to find the statement they want to share.

Set the stage for the whole-class discussion

Mrs. Schineller uses small-group work time to determine which student will talk about particular statements and justifications. She tells individual students what she will call on them to talk about and in what order.

For more information on activities that can help teachers use small-group discussions to increase the productivity of the whole-class discussion that follows, see Chapter 2.

Video Clip 8D: Analyzing Data from a Bar Graph, Part B
(Mrs. Schineller, Grade 3)

In this clip, we will see Mrs. Schineller enact the part of her lesson plan that fo-cuses on using the phrase *times as many* to compare the data in the two categories. You will notice that Mrs. Schineller was absolutely on target in anticipating that students would have difficulty stating this particular comparison. She relies on a variety of talk moves to help her students work their way through this confusion. As you watch the clip, identify and think about when the following talk moves occur.

Who Can Add On? and Who Can Repeat?

Mrs. Schineller begins this part of the lesson by calling on Margo, who struggles to deliver her comparison in a concise and articulate manner. When Margo struggles to clarify her thinking, Mrs. Schineller uses the move *Who can add on?* to try to bring clarity to Margo's statement. When Zoe gives her formulation of the same statement, she goes on to justify it by showing that the length of the bar that represents the data in the After column is about three times as tall as the bar that represents the data in the Before column. Mrs. Schineller uses the move *Who can repeat?* to give the other students a chance to think about Zoe's statement.

Press for Reasoning

After Sophia restates Zoe's conclusion, Mrs. Schineller asks her to justify how she knows the statement is true. When Sophia comes to the board to show that three of the smaller bars are approximately the same length as the taller bar, all of the stu-dents get a chance to develop their own understanding of multiplicative comparisons.

In Clip 8D, we can see Mrs. Schineller working on at least three of the four steps of productive math talk. She asks students to share their thinking, justify their reasoning, and respond to the thinking of others. Might Mrs. Schineller have used different talk moves to accomplish these same goals? Yes, this is entire possible. For instance, Mrs. Schineller might have asked more students to repeat Zoe's statement to give more students practice talking about *times as many* graphing conclusions. Or she might have used *turn and talk* to give all students the oppor-tunity to state this conclusion. What's important to keep in mind, however, is that decisions about talk moves and formats should always serve the larger goal of developing student reasoning about the key mathematical ideas of the lesson.

FOUR STEPS...

Asking students to justify their mathematical claims supports Step 3: Helping Students Deepen Their Own Reasoning (see "Four Steps Toward Productive Talk," Chapter 1, page 10). It also reinforces the idea that mathematics makes sense!

Video Clip 8E: Analyzing Data from a Bar Graph, Part C
(Mrs. Schineller, Grade 3)

FOUR STEPS...

Asking students to work together to provide one complete justification supports Step 4: Helping Students Engage with the Reasoning of Others (see "Four Steps Toward Productive Talk," Chapter 1, page 10).

In this third and final clip from Mrs. Schineller's graphing lesson, students talk about the comparison that uses the phrase *more than half*. Students conclude that "more than half of the students prefer to do their homework before dinner than after," and then justify how they know this statement is accurate using quantitative reasoning. In the footage featured, we will see Mrs. Schineller use talk moves to help students present this justification in smaller steps so that the other students can follow along and learn from it. Specifically, observe how she manages the discussion to address the two questions, "How many people were surveyed in total?" and "How do we use the total number of students surveyed to find the number that represents half of this total?"

How many people were surveyed in total?

Mrs. Schineller calls on Franchesca to say, "More than half of the people chose to do their homework before dinner." After asking several students to repeat this statement, Mrs. Schineller calls on James to begin the work of justifying why this statement is true. James tries to explain how he used a number line strategy to find the total number of people surveyed, but struggles to make his reasoning clear. Mrs. Schineller calls on Franchesca to help James clarify his reasoning.

How do we use the total number of students surveyed to find the number that represents half of this total?

FOUR STEPS...

The talk move *Who can repeat?* supports Step 2: Helping Students Orient to the Thinking of Others (see "Four Steps Toward Productive Talk," Chapter 1, page 10).

Mrs. Schineller calls on Lucas to explain why finding the total number of people surveyed helps justify why the statement that "more than half of us prefer to do our homework before dinner" is true. Lucas explains that once you find half of the total, you can see that the bar that represents the data for those who choose *before dinner* is higher than that number. Mrs. Schineller uses the talk move *Who can repeat?* to give other students the time to think about Lucas' reasoning. After correcting Lucas's calculation error, Mrs. Schineller asks Lucas to once again explain why it was important to find half of the total number of people surveyed. She then uses *Who can repeat?* four times in succession to focus all of the students' attention on this idea. Finally, she summarizes the steps of the justification herself.

Updating the Lesson Plan After It's Taught

Just as there is a need to help students summarize the important information gleaned from classroom discussions, it is also important for teachers to summarize the questions and talk moves they used in their lessons in their own notes.

Whenever you use a talk lesson, take the time to add notes about students' insights, difficulties, and changes that you might want to make next time. Mrs. Schineller reflected on her graphing lesson and made several notations on her lesson plan. First, she put a star next to the fourth bullet of the "Anticipating Confusion" section as a way to note that the *times as many* statement was possibly even more challenging than she had anticipated. Mrs. Schineller also wrote a note under "Planning the Implementation" to remind herself to use the talk move *stop and jot* when students talked about the phrase *three times as many*. She noticed that only a few students participated in this part of the discussion and believes that this talk move may have encouraged more participation by giving students time to think about the statement and seek clarification from their partners as needed.

> Whenever you use a talk lesson, take the time to add notes about students' insights, difficulties, and changes that you might want to make next time.

Discussion and Reflection

1. Some teachers have used video clips of actual classroom discussions to introduce their students to productive math talk. Depending on the age and background of your students, you may wish to use several of the video clips from this resource in a similar manner. Which clips that you have viewed so far do you think would be most helpful to your students? Why?

2. Some teachers find that the "Asking Questions" part of lesson planning is the most challenging because they aren't sure what questions to ask. Describe what is meant by high-level questions. What resources might help you determine the mathematical goals and related high-level questions when writing talk-based lesson plans?

3. If you have tried using discussion in your classroom, describe what you found was most helpful in planning the use of talk. If you have not yet tried to use talk with students, write a talk lesson plan using the steps described in this chapter.

For professional development sessions and additional video clips that go with this chapter, see:

*Classroom Discussions in Math: A **Facilitator's Guide** to Support Professional Learning of Discourse and the Common Core* (Anderson, Chapin, and O'Connor 2011).

ISBN: 978-1-935099-12-3

Troubleshooting Common Math Talk Problems and Concerns

(Continued)

About This Chapter

As experienced teachers know, any class can present obstacles or unexpected difficulties. This is particularly true when you, the teacher, decide to try something new. In our experience, students may or may not take to all of the methods described in this resource. Some may easily begin to participate in talk, while others may not seem to want to participate at all. As you monitor your progress, it's a good idea to keep track of the difficulties you encounter. In this final chapter we examine the most common problems and what teachers have done in the past to make improvements. We conclude with insights from asking students in our Project Challenge research how they feel about math talk.

Common Problems and Concerns

1. My students won't talk!
2. The same few students do *all* the talking!
3. Should I call on students who do not raise their hands?
4. My students will talk, but they won't listen.
5. "Huh?" How do I respond to incomprehensible contributions?
6. Brilliant, but did anyone understand?
7. I have students at *very* different levels.
8. What should I do when students are wrong?
9. This discussion is not going anywhere . . . .
10. Students' answers are so superficial!
11. What if the first student to speak gives the right answer?
12. What should I do for English language learners?
13. I'm falling behind in my curriculum.
14. Students are off-task while working in small groups.
15. The parents of my students have a lot of questions about all of this talking.

My Students Won't Talk!

Many students are used to a traditional classroom, in which the teacher normally does most of the talking and occasionally asks students to answer questions. It's a big change to ask them to talk about their thinking and respond to other students' contributions. In some classrooms, the teacher will be met with silence at first. This can be unnerving, and even demoralizing. So the first thing to do is to ask yourself a few questions.

Are the students silent because they have not understood a particular question?

Make sure that whether the question comes from you or from another student, they have heard it a few times and have had time to think about it. If it's your question, ask several students to restate it; if it's a student's question, either revoice it yourself or ask another student to repeat it. Be sure that any question is repeated and clarified.

Do the students understand why you are asking them to repeat what others have said, or to explain their reasoning?

For detailed lesson plans on introducing your students to math talk, see Chapter 8.

If you have given an introductory lesson about the reasons for these talk moves, you might revisit that. You might ask, "Why do you think I'm asking you to repeat what the previous speaker said?" Or "Why do you think I'm asking you whether you agree with another student's reasoning?" This will give students an opportunity to review the reasons that everyone must understand what is said, and everyone must pay attention so that they can understand.

Are the students experiencing an attack of either mass shyness or mass confusion?

If you have clarified questions and there is still no answer, it may be that your students are having an attack either of mass shyness or mass confusion! Sometimes it's hard to tell the difference. Early on in the process of starting to use talk, students may be hesitant to think out loud in front of their classmates. If you are confronted with silence from the whole class, have your students use partner talk for two minutes to clarify their thinking and practice their answers with one another. If they still don't seem to be able to talk about the ideas, you may have to step back and pose a simpler but related question. Don't give up!

Is there a pattern of discourteous or disrespectful comments or noises?

If many of your students seem reluctant to speak, make sure that it is not because of a pattern of discourteous or disrespectful comments or noises. Even the presence of one or two students rolling their eyes at the contributions of others may be a deterrent to participation.

Are students' social or cultural backgrounds in conflict with the expectations to talk?

In some cases reluctance to talk may be a function of an individual child's personality. In other cases it may be a family or cultural norm. In some families or communities, children are encouraged to observe and to learn through quiet apprenticeship. Children in these families or communities are not supposed to hold forth about their nascent ideas. It may be particularly frowned upon for girls to actively speak out. When you ask such children to explain their mathematical reasoning, that behavior may be in conflict with what they are used to, although they may not be able to explain this to you. It will take time and patience to encourage quiet children to speak up voluntarily.

For additional information on how to involve more students in your discussions, see Chapter 2.

Teacher Reflection: Quiet Students

Mrs. O'Connor

One teacher we worked with during Project Challenge had a group of fourth-grade girls and boys from Puerto Rico and Central America who were particularly quiet. They were eager and cooperative students but she could not get them to volunteer, and when she called on them they were so quiet that no one could hear them. Repeated requests for them to speak up did not seem to result in louder contributions. Finally, after several months, the teacher spoke to them outside of class as a group. She told them that their contributions were very valued and that they needed to learn to

(Continued)

participate, even if it might seem challenging. To help get the process started, she said she expected each of them to raise his or her hand at least once every lesson: to ask a question, to answer a question, or even just to ask "Could you repeat that?" The students looked relieved, she said, to have the decision to participate made for them. After that, each one began to enter into the conversation and eventually even started to speak loudly enough for everyone to hear. For these particular children, however, the process took the better part of a year.

The Same Few Students
Do *All* the Talking!

Most teachers find that when they begin the process of asking students to talk, there are a few who immediately blossom into really big talkers. Just as with the quiet students, this can be an individual personality trait, or it can be a family or cultural norm. In some families and communities, children who talk a lot, who freely offer their opinions, are considered bright or personable, and their talk is encouraged. When these students are asked to talk in school, they have an advantage. Just like children who have played baseball since age two have an advantage on the playground, when these children get into the game of academic talk in elementary school, they will be way ahead of others in their skills. If you have such students in your class, they will usually jump to answer your questions. Other students will quickly decide that they don't need to force themselves to do the work of participating: These two or three monopolizers will do the work for them.

The teacher then has a problem: The few will gladly take the floor and discuss whatever needs discussion, and the silent majority will become less and less willing to participate. If you see this pattern starting, it's a good idea to nip it in the bud. How? Consider the following suggestions.

Use Your Wait Time

For more information on wait time, see Chapter 1.

First, be determined: Use your wait time. When you ask a question, and those same two or three hands go up first, keep waiting. Be explicit with your students about your use of wait time. Sometimes when teachers begin to increase their wait time, students are taken aback and wonder why the teacher is not calling on them right away. You might say, "All good mathematicians need time to think. So, I'm trying really hard to make sure that I give you time to think about the question before we hear one person's answer."

> All good mathematicians need time to think. So, I'm trying really hard to make sure that I give you time to think about the question before we hear one person's answer.

Repeat the Question

You may decide to repeat the question in order to provide additional thinking time for students who may want to participate, but who don't feel ready to do so. When other students finally do raise their hands, call on several of them and have them repeat one another's contributions. If you wait ten, twenty, or thirty seconds and still only the usual two or three hands appear, don't give in. Use partner talk to solicit more participation. You might say, "This is a tough but important question. Turn and talk with the person next to you for thirty seconds about this question." Many teachers report that when they do this, the room erupts with talk. In this case, call the students back together, and once again ask for volunteers to speak. Usually, the number of raised hands is much larger than it was initially.

> This is a tough but important question. Turn and talk with the person next to you for thirty seconds about this question.

Arrange Individual Meetings

Just as we suggested meeting individually with students who are hesitant to talk, we would encourage you to meet privately with students who monopolize the floor. You might say, "I see your hand up a lot. I'm not ignoring you, but my job as the teacher is to make sure all students participate. So since your hand is up almost all the time, you might want to think about this. Decide before you raise your hand whether this is something you really want to comment on. Remember, you can always come and talk to me after class about the problem."

Take Advantage of Small-Group Discussions

Small-group discussion time offers a great opportunity to increase the number of students who speak during the whole-class discussion. As you circulate among students working in small groups, listen in on their conversations. If you hear a particularly quiet student articulate an insightful idea, ask an important question, or describe an effective solution strategy, ask that student if she or he would be willing to share the contribution later with the entire class.

Assign Random Speakers

You may also consider assigning random speakers as representatives of their small groups. Notify these students in advance that they will speak during the whole-class discussion. For example, in a discussion about solution methods, say, "In a moment, I'm going to call on several small groups to tell us how they solved the problem. The person in each group with the birthday closest to today will speak for each group. So, in your small groups, determine who that person is, decide what you want that person to say, and have that person practice what he or she is going to say."

Build on Contributions

For additional information on how to involve more students in your discussions, see Chapter 2.

Sometimes you may feel that the few who raise their hands early and often are the most able, and that you want to use what they have to say. Their contributions may be the most dynamic, the most illuminating in terms of getting other students to understand the issues. We encourage you to use the insights of those students. Build on their contributions. Just make sure that you don't fall into the habit of relying on them to support your use of talk to the exclusion of other, less clear or less confident students. Your goal is to build a classroom community in which everyone can participate.

Should I Call on Students Who Do Not Raise Their Hands?

For many teachers, one of the toughest parts of using student talk in the classroom is deciding whether to call on students who never volunteer. In every classroom there will be one or two students who are truly reluctant to say anything. Are they benefiting from the use of talk in the classroom if they never talk and only listen? The little research that exists on the question seems to indicate that students certainly can benefit by listening. They can learn without talking. However, as we argued in Chapters 1 and 2, there are benefits to participating in talk, from attention and motivation to clarification of understanding and improvement in language facility. So, how should you handle the few cases where you get the distinct feeling that you are torturing the students by waiting for them to answer a question? Consider the following.

> Students certainly can benefit by listening. They can learn without talking. There are benefits to participating in talk, from attention and motivation to clarification of understanding and improvement in language facility.

Arrange Individual Meetings

Some teachers feel that if they call on such students they may actually harm them. In our view, if you are sensitive and supportive, you will actually help such students, rather than harm them. Once again, we recommend talking to each student privately. Ask the student about his or her concerns and reluctance. Try to come up with a plan that will let the student dip a toe in the water, so to speak. A few planned contributions can build confidence, and the student may overcome a barrier that will help him or her in other areas of life as well. Your efforts with such students may continue over a number of months.

Take Advantage of Partner Talk

Call on reluctant students right after partner talk, when they have had a chance to practice with a partner. Ask: "What did you and your partner come up with?" Or, "Tell us one thing that you learned from talking with your partner." You may also wish to work with such students during partner talk to help them prepare what they will say.

Give Students the Right to Pass

Remind students of their right to "pass" when you call on them. The obligation to participate in a discussion does not equate to an obligation to give answers on demand. Rather, it means that students are expected to communicate about what they are thinking and what they need to help them learn. So, students who need more time to help them learn have the right to this time. You might

> Remember, if I call on you and you need more time to think about your answer, that's no problem. Just say, 'I need more time.' Or, 'Can you come back to me?'

say, "Remember, if I call on you and you need more time to think about your answer, that's no problem. Just say, 'I need more time.' Or, 'Can you come back to me?'" When a student does ask for more time, be sure to remember to revisit with this student later in the discussion.

Ask Each Student to Make at Least One Contribution

For a video example of a teacher explaining to students what they might do if she calls on them to speak and they are not ready to respond, see Video Clip 8B, If I Call on You . . . in Chapter 8.

A more general issue related to this is how we call on students every day. Should we call only on those students whose hands are raised, or should we try to distribute the turns equally throughout the class? This is a difficult issue, and different teachers will have distinct views on it. In our view, the most effective approach is to try to get all students to make a significant contribution at least once every few lessons. And in order to get them over the hurdle of speaking out loud in a group, it may also be a good idea to have each student say at least one thing every day, even a minor request for clarification.

My Students Will Talk, But They Won't Listen

You may be fortunate to have a class full of students who are willing to talk and share their reasoning. However, these same students may have another problem: They may be so involved in talking that they don't listen well. Instead of listening to one another's contributions and building on the idea of the preceding speaker, they may interrupt, talk over one another, and contribute ideas that all but ignore the previous contributions. Sometimes small groups of friends may talk together while others are talking in the large group. There may even be some discourteous or disrespectful talk about others' contributions. How can you get students to listen respectfully to one another and think together as a class?

Remind Students of Their Discussion Rights and Obligations

Start by having a talk with the whole class. Remind students that each of them has the right to be heard, but that this means they have a corresponding obligation to listen.

Ask Students to Repeat What Another Student Said

Start to rely more heavily on the move of asking students to repeat what the previous speaker has just said. If they are not able to do this, use whatever classroom sanctions you have in place to let them know that this is a serious obligation.

One teacher had students in fourth grade who were not very good at making their contributions connect with those of the previous speaker. He ended up with lots of disjointed talk, where one student's turn had no obvious connection to the next. For a while he tried to draw the connections for them, but finally he decided to ask them to start each turn by saying either of two things: "I agree/disagree with what [the previous speaker] said because . . ." or "I want to add on to what [the previous speaker] said . . . ."

We think you will find that if you are consistent, asking students to respond specifically to one another's contributions, students will begin to internalize the obligation to listen to others and think about what they have said.

For detailed lesson plans on introducing your students to math talk, see Chapter 8.

"Huh?" How Do I Respond to Incomprehensible Contributions?

As we have shown in some of the examples in previous sections, students' responses are sometimes almost impossible to understand. What should one do when a student produces a really unintelligible utterance? What if it is so incomprehensible that you cannot even begin to rephrase it because you just haven't understood any of it? The temptation is simply to say, "Oh, I see. How interesting," and quickly move on to another student. This way we can avoid embarrassing ourselves and the student at the same time! However, in the long run, this will really undermine your purposes. You want students to practice becoming clearer in their thinking and talking. What better place to start than with a student who is very unclear? You want students to learn that it is worth the struggle to try to clarify one's meaning. If you pass over unclear students, other students will learn that it's better to avoid embarrassment than to engage in the struggle for clarity.

> You want students to practice at becoming clearer in their thinking and talking. What better place to start than with a student who is very unclear?

If you are working hard to engage students in challenging mathematics, you will not be able to avoid this problem. People—whether adults or children—who are talking about something new and complicated tend to sound unclear. As comprehension gets more difficult, fluency and clarity decrease. In our experience, when teachers introduce a new and challenging mathematics topic, up to half of all contributions in a class may be very difficult to comprehend. So what can be done? Consider the following.

Revoice and Repeat

For more information on the talk moves revoicing and repeating, see Chapter 1.

First, use the talk moves revoicing and repeating. Try to repeat even a few words the student has said. If you can't do this, ask another student to do so. Unlikely as it seems, we have often seen students give wonderful renditions of what we found incomprehensible. In a way, this makes sense. You are up at the front of the class, trying to keep track of twenty-five different individuals and the contents of the lesson as well. Students can afford to sit at their desks listening. They may have understood something that got by you. Keep trying until you get at least a partial insight into what the student was saying. Remember to ask: "Is that what you said?" when either you revoice or another student repeats the original speaker's idea. In an effort to understand a contribution, listeners can often misinterpret what was said, and the student's original point can morph into something quite different in intent from the speaker's original statement.

Say More . . .

For more information on the talk move, "Say more . . ." see Chapter 1.

Use the talk move *Say more* . . . to help the student expand on their original contribution. If the additional information does not provide clarity to their prior remark, don't hesitate to use this move once again (for example, "OK, that helped clarify things a bit. But I still need a little bit more help making sure I understand. Keep going."). Remind students that communication takes time and effort and ask them to be patient with you as you strive to understand their thinking.

Show What You're Thinking

You can also ask students if they would like to come up to the board to show the class what they are thinking. Even in classroom discussions, a picture is still worth a thousand words. It is important, however, not to let the students' written representation (for example, equation or picture) supplant their verbal description. Once students record the representation where everyone can see it, ask them to explain what they have shown. Then, ask several other students to explain what the representation shows and repeat what their classmates have said.

Give It Another Try Later?

There will occasionally be times when neither you nor anyone else can understand what a particular student is saying. If you need to move on, you can say to the student something like this: "Well, I guess we haven't really understood your contribution. See if you can work on it, and if you want to give it another try later, I'll come back to you." The student may or may not want to pursue it later, but at least you have conveyed the message that each student's ideas are worth struggling with.

Brilliant, But Did Anyone Understand?

Occasionally a student will make a mathematically brilliant contribution, or one that at least has the potential to raise some important issues for discussion. But as you look around the room, you wonder whether you and the student are the only two people in the room who have understood what the student said. What are you to do?

Can You Repeat That?

First, start by asking the student to repeat. Say something like: "Wow, that sounds really interesting, but I got lost in the middle. Can you repeat that?" Next, ask several other students to repeat or rephrase the contribution. This alerts them that they all have to pay attention to what has been said. Make sure that you ask the originator of the idea whether he or she agrees with the other students' interpretations. If the originator does not agree, he or she will have to repeat and clarify the idea. Even if the originator does agree, have several students in succession try to repeat the idea. If the idea is really important, having multiple students repeat it will ensure that most of them understand it, and that many of them will appreciate its significance as the discussion proceeds. In fact, you may even want to use one to two minutes of partner talk here to give everyone in the class the opportunity to repeat and make sense of the idea.

> For more information on the talk move *Who can repeat?* see Chapter 1.

If the contribution is a lengthy one, don't be afraid to interrupt the speaker so that the other students are called upon to repeat the statement in parts rather than in its entirety. After the speaker makes one key point or describes one step in his or her thinking, say, "Let me interrupt you for a moment. Torrence, can you repeat what Diane just said?" Many times students are unable to repeat a comment because the comment is simply too long. Asking the speaker to stop at key points gives students time to think so that they can continue to follow along with the reasoning step by step.

Should you pitch in at this point, attempting to give yet another rendition of what the original student said? In our view, although it's tempting to take over and revoice the student's excellent contribution yourself, we think you should refrain, if you can. By allowing other students

> In our view, although it's tempting to take over and revoice the student's excellent contribution yourself, we think you should refrain, if you can.

to try first, before you step in, you focus everyone's attention on the contribution, and you allow the originator to get credit for the insight. It also reinforces the joint, collaborative nature of the discussion. You can play a role, however, in determining the extent that all students understand the contribution, and in moving the conversation forward to aspects that they still may not understand.

Write It Down

For more information on the talk move *revoicing*, see Chapter 1.

You may also use the board as a revoicing tool. You can scribe what other students say as they rephrase the originator's idea. Students may also scribe or illustrate their points. Sometimes slowing down the process enough to write things down allows you to get a clearer idea of how to proceed. And getting across the importance of a difficult new idea or an original observation can take a long time. We once watched the important idea of one student slowly become clear to other students over the course of two different lessons.

I Have Students at *Very* Different Levels

Most teachers are confronted with a wide range of backgrounds and abilities in their classrooms. If you are trying to get the students to focus on the same problem, what do you do if some of the students do not understand the problem? How can you have a discussion when your students are at very different levels?

Pair Students of *Similar* Ability

We first suggest pairing students of similar ability and of compatible personality. What do we mean by similar ability and compatible personality? This is something that a teacher can discover only through getting to know the students. It doesn't necessarily mean pairing boys with boys and girls with girls, but rather is based on your intuition of which students will be able to talk to one another in a productive way. This may sometimes mean that a weaker student is paired with a student on grade level. Or a student on grade level may be paired with one of the most able students in the room. The only real proviso is to avoid pairing the very strongest students with the very weakest students.

Avoid Grouping Weaker Students with Stronger Students

Many teachers follow the practice of grouping weaker students with stronger students, because they believe that high-achieving students can help the weaker students understand the material. In our experience, in talk-intensive classrooms, this often does not work well. What happens is that high-achieving students quickly come to an understanding and present a solution, and the talk ceases long before the weaker student can participate in thinking through the problem. Even when the higher-achieving student tries to explain his or her reasoning in a sort of expository or lecture style, there is no guarantee that the weaker student will benefit. Often the weaker student takes on a very passive role as a learner, and this is the opposite of what we are trying to foster.

Switch Partners at Regular Intervals

Some teachers randomly assign partners, and this can work as well. However even in this case, you want to think carefully to avoid problems. In our experience, if you want to get the most out of this model of using talk, you might do well to pair students of similar ability, at least part of the time. Then consider switching partners at regular intervals, and if you see that a partnership is not working, don't be afraid to intervene and change partners.

Use Flexible Grouping

It's important to note that pairing students of similar ability may or may not involve assigning students different tasks. For example, it's possible to give students who understand quickly an additional question or challenge that they can do while other students work with the main assignment. This also allows the teacher to provide more scaffolding and support to groups and pairs that need it. What we are aiming for is flexible grouping based on what students know about a particular area, and based on what the teacher has perceived about their ways of interacting.

For more tips on working with small groups, see Chapter 2.

What Should I Do When Students Are Wrong?

Discussions like the ones you will experience are often full of mistakes of various kinds. In the process of working through a problem, students may use a word incorrectly. They may use a computational procedure incorrectly. Their answers may be wrong, sometimes strikingly wrong. Your task is to figure out how to respond. Our suggestions here fall into two broad categories: how to handle students' feelings about being wrong, and how to allocate time to their mistakes.

It's OK to Be Wrong

First, we'd like to point out that this kind of instruction requires students to agree and disagree with one another at some point. Often, in this atmosphere of inquiry, students will notice when someone says something wrong, or two students will come up with different answers. For most students, being wrong is not pleasant, and not trivial. Many students will still have the idea that success in mathematics means being right, not being a strong thinker. It is helpful to explicitly discuss the value of wrong answers, and the unavoidability of mistakes and errors. Errors can be repositioned as a source of new knowledge. Teach your students to say, "I'd like to revise my thinking" or the phrase that often pops up spontaneously in a good discussion: "I disagree with myself!"

> It is helpful to explicitly discuss the value of wrong answers, and the unavoidability of mistakes and errors.

It's very important to monitor the norms of respectful discourse at points like these, when a student has come up with a wrong answer. You do not have to avoid calling attention to a wrong answer, but you do need to continue to reassure students that it's OK to be wrong, and that all students must be sensitive to the feelings of someone who has publicly made a mistake.

Allocating Time to Mistakes

Second, it will sometimes be the case that you will be in the middle of a good discussion where a student is making an important mathematical point. In the middle of making this point, the student will say something incorrect, such as "five times eight is forty-eight." You might wonder: Should you stop the discussion to correct this error, at the risk of derailing a conversation where students are getting intellectually involved? We encourage you to be sensitive to the flow of discussion. If students are dealing with new and difficult ideas, and the point of the discussion is to get clarity about concepts and ideas, it might be perfectly acceptable to ignore a minor mistake.

> Should you stop the discussion to correct this error, at the risk of derailing a conversation where students are getting intellectually involved?

However, if you are in a review, or in a discussion in which you are going over something that has become familiar to students, that is a good time to insist on high standards of correctness.

Telling

Finally, you should also remember that you can continue to use direct instruction or more traditional forms of "telling" during a whole-class discussion. If students are converging on the wrong solution, developing a misguided generalization, or misusing an algorithm, do not be afraid to step in and provide the necessary course correction. In these instances, pointing out inconsistencies and errors, providing a missing definition or skill, and modeling certain procedures may be exactly what is needed to shift the productivity of the discussion back into high gear.

This Discussion Is Not Going Anywhere . . . .

Sometimes you may get the impression that although your students are willing to talk and listen respectfully, the conversation is slow, repetitive, and even dull at times. If this is happening consistently, ask yourself whether you are "beating a dead horse" and going over material after the majority of students have understood. If you feel that there is too much repetition, you may be asking too many students to repeat ideas that they have already made sense of. Consider doing the following.

Take a Quick Formative Assessment

Use the small-group time that typically precedes the whole-group discussion to do a quick, formative assessment of students' thinking. For example, if most student groups are successfully solving a problem using a particular strategy, there may not be a need to explore this strategy further during the whole-group discussion. Rather, look and listen for effective and efficient strategies that groups are using with limited success and use those as the focus of your whole-group discussions. Discussions around the mathematics with which students are not yet proficient have the greatest potential to increase understanding.

> Look and listen for effective and efficient strategies that groups are using with limited success and use those as the focus of your whole-group discussions.

Revisit the Level of Your Questions

Another issue may be the level of your questions. If there are too many low-level questions, you may not have appropriate fodder for a high-level, exciting discussion. It helps to work with colleagues on this issue. You might ask someone to come in and observe you, to see if your use of the tools of talk could be sharpened.

Keep Sight of Your Mathematical Goals

For more guidance on determining mathematical goals and questions for talk-based mathematics lessons, see Chapter 8.

Sometimes the problem is that students are introducing interesting but tangential questions, and although the discussion is lively, you are not making progress toward your mathematical goals. It's important to remember that you cannot follow up on every single point. In order to keep the discussion moving, you will have to ignore some things and move other topics to the forefront. This is why planning is so important—it's easy to lose sight of your goals and get off track with interesting but tangential questions.

Students' Answers Are So Superficial!

At the beginning of this process, as you first begin to use talk intensively, students may not know how to respond. They will rely on the strategy they have used before, namely, to provide a one-word answer to the teacher's question, as in the following example:

1. **Ms. G:** So what method do you think you'll use to solve this problem?
2. **Phil:** Subtract. [No response from Ms. Glass] Yes, subtract!

This is a typical response from a student who has not had much experience carefully thinking through a problem and presenting reasons for his responses. What should Ms. Glass do here? One option is to ask Phil why he thinks the method should be to use subtraction. Imagine, however, that Phil responds: "I don't know." What next? Ms. Glass could refer him back to the problem, asking him again why subtraction seemed to him to be a good method. Or she may ask him to describe the features of the problem that helped him decide to subtract. Upon rereading the problem, Phil may actually think more deeply about the problem, rather than simply trying to supply a one-word answer that in another class would be sufficient.

The principle here is that the teacher must continue to focus on reasoning: Ask students to justify their decisions, whatever sort of decisions those are. Don't be afraid to press them for evidence of reasoning. Students we have worked with have told us that they appreciate the experience of being made to think more deeply. Although they do say that they feel pressured sometimes, they enjoy the fact that mathematics starts to make sense because they are forced to make sense of it.

What If the First Student to Speak Gives the Right Answer?

Imagine you have posed a problem to your students and after giving them time to solve the problem with a partner, you then begin the whole-class discussion. You ask, "Who can tell us how they began to solve the problem?" The first student you call on gives a coherent, articulate explanation of the correct answer. What do you do? Put aside your plans for a discussion? Move on? Not yet.

Recall What You Heard in Pairs or Small Groups

First, recall what you observed and heard when students were working in pairs or small groups to solve the problem. Did most of them solve the problem correctly before the whole-class discussion began? If so, you may wish in the whole-class discussion to ask several other students to repeat the speaker's statement and explain why they agree or disagree with its reasoning. Then, ask everyone to turn and talk with the person next to them about whether they agree or disagree with the speaker's comment, and listen to see if most can do so successfully. If the students can, it is not necessary to continue the discussion of a comment that most, or all, students understand. After all, classroom talk is productive when it allows students to progress in their understanding, not simply reaffirm what they already know.

> Classroom talk is productive when it allows students to progress in their understanding, not simply reaffirm what they already know.

Revisit the Student's Answer Later On

If the students you call on to respond to the speaker's comment cannot do so successfully, you may wish to use the techniques described in the section "Brilliant, but did anyone understand?" Or, you may feel that this comment will have much greater significance if discussed later on. Perhaps students do not seem clear on the constraints of the problem, nor are they sure of which strategies to use. Maybe most have solved the problem incorrectly and need clarification of their misconceptions before discussing the correct solution. In this case you may say to the student, "You have given us a lot to think about. I know I need to back up a little bit and think more about making sense of the problem and deciding which strategy to use and why. I'm going to ask if you would be willing to say your comment again a little later on. I know it is going to be helpful to all of us."

Decide Who You Will Call On and in What Order

Further, if you wish to avoid this scenario in future discussions, use the partner- or small-group discussion time to decide who you will call on and in what order. For example, you may wish to begin the discussion by calling on several students whom you heard restate the problem and question articulately and thoroughly, even though their solution strategies may have had problems. Then, you may wish to call on students who explored different ways to solve the problem, progressing in difficulty and complexity. Notifying these students in advance that you plan to call on them also increases the productivity of the whole-group discussion. The more you know about what your students understand and the more prepared they are to speak, the more strategically you can use their contributions in a whole-class discussion.

Pose a More Difficult Problem

If you have time, you can capitalize on students' understanding by posing a similar but more difficult problem or problem extension for students to discuss. This will allow you to reach the mathematical goals of your lesson while still engaging the students in productive discourse.

What Should I Do for English Language Learners?

Three-quarters of the students with whom we worked in Project Challenge were English language learners (see *The Research: Project Challenge* in Appendix A). Yet they all made tremendous progress in classrooms using intensive talk. Teachers with English language learners should not shy away from using this approach to mathematics, but it helps to think carefully about the demands of the talk moves and formats we have introduced here.

Use Wait Time

First, make sure that you give students plenty of time. Use wait time consistently and patiently. Waiting up to thirty seconds may be necessary, and if you have many native English speakers mixed in with your English language learners, you will have to model for them the value of waiting.

Understand the Timeline for Readiness

Second, it may take longer into the year before such students are ready to handle the demands of talking, repeating other students' contributions, or making their own. Think carefully about putting them on the spot. But as the year progresses, do not assume that you must simply leave them out of the discussion. Talk with students outside of class to encourage them to ask a question, or to ask for clarification.

I'm Falling Behind in My Curriculum

Teachers who are new to using talk in their classrooms typically report falling behind in their curriculum as one of their concerns. They find that asking students to explain and clarify their reasoning and respond to and repeat each other's ideas turns a one-day lesson into a two- or three-day event. In the face of this dilemma, teachers often revert back to direct instruction techniques in order to "catch up" but then worry that their students aren't getting better at using talk to learn mathematics. These are all typical and understandable concerns. Unfortunately, there are no quick and easy answers to managing the time pressures of teaching mathematics using any form of instruction. However, we have found that teachers who stick with talk do get better at managing instructional time. Keep in mind the following suggestions.

> **MATH TALK TIP**
>
> ### Use Math Talk to Support Students' Language Learning
>
> We found in Project Challenge that the talk moves and talk formats introduced in this resource actually support language learning as well as mathematical thinking. There are ideas and practices throughout the resource that will help students who are learning English. For example, *revoicing* can clarify students' contributions and *Who can repeat?* can help make others' contributions clearer to them. In Chapters 3 and 7, the emphases on definitions, concepts, and representations are particularly relevant for English language learners. Over time, the experience of listening closely, repeating their classmates' explanations, and making their own contributions will push your students ahead in English as well as mathematics.

See Chapter 8 for more guidance on planning questions and other important components of talk-based lessons.

Plan Your Discussion Questions in Advance

We suggest that you plan your discussion questions in advance. Choose two or three questions that focus on the mathematical objectives of the lesson. Make sure that these questions are open-ended in either approach or answer. Use the talk moves described in Chapter 1 only when discussing these key questions.

Combine or Consolidate Lessons

Teachers who use talk-based instruction with their textbook series sometimes find that the discussions allow them to make adjustments to their curriculum. Sometimes students' comments reveal that they know more than what the textbook lesson assumed. For example, if several student groups use a strategy that is not covered until later in the chapter, the teacher may decide to focus the entire whole-class discussion on this strategy. This allows the teacher to move forward in the curriculum by either combining or consolidating lessons. In addition, talk encourages students to connect new ideas to previous understandings. Review of important mathematical concepts and skills often occurs naturally. Thus, teachers sometimes find that they no longer need to devote entire class periods to review.

Students Are Off-Task While Working in Small Groups

For more tips on using the small-group discussion format, see Chapter 2.

Human beings are inherently social. Any adult who has ever worked in a cooperative group knows that a certain amount of socializing in a group setting is inevitable. Nonetheless, it is serious concern when the social aspect of the group interferes with and prevents learning from taking place. While off-task behavior is detrimental to any type of teaching, it is particularly problematic with discourse-intensive instruction. Students who do not engage in small-group discussions will likely be unable to participate in whole-class discussions in a meaningful way.

Why Are My Students Off-Task?

There are a number of reasons why small-group talk may be unproductive. Ask yourself the following questions.

Are the questions I've given small groups to discuss complex enough?

First, the questions the groups are to discuss may not be complex enough to support talk from multiple perspectives. If a question (for example, "Identify the parallel and perpendicular lines in the diagram") can be answered with a one-word response, students will quickly answer and then start talking about nonmathematical topics. Another reason small groups get off-task is because a task or question (for example, "Explain your method for solving this problem") doesn't provide enough fodder for all group members to stay engaged. Often only one or two students share their ideas and methods and the other students state that they agree with them. In this case, the question may be a good one but the talk format has not supported all students articulating their reasoning. Grouping students into pairs may provide a quick and easy solution.

Do students feel accountable and motivated to stay on-task?

What if the question posed to a group is a good, complex one and students are still off-task? What should you do? One way to make sure that students work productively in their small groups is to be very explicit about their accountability to the whole class. This can be accomplished by assigning each group a specific question or one part of a multistep problem or task to discuss later with the entire class. Alternatively, you may assign each member in the class to be the designated speaker for a particular question or problem step. In reality, you will not call on every student to speak about every question or problem. But anticipating that you might call on them to speak will likely motivate students to stay on-task.

The Parents of My Students Have a Lot of Questions About All of This Talking

If students enter your class only having experienced traditional mathematics instruction, they will likely have a lot to tell their parents after school about what's going on in math class. Some students may express concerns to their parents about talking in math class—even if they don't share those concerns with you. Other students may tell their parents how much they are enjoying your class discussions, but their parents may have their own questions and concerns about your new forms of talk. Here are a few tips for talking with parents.

> **MATH TALK TIP**
>
> ### Talking to Principals and Administrators
>
> The information here can also be helpful when talking to principals and department chairs about your new forms of talk.

Use the Talk Moves

If parents wish to speak with you more about your emphasis on student discussion, it is important to find out specifically what their concerns and questions are. As you talk with parents, you might find it helpful to use some of the talk moves we describe in this resource. For example, if a parent shares that their child seems anxious about talking in front of the class, you may say, "So, you are concerned that our classroom discussions may be stressful to your child. Is that right?" After the parent verifies or clarifies, ask them to say more (e.g., "Tell me a little bit more so I can be sure I understand.").

Explain Your Reasons for Using Classroom Discussions

As you talk with parents, you should be prepared to explain to them your reasons for using discussion in math class. Talk to your students' parents about how discussion and reasoning are emphasized throughout the Common Core State Standards for Mathematics. Use the "Why Use Talk in Mathematics Classrooms?" section in the front of this resource to describe the cognitive and social benefits of student discussion.

Describe How You Help Students Learn to Participate in Discussions

Talk about the strategies you use to help students become successful participants during your class discussions. Focus your description so that it is relevant to each parent's specific concerns. For example, if a parent is concerned that his or her child feels "put on the spot" when called on to speak during a whole-class discussion, explain how you work with students during small-group work time to help them develop responses that can later be shared with the whole class.

Assure Parents of a Balanced Instructional Approach

Finally, it is important to assure parents that your use of discussion is one part of a balanced instructional approach. Even though discussions will be a regular part of math class this year, students will also be given lots of opportunities to work independently on computation and problem-solving exercises.

Reassurance from Project Challenge Students

As you begin these new practices, you may be sensitive to negative reactions from students. Many people respond to new practices with complaints or resistance. You may feel that requiring students to listen to each person's contribution is too demanding, or that waiting twenty seconds for a student's answer puts too much pressure on them. We have some reassurance from some of our students in Project Challenge, the project described in Appendix A. Recall that about 75 percent of the students in the low-income urban schools we worked in were second-language learners of English, as were the Project Challenge students. We had had concerns since the beginning of the program about the challenges they might experience in our talk-intensive classrooms.

See Appendix A.

Although we had seen tremendous growth, we wanted to know how they felt about it. So at the end of the fourth year of Project Challenge, we took some class time to ask one hundred seventh-grade students for their reactions to our four-year focus on productive talk. The following examples reveal what students said and wrote about talking and listening.

> At the end of the fourth year of Project Challenge, we took some class time to ask one hundred seventh-grade students for their reactions to our four-year focus on productive talk.

Was being required to listen to each other helpful or not helpful?

When asked, "Was being required to listen to each other helpful or not helpful?" approximately 95 percent of the students surveyed responded "helpful." When asked why he thought listening was helpful, Anton made the following remark: "Sometimes [math] is confusing but when you listen carefully, you can figure out how to do the math slowly, or little by little, and you find out how to do it." Anton's comment is that of an experienced and effective listener. He knows that listening does not make understanding instantaneous or automatic. Rather, as he says himself, listening helps learning *slowly, or little by little*. And how does this happen? It happens when students have conversations about mathematics, often revoicing an idea over and over again, until peers reach a common understanding of an idea. The listening

> Sometimes [math] is confusing but when you listen carefully, you can figure out how to do the math slowly, or little by little, and you find out how to do it.

continues as students comment on why they agree or disagree with an idea. All the while, the listeners are learning from the students who are talking. Anton not only knows how to listen but also sees its value in his learning.

Mel offers a perspective on how talking and listening go hand-in-hand in learning mathematics. He says, "It helped us when we got to hear other people's answers. We can add things to our answers to make them better than [the solution] we had originally from the question that we had to answer." Mel's comment targets one of the very core benefits of listening—helping us figure out what to say and how to say it. Mel knows that we listen not for the sake of listening, but so that we can broaden what we know about a subject and thus get better at speaking about it. He knows this because he has been encouraged and expected to listen to his classmates and then use their statements to form and articulate his own reasoning.

Brianna's comment mirrors Mel's remark. She writes: "Listening to each other is helpful because if we don't listen to each other, how can we understand what each of us has to say?" Aaron writes: "It's helpful because if it was not required [to listen] I wouldn't pay attention." Jan says, "You can see other people's points of view. People can correct their mistakes by hearing others." These comments are from students who participated in talk-intensive classes. But their comments show that they understand the benefits of listening. And that's what is required if students are going to use listening as a learning tool as they continue with their studies.

Was having to talk to others about math helpful or not helpful?

When asked, "Was having to talk to others about math helpful or not helpful?" approximately 88 percent of the students responded "helpful." Jan notes that it is important to explain yourself in math class because, "In real life, if you can't explain and don't have evidence, it doesn't count." Aaron, who writes that listening forces him to pay attention, thinks, "It's helpful [to talk] because I could ask questions." Barry says, "I like the talking to your neighbor or partner thing because if somebody doesn't really understand something and they talk to their partner, their partner can help them understand it so you get to go on without being confused or having trouble." These students can articulate the benefits of talk because they have experienced

> In real life, if you can't explain and don't have evidence, it doesn't count.

these benefits regularly and consistently in their mathematics classes. By talking about their reasoning and receiving the support to do so, students come to realize that it is important to be as clear as possible, provide supporting evidence, and use talk as an opportunity to get clarification and understanding.

During the discussion about talking and listening, Tina and Mrs. Anderson had an exchange that shows that even when students are uncomfortable with talk, they still see its worth. Mrs. Anderson asked Tina if she liked being called on in discussions. This is the conversation that ensued.

1. **Tina:** Sometimes you push me to say the answer and I really don't know the answer.

2. **Mrs. A:** What happens if I keep pushing you and you still don't know the answer?

3. **Tina:** I tell you I don't know.

4. **Mrs. A:** And then what happens?

5. **Tina:** You go to call on a different person.

6. **Mrs. A:** So how does that make you feel?

7. **Tina:** Better.

8. **Mrs. A:** And when I call on another person what are you doing?

9. **Tina:** Listening.

10. **Mrs. A:** And then do you usually raise your hand after that? [Tina shakes her head no.] Why not?

11. **Tina:** 'Cause you'll usually just come right back and ask me.

12. **Mrs. A:** And when I come back automatically, then how do you feel?

13. **Tina:** Better because then I would know the answer.

It is not easy or enjoyable for students, or anyone, to admit that they do not know something. But the fact remains that not knowing answers is a normal part of life. And because it is, saying so should be a part of talking in math class. Students should be allowed to say when they do not know or cannot explain something. Some teachers are surprised when we push to revisit a student after he or she admits to not knowing an answer. They think that it puts too much pressure on a student who already has admitted that he or she lacks understanding. Tina's comments indicate that the opposite is true. Tina admits that she feels better when Mrs. Anderson goes on to speak with another student; it takes the pressure off of her. But while the other student is speaking, Tina is listening. So, instead of the discussion continuing without a contribution from

> **Students appreciate being revisited because it gets them past the discomfort of "not knowing the answer" and on to being a contributor to the discussion.**

Tina, Mrs. Anderson comes back to her. This gives Tina a chance to show what she has gained from listening, and she gets to contribute to the discussion. This, Tina says, makes her feel better. Tina's comments suggest that students appreciate being revisited because it gets them past the discomfort of "not knowing the answer" and on to being a contributor to the discussion.

When asked how she felt about the expectation to contribute to class discussions, Kara responded that she didn't like it. She said, "Some girls don't really know the answer or are shy and don't want to speak." When asked whether she felt that there was a payoff to speaking despite being shy or unsure, Kara said, "Sometimes it's worth it because you end up knowing the answer but you didn't know it before." Ryan told us that he did not like being called on to talk because when he was not paying attention, it was embarrassing. He then went on to say, "If I got called on and wasn't paying attention, I was afraid I would get called on again so I started paying attention." Both Kara and Ryan are quite honest in their feelings about required participation—they don't like it. But both also name benefits to it—it helps them pay attention and learn new information.

The Authors' Story: Gayle's Transformation

We end this chapter with one last striking example that convinced us that classroom talk was a difficult but rewarding endeavor. This example centers on Gayle, a Project Challenge student. When Gayle began Project Challenge in fourth grade, she did not say much at all in class. Watching Gayle and her partners complete a project, her fourth-grade teacher remarked, was like watching a silent movie. Gayle struggled on her weekly quizzes and did not seem to be benefiting from this instructional approach.

> **Watching Gayle and her partners complete a project, her fourth-grade teacher remarked, was like watching a silent movie.**

Yet over the course of fifth grade, Gayle began to change. Her fifth-grade teacher worked hard to get Gayle to speak in class. When called on, Gayle would often respond with a short to long period of silence, which was then followed by a short, barely audible response. Her teacher continued to call on Gayle, and each time her responses got a little louder, a little longer, and a little more sensible. While her evolution was slow but steady, one particular example of her emergence comes to mind. Gayle's class was discussing the sum of angles in a triangle. The question posed to the class was whether it was necessary to measure all three angles in order to determine the measure of each. Many students maintained that it was necessary when Gayle spoke up with this comment: "You don't need to measure all the angles because the sum is one hundred eighty degrees. So if you know that two of them are one hundred twenty degrees, you just ask yourself, 'What plus one hundred twenty is one hundred eighty?' and that gives you the answer." After she made this comment, Gayle's classmates were asked what they thought of her idea. As they were speaking, most in support but some still dubious, Gayle's teacher looked back at Gayle and saw her straighten her posture, throw her shoulders back, and while maintaining a serious look on her face, beam with quiet confidence. At the end of the program, Gayle was described by her seventh-grade teacher as still quiet but articulate, responsive, and engaged. Of talking and listening, Gayle writes: "It was helpful to listen and talk to each other because I got to listen to how people thought about problems and why they agreed or not, and I got to talk to people and tell them what I thought about certain things."

Gayle's transformation occurred because she had teachers who were determined to get their students to talk productively about their mathematical understanding. None of those teachers said it was easy. All said, without hesitation, that it was worthwhile. As you begin to use talk in your own class, you will help students change like Gayle did.

Gayle's transformation occurred because she had teachers who were determined to get their students to talk productively about their mathematical understanding.

Discussion and Reflection

1. Which of the challenges described in the first part of this chapter have you experienced? Which of the authors' suggestions helped you overcome these challenges? What other strategies have worked?

2. Calling on students is a particularly emotional and complex issue. What do you think about calling on students who have not raised their hands to speak? Do you think calling on them is an effective instructional strategy? Why or why not?

3. In the last part of this chapter, "Reassurance from Project Challenge Students," the authors describe what happened when they asked their students to react to the use of productive talk in math class. Ask your students what they think about talking in math class. Specifically, ask them to describe how they think talk has or has not helped them learn math.

Appendices

Appendix A

The Research: Project Challenge

What is the basis for the descriptions and recommendations you will find in this resource? One source is the research and literature that deals with classroom talk and student learning. We include an appendix of these references for readers who want to learn more. However in addition, we have our own research experience in the planned use of classroom discourse to support students' thinking and reasoning in mathematics. We call this "Project Challenge." Through this project we have seen tremendous changes take place in classrooms and in students over a period of four years in one low-income urban school district.

From 1998 through 2002, we implemented Project Challenge, an intervention project funded by the Jacob K. Javits program of the United States Department of Education. The Javits Program was specifically looking for projects that would increase the number of ethnic and linguistic minority students in programs for gifted and talented students. For many years it has been the case that programs for gifted and talented students served primarily white, affluent students. In many poor urban districts, where students are primarily nonwhite and where many are English language learners, there have been few programs for gifted and talented students. When we started out, the goals of Project Challenge were to identify English language learners, minority students, and economically disadvantaged elementary and middle school students who had potential talent in mathematics, and to provide them with a reform-based mathematics curriculum that focused on mathematical reasoning and communication. We hoped that by combining a solid curriculum, instruction based on mathematical understanding, and a heavy emphasis on talk and communication about mathematics, we would be able to help these students become robust learners of mathematics: learners able to think deeply and insightfully, learners who would not give up when a problem was difficult, and learners who would legitimately come to think of themselves as mathematically able.

From the beginning, obstacles to these goals appeared with regularity. First, the students in the schools we worked with were not high-performing students. The district had no programs at all for gifted or talented students. Some teachers and administrators suggested that there were very few gifted students in the system. About 85 percent of the district's students qualify for free or reduced-price lunch, and over 75 percent speak a language other than English at home. We began by evaluating the six hundred or so students in the fourth grade in September of 1998 to see if we could identify about one hundred to participate in the project starting later in the fall. On alternative assessments (created to reflect the local curriculum) and on standardized assessments of aptitude, very few of the students performed at a level that would indicate any special talent in mathematics. Of the approximately six hundred students we evaluated each year over the four years of the project, less than a dozen stood out each year as obviously talented in mathematics.

> Many students probably had abilities and interests in mathematics that could be nurtured and developed, even if these did not show up at the time on standardized tests. We were looking for potential in mathematics, not demonstrations of accomplishment.

But our assumption in designing this intervention was that many students probably had abilities and interests in mathematics that could be nurtured and developed, even if these did not show up at the time on standardized tests. We were looking for potential in mathematics, not demonstrations of accomplishment. Each year, using teacher recommendations, student work, some standardized measures of aptitude, and records of prior achievement in mathematics, we selected about one hundred students to begin participating in a daily mathematics curriculum, organized into four classes each containing about twenty-five students. These students closely mirrored the demographic profile of all students in the district in terms of ethnicity and home language.

We worked with many teachers to combine solid curriculum materials (*Investigations in Number, Data, and Space* in fourth grade and *Connected Mathematics* in grades 5–7) with the strategic use of various forms of classroom talk. We instituted weekly quizzes as a way to reinforce the importance of studying and remembering the content introduced during each week. We gave each teacher daily "warm-up" problems in logic and spatial reasoning to work through with students every morning before classes began. In addition, we introduced major projects that students worked on at the end of the year, culminating in a mathematics fair. Other students and parents were invited to this fair.

From the beginning, we attempted to incorporate various forms of classroom talk into the mathematics work. During the first year, the one hundred students in our first cohort were in fourth grade. Many of them were reluctant to talk in class, or to speak loudly enough so that others could hear. Others were confused by the new forms of activity and participation, and still others resisted the whole process. But we persisted, working alongside committed teachers who worked hard to put these new forms of instruction into place. Gradually, we began to see real changes in the ways our students were thinking and talking. After about seven or eight months of our first year's efforts, we noticed that students' reasoning had become more complex, more sophisticated, and more recognizably mathematical. Students were better able to give clear explanations for their problem solutions, their use of language became more precise, and their communication skills improved noticeably.

As our first cohort of students moved through fifth grade, we started to see results that were more striking. Even students who had been nearly silent the entire first year of the program began to speak up, explain their thinking, respond to other students' contributions, and ask and answer questions that reflected a growing interest in mathematics as well as a growing ability to think mathematically. Other teachers who taught these students in their language arts and social studies classes began to comment on their striking ability to verbalize their thoughts and explanations. Parents who had previously seemed disconnected from the program began to communicate that they were very happy with their children's growing interest in mathematics.

> Even students who had been nearly silent the entire first year of the program began to speak up, explain their thinking, respond to other students' contributions, and ask and answer questions that reflected a growing interest in mathematics as well as a growing ability to think mathematically.

In addition, we got very strong support for our efforts in the form of results on standardized tests. At the beginning of the program, we administered the Test of Mathematical Abilities, Second Edition (TOMA 2) to our first cohort of students. Only 4 percent were rated as "Superior" or "Very Superior" (which indicates a "high probability of giftedness in mathematics") and 23 percent were rated as "Above Average." The remaining 73 percent were rated as "Average" or "Below Average" in their mathematical abilities. After two years in the program, however, we again tested those students who had remained in the program (approximately eighty). After two years, 41 percent were now "Superior" or "Very Superior," and 36 percent more were "Above Average." Only 23 percent of our first cohort were classified as having "Average" ability in mathematics after two years in the program, and none were "Below Average."

In order to examine student achievement growth over time, we also used data from the California Achievement Test (CAT). After three months in the project, our first one hundred students scored better on the CAT than 70 percent of a national sample. This score undoubtedly indicated that we had identified students who did have potential ability in mathematics. Two years later these same students took the CAT mathematics subtest again. This time, they scored better, on average, than 91 percent of a national sample. Furthermore, after three years in the program, 90 percent of the one hundred sixth graders in our first cohort placed in the top two categories on the Massachusetts state assessment (MCAS) in mathematics, a rate greater than that of nearby affluent suburbs.

The growth in achievement has continued for students who entered the program after the first year. We have compared the growth of the second cohort—roughly one hundred students who entered the program as fourth graders in the second year of Project Challenge. Like the first cohort of one hundred, their achievement growth was significant; in two years that cohort went from having a mean total mathematics score at the 74th percentile to a ranking at the 91st percentile. We found similar results for the third and fourth cohorts.

To what can we attribute these results? First, we attribute them to the very hard work of the teachers and students involved in the program. Second, we believe that a well-planned mathematics curriculum that emphasizes student understanding is a critical centerpiece to our story. The supporting activities—the projects, the weekly quizzes, the daily logic problem warm-ups, and an emphasis on high levels of achievement all played an important part in the high levels of performance we saw our students achieve. In addition, we believe that these results are due in part to the very productive use of classroom discourse in these classes, something we have carefully scaffolded since the beginning of the project. We think there are a variety of reasons why the classroom talk that occurred between students and teachers in these classrooms was supportive of mathematical thinking and learning:

- Talk about mathematical concepts and procedures caused misconceptions to surface and helped the teachers recognize and address what students did and did not understand.

- Discourse formats, such as extended group discussion and partner talk, played a part in helping students improve their ability to reason logically: When one student made a claim, the teacher would ask for evidence to support the claim. Examples or counterexamples to the claim provided fodder for reasoning. Over four years, this had a noticeable impact.

- Allowing students to talk about their thinking and problem solving gave them more to observe and listen to, and more chances to participate in mathematical thinking. This pushed them beyond their incomplete, shallow, or passive knowledge by making them aware of discrepancies between their own thinking and that of others.

- Classroom discussion provided motivation: Students became more motivated through taking an interest in their peers' claims and positions within a discussion.

In short, we believe that the ways we used talk in the classroom helped these students make their thinking public; it helped students to explicate and elaborate their reasoning; it allowed them to model, build on, and add to the development of complex ideas; and in at least some cases, it provided a socially grounded motivation to learn.

None of the participants would say that the work of Project Challenge has been easy. In some ways, our experiments with using classroom discourse to promote student learning have been the most challenging aspect of the program. But we believe that our results—the whole range of our results, from test scores to student testimonials—indicate that productive talk was a crucial part of the program. It enabled these low-income students, three-quarters of whom spoke a language other than English at home, to become mathematically articulate. They learned to express their mathematical thoughts to their peers and to their teachers. This was a formative experience for them, and it was a formative experience for us as well. Our experiences with Project Challenge are a large part of the reason that we decided to write this resource, so that teachers who wish to support the learning of their students could build on what we have learned.

> We believe that our results— the whole range of our results, from test scores to student testimonials—indicate that productive talk was a crucial part of the program.

Appendix B

Lesson Plans

Kindergarten: Using *More* and *Less* to Describe the Data in a Graph

Overview

In this lesson, adapted from *Minilessons for Math Practice, Grades K–2* by Rusty Bresser and Caren Holtzman (Math Solutions 2006), students determine whether their shoes do or do not have shoelaces. They place a sticker in the appropriate column on a two-column graph. Students compare the number of people who are and are not wearing shoelaces. Students also talk about how to use the graph to determine how many students are present in class today.

> For more information about this lesson, see Chapter 7, "Talking About Mathematical Terminology, Symbols, and Definitions." You can also watch video clips of this lesson from an actual kindergarten classroom. Refer to the table at the front of this resource for more information.

Time

approximately 20 minutes

Materials

graph paper
sticky notes with students' names (one name per sticky note)

Vocabulary

less
more

Teaching with the Common Core

K.CC Compare Numbers
K.MD Classify objects and count the number of objects in each category.

Identifying the Mathematical Goals

Students will

- use the length of the columns on the graph to compare the data using the words *more* and *less*

- count the number of pieces of data in each column and use numbers to compare the data using the words *more* and *less*
- use the graph to determine the total number of students present in class today

Anticipating Confusion

- Students may not associate longer with more. They may not understand that the longer column on the graph indicates that more people are in that column as compared with the other column.

Asking Questions

- Is the number of people wearing shoelaces more or less than the number of people not wearing shoelaces? How do you know?
- How can we use numbers to explain whether more people are wearing shoelaces?
- How can we use the graph to explain whether more people are wearing shoelaces?
- How can we use the graph to find out how many students are in class today?

Planning the Implementation

1. Ask students to check to see if they are wearing shoelaces.
2. Show students the graph with the title "Are you wearing shoelaces today?" Give each student a sticker with his or her name on it. Ask each student to come up and post the sticker in the correct column.
3. Ask students, "Is the number of people wearing shoelaces more or less than the number of people not wearing shoelaces? How do you know?"
4. Explain to students that they will talk about this question with their math partners. To help them with this, model a *turn and talk* with one student. (See Chapter 1 for more information on turn and talk.) Talk with this student about the question while the other students listen. Then, ask the students what they noticed about your turn and talk—how did the two speakers help each other?
5. Ask students to turn and talk with their partners about the question, Is the number of people wearing shoelaces more or less than the number of people not wearing shoelaces? How do you know?
6. Conduct a whole-class discussion of students' answers.
7. Ask students, "How can you use the graph to find out how many students are in class today?" Share ideas.

Kindergarten: Decomposing the Number Seven

Overview

In this activity, based on *Teaching Number Sense: Kindergarten* by Chris Confer (Math Solutions 2005), students use the seven of hearts playing card to focus on decomposing the number seven into smaller groups. First, students count the number of hearts on the card. Then, they talk about the small groups of hearts that they see within the total of seven. The teacher records what they see in the form of an addition number sentence. Student talk focuses on connecting the number sentence to the groups that they see.

For more information about this lesson, see Chapter 7, "Talking About Mathematical Terminology, Symbols, and Definitions." You can also watch video clips of this lesson from an actual kindergarten classroom. Refer to the table at the front of this resource for more information.

Time

approximately 20 minutes

Materials

the seven of hearts playing card, 4–5 copies, enlarged so that copies can be seen by all students (cover the small heart beneath each numeral) markers or crayons

Vocabulary

add
groups
plus sign
sum

Teaching with the Common Core

K.OA Decompose numbers less than or equal to 10 into pairs in more than one way, for example, by using objects or drawings, and record each decomposition by a drawing or equation (for example, $5 = 2 + 3$ and $5 = 4 + 1$).

From *Classroom Discussions in Math: A Teacher's Guide for Using Talk Moves to Support the Common Core and More, Grades K–6. A Multimedia Professional Learning Resource* by Suzanne H. Chapin, Catherine O'Connor, and Nancy Canavan Anderson. © 2013 Scholastic Inc. Permission granted to photocopy for nonprofit use in a classroom or similar place dedicated to face-to-face educational instruction.

Identifying the Mathematical Goals

Students will

- learn that the number seven can be broken into smaller groups in many different ways
- learn that the counting sequence can be used to count individual items as well as groups of items
- learn how to use an addition number sentence to record how they see groups of numbers within the number seven

Anticipating Confusion

- Students may have difficulty writing a number sentence that represents the way that they see groups of hearts within the seven hearts.
- Students may not understand why the total number of groups of hearts is not the same as the total number of hearts on the card.

Asking Questions

- What does the number 7 tell us about the card?
- When you look inside these seven hearts, do you see any little groups inside there?
- *After writing a number sentence for each student's representation:* Where do you see [one part of the number sentence] on the card?
- *After a student shows a certain number of groups:* If there are only [certain number of] groups here, how can there be seven hearts?

(*continued*)

Planning the Implementation

1. Gather students in the meeting area. Show one large copy of a seven of hearts playing card. As a class, count the hearts. Ask students, "What does the seven on the top and bottom of the card tell us?"

2. Ask students, "When you look at these seven hearts, do you see any little groups inside there? For example, I see two hearts here [circle the two hearts below the group of five]. What else do you see?" Call on a volunteer to come up and circle other groups. Ask each volunteer to describe what he or she circled. Then, ask other students to repeat each student's description.

3. Note to students that all of the hearts have been circled.

4. Record a number sentence for what the student saw. Explain how each part of the number sentence relates to the drawing. For example, if the student circled a group of five and a group of two, say, "This is how a mathematician might record these groups. I'm going to write a five because it goes with this group of five [point to the top five hearts]." Write + 2 and say, "[Student] also saw this group of two hearts [point to the bottom two hearts]. How many hearts does that make altogether?" When students say, "Seven," write = 7 so that the number sentence reads 5 + 2 = 7.

5. Move this card to the side. Post another blank copy of the large seven of hearts card. Ask for another way to see these hearts. Wait at least ten seconds before calling on a student to draw and describe the groups he or she sees. Then, ask other students to repeat the description of what their

classmate circled. Record a number sentence for this student's thinking at the bottom of the card. Connect each part of the number sentence back to the groups of hearts on the card. For example, say, "The number sentence shows a three. Where do you see a three on the card?"

6. Practice counting groups as a whole class.

7. Repeat steps 5 and 6. Push on the idea of the difference between number of hearts and number of groups. For example, if a student draws a group of three, a group of two, and a group of two, say, "I'm confused. If there are only three groups here, how can there be seven hearts?" Share ideas.

8. Post all copies of the card. Say, "What do you notice is the same about these cards? What is different?" Share ideas. Again, ask students to repeat each other's ideas.

9. Summarize by explaining that they can see that inside the seven hearts there are smaller groups of hearts. Many of them saw these smaller groups in different ways. No matter which way someone saw the groups, there were always seven hearts total on each card.

Grade 1: Number Patterns on the Hundreds Chart

Overview

This minilesson focuses on number and counting patterns. The teacher uses a range of methodologies to help students build knowledge. He or she has students count aloud to establish auditory patterns and learn number names; also incorporate physical movements and link these to counting patterns for fives and tens. The hundreds chart is a focus of the lesson—as students say the numbers, their words are connected to the symbols on the chart. Toward the end of the minilesson, students play a game, *Magnet Man—on the Move!*, where they are asked to identify a mystery number that Magnet Man lands upon; they then count using different counting patterns to get from zero to the mystery number.

For more information about this lesson, see Chapter 3, "Talking About Mathematical Concepts." You can also watch video clips of this lesson from an actual first-grade classroom. Refer to the table at the front of this resource for more information.

Time

approximately 20 minutes

Materials

magnetic hundreds chart
magnetic clips in the form of a man

Vocabulary

pattern

Teaching with the Common Core

1.NBT Extend the counting sequence. Understand place value.

From *Classroom Discussions in Math: A Teacher's Guide for Using Talk Moves to Support the Common Core and More, Grades K–6. A Multimedia Professional Learning Resource* by Suzanne H. Chapin, Catherine O'Connor, and Nancy Canavan Anderson. © 2013 Scholastic Inc. Permission granted to photocopy for nonprofit use in a classroom or similar place dedicated to face-to-face educational instruction.

Identifying the Mathematical Goals

Students will

- review counting by ones, fives, and tens from zero to one hundred
- explore counting patterns such as counting by elevens or counting by tens starting at any number
- identify numbers on a hundreds chart and share different counting patterns to reach the numbers
- be able to apply another student's counting pattern to find a mystery number

Anticipating Confusion

- Students may not be able to identify different numbers.
- Students may have difficulty counting on by tens from any number.
- Students may have difficulty identifying counting patterns or counting by numbers other than ones.
- Students may be able to count by rote but not identify patterns.

Asking Questions

- What number do we say before x [the number]? After x [the number]?
- What pattern are you using to count by?
- How did you get to x [the number]? What counting pattern did you use? Share with me how you counted.
- Why do we get to x [the number] faster when counting by tens than when counting by twos?

Planning the Implementation

1. Have students gather on the floor in front of an easel on which there is a magnetic hundreds chart. As you point to each numeral, have students count by ones from one to one hundred. Select pairs of students to count certain groupings of the numbers (for example, twenty-one to thirty).

(continued)

2. Pick a number, such as sixty-five. Ask students to count by different amounts to get to sixty-five. Help students establish a pattern that gets them close to the number, if not right to it. For example, students might count by fives to reach sixty-five. They also could count by twos to sixty-four and then count one more to sixty-five, or they might count by elevens to sixty-six and count backward by one. Students might even count by tens starting at five and land right on sixty-five! Ask students to repeat each other's counting patterns.

3. Pick other numbers and ask many students how they counted to those numbers. Again have students repeat other students' patterns.

4. You might also want to have students review rote counting by fives and by tens. Use the hundreds chart to help students count by tens starting at any number such as 3 (for example, 13, 23, 33, 43, 53, 63, . . .). Ask students to share the patterns they notice in the numerals, such as "There is a three in the ones place each time, but the tens place increases repeatedly by ten."

5. Play the game *Magnet Man—on the Move!* at least four times. In this game, the teacher places the magnet on a number. Students must identify the number and then count to it. Make connections between counting patterns such as counting by tens from different starting numbers. For example, if a student counts by tens from three and another student counts by tens from five, ask them how their counting patterns are alike. Or after you have practiced counting by tens from any number, ask students to apply this pattern to reach the magnet.

From *Classroom Discussions in Math: A Teacher's Guide for Using Talk Moves to Support the Common Core and More, Grades K–6. A Multimedia Professional Learning Resource* by Suzanne H. Chapin, Catherine O'Connor, and Nancy Canavan Anderson. © 2013 Scholastic Inc. Permission granted to photocopy for nonprofit use in a classroom or similar place dedicated to face-to-face educational instruction.

Grade 1: Adding Three Numbers

Overview

In this lesson, students find the sum of three addends. Working with a partner, students take turns drawing three number cards from a deck of number cards and placing them on a template. Students find the sum of the three numbers, tell that sum to their partners, and explain the strategies they used to calculate the sum. Following, students share their strategies during a whole-class discussion.

> For more information about this lesson, see Chapter 4, "Talking About Computational Procedures." You can also watch video clips of this lesson from an actual first-grade classroom. Refer to the table at the front of this resource for more information.

Time

approximately 45 minutes

Materials

numeral cards
numeral card template

Vocabulary

addend
counting up from *or* counting on
sum

Teaching with the Common Core

1.OA Understand and apply properties of operations and the relationship between addition and subtraction. Add and subtract within 20.

Identifying the Mathematical Goals

Students will

- find the sum of three addends using efficient and effective strategies

Anticipating Confusion

- Students may not understand that they can change the order of the three cards to create sums that are easier to calculate.
- Students may misuse the *counting up from* strategy. They may use the first addend as the first number in the count that represents the second addend (for example, 6 + 3 is 6, 7, 8).

Asking Questions

- What strategy did you use to find the sum?
- When your partner explained how he or she got the sum, how did you know if your partner was right?
- How can we use our strategies for finding the sum of two numbers to find the sum of three numbers?
- Tell me how to find the sum of three numbers by *counting up from one of the three numbers*.
- If we move the cards around on the template, how might that help us find the sum? Does the sum change when we move the cards?

Planning the Implementation

1. Explain the activity to the whole class. In this activity, students will work with a partner. Working with a partner, students will take turns drawing three number cards from a deck of number cards and placing them on a template similar to the one below.

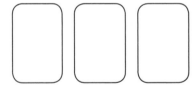

   Students will find the sum of the three numbers, tell that sum to their partners, and explain the strategies they used to calculate the sum.

2. Review important vocabulary terms such as *sum, counting up from*, and *doubles*. Remind students of strategies that they have used to find the sum of two numbers.

From *Classroom Discussions in Math: A Teacher's Guide for Using Talk Moves to Support the Common Core and More, Grades K–6. A Multimedia Professional Learning Resource* by Suzanne H. Chapin, Catherine O'Connor, and Nancy Canavan Anderson. © 2013 Scholastic Inc. Permission granted to photocopy for nonprofit use in a classroom or similar place dedicated to face-to-face educational instruction.

3. Students complete the activity in pairs. Make sure students are explaining their strategies to their partners. Make sure that students give their partners time to think without blurting out the answers. Ask students to share particular strategies during the subsequent whole-class discussion. Write down the three numbers so that both you and the students remember what they will talk about.

4. Students share their strategies during a whole-class discussion. Ask each speaker's partner to repeat his or her strategy. Then, call on other students to repeat. Ask students to describe additional strategies for the same computation.

Grade 2: Teaching Subtraction Strategies

Overview

In this lesson, students talk about how to subtract whole numbers by decomposing the subtrahend in parts. The teacher begins by posting an example of a subtraction computation that is partially completed using the strategy of decomposition. The teacher asks students to figure out what should be the next step in the strategy. Following, the teacher posts two different representations of the same subtraction strategy as a way to draw students' attention to the relationships between the strategy and its underlying concepts.

> For more information about this lesson, see Chapter 4, "Talking About Computational Procedures." You can also watch video clips of this lesson from an actual second-grade classroom. Refer to the table at the front of this resource for more information.

Time

approximately 30 minutes

Materials

whiteboard or interactive whiteboard

Vocabulary

difference
friendly number
number line
round number
subtrahend

Teaching with the Common Core

2.NBT Use place value understanding and properties of operations to add and subtract.
2.NBT. Explain why addition and subtraction strategies work, using place value and the properties of operations.

From *Classroom Discussions in Math: A Teacher's Guide for Using Talk Moves to Support the Common Core and More, Grades K–6. A Multimedia Professional Learning Resource* by Suzanne H. Chapin, Catherine O'Connor, and Nancy Canavan Anderson. © 2013 Scholastic Inc. Permission granted to photocopy for nonprofit use in a classroom or similar place dedicated to face-to-face educational instruction.

Identifying the Mathematical Goals

Students will
- find the difference of two whole numbers by decomposing the subtrahend

Anticipating Confusion

- Students may not understand that when a number is decomposed into smaller parts, the total value of those parts must equal the value of the original number.
- Students may not hold the value of the subtrahend constant during the process of decomposition.

Asking Questions

- Describe what you see when you look at this subtraction strategy (refer to diagrams in the section entitled, "Planning the Implementation"). What did the student do first? Why?
- What should be the next step in completing the subtraction? Why?
- If you perform the subtraction in more than one step, how do you know when you have found the final answer?
- When we decompose or break up a number into smaller pieces in order to subtract it, what does that look like on a number line? What does that look like in a picture of tens and ones?

Planning the Implementation

1. Post the image below on the board and explain the purpose of the task to students. For example, you might say, "One of the ideas that we have talked a lot about lately is how to use friendly numbers to help us solve subtraction problems. We have also been talking a lot about how we can show our thinking using an open number line. Today, we are going to talk about the computation 26 minus 8. Let's imagine that a friend tried to compute this difference using a number line. The friend started at 26 and then subtracted 6 to get to 20. But then he got stuck. What would tell the friend to do next? Why? Talk to your partner about this."

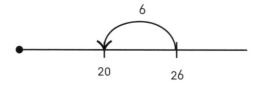

2. As students work in pairs, listen for students who explain that the next step should be taking away take 2 since 6 plus 2 is 8 and that's the number we want to subtract. Ask these students if they would be willing to share that idea with the whole class.

3. Conduct a whole-class discussion. Begin by calling on the students who you had previously asked to speak. Use the talk move *press for reasoning* to keep the discussion focused on decomposition (e.g., "How do you know that 'take away 2' should be the next step? Why 2 if the original problem was to take away 8?"). It is important that students articulate the relationship between the parts of the subtrahend and its original value (e.g., "It makes sense to take away 2 because 6 plus 2 is 8 and 8 is the value of the original subtrahend."). Then ask, "Who agrees or disagrees? Can you tell us why?" to encourage students to engage with each other's reasoning.

4. You may wish to extend this lesson by posting a similar problem (e.g., $45 - 8$) or a more difficult problem with a two-digit subtrahend that can be decomposed into more than two parts (e.g., $45 - 18$). As with steps 1-3 above, post work that shows the steps of the procedure but stop right before the step that is particularly problematic for your students. For example, show how the 18 in $45 - 18$ can be decomposed into $10 + 5 + 3$ and that $45 - 10 = 35$ and $35 - 5 = 30$. However, do not record the last step of $30 - 3$. (See example below.) Give students some time to reflect on the strategy as it has been completed so far and to decide what to do next. During the discussion, focus the student talk on the step of the procedure that is often misunderstood ($30 - 3$). Ask students, "What do you think we should do next?" Use *turn and talk* and then conduct a whole-class discussion of students' ideas.

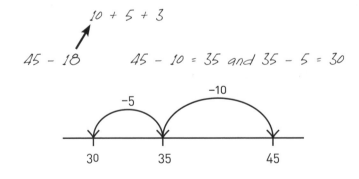

From *Classroom Discussions in Math: A Teacher's Guide for Using Talk Moves to Support the Common Core and More, Grades K–6. A Multimedia Professional Learning Resource* by Suzanne H. Chapin, Catherine O'Connor, and Nancy Canavan Anderson. © 2013 Scholastic Inc. Permission granted to photocopy for nonprofit use in a classroom or similar place dedicated to face-to-face educational instruction.

5. Post an image on the board that shows one subtraction computation solved via decomposition but represented using a number line and a picture of tens and ones. (See example below.) Ask the students to talk about how the two images are similar and different. For example, you might say, "We have been learning how to subtract numbers using both open number lines and pictures of tens and ones. Let's imagine that what's posted here shows two students' strategies for solving 34 minus 6. One student used a number line and the other used a picture of tens and ones. Even though these strategies look different, they also have a lot in common. How are the number line and picture strategies similar? Talk to your partner."

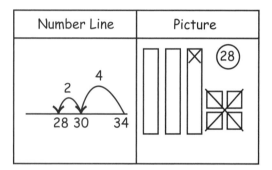

6. As students work in pairs, listen in on their conversations for the following key ideas. Ask these students if they would be willing to share their ideas with the class.

   i. Both students took away 4 first.

   ii. It makes sense to take away 4 first since 34 – 4 is an easy problem; it gets you to a friendly or round number.

   iii. Both students took away 2 as their next step; this makes sense because 4 + 2 is 6 and 6 is what we want to subtract.

7. Conduct a whole-class discussion of students' ideas. Use the talk move *Who can repeat?* after a student says one of the key points in step 6. Use the talk move *press for reasoning* to focus the discussion on why it makes sense to perform the subtraction by taking away 4 and then 2. Also focus on the relationship between the numbers 2, 4, and 6.

8. Close by asking the students to turn and talk with their partners about the ideas brought up in the discussion. Then, summarize the key ideas of the lesson. For example, explain that one way to subtract numbers is to break the number that is being subtracted (the subtrahend) into smaller and friendly parts. We must make sure that all of the smaller parts add up to the same value as the original number. Explain that this strategy of breaking apart numbers can be represented in a different ways. We can show it on a number line as well as using pictures of tens and ones.

Grade 2: Making Sense of One-Half

Overview

In this lesson, students explore the word *half* as a relational word—a word whose meaning shifts depending on the *of* phrase that follows it. Students explain why 30 minutes is equal to half an hour even though 30 cents is not equal to half a dollar.

For more information about this lesson, see Chapter 7, "Talking About Mathematical Terminology, Symbols, and Definitions." You can also watch video clips of this lesson from an actual second-grade classroom. Refer to the table at the front of this resource for more information.

Time

approximately 20 minutes

Materials

whiteboard or interactive whiteboard

Vocabulary

cents
dollar
half
hour
parts
whole

Teaching with the Common Core

2.MD Work with time and money
Practice 6: Attend to precision.

Identifying the Mathematical Goals

Students will

- understand that the meaning of the word *half* shifts depending on the *of* phrase that follows it, and
- understand that, in any particular context, the quantity named by the word *half* depends upon the quantity of the whole

Anticipating Confusion

- Students may associate the number 30 with the word *half* since there are 30 minutes in half an hour.
- Students may not understand why there are not 30 cents in a half a dollar even though there are 30 minutes in half an hour.

Asking Questions

- Since 30 minutes is equal to half an hour, is 30 cents equal to half a dollar? Why or why not?
- How many minutes are in an hour? How does this help us make sense of why there are 30 minutes in half an hour?
- How many cents are in a dollar? How does this help us make sense of why half a dollar is *not* equal to 30 cents? How does this help us find the correct number of cents in half a dollar?
- We can talk about half an hour as 30 minutes or half a dollar as 50 cents. Why does the same word, *half*, have different meanings?

Planning the Implementation

1. Explain to students that this year they are going to learn a lot about the word *half* and how it is used to describe things like time and money. Ask students how many minutes are in half an hour. Agree as a class that the answer is 30.
2. Post the following question on the board. "If half an hour is 30 minutes, is half a dollar equal to 30 cents?" Ask students to talk about this question in their small groups. Listen in to small group discussions in order to decide which students to call upon to share and in what order during the whole-class discussion.

3. Begin the whole-class discussion. Scribe students' comments on the board as they offer them. When a student talks about how the size of *half* depends on the size of the whole, use the talk move *Who can repeat?* to help other students focus on this idea. When a student rejects the claim that 30 cents is equal to half a dollar by connecting the size of *half* to the size of the whole, ask, "What do you think about that?" to encourage other students to engage with that idea.

4. Before the end of the discussion, use *turn and talk* to give students a chance to think about the key ideas that have been discussed so far in the discussion.

5. Summarize the key ideas. Say, "We learned that even though a half of an hour is 30 minutes, a half of a dollar is not equal to 30 cents. We thought about the size of one dollar as compared to the size of one hour. An hour is equal to 60 minutes but a dollar is equal to 100 cents, not 60 cents. So half of a dollar is 50 cents since 50 plus 50 is 100." Re-assure students that it's okay if they are still confused about why the same word, *half*, can have different meanings. Explain to students that this is a difficult topic that they will revisit again over the course of the school year.

Grade 3: The Birthday Party Problem

Overview

In this lesson, students are presented with one multistep word problem. This problem is about buying juice and is complex because of the many conditions students must consider. It also is complex because of the language used to express certain relationships. At the start of the lesson, the teacher asks students to talk about the problem, making sure they understand what is being asked and how the conditions dictate the number of possible cans of juice. Then students work in small groups to solve the problem. The teacher checks in with each small group and uses this knowledge to select students to present. The class concludes with a discussion of the various solution methods to the problem.

For more information about this lesson, see Chapter 5, "Talking About Solution Methods and Problem-Solving Strategies." You can also watch video clips of this lesson from an actual third-grade classroom. Refer to the table at the front of this resource for more information.

Time

approximately 45 minutes

Materials

paper and pencil for each student

Vocabulary

at least
no more than
six-pack
four-pack

Teaching with the Common Core

3.OA Represent and solve problems involving multiplication and division.

From *Classroom Discussions in Math: A Teacher's Guide for Using Talk Moves to Support the Common Core and More, Grades K–6. A Multimedia Professional Learning Resource* by Suzanne H. Chapin, Catherine O'Connor, and Nancy Canavan Anderson. © 2013 Scholastic Inc. Permission granted to photocopy for nonprofit use in a classroom or similar place dedicated to face-to-face educational instruction.

Identifying the Mathematical Goals

Students will

- apply their understanding of the phrases *at least* and *no more than* to the solution of a problem
- focus on understanding the given information in a word problem
- practice explaining their solution methods and making sense of other solution methods
- connect groupings of four and groupings of six to multiplying by four and six, respectively

Anticipating Confusion

- Students may not understand how to use the facts that grape juice and apple juice come in four- and six-packs, respectively.
- Students may not realize that the phrase *at least twenty-six but no more than thirty cans* means that they can buy 26, 27, 28, 29, or 30 cans of juice.
- Students may find it confusing that there are multiple solutions that satisfy the conditions in the problem.
- Students may not see the connections between different solution methods.

Asking Questions

- What are some of the facts in the problem that we have to consider?
- What does it mean that we have to buy "at least twenty-six cans"? Does this mean we can buy exactly twenty-six cans? Why or why not?
- The problem states that we have to buy at least twenty-six cans but no more than thirty cans. How many cans can we buy? Does this mean we can buy exactly twenty-six? Exactly thirty? Explain.
- How can we use multiplication to find the number of cans of juice? Explain your thinking.
- Explain how you checked that your solution satisfied all the conditions of the problem.
- How are these two solutions the same? How are they different?

Planning the Implementation

1. Introduce the following problem and post it so students can see it.

The Birthday Party Problem

Mrs. Foley needs to buy drinks for her daughter's birthday party. She wants to buy both apple juice and grape juice. Cans of apple juice are sold in 6-packs. Cans of grape juice are sold in 4-packs. Mrs. Foley needs to buy at least 26 but no more than 30 cans of juice. How many packs of apple juice might she buy? How many packs of grape juice might she buy? Show or explain how you got your answer.

Ask students to read the problem silently to themselves and then turn to the person next to them and put the problem in their own words.

2. Next ask the students to explain what the problem is about. Ask for volunteers to repeat parts of a student's answer. If necessary, interrupt the speaker so that students are only being asked to repeat a small part of a longer statement.

3. Continue to discuss all of the conditions of the problem including that apple juice comes in six-packs, grape juice comes in four-packs, Mrs. Foley wishes to buy both types of juice, and that she needs to buy at least twenty-six cans but no more than thirty cans. Once students are secure in their understanding of the problem, ask them to find solutions to the problem.

4. Allow students to work in small groups of two or three to find solutions. Work with different groups to provide direction where needed. Other students may need to practice explaining their solution steps and reasoning behind the steps to you. There are multiple solutions for this problem. Encourage students to find at least two solutions.

1.

Apple	Grape
1 pack	6 packs
6 cans	24 cans
Total: 30 cans	

2.

Apple	Grape
1 pack	5 packs
6 cans	20 cans
Total: 26 cans	

3.

Apple	Grape
2 packs	4 packs
12 cans	16 cans
Total: 28 cans	

From *Classroom Discussions in Math: A Teacher's Guide for Using Talk Moves to Support the Common Core and More, Grades K–6. A Multimedia Professional Learning Resource* by Suzanne H. Chapin, Catherine O'Connor, and Nancy Canavan Anderson. © 2013 Scholastic Inc. Permission granted to photocopy for nonprofit use in a classroom or similar place dedicated to face-to-face educational instruction.

4.

Apple	Grape
3 packs	2 packs
18 cans	8 cans
Total: 26 cans	

5.

Apple	Grape
3 packs	3 packs
18 cans	12 cans
Total: 30 cans	

6.

Apple	Grape
4 packs	1 pack
24 cans	4 cans
Total: 28 cans	

5. Begin the whole-class discussion by calling on a pair you spoke with during partner work time. Ask at least two or three students to repeat each part of their explanation. Stop the speaker mid-explanation, as needed, so that students are only asked to repeat a small part of a longer solution method. Also, record students' statements where everyone can see them.

6. Continue having students explain solution methods. Be sure that at the end of the solution, everyone checks that all the conditions of the problem were met. Ask, "Who else got the same answer?" Call on students to explain how they got the answer. Even if a student says, "I did the same thing," ask him or her to explain the solution method again.

7. Next ask, "Who got a different answer?" Again, ask students to repeat small portions of each solution method as it is presented.

8. Summarize the different solutions by posting them. Review the key conditions in the problem and how all of the methods satisfy the conditions.

Grade 3: Four Strikes and You're Out

Overview

In this lesson, based on *Teaching Arithmetic: Lessons for Addition and Subtraction, Grades 2–3* by Bonnie Tank and Lynne Zolli (Math Solutions 2001), students analyze practice games from the game *Four Strikes and You're Out*. The teacher shows students a partially completed game and students discuss possibilities for the next guess based on known information about the game, including filled-in digits, strikes, and sums of tens and ones.

For more information about this lesson, see Chapter 6, "Talking About Mathematical Reasoning." You can also watch video clips of this lesson from an actual third-grade classroom. Refer to the table at the front of this resource for more information.

Time

approximately 20 minutes

Materials

overhead transparency of game board

Vocabulary

addend
digit
sum

Teaching with the Common Core

3.NBT Fluently add and subtract within 1000 using strategies and algorithms based on place value, properties of operations, and/or the relationship between addition and subtraction.
Practice 2: Reason abstractly and quantitatively.
Practice 3: Construct viable arguments and critique the reasoning of others.

From *Classroom Discussions in Math: A Teacher's Guide for Using Talk Moves to Support the Common Core and More, Grades K–6. A Multimedia Professional Learning Resource* by Suzanne H. Chapin, Catherine O'Connor, and Nancy Canavan Anderson. © 2013 Scholastic Inc. Permission granted to photocopy for nonprofit use in a classroom or similar place dedicated to face-to-face educational instruction.

Identifying the Mathematical Goals

Students will

- use deductive reasoning, mental arithmetic, and knowledge about place value to find missing addends in an addition number sentence

Anticipating Confusion

- Students may not understand that a number that has not yet been guessed can be eliminated as a possibility based on other information about missing and filled-in digits.

Asking Questions

- Based on the information that is already filled in on the template, which number or numbers would make a good next guess? Why? Which number or numbers would not make a good next guess? Why not?
- How can we use a number that is a strike to help us make a good next guess?

Planning the Implementation

1. Explain to students that they will use practice games of *Four Strikes and You're Out* so that they can learn strategies that may help them during their next round of the game. Explain that you will show them a game and they should pretend that two imaginary people are playing this game. Some of the digits have already been correctly identified and some strikes have been recorded too. Students will look at the information and use that to think about which numbers would make good next guesses and which numbers would not make good next guesses.

2. Post the game below on the overhead. Ask students to take sixty seconds to note what has already been guessed correctly and incorrectly and to think about what they might guess next and why and what they would not guess next and why.

$$\underline{}\ 0 \ + \ \underline{}\ 1 \ = \ 81 \qquad \underline{strikes}$$
$$\cancel{0}\ \cancel{1}\ 2\ \cancel{3}\ 4\ 5\ 6\ \cancel{7}\ \cancel{8}\ 9 \qquad XX$$

3. Ask students to talk in pairs about what they would and would not guess for their next number. As students talk in pairs, listen in on several pairs' conversations (see Chapter 1 for more information on turn and talk). Listen for students who are explaining why five is not a good guess. Listen for students who are explaining why two and six as well as four would make good next guesses. Tell those students that you will call on them during the whole-class discussion. Help those students formulate a good response.

4. Call students together for a whole-class discussion. Begin the whole-class discussion by talking about what would *not* make a good next guess. Call on a student who will tell why five is not a good guess. Ask several students to repeat this idea and then explain if they agree or disagree, and why. Also, use turn and talk so that every student has a chance to think about why five would not make a good next guess.

5. Share ideas for good next guesses. Again, ask students to first repeat a student's idea for a good next guess and then explain if they agree or disagree, and why.

6. Summarize. Explain to students that this practice game shows that they can use number facts—pairs of numbers that add to a particular sum—as well as information about what numbers are strikes to help them make their next guess when playing the game.

Grade 4: Perimeters of Rectangles with a Fixed Area

Overview

This lesson is part of an instructional module on area and perimeter and can be used once students have an understanding of both measures. At the start of the lesson, students review the meaning of area and perimeter; the teacher helps them articulate the differences between the two measures. Emphasis is placed on the fact that the units they have used to measure perimeter are inches whereas the units they have used to measure area are square inches. Next, students are asked to find the dimensions of all possible rectangles with an area of 20 square inches and determine the perimeter of each. Students discover that there are three distinct rectangles: 1 by 20 inches (P = 42 inches), 2 by 10 inches (P = 24 inches) and 4 by 5 inches (P = 18 inches). They conclude that long, thin rectangles have a greater perimeter than rectangles that are more squarelike and spend time discussing why.

For more information about this lesson, see Chapter 3, "Talking About Mathematical Concepts." You can also watch video clips of this lesson from an actual fourth-grade classroom. Refer to the table at the front of this resource for more information.

Time

approximately 45 minutes

Materials

chart paper and markers
square tiles
grid paper
optional: interactive whiteboard

Vocabulary

area
perimeter
units

Teaching with the Common Core

3.MD Recognize perimeter as an attribute of plane figures and distinguish between linear and area measures. Solve real-world and mathematical problems involving perimeters of polygons, including finding the perimeter given the side lengths, finding an unknown side length, and exhibiting rectangles with the same perimeter and different areas or with the same area and different perimeters.
4.MD Apply the area and perimeter formulas for rectangles in real-world and mathematical problems.

Identifying the Mathematical Goals

Students will

- review the units used when determining the perimeter and area of rectangles (inches and square inches, in this case)
- learn that rectangles with the same area but different dimensions do not necessarily have the same perimeter
- articulate how the shape of a rectangle affects the perimeter of the shape

Anticipating Confusion

- Students may confuse measuring perimeter with measuring area.
- Students' definition of *perimeter* may not include that it is the length or distance around the outside of a figure.
- Students may not understand how the shape of a rectangle affects its perimeter.
- Students may not see how 20 square inches can be rearranged to form different rectangles.
- Students may have difficulty explaining why the rectangles have different perimeters.
- Students may refer to perimeter devoid of units of any kind and not realize the importance of the type of unit.

Asking Questions

- What does it mean to find the perimeter of a rectangle?
- A student last year said that perimeter is the outside of a rectangle. What can we add to this explanation to make it more accurate?

From *Classroom Discussions in Math: A Teacher's Guide for Using Talk Moves to Support the Common Core and More, Grades K–6. A Multimedia Professional Learning Resource* by Suzanne H. Chapin, Catherine O'Connor, and Nancy Canavan Anderson. © 2013 Scholastic Inc. Permission granted to photocopy for nonprofit use in a classroom or similar place dedicated to face-to-face educational instruction.

- What is the difference between area and perimeter?
- How can you change a 1-by-20-inch rectangle into to a 2-by-10-inch rectangle? How does the perimeter change? Where did the perimeter go? Explain your thinking.
- What effect does the shape of a rectangle have on its perimeter? Explain.
- How do you know if you have found all possible rectangles with an area of 20 square inches?

Planning the Implementation

1. Have students talk about their knowledge of the terms *perimeter* and *area* by asking, "If I were to measure the perimeter of a rectangle, what feature of it would I be measuring? And what about area? What does it mean to find the area of a rectangle?" Conduct a whole-class discussion about this.

2. Present the following investigation. You may wish to post or write the following where everyone can see it.

Area and Perimeter Investigation

Use square tiles to create all possible rectangles with an area of 20 square tiles.

Find the perimeter of each rectangle.

Why does it make sense that some perimeters are greater than others?

Compare and contrast the rectangles with the greatest and least perimeters.

3. As students work, talk with different pairs about the following questions. Think about whom you will call upon during the whole-class discussion.
   a. How do you know that you have found all possible rectangles?
   b. How is it possible that rectangles with the same area have different perimeters?
   c. Why are some perimeters greater than others?
   d. Compare and contrast the rectangles with the greatest and least perimeters.

4. Right before starting the whole-class discussion, draw a 1-by-20, a 2-by-10, and a 4-by-5-inch rectangle on the board. Label the dimensions of each rectangle. Then conduct a discussion about each of the questions above.

   a. Ask: "How did you know when you found all possible rectangles with an area of twenty square inches?"

     Call on students with whom you spoke during partner work time and use the *Who can repeat?* talk move. A student's response might be "We used the factors of twenty. We did one by twenty, two by ten, and four by five. Those are all of the factors, so those are all of the rectangles."

   b. Discuss: "Three rectangles have the same area of twenty square inches. How is it possible they have different perimeters?" Possible responses might be

      • The rectangles don't all have the same perimeter because some of them have more squares going around their borders than others (different dimensions).

      • The rectangles don't all have the same perimeter because they are different sizes—some are long and thin but others are short.

   c. Ask: "What do you notice about the rectangle with the greatest perimeter? How would you describe that rectangle?" Students are likely to describe the rectangle as long and skinny. Require students to explain why a long and skinny rectangle has a greater perimeter than a differently shaped rectangle.

5. Use an interactive whiteboard or grid paper to show how square units are moved from the border of the 1-by-20-inch rectangle to inside the 2-by-10-inch rectangle. Ask, "What do you notice is happening to the perimeter when I turn a one-by-twenty-inch rectangle into a two-by-ten rectangle? Turn and talk with your partners about this." Share ideas and ask several students to repeat each other's statements.

6. Continue discussing that the 4-by-5-inch rectangle has the least perimeter of the three. Students might mention that this rectangle has the least perimeter because a lot of the squares are inside the rectangle and not part of the border.

7. Finish the discussion by asking, "So if we know the area of a rectangle, do we also know its perimeter? Why or why not? Talk to your partners." Listen as pairs talk. Listen for a student to say, "No because there are lots of different rectangles that have the same area but they will have different perimeters." Tell this student that you will call on him or her during the whole-class discussion.

8. Conclude by asking students to summarize what they learned. In general, it is important for students to articulate that rectangles can have the same area but different perimeters. They might also mention that if two rectangles have the same area but one is long and skinny and the other is more compact, then the long and skinny rectangle will have a greater perimeter. This is because more of the square inches have a side along the exterior of the rectangle.

Grade 4: Reasoning About Factors and Multiples

Overview

In this lesson, students solve a mystery number puzzle about factors and multiples. Students begin by reviewing the terms *factor* and *multiple*. Students solve the mystery number puzzle with a partner. Then, students discuss their strategies and solutions in a whole-class discussion.

> For more information about this lesson, see Chapter 7, "Talking About Mathematical Terminology, Symbols, and Definitions." You can also watch video clips from a related lesson taught in an actual fourth-grade classroom. Refer to the table at the front of this resource for more information.

Time

approximately 20 minutes

Materials

chart paper
paper and pencils

Vocabulary

factor
multiple

Teaching with the Common Core

4.OA Gain familiarity with factors and multiples.

Identifying the Mathematical Goals

Students will

- identify factors and multiples of numbers
- use deductive reasoning to identify numbers with particular characteristics

From *Classroom Discussions in Math: A Teacher's Guide for Using Talk Moves to Support the Common Core and More, Grades K–6. A Multimedia Professional Learning Resource* by Suzanne H. Chapin, Catherine O'Connor, and Nancy Canavan Anderson. © 2013 Scholastic Inc. Permission granted to photocopy for nonprofit use in a classroom or similar place dedicated to face-to-face educational instruction.

Anticipating Confusion

- Students may think that factors of a number are always less than the number itself.
- Students may think that multiples of a number are always greater than the number.
- Students may confuse factors and multiples. For example, they may think the factors of 2 are 2, 4, 6, 8, and so on.

Asking Questions

- What is a factor of a number?
- What is a multiple of a number?
- What are some ways that we can find factors of a number?
- What are some ways that we can find multiples of a number?

Planning the Implementation

1. Gather students for a whole-class discussion. Explain that students are going to solve a mystery number puzzle with clues that often use the words *factor* and *multiple*. Review what students know about the words *factor* and *multiple*.

   a. When a student says, "A factor is a number that when multiplied by another number gives a product," write that where everyone can see it. Ask several students to repeat this.

   b. When a student says, "A multiple is a number you say when you skip-count by a certain number," write that where everyone can see it. Ask several students to repeat this.

2. Post the following mystery puzzle where everyone can see it:

Mystery Number Puzzle

Clue 1: I am a factor of 40.
Clue 2: I am a two-digit number.
Clue 3: I am a multiple of 8.
Who am I?

Ask students to solve the puzzle with a partner. As students work, look for a student who is using strategies such as making a list of the factors of forty and then crossing off numbers from this list as he or she reads the other clues. Ask that student to share his or her strategy during the whole-class discussion.

3. Conduct a whole-class discussion of the puzzle. Call on students with whom you had spoken earlier. Ask them to share their solution strategies. Ask several students to repeat each part of a solution strategy as it is presented.

4. After the first presenter crosses out all single-digit factors of forty, spend time discussing the third clue, *I am a multiple of 8*. Once the student identifies that the mystery number is forty, ask other students to explain why they either agree or disagree. Ask other students to explain why they agree or disagree that forty is a multiple of eight. Ask students how they know that ten and twenty can't be the mystery number.

5. Continue until the puzzle is solved. Reread the clues to make sure that the solution fits all of the criteria. When revisiting the first clue, ask students to explain why they either agree or disagree that forty is a factor of forty.

6. Ask for volunteers to explain how they solved the puzzle using different solution strategies.

7. Summarize the learning from the lesson. Ask students, "What did you need to know about factors and multiples in order to solve the puzzle?"

Grade 5: Teaching Division Strategies

Overview

In this lesson, the teacher uses a string of related computations to help students learn how to use partial quotients to divide whole numbers.

For more information about this lesson, see Chapter 4, "Talking About Computational Procedures."

Time

approximately 20 minutes

Materials

whiteboard, markers

Vocabulary

dividend
divisor
partial quotient
quotient

Identifying the Mathematical Goals

Students will

- learn how to use the quotients of related and easier division computations to derive other quotients.

Teaching with the Common Core

5.NBT Find whole-number quotients of whole numbers . . . using strategies based on place value, the properties of operations, and/or the relationship between multiplication and division.

Anticipating Confusion

- Students may not understand why partial quotients can be added to find quotients of related computations.
- Students may not understand how to use interpretations of division to reason about division computational procedures.

Asking Questions

- What are some different ways to interpret an expression such as $624 \div 6$?
- Why does breaking the number 624 into 600 and 24 help us compute $624 \div 6$?
- Why does it make sense to add the quotients of $600 \div 6 = 100$ and $24 \div 6 = 4$ to compute $624 \div 6$? Why are we *adding* to find a quotient?

Planning the Implementation

1. Explain to students that this lesson focuses on dividing whole numbers. Specifically, students will learn how to use well-known quotients to find the quotients of more difficult computations.
2. Post the computation $24 \div 6 = N$ on the board and ask students to interpret the equation. For example, you might say, "We can read this as 24 divided by 6." But what does that really mean?"
3. Ask students to turn and talk about this with a partner. As they talk, listen for students who are interpreting the division in terms of equal grouping (i.e., the number in each group if 24 is divided into 6 groups), repeated subtraction (i.e., the number of groups when groups of 6 are repeatedly subtracted from 24) and missing factor (i.e., 6 times some unknown factor, N, equals 24).
4. Reconvene the discussion and ask students to share different interpretations. If students do not mention either equal grouping or repeated subtraction, describe these yourself.
5. Ask students to compute $600 \div 6$.
6. Ask students to compute $24 \div 6$.
7. Post $624 \div 6$ on the board. Ask students to interpret the expression. Ask them to turn and talk with their math partners about this. As they talk, listen for students who are interpreting the expression using the idea of equal grouping (i.e., the size of each group if 624 is shared equally among 6 groups).

From *Classroom Discussions in Math: A Teacher's Guide for Using Talk Moves to Support the Common Core and More, Grades K–6. A Multimedia Professional Learning Resource* by Suzanne H. Chapin, Catherine O'Connor, and Nancy Canavan Anderson. © 2013 Scholastic Inc. Permission granted to photocopy for nonprofit use in a classroom or similar place dedicated to face-to-face educational instruction.

8. Reconvene the whole-class discussion. Call on a student who interpreted the computation using the idea of equal grouping. After this student gives his or her response, use the talk move *Who can repeat?* to give other students a chance to think about that interpretation.

9. Next ask the students to use their classmate's interpretation and the two earlier computations to compute 624 ÷ 6. Ask students to talk about this with their partners.

10. After a few minutes of partner talk, reconvene the whole-class discussion. Call on students to explain their reasoning. Use the talk move *press for reasoning* to encourage students to connect their strategies to the underlying division concepts. For example, if a student says that she found the quotient of 624 ÷ 6 by adding the quotients of 600 ÷ 6 = 100 and 24 ÷ 6 = 4, ask, "Why does it make sense to add those two quotients? How are those two computations related to 624 ÷ 6?" Then ask other students to explain their classmate's thinking in their own words. (After this discussion, open the floor to students who interpreted the expression differently and/or used a different computational strategy.)

11. Post another computation such as 648 ÷ 6 and ask students to explain their computational strategies. Following, if students seem ready, post a computation such as 594 ÷ 6 to see if they can solve this problem by thinking about 594 as 600 – 6.

12. Summarize the key ideas of the lesson. Say, "When we see a division computation to which we don't immediately know the answer, we can use related computations to help us. We can look inside the dividend for smaller numbers that we can easily divide by the divisor. Once we perform these computations, we can add the partial quotients to find the quotient of the original computation." Explain to students that they will be talking more about this division strategy and others in upcoming lessons.

Grade 5: Volume of Rectangular Prisms

Overview

In previous lessons, students built rectangular prisms using cubic units and determined the volume of the prisms by counting cubes. Students started to devise methods for finding the volume of any rectangular prism without counting. In this lesson, students continue their work on developing a method for determining the volume of any rectangular prism. They share their methods with each other and discuss similarities and differences between the methods. One goal of the lesson is to help students articulate how volume can be determined by finding the number of cubes in each layer of a prism. If students know the number of cubes in one layer, they can multiply that amount by the number of layers, or height of the rectangular prism. The method of multiplying the dimensions is then connected to the idea of layers.

> For more information about this lesson, see Chapter 6, "Talking About Mathematical Reasoning." You can also watch video clips of this lesson from an actual fifth-grade classroom. Refer to the table at the front of this resource for more information.

Time

approximately 45 minutes

Materials

interlocking cubes
3-by-4-by-5 rectangular prisms, 1 per group of 3–4 students

Vocabulary

cubic units
rectangular prism
volume

From *Classroom Discussions in Math: A Teacher's Guide for Using Talk Moves to Support the Common Core and More, Grades K–6. A Multimedia Professional Learning Resource* by Suzanne H. Chapin, Catherine O'Connor, and Nancy Canavan Anderson. © 2013 Scholastic Inc. Permission granted to photocopy for nonprofit use in a classroom or similar place dedicated to face-to-face educational instruction.

Teaching with the Common Core

5.MD Understand concepts of volume and relate volume to multiplication and addition.

Identifying the Mathematical Goals

Students will

- learn a method for finding the volume of a rectangular prism based on the number of layers in the prism
- connect the method of multiplying the dimensions to finding the number of cubes in the base layer ($l \times w$) and multiplying by the height h
- review the units used when determining volume of rectangular prisms (cubes or cubic units)

Anticipating Confusion

- Students may confuse measuring volume with measuring surface area.
- Students may not visualize a prism as consisting of layers of cubes.
- Students may refer to volume devoid of units of any kind and not realize the importance of the type of unit.

Asking Questions

- What does it mean to find the volume of a prism?
- How can we use multiplication to find the number of cubes in one layer of a rectangular prism?
- How can we use multiplication to find the total number of cubes in a rectangular prism?
- Explain why your method works to find volume.
- How is multiplying the dimensions to find the volume similar to using the layers approach?
- What type of units are needed to measure volume? Why do we use that unit instead of others such as . . . [fill in depending on response from students].

Planning the Implementation

1. Begin this lesson by reviewing the terms *rectangular prism, volume,* and *cubic unit.* Ask students, "What does each term mean?" Conduct a brief whole-class discussion about each definition.

2. Connect to the previous class periods where students spent time finding the volume of rectangular prisms: "Over the past few days, many of you have developed methods for finding the volume of any rectangular prism. Today, I'd like for us to talk as a whole class about our methods." Write the following where everyone can see it: *Method for finding the volume of a rectangular prism.* Say, "As a group, develop a method for finding the volume of a rectangular prism." Let students work in groups of three or four for about eight to ten minutes. Give the groups interlocking cubes to help them develop their methods.

3. Post each group's method where everyone can see it. Withhold comments or corrections. If groups have identical methods, post the methods both times.

4. Say, "We have several different methods. Before we think about whether they work for all prisms, let's test them with one prism. With your partner, see if you can apply each of the methods displayed to a three-by-four-by-five-unit prism. If you get stuck, think about how you might edit the method so that it works. If the method does work, think about why it works and whether it will work for all rectangular prisms." Give students time to do this with their partners.

5. Conduct a whole-class discussion to discuss certain methods.

    a. Briefly discuss which methods may need a little revision or editing. If a student makes a suggestion on how to revise a method that he or she did not write, check back with the students who wrote it. For example, you might ask, "What do you think about that suggestion? Do you think it makes sense to add it to what you wrote? Why?"

    b. Pick the methods you would like everyone to discuss based on the mathematics. Namely, focus the discussion on methods that involve layering—finding the number of cubes in one layer by multiplying length × width, then multiplying this by the number of layers, which is the height of the prism. Any time a student uses language associated with layering, ask at least two other students to repeat it. Ask students if they agree or disagree that the method would work for all rectangular prisms, and why.

From *Classroom Discussions in Math: A Teacher's Guide for Using Talk Moves to Support the Common Core and More, Grades K–6. A Multimedia Professional Learning Resource* by Suzanne H. Chapin, Catherine O'Connor, and Nancy Canavan Anderson. © 2013 Scholastic Inc. Permission granted to photocopy for nonprofit use in a classroom or similar place dedicated to face-to-face educational instruction.

c. If a group has suggested multiplying length × width × height, first have students discuss why this method works. Ask other students to explain why they agree or disagree that this method would work for all rectangular prisms. Then ask, "How is this method similar to the layering method? How is it different?" Share students' ideas.

6. Summarize the key mathematical points. Say, "We have discussed several different methods but all of these methods have one thing in common. They all involve finding the volume by determining the number of cubes in one layer and then multiplying that by the number of layers."

Grade 6: Area of a Parallelogram, $A = bh$

Overview

This lesson is part of an instructional unit on area formulas (triangles, parallelograms, rectangles, and trapezoids). At the start of the lesson, students review the difference between units and square units; the teacher reminds them of the need to label dimensions and areas. Next, students are asked to work on a task where they cut different parallelograms into two pieces and then reform the two pieces into rectangles. Students determine the area of the rectangles and during whole-class discussion, discuss the formula, $A = bh$. The emphasis is on understanding the relationship between the formulas for area of a rectangle and area of a parallelogram with the same base and height measures.

For more information about this lesson, see Chapter 3, "Talking About Mathematical Concepts."

Time

approximately 40 minutes

Materials

grid paper
Reproducible: Area of a Parallelogram

Vocabulary

area
base
dimensions
height
perpendicular

Teaching with the Common Core

6.G: Find the area of right triangles, other triangles, special quadrilaterals, and polygons by composing into rectangles or decomposing into triangles and other shapes.
Practice 5: Use appropriate tools strategically.
Practice 6: Attend to precision.

From *Classroom Discussions in Math: A Teacher's Guide for Using Talk Moves to Support the Common Core and More, Grades K–6. A Multimedia Professional Learning Resource* by Suzanne H. Chapin, Catherine O'Connor, and Nancy Canavan Anderson. © 2013 Scholastic Inc. Permission granted to photocopy for nonprofit use in a classroom or similar place dedicated to face-to-face educational instruction.

Identifying the Mathematical Goals

Students will

- review the type of units used to measure the dimensions and area of a parallelogram
- learn that the area of a parallelogram can be found by multiplying the base length times the height of the parallelogram
- articulate the relationship between the area of a parallelogram and a rectangle with the same base length and height

Anticipating Confusion

- Students may confuse units with square units.
- Students may not understand how to determine the height of all parallelograms.
- Students may have difficulty explaining why the formula for the area of a parallelogram can be found by multiplying the base length times the height of the parallelogram.

Asking Questions

- What are you measuring when you find the area of a parallelogram?
- What are the dimensions of a parallelogram? Why can't we use length and width, like we do with a rectangle?
- Does the base length stay the same when the parallelogram is transformed into a rectangle? Why or why not?
- How do you determine the height of a parallelogram?
- What does it mean for two line segments to be perpendicular to each other?
- Does the height stay the same when the parallelogram is transformed into a rectangle? Why or why not?

Planning the Implementation

1. Ask students to talk about their knowledge of the units used to measure the dimensions and areas of parallelograms: "If I were to measure the base or height of a parallelogram, what am I measuring? How do I determine the height of any parallelogram?" And what about area? What are you measuring when you find the area of a parallelogram?" Conduct a whole-class discussion about these questions.

2. Present the following investigation and pass out two copies of the reproducible "Area of a Parallelogram" to each student. Students cut out one copy of each parallelogram, cut each parallelogram along a height, and recompose the two into rectangles. They then compare the rectangles to the original parallelograms.

Make two copies of parallelograms A, B, and C below. Cut out both sets of parallelograms. On one set, draw in a segment to show the height. Cut along the height to form two pieces. Reshape the pieces into a rectangle.

a) What are the bases and heights of the rectangles formed using parallelograms A, B, and C?

b) What are the base and height of parallelograms A, B, and C?

c) Why are the dimensions of the parallelograms and their corresponding rectangles the same?

d) Use what you know about the area of a rectangle to determine the areas of parallelograms A, B, and C.

e) What generalizations can you make about the area of a parallelogram?

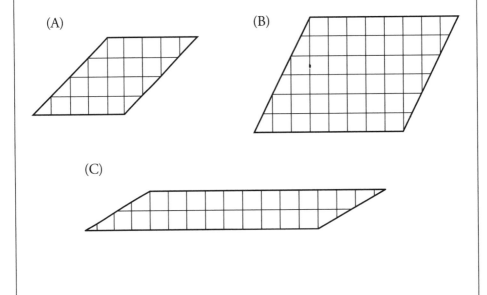

(A)

(B)

(C)

From *Classroom Discussions in Math: A Teacher's Guide for Using Talk Moves to Support the Common Core and More, Grades K–6. A Multimedia Professional Learning Resource* by Suzanne H. Chapin, Catherine O'Connor, and Nancy Canavan Anderson. © 2013 Scholastic Inc. Permission granted to photocopy for nonprofit use in a classroom or similar place dedicated to face-to-face educational instruction.

3. Ask a student to explain how to determine the height of a parallelogram. Encourage them to use the term *perpendicular.* Make sure students understand that for all parallelograms that are not rectangles, the height is *not* one of the dimensions.

4. As students work, talk with different pairs about the following questions.

   a. What is the base and height of the parallelogram? What is its area?

   b. What is the base and height of the rectangle? What is its area?

   c. Why are the areas the same?

   d. Can you transform any parallelogram into a rectangle? Explain.

   e. Explain why the formula for the area of a parallelogram is $A = bh$.

5. Use an interactive whiteboard or grid paper and have a student show how to transform a parallelogram into a rectangle. Ask students to share what is the same as before and what is different. Discuss the questions above. Use the talk move *Who can repeat?* to focus students' attention on the key ideas of the lesson. Use the move *press for reasoning* to encourage students to justify why the area of the parallelogram does not change when it is transformed into a rectangle. Use the talk move *What do you think about that?* to encourage students to respond to each other's explanations.

6. Summarize students' contributions and conclusions. Write key points on the board for students to put into their notes.

Area of a Parallelogram (Reproducible)

Directions:

Make two copies of parallelograms A, B, and C below. Cut out both sets of
parallelograms. On one set, draw in a segment to show the height. Cut along
the height to form two pieces. Reshape the pieces into a rectangle.

a) What are the bases and heights of the rectangles formed using
parallelograms A, B, and C?
b) What are the base and height of parallelograms A, B, and C?
c) Why are the dimensions of the parallelograms and their corresponding
rectangles the same?
d) Use what you know about the area of a rectangle to determine
the areas of parallelograms A, B, and C.
e) What generalizations can you make about the area of a parallelogram?

(A)

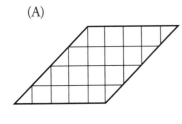

(B)

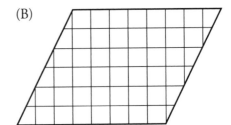

(C)

 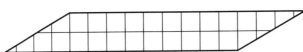

From *Classroom Discussions in Math: A Teacher's Guide for Using Talk Moves to Support the Common Core and More, Grades K–6. A Multimedia Professional Learning Resource* by Suzanne H. Chapin, Catherine O'Connor, and Nancy Canavan Anderson. © 2013 Scholastic Inc. Permission granted to photocopy for nonprofit use in a classroom or similar place dedicated to face-to-face educational instruction.

Grade 6: Placing Fractions on a Number Line

Overview

In this lesson, students determine which of two fractions is the better choice for a given location on a number line. Students work with a partner to make and justify their choice. Then students share their strategies in a whole-class discussion.

For more information about this lesson, see Chapter 4, "Talking About Computational Procedures." You can also watch video clips of this lesson from an actual sixth-grade classroom. Refer to the table at the front of this resource for more information.

Time

approximately 20 minutes

Materials

paper and pencils
chart paper
optional: interactive whiteboard

Vocabulary

denominator
distance
equivalent fraction
numerator
percent
unit

Teaching with the Common Core

6.NS Understand a rational number as a point on the number line. . . . Find and position integers and other rational numbers on a horizontal and vertical number line diagram. Apply and extend previous understandings of numbers to the system of rational numbers.

Identifying the Mathematical Goals

Students will

- use equivalent fractions, fraction comparison strategies, and percents to place fractions on a fraction number line

Anticipating Confusion

- Students may not make use of the location of 1, or $\frac{4}{4}$, to complete the task.
- Students may place 1 to the far right of the number line.
- If students use percents to complete the task, they may struggle to write seven-eighths as a percent.

Asking Questions

- How can we use the location of the fraction $\frac{1}{4}$ to find other fractions on the number line?
- Compare three-fourths and three-fifths. Which is greater? How do you know?
- Compare three-fourths and seven-eighths. Which is greater? How do you know?
- If a fraction is greater than three-fourths, where is it located in relation to $\frac{3}{4}$ on the number line?

Planning the Implementation

1. Post the number line below. Read the question.

   Which is a better choice, $\frac{3}{5}$ or $\frac{7}{8}$, for the location marked A on the number line?

2. Review the terms *distance* and *unit*. Ask students to explain what it means for a location to be marked $\frac{1}{4}$ using the words *distance* and *unit*.

3. Pass out a copy of the fraction number line task to each student. Explain that students need to work with a partner to determine which fraction, $\frac{3}{5}$ or $\frac{7}{8}$, is the better choice for the location marked A. Explain that students

must develop a convincing argument for their choice. During the whole-class discussion later on, they may have the option of using an interactive whiteboard to help them, but they must also think about how to explain the steps in their strategy to make a convincing argument.

4. As students work in pairs, listen and look for students who use the following two strategies. Ask these students to share their strategies with the class during the whole-class discussion.

Strategy 1

Repeat the distance from 0 to $\frac{1}{4}$ to find $\frac{2}{4}$, $\frac{3}{4}$, and $\frac{4}{4}$. Point A is about halfway between $\frac{3}{4}$ and $\frac{4}{4}$. The number $\frac{7}{8}$ is halfway between $\frac{3}{4}$ and $\frac{4}{4}$ because $\frac{3}{4} = \frac{6}{8}$ and $\frac{4}{4} = \frac{8}{8}$. So, it is the better choice. Also, $\frac{3}{5}$ is less than $\frac{3}{4}$ since fifths are smaller than fourths. So, $\frac{3}{5}$ is located to the left of $\frac{3}{4}$ whereas Point A is to the right of $\frac{3}{4}$.

Strategy 2

Convert $\frac{1}{4}$ to 25 percent. Then repeat this distance to find 50 percent, 75 percent, and 100 percent. A is between 75 percent and 100 percent, but $\frac{3}{5}$ is only 60 percent, so it can't be the better choice. Seven-eighths is more than 75 percent since 75 percent $= \frac{3}{4} = \frac{6}{8}$.

5. Begin by calling on a student who will talk about strategy 1. The student can either come up to the interactive whiteboard or talk from his or her seat. Ask other students to repeat key parts of the method. Use *turn and talk* as needed. (See Chapter 1 for more information on turn and talk.)

6. Ask students to address why seven-eighths is a *better* choice than three-fifths. In other words, even if seven-eighths is a good choice, how do they know that three-fifths is not the better choice?

7. Continue with a student who will talk about strategy 2. Ask other students to repeat key parts of the method.

8. Ask students to talk about different ways to convert seven-eighths to a percent.

9. Ask for volunteers to present other strategies for finding the better choice for A.

10. Summarize the learning from the task. Ask students, "What skills and ideas about fractions did you use in order to complete this task?"

Appendix C: **Lesson Planning Template**

Lesson Title

Time

Materials

Vocabulary

Identifying the Mathematical Goals

Anticipating Confusion

Asking Questions

Planning the Implementation

References

This list includes useful references that have influenced our work. We recommend them for those who want to learn more about productive math talk.

Bickmore-Brand, J., ed. 1993. *Language in Mathematics.* Portsmouth, NH: Heinemann.

Bransford, J., A. Brown, and R. Cocking, eds. 2000. *How People Learn: Brain, Mind, Experience, and School.* Washington, DC: National Academy Press.

Bresser, R., and C. Holtzman. 2006. *Minilessons for Math Practice, Grades K–2.* Sausalito, CA: Math Solutions.

Burns, M. 2007. *About Teaching Mathematics: A K–8 Resource.* 3d ed. Sausalito, CA: Math Solutions.

Cai, J., and J. Moyer. 2008. "Developing Algebraic Thinking in Earlier Grades: Some Insights from International Comparative Studies." In *Algebra and Algebraic Thinking in School Mathematics,* edited by C. E. Greenes and R. Rubenstein (pp. 169–82). Reston, VA: National Council of Teachers of Mathematics.

Chapin, S., and A. Johnson. 2006. *Math Matters: Understanding the Math You Teach, Grades K–8.* 2d ed. Sausalito, CA: Math Solutions.

Chapin, S., and C. O'Connor. 2007. "Academically Productive Talk: Supporting Students' Learning in Mathematics." In *The Learning of Mathematics,* edited by W. G. Martin, M. Strutchens, and P. Elliott (pp. 113–28). Reston, VA: National Council of Teachers of Mathematics.

Chazan, D., & D. Ball. 1999. "Beyond Being Told Not to Tell." *For the Learning of Mathematics* 19: 2–10.

Clark, P. G., K. C. Moore, and M. P. Carlson. 2008. "Documenting the Emergence of 'Speaking with Meaning' as a Sociomathematical Norm in Professional Learning Community Discourse." *The Journal of Mathematical Behavior* 27 (4): 297–310.

Cobb, P., T. Wood, and E. Yackel. 1993. "Discourse, Mathematical Thinking, and Classroom Practice." In *Contexts for Learning: Sociocultural Dynamics in Children's Development,* edited by E. A. Forman, N. Minick, and C. A. Stone (pp. 91–119). New York: Oxford University Press.

Cohen, E. G. 1994. "Restructuring the Classroom: Conditions for Productive Small Groups." *Review of Educational Research* 64 (1): 1–35.

Cohen, E. G., and R. A. Lotan. 1995. "Producing Equal Status Interaction in the Heterogeneous Classroom." *American Educational Research Journal* 32 (1): 99–120.

Confer, C. 2005. *Teaching Number Sense: Kindergarten.* Sausalito, CA: Math Solutions.

Delpit, L. 1995. *Other People's Children: Cultural Conflict in the Classroom.* New York: New Press.

Delpit, L., and J. K. Dowdy, eds. 2002. *The Skin That We Speak: Thoughts on Language and Culture in the Classroom.* New York: New Press.

Donovan, M. S., and J. Bransford, eds. 2005. *How Students Learn: Mathematics in the Classroom.* Washington, DC: National Academy Press.

Economopoulos, K., J. Mokros, R. Corwin, and S. Russell. 1995. *From Paces to Feet: Measuring and Data.* Palo Alto, CA: Dale Seymour.

Edwards, A. D., and D. P. G. Westgate. 1994. *Investigating Classroom Talk.* 2d ed. Bristol, PA: Falmer Press.

Edwards, D., and N. Mercer. 1987. *Common Knowledge: The Development of Understanding in the Classroom.* 2d ed. London and New York: Methuen.

Elliott, P., and C. Garnett, eds. 2008. *Getting into the Mathematics Conversation: Valuing Communication in Mathematics Classrooms.* Reston, VA: National Council of Teachers of Mathematics.

Enyedy, N., L. Rubel, V. Castellón, S. Mulhopadhyay, I. Esmonde, and W. Secada. 2008. "Revoicing in a Multilingual Classroom." *Mathematical Thinking and Learning: An International Journal* 10 (2): 134–62.

Gallas, K. 1995. *Talking Their Ways into Science: Hearing Children's Questions and Theories, Responding with Curricula.* New York: Teachers College Press.

Gavelek, J. R., and T. E. Raphael. 1996. "Changing Talk About Text: New Roles for Teachers and Students." *Language Arts* 73: 182–92.

Godfrey, L., and M. C. O'Connor. 1995. "The Vertical Hand Span: Nonstandard Units, Expressions, and Symbols in the Classroom." *Journal of Mathematical Behavior* 14: 327–45.

Goldenberg, C. 1999. "Instructional Conversations: Promoting Comprehension Through Discussion." *The Reading Teacher* 46: 316–26.

Gooding, A., and K. Stacey. 1993. "Characteristics of Small Group Discussion Reducing Misconceptions." *Mathematics Education Research Journal* 5 (1): 60–73.

Hatano, G., and K. Inagaki. 1991. "Sharing Cognition Through Collective Comprehension Activity." In *Perspectives on Socially Shared Cognition*, edited by L. Resnick, R. Levine, and S. Teasley. Washington, DC: APA.

Heath, S. B. 1983. *Ways with Words: Language, Life, and Work in Communities and Classrooms.* Cambridge, U.K., and New York: Cambridge University Press.

Hicks, D. 1995. "Discourse, Learning, and Teaching." *Review of Research in Education* 21: 49–95.

Hiebert, J., and T. P. Carpenter. 1992. "Learning and Teaching with Understanding." In *Handbook of Research on Mathematics Teaching and Learning*, edited by D. A. Grouws (pp. 65–97). New York: Macmillan.

Inagaki, K., E. Morita, and G. Hatano, 1999. "Teaching Learning of Evaluative Criteria for Mathematical Arguments Through Classroom Discourse: A Cross National Study." *Mathematical Thinking and Learning* 1 (2): 93–111.

Khisty, L. L., and K. B. Chval. 2002. "Pedagogic Discourse and Equity in Mathematics: When Teachers' Talk Matters." *Mathematics Education Research Journal* 14 (3): 154–68.

K–8 Publishers' Criteria for the Common Core State Standards for Mathematics. 2002. Found at: http://www.corestandards.org/assets/Math_Publishers_Criteria_K-8_Summer%202012_FINAL.pdf

Jensen, R., ed. 1993. *Research Ideas for the Classroom: Early Childhood Mathematics.* New York: Macmillan.

Keefer, M. W., C. M. Zeitz, and L. B. Resnick. 2000. "Judging the Quality of Peer Led Student Dialogues." *Cognition and Instruction* 18 (1): 53–81.

Khisty, L. L. 1995. "Making Inequality: Issues of Language and Meanings in Mathematics Teaching with Hispanic Students." In *New Directions for Equity in Mathematics Education*, edited by W. Secada, E. Fennema, and L. B. Adajian (pp. 279–97). Cambridge, U.K., and New York: Cambridge University Press.

Kieran, C., and L. Chalouh. 1993. "Prealgebra: The Transition from Arithmetic to Algebra." In *Research Ideas for the Classroom: Middle Grades Mathematics*, edited by D. Owens (pp. 179–98). New York: Macmillan.

Kilpatrick, J., J. Swafford, and B. Findell, eds. 2001. *Adding It Up: Helping Children Learn Mathematics.* Washington, DC: National Academy Press.

Lamon, S. 2006. *Teaching Fractions and Ratios for Understanding.* 2d ed. Mahwah, NJ: Lawrence Erlbaum.

Lampert, M. 1990. "Connecting Inventions with Conventions." In *Transforming Children's Mathematics Education: International Perspectives*, edited by L. P. Steffe and T. Wood (pp. 253–64). Hillsdale, NJ: Lawrence Erlbaum.

———. 2001. *Teaching Problems: A Study of Classroom Practice.* New Haven, CT: Yale University Press.

Lampert, M., and M. L. Blunk, eds. 1998. *Talking Mathematics in School: Studies of Teaching and Learning.* Cambridge, U.K., and New York: Cambridge University Press.

Lampert, M., P. Rittenhouse, and C. Crumbaugh. 1996. "Agreeing to Disagree: Developing Sociable Mathematical Discourse in School." In *Handbook of Psychology and Education: New Models of Learning, Teaching, and School*, edited by D. R. Olson and N. Torrance (pp. 731–64). Oxford, U.K.: Basil Blackwell.

Lappan, G., J. Fey, W. Fitzgerald, S. Friel, and E. Phillips. 2002. *How Likely Is It?* Upper Saddle River, NJ: Prentice Hall.

Lemke, J. 1990. *Talking Science: Language, Learning, and Values.* Norwood, NJ: Ablex.

McKeown, M. G., I. L. Beck, R. L. Hamilton, and L. Kucan. 1999. *"Questioning the Author" Accessibles: Easy-Access Resources for Classroom Challenges.* Bothell, WA: The Wright Group.

McNamara, J., and M. M. Shaughnessy. 2010. *Beyond Pizzas and Pies: 10 Essential Strategies for Supporting Fraction Sense.* Sausalito, CA: Math Solutions.

Mehan, H. 1979. *Learning Lessons: Social Organization in the Classroom.* Cambridge, MA: Harvard University Press.

Moschovich, J. 1999. "Supporting the Participation of English Language Learners in Mathematical Discussions." *For the Learning of Mathematics* 19 (1): 11–19.

———. 2000. "Learning Mathematics in Two Languages: Moving from Obstacles to Resources." In *Changing the Faces of Mathematics: Multiculturalism and Gender Equity,* edited by W. Secada (pp. 85–93). Reston, VA: National Council of Teachers of Mathematics.

Moses, R. P., M. Kamii, S. Swap, and J. Howard. 1989. "The Algebra Project: Organizing in the Spirit of Ella." *Harvard Educational Review* 59 (4): 423–43.

Murray, M. 2004. *Teaching Mathematics Vocabulary in Context.* Portsmouth, NH: Heinemann.

National Council of Teachers of Mathematics. 2000. *Principles and Standards for School Mathematics.* Reston, VA: National Council of Teachers of Mathematics.

National Governors Association Center for Best Practices, Council of Chief State School Officers. 2010. *Common Core State Standards for Mathematics.* Washington, DC: National Governors Association Center for Best Practices, Council of Chief State School Officers.

National Research Council. 2000. *How People Learn.* Washington, DC: National Academy Press.

Nystrand, M. 1997. *Opening Dialogue: Understanding the Dynamics of Language and Learning in the English Classroom.* New York: Teachers College Press.

O'Connor, M. C. 1998. "Language Socialization in the Mathematics Classroom: Discourse Practices and Mathematical Thinking." In *Talking Mathematics in School: Studies of Teaching and Learning,* edited by M. Lampert and M. L. Blunk (pp. 17–55). Cambridge, U.K., and New York: Cambridge University Press.

———. 2001. "'Can Any Fraction Be Turned into a Decimal?' A Case Study of a Mathematical Group Discussion." *Educational Studies in Mathematics* 46: 143–85.

O'Connor, M. C., and S. Michaels. 1996. "Shifting Participant Frameworks: Orchestrating Thinking Practices in Group Discussion." In *Child Discourse and Social Learning,* edited by D. Hicks (pp. 63–102). Cambridge, U.K., and New York: Cambridge University Press.

Orsolini, M., and C. Pontecorvo. 1992. "Children's Talk in Classroom Discussions." *Cognition and Instruction* 9: 113–36.

Owens, D., ed. 1993. *Research Ideas for the Classroom: Middle Grades Mathematics.* New York: Macmillan.

Paratore, J. R., and R. L. McCormack, eds. 1997. *Peer Talk in the Classroom: Learning from Research.* Newark, DE: International Reading Association.

Pimm, D. 1987. *Speaking Mathematically: Communication in Mathematics Classrooms.* London: Routledge & Kegan Paul.

Polya, G. 1945. *How to Solve It.* Princeton, NJ: Princeton University Press.

Rectanus, C. 2006. *So You Have to Teach Math? Sound Advice for Grades 6–8 Teachers.* Sausalito, CA: Math Solutions.

Rowe, M. B. 1986. "Wait Times: Slowing Down May Be a Way of Speeding Up." *Journal of Teacher Education* 37 (1): 43–50.

Russell, S. J. 1999. "Mathematical Reasoning in the Elementary Grades." In *Developing Mathematical Reasoning in Grades K–12*, edited by L. V. Stiff and F. R. Curcio (pp. 1–12). Reston, VA: National Council of Teachers of Mathematics.

Russell, S. J., and R. B. Corwin. 1993. "Talking Mathematics: 'Going Slow' and 'Letting Go'." *Phi Delta Kappan* (March): 555–58.

Schleppegrell, Mary J. 2007. "The Linguistic Challenges of Mathematics Teaching and Learning: A Research Review." *Reading & Writing Quarterly: Overcoming Learning Difficulties* 23 (2): 139–59.

Schuster, L., and N. C. Anderson. 2005. *Good Questions for Math Teaching: Why Ask Them and What to Ask, Grades 5–8.* Sausalito, CA: Math Solutions.

Secada, W., E. Fennema, and L. B. Adajian, eds. 1995. *New Directions for Equity in Mathematics Education.* Cambridge, U.K., and New York: Cambridge University Press.

Sfard, A. 2001. "There Is More to Discourse than Meets the Ears: Looking at Thinking as Communicating to Learn More About Mathematical Learning." In *Learning Discourse,* edited by C. Kieran, E. Forman, and A. Sfard (pp. 13–57). Dordrecht: Kluwer Academic Publishers.

Sheffield, L., and D. Cruikshank. 2001. *Teaching and Learning Elementary and Middle School Mathematics.* 4th ed. New York: John Wiley & Sons.

Smith, M. S., and M. K. Stein. 2011. *Five Practices for Orchestrating Productive Mathematics Discussions.* Reston, VA: National Council of Teachers of Mathematics.

Stacey, K., and M. MacGregor. February 1997. "Ideas About Symbolism That Students Bring to Algebra." *Mathematics Teacher* 90 (2): 110–13.

Stein, M. K., M. S. Smith, M. A. Henningsen, and E. A. Silver. 2000. *Implementing Standards-Based Mathematics Instruction: A Casebook for Professional Development.* New York: Teachers College Press.

Tank, B., and L. Zolli. 2001. *Teaching Arithmetic: Lessons for Addition and Subtraction, Grades 2–3.* Sausalito, CA: Math Solutions.

Van Zee, E. H., and J. Minstrell. 1997. "Using Questioning to Guide Student Thinking." *Journal of the Learning Sciences* 6 (2): 227–69.

Van Zee, E. H., M. Iwasyk, A. Kurose, D. Simpson, and J. Wild. 2001. "Student and Teacher Questioning During Conversations About Science." *Journal of Research in Science Teaching* 38 (2): 159–90.

Wagner, S., and S. Parker. 1993. "Advancing Algebra." In *Research Ideas for the Classroom: High School Mathematics,* edited by P. Wilson (pp. 119–39). New York: Macmillan.

Wells, G. 1985. *Language at Home and School.* Cambridge, U.K., and New York: Cambridge University Press.

———. 1999. *Dialogic Inquiry: Toward a Sociocultural Practice and Theory of Education.* Cambridge, U.K., and New York: Cambridge University Press.

White, D. Y. 2003. "Promoting Productive Mathematical Classroom Discourse with Diverse Students." *The Journal of Mathematical Behavior* 22 (1): 37–53.

Whitin, P., and D. Whitin. 2000. *Math Is Language Too: Talking and Writing in the Mathematics Classroom.* Urbana, IL: National Council of Teachers of English.

Willes, M. 1983. *Children into Pupils: A Study of Language in Early Schooling.* London: Routledge & Kegan Paul.

Wood, T. 1999. "Creating a Context for Argument in Mathematics Class." *Journal for Research in Mathematics Education* 30: 171–91.

Wood, T., and E. Yackel. 1990. "The Development of Collaborative Dialogue in Small Group Interactions." In *Transforming Early Childhood Mathematics Education: An International Perspective,* edited by L. P. Steffe and T. Wood (pp. 244–52). Hillsdale, NJ: Lawrence Erlbaum.

Yackel, E., P. Cobb, and T. Wood. 1991. "Small Group Interactions as a Source of Learning Opportunities in Second Grade Mathematics." *Journal for Research in Mathematics Education* 22: 390–408.

Index